Interpreting and Judging Petrarch's *Canzoniere* in Early Modern Italy

I0662893

LEGENDA

LEGENDA is the Modern Humanities Research Association's book imprint for new research in the Humanities. Founded in 1995 by Malcolm Bowie and others within the University of Oxford, Legenda has always been a collaborative publishing enterprise, directly governed by scholars. The Modern Humanities Research Association (MHRA) joined this collaboration in 1998, became half-owner in 2004, in partnership with Maney Publishing and then Routledge, and has since 2016 been sole owner. Titles range from medieval texts to contemporary cinema and form a widely comparative view of the modern humanities, including works on Arabic, Catalan, English, French, German, Greek, Italian, Portuguese, Russian, Spanish, and Yiddish literature. Editorial boards and committees of more than 60 leading academic specialists work in collaboration with bodies such as the Society for French Studies, the British Comparative Literature Association and the Association of Hispanists of Great Britain & Ireland.

The MHRA encourages and promotes advanced study and research in the field of the modern humanities, especially modern European languages and literature, including English, and also cinema. It aims to break down the barriers between scholars working in different disciplines and to maintain the unity of humanistic scholarship. The Association fulfils this purpose through the publication of journals, bibliographies, monographs, critical editions, and the MHRA Style Guide, and by making grants in support of research. Membership is open to all who work in the Humanities, whether independent or in a University post, and the participation of younger colleagues entering the field is especially welcomed.

ALSO PUBLISHED BY THE ASSOCIATION

Critical Texts
Tudor and Stuart Translations • *New Translations* • *European Translations*
MHRA Library of Medieval Welsh Literature

MHRA Bibliographies
Publications of the Modern Humanities Research Association

The Annual Bibliography of English Language & Literature
Austrian Studies
Modern Language Review
Portuguese Studies
The Slavonic and East European Review
Working Papers in the Humanities
The Yearbook of English Studies

www.mhra.org.uk
www.legendabooks.com

ITALIAN PERSPECTIVES

In the light of growing academic interest in Italy and the reorganization of many university courses in Italian along interdisciplinary lines, this book series, founded by Maney Publishing under the imprint of the Northern Universities Press and now continuing under the Legenda imprint, aims to bring together different scholarly perspectives on Italy and its culture. *Italian Perspectives* publishes books and collections of essays on any period of Italian literature, language, history, culture, politics, art, and media, as well as studies which take an interdisciplinary approach and are methodologically innovative.

APPEARING IN THIS SERIES

Managing Editor
Dr Graham Nelson, 41 Wellington Square, Oxford OX1 2JF, UK
www.legendabooks.com

Interpreting and Judging Petrarch's *Canzoniere* in Early Modern Italy

Edited by Maiko Favaro

LEGENDA

Italian Perspectives 49
Modern Humanities Research Association
2021

Published by Legenda
an imprint of the Modern Humanities Research Association
Salisbury House, Station Road, Cambridge CB1 2LA

ISBN 978-1-781885-72-7 (HB)
ISBN 978-1-78188-584-0 (PB)

First published 2021

Copy-Editor: Dr Ellen Jones

CONTENTS

ACKNOWLEDGEMENTS

I would like to express my warmest thanks to the general editor of *Italian Perspectives*, Simon Gilson, who has followed the preparation of this volume from the earliest stages with the utmost care and interest. He has always provided his invaluable help with extraordinary generosity and promptness. The volume has remarkably benefited from his renowned expertise on Petrarch's *Canzoniere* and his exegetical reception. I wish to also thank the two anonymous peer-reviewers, who have offered excellent advice to improve the book. I am grateful to the editorial board at Legenda for accepting the proposal. In particular, I would like to thank Graham Nelson for his very kind availability and skilful guidance through all the stages to publication.

The publication of this volume is part of my Marie Skłodowska-Curie IF project, which has received funding from the European Union's Horizon 2020 research and innovation programme (grant agreement No 653443; host institution: Freie Universität Berlin; supervisor: Prof. Dr. Bernhard Huss).

M.F., January 2021

NOTES ON THE CONTRIBUTORS

Cristina Acucella graduated from the University of Basilicata, where she worked on Baroque fairytale and the dream of the beloved from Petrarch to Marino. She took part in two digital humanities projects (a PRIN on the *Orlando Furioso* and an ERC on Anton Francesco Doni). She earned a PhD in Philology and Italian literature at the University of Florence, in co-supervision with the University of Bonn and the Sorbonne in Paris. She published an annoted edition of Chiara Matraini's *Lettere e Rime* (Firenze University Press, 2018). Her publications also focus on sixteenth-century illustrated editions of the *Orlando Furioso*, the relationship between poetry and painting, and the *Vita* of Benvenuto Cellini. She is currently a researcher at the Università della Basilicata working on unpublished Renaissance texts and 'cinquecentine' from the Kingdom of Naples.

Guglielmo Barucci is Associate Professor of Italian Literature at the University of Milan. His interests embrace Dante's *Comedy* and Renaissance genres, culture, and literature. He is the author of *'Simile a quel che talvolta si sogna'. I sogni del 'Purgatorio' dantesco* (Le Lettere, 2012); *Le solite scuse. Un genere epistolare del Cinquecento* (FrancoAngeli, 2009); *I segni e la storia. Modelli tacitiani nella 'Storia d'Italia' del Guicciardini* (LED, 2004). Currently he is mainly working on Renaissance fables.

Laura Benedetti is the Laura and Gaetano Professor of Contemporary Italian Culture at Georgetown University (USA). Her publications span seven hundred years, from Boccaccio to Elena Ferrante, and include *La sconfitta di Diana. Un percorso per la 'Gerusalemme liberata'*; *The Tigress in the Snow: Motherhood and Literature in 20th-Century Italy* (winner of the Flaiano International Prize); the edition and English translation of Lucrezia Marinella's *Exhortations to Women and to Others if They Please*; and the novels *Un paese di carta* and *Secondo piano*. She has received fellowships from the Renaissance Society of America, the Bogliasco Foundation, and the Gladys Krieble Delmas Foundation.

Giacomo Comiati is a Postdoctoral Research Fellow at the University of Oxford within the AHRC-funded project 'Petrarch Commentary and Exegesis in Renaissance Italy, c.1350–c.1650'. He previously worked as postdoctoral fellow at the Dahlem Humanities Centre of the Freie University in Berlin and the Institute of Advanced Studies at the University of Warwick. He studied Italian Modern Philology and Literature in Padua, where he also attended the Scuola Galileiana di Studi Superiori, and then obtained his PhD in Italian Studies from the University of Warwick with a dissertation devoted to the influence of the Latin poet Horace on sixteenth-century Italy (2016). His research interests mainly concern Renaissance

Italian literature, fifteenth- and sixteenth-century poetry in Latin and Italian, Renaissance exegesis, and the Early-Modern reception of Latin antiquity.

Maiko Favaro is Lecturer of Italian Literature at the University of Fribourg (Switzerland). He studied at the Scuola Normale Superiore and the University of Pisa. He was Marie Skłodowska-Curie Fellow at the Freie Universität Berlin. His research mainly focuses on Renaissance literature, in particular Petrarchism, love treatises, epic-chivalric poetry, and Torquato Tasso. His books include *'L'ospite preziosa'. Presenze della lirica nei trattati d'amore del Cinquecento e del primo Seicento* (Pacini Fazzi, 2012); *Dea del cielo o figlia di Eva? La donna nella cultura italiana fra Rinascimento e Controriforma* (Museo Petrarchesco Piccolomineo, 2017); *Dante da una prospettiva friulana. Sulla fortuna della 'Divina Commedia' in Friuli dal Risorgimento ad oggi* (Forum, 2017); *Ambiguità del petrarchismo. Un percorso fra trattati d'amore, lettere e templi di rime* (FrancoAngeli, 2021); *Le virtù del nobile. Precetti, modelli e problemi nella letteratura del secondo Cinquecento* (I libri di Emil, 2021). He co-edited (with Bernhard Huss) the volume *Intedisciplinarità del petrarchismo. Prospettive di ricerca fra Italia e Germania* (Olschki, 2018). He is the recipient of the Canadian Society for Italian Studies Award 2011 and the Premio Tasso 2016.

Andrea Lazzarini is Research Fellow at the University of Modena and Reggio Emilia. His main research interests are seventeenth-century Italian authors (Alessandro Tassoni, Giovan Battista Marino, Tommaso Stigliani, Francesco Bracciolini) and the Neapolitan literature of the same period (Giulio Cesare Cortese and Giovan Battista Basile). He is also interested in the fortune of Petrarch's *Canzoniere*, the relationship between literature and figurative arts, and the history of the Italian language in the sixteenth and seventeenth centuries. He is Assistant Editor of the journal *Studi secenteschi*.

Simona Oberto is Akademische Rätin a.Z. at the Albert-Ludwigs-Universität Freiburg (Germany). She is specialized in Medieval Italian Literature and Renaissance Studies, in the field of which she investigated the role of sixteenth-century Italian academies in the gradual dissolution of Petrarchism, with a special focus on their relationship to Pietro Bembo. Her current research is concentrated on Nineteenth-Century French Literature. Her publications include: *Poetik und Programmatik der akademischen Lyrik des Cinquecento* (Winter, 2016); 'Die Impresa als Ausdruck dichterischer Programmatik in den italienischen Akademien des 16. Jahrhunderts' (*Germanisch-Romanische Monatsschrift*, 66, 2, 2016); and 'What happens to Aristotle in practice? Sperone Speroni's *Canace* before the background of the *Accademia degli Infiammati* and *Elevati*' (*Horizonte*, n.s., 2, 2017).

Lorenzo Sacchini is Research Fellow at the University of Leeds where he is collaborating on the three-year AHRC collective project 'Petrarch Commentary and Exegesis in Renaissance Italy, c.1350–c.1650', co-led by the University of Leeds and Oxford. He specializes in the Italian literature of the sixteenth and seventeenth centuries. His monograph, *Identità, lettere, virtù. Le lezioni inedite degli Accademici Insensati di Perugia (1561–1608)*, was published in 2016 (I libri di Emil). His publications include various articles on late Renaissance Italian literature, academy culture, and Petrarch's reception.

Giacomo Vagni is a Swiss National Science Foundation Fellow at the University of Lausanne, where he studies the modern reception of sixteenth-century lyric poetry. He obtained his PhD at the Catholic University of Milan (2013) and worked on two projects at the University of Fribourg (2014–2018) on the poems of Giuliano di Lorenzo de' Medici and the dialogues of Torquato Tasso. He edited Baldassarre Castiglione and Cesare Gonzaga's poems (I libri di Emil, 2015), and the proceedings of the conference *Lirica in Italia 1494–1530. Esperienze ecdotiche e profili storiografici*, which he organized with Uberto Motta (I libri di Emil, 2017). He is also interested in the humanistic culture of Renaissance Rome, and the letters of Baldassarre Castiglione and Pietro Bembo.

LIST OF ILLUSTRATIONS

FIG. 5.1. Cover of *Rime de gli Academici Occulti con le loro imprese et discorsi*. Venice, Biblioteca Nazionale Marciana, D 063 D 078. Reproduced by courtesy of the Ministero dei Beni e delle Attività Culturali e del Turismo–Biblioteca Nazionale Marciana.

FIG. 5.2. *Rime de gli Academici Occulti con le loro imprese et discorsi*. Venice, Biblioteca Nazionale Marciana, D 063 D 078, fol. 8^r. Reproduced by courtesy of the Ministero dei Beni e delle Attività Culturali e del Turismo–Biblioteca Nazionale Marciana.

FIG. 5.3. *Rime de gli Academici Occulti con le loro imprese et discorsi*. Venice, Biblioteca Nazionale Marciana, D 063 D 078, fol. 119^r. Reproduced by courtesy of the Ministero dei Beni e delle Attività Culturali e del Turismo–Biblioteca Nazionale Marciana.

NOTE ON TRANSLATIONS

All English translations are the authors' own, unless otherwise specified.

INTRODUCTION

Maiko Favaro

1. The Commentary Tradition on Petrarch's *Canzoniere* (15th–18th Centuries)

Any exploration of the exegetical tradition of Petrarch's *Canzoniere* in Early Modern Italy presents us with a broad and complex subject because of its many ramifications as well as the large number of texts involved. Nonetheless, it is possible to distinguish some different stages in such a tradition. Therefore, in the first part of this introduction we will provide an overview of that earlier tradition and relevant scholarship before turning to discuss the chapters in the present volume.

Even if the Florentine Luigi Marsili had discussed 'O aspettata in ciel' and 'Italia mia' in the late fourteenth century,[1] the first sustained attempts to comment on Petrarch's *Canzoniere* date back to the early fifteenth century. Therefore, it seems appropriate to begin our overview at this point. The main features of Petrarch's reception in the Quattrocento were brilliantly illustrated by Carlo Dionisotti in a celebrated article.[2] Humanists were more interested in Petrarch's Latin works,

1   On Marsili's commentary, see Gino Belloni, *Laura tra Petrarca e Bembo. Studi sul commento umanistico-rinascimentale al 'Canzoniere'* (Rome-Padua: Antenore, 1992), pp. 1–57.

2   See Carlo Dionisotti, 'Fortuna del Petrarca nel Quattrocento', *Italia medioevale e umanistica*, 17 (1974), 61–113 (later in Carlo Dionisotti, *Scritti di storia della letteratura italiana*, ed. by Tania Basile, Vincenzo Fera, and Susanna Villari, 5 vols (Rome: Edizioni di Storia e Letteratura, 2008–), III (2010), 93–136). For an overview of fifteenth-century commentaries, see also Gino Belloni, 'Commenti petrarcheschi', in *Dizionario critico della letteratura italiana*, dir. by Vittore Branca, with the collaboration of Armando Balduino, Manlio Pastore Stocchi, and Marco Pecoraro, 4 vols (Turin: Utet, 1986), II, 22–30; Nadia Cannata, 'Petrarch Commentaries', in *The Oxford Companion of Italian Literature*, ed. by Peter Hainsworth and David Robey (Oxford: Oxford University Press, 2005) <https://www.oxfordreference.com/view/10.1093/acref/9780198183327.001.0001/acref-9780198183327-e-2436> [accessed 16 July 2019]. More broadly on Petrarch's reception and editions in the fifteenth and sixteenth centuries, see Corrado Bologna, 'Tradizione testuale e fortuna dei classici italiani', in *Letteratura italiana*, ed. by Alberto Asor Rosa, 17 vols (Turin: Einaudi, 1982–2000), VI: *Teatro, musica, tradizione dei classici* (1986), pp. 445–928; Paolo Trovato, *Con ogni diligenza corretto. La stampa e le revisioni editoriali dei testi letterari italiani (1470–1570)* [1991] (Ferrara: UnifePress, 2009), pp. 121–328; Brian Richardson, *Print Culture in Renaissance Italy: The Editor and the Vernacular Text, 1470–1600* (Cambridge: Cambridge University Press, 2002), pp. 20–228; Paola Vecchi Galli, 'Petrarca fra Tre e Quattrocento', in *Storia della letteratura italiana*, dir. by Enrico Malato, XI: *La critica letteraria dal Due al Novecento*, coord. by Paolo Orvieto (Rome: Salerno, 2003), pp. 161–88; Paola Vecchi Galli, 'Petrarca nel Cinquecento', in *Storia della letteratura italiana*, XI, 325–51; Amedeo Quondam, 'Sul Petrarchismo', in *Il Petrarchismo. Un modello di poesia per l'Europa*, ed. by Loredana Chines, Floriana Calitti, and Roberto Gigliucci, 2 vols (Rome: Bulzoni, 2006), pp. 27–92; Amedeo Quondam, 'Sul Petrarchismo. Dieci anni dopo', in *Petrarca, l'Italia, l'Europa. Atti del Convegno di Studi (Bari, 20–22*

while they had some reservations about his vernacular writings, in particular the *Canzoniere*. That was not only because of the choice of vernacular language, but also because of the subject of love, which was considered as unworthy of attention. Indeed, some fifteenth-century commentators (like Filelfo and Patrizi the Elder) seem to have expounded the *Canzoniere* with a degree of reluctance, having done so above all to please their patrons. Thanks to their moral-allegorical content, Petrarch's other vernacular poetry, the *Trionfi*, were more popular in the fifteenth century.[3] In the first half of the Quattrocento, the greatest promoter of commentaries on Petrarch's *Canzoniere* was undoubtedly Filippo Maria Visconti, duke of Milan from 1412 to 1447.[4] Visconti, with his remarkable curiosity for Florentine language and literature, was fond of the *Canzoniere*. Thanks to him, almost all the earliest commentaries on Petrarch's masterpiece were written in Milan between the 1420s and 1440s, including those of Pier Candido Decembrio, Pietro Lapini da Montalcino, also known as Pietro Ilicino (father of Bernardo, the author of an important commentary on the *Trionfi* published in 1475), Guiniforte Barzizza, and Francesco Filelfo. Decembrio is also the author of a biography of Petrarch. His commentary — now lost — was written between the 1420s and 1430s.[5] Ilicino's commentary, compiled before 1447, is also lost. Instead, a short fragment of commentary on *Voi ch'ascoltate* speech marks by Guiniforte Barzizza — better known for his on Dante's *Inferno* — is preserved in a manuscript housed at the Bibliothèque Nationale de France.[6] However, the fifteenth-century commentary that has attracted most attention from scholars in the last decades is undoubtedly that by the celebrated humanist Francesco Filelfo, probably the foremost Greek scholar of his generation.[7] Filelfo's commentary, written in 1444–

maggio 2015), ed. by Elisa Tinelli, foreword by Davide Canfora (Bari: Edizioni di Pagina, 2016), pp. 243–58.

3   On the manuscripts of the *Trionfi*, see Simona Brambilla, 'I mercanti lettori del Petrarca', *Verbum*, 7.1 (2005), 185–219.

4   See Massimo Zaggia, 'Appunti sulla cultura letteraria in volgare a Milano nell'età di Filippo Maria Visconti', *Giornale storico della letteratura italiana*, 170.550 (1993), 161–219, and 170.551 (1993), 321–82; Antonia Tissoni Benvenuti, 'Il commento per la corte', in *Intorno al testo. Atti del Convegno di Urbino (1–3 ottobre 2001)* (Rome: Salerno, 2003), pp. 195–221.

5   See Gabriella Mezzanotte, 'Pier Candido Decembri e la *Vita* del Petrarca attribuita a Antonio da Tempo', *Studi Petrarcheschi*, n.s., 1 (1984), 211–24.

6   See Luca Marcozzi, 'Tra Da Tempo, Filelfo e Barzizza: biografia sentimentale e allegoria morale nei commenti quattrocenteschi al Canzoniere di Petrarca', *Italianistica*, 33.2 (2004), 163–77, reprinted in Luca Marcozzi, *Petrarca platonico: Studi sull'immaginario filosofico del canzoniere*, 2nd edn (Rome: Aracne, 2011), pp. 173–98; Federico Ruggiero, 'Il commento di Guiniforte Barzizza a "Voi ch'ascoltate": edizione, cronologia, proposte', in *La lirica in Italia dalle Origini al Rinascimento*, ed. by Lorenzo Geri and Marco Grimaldi, *Studi (e testi) italiani*, 38 (2016), 105–25.

7   On Filelfo's commentary, see Ezio Raimondi, 'Francesco Filelfo, interprete del *Canzoniere*', *Studi Petrarcheschi*, 3 (1950), 143–64; Vincenzo Fera, 'Itinerari filologici di Francesco Filelfo', in *Francesco Filelfo nel quinto centenario della morte. Atti del XVII Convegno di studi maceratesi (Tolentino, 27–30 settembre 1981)* (Padua: Antenore, 1986), pp. 89–135; Rossella Bessi, 'Sul commento di Francesco Filelfo ai *Rerum Vulgarium Fragmenta*', *Quaderni petrarcheschi*, 4 (1987), 229–70; Rossella Bessi, 'Filelfo commenta Petrarca', *Schifanoia*, 15–16 (1995), 91–98; Rossella Bessi, *Umanesimo volgare. Studi di letteratura fra Tre e Quattrocento* (Florence: Olschki, 2004), pp. 23–61; Marcozzi, 'Tra Da Tempo, Filelfo e Barzizza'; Luca Verrelli, 'Il proemio del *Commento* di Francesco Filelfo ai *Rerum Vulgarium Fragmenta*: ipotesi

47, was first published in 1476 (Bologna: Annibale Malpigli), just six years after the *editio princeps* of the *Canzoniere*, which was published in 1470 in Venice by Wendelin of Speyer. Since Filelfo's commentary was unfinished (it covers only poems 1–136), the mediocre humanist Girolamo Squarzafico completed it in 1484 as part of a later Venetian edition printed by Piero de' Piasi.[8] In his annotations, Filelfo dwelled above all on the meaning of the most difficult passages and the classical sources. Filelfo-Squarzafico's commentary was often published together with another one falsely attributed to Antonio da Tempo, an important metricist of the fourteenth century.[9] The latter, first published in 1477 (Venice: Domenico Siliprandi), was much shorter than Filelfo's, and could not rival its popularity. The so-called da Tempo's commentary pays attention especially to the subjects of the poems and their classical sources. Another interesting environment for fifteenth-century exegesis on Petrarch was the Aragonese court in Naples, to which we owe Francesco Acciapaccia's and Francesco Patrizi the Elder's commentaries. Acciapaccia's commentary, preserved by a Parisian manuscript, was compiled around 1467–73. It considers only Petrarch's sonnets, madrigals and ballads, and almost exclusively from a moral point of view. Both because of this and its limited value, it had an almost private circulation, and was soon forgotten.[10] Patrizi, a humanist and bishop of Gaeta, is especially known for his *De institutione reipublicae* and *De regno et regis institutionis*, which enjoyed a considerable editorial success and have been studied with regard to Machiavelli's political writings. He wrote the first version of his Petrarchan commentary (still unpublished) before 1478. Patrizi's peculiar attention to the metrical aspects and the order of the poems is remarkable.[11] Scholars have also devoted much attention to the atypical and fascinating commentary by the poet and artist Antonio Grifo (c. 1530–c. 1510), probably Venetian, who was active at the Sforza court in Milan at the end of the fifteenth century. On a copy of the *editio princeps* of the *Canzoniere* (1470), now at the Biblioteca Civica Queriniana of Brescia, he commented on the poems with handwritten annotations and lavish coloured illustrations.[12] Generally

preliminari', *Medioevo e Rinascimento*, 28 (2014), 95–125; Nicoletta Marcelli, 'Filelfo "volgare": Stato dell'arte e linee di ricerca', in *Philelphiana. Nuove prospettive di ricerca sulla figura di Francesco Filelfo*, ed. by Silvia Fiaschi (Florence: Olschki, 2015), pp. 47–81.

8   On Squarzafico, see Josef Allenspach and Giuseppe Frasso, 'Vicende, cultura e scritti di Gerolamo Squarzafico, Alessandrino', *Italia medioevale e umanistica*, 23 (1980), 233–92.

9   On this commentary, see Marcozzi, 'Tra Da Tempo, Filelfo e Barzizza'.

10   See Olga Silvana Casale and Laura Facecchia, 'Un (quasi) sconosciuto commento quattrocentesco al *Canzoniere* di Petrarca', *Filologia e critica*, 23 (1997), 240–63; Marcozzi, 'Tra Da Tempo, Filelfo e Barzizza', 165.

11   On Patrizi, see Matteo Maria Quintiliani, 'Patrizi, Francesco', *Dizionario biografico degli italiani* (Rome: Istituto dell'Enciclopedia italiana, 1960–), LXXXI (2014), 730–32; Gabriele Pedullà, 'Francesco Patrizi e le molte vite dell'umanista', in *Atlante della letteratura italiana*, ed. by Sergio Luzzatto and Gabriele Pedullà (Turin: Einaudi, 2010), I, 457–64. On his commentary, see Laura Paolino, 'Per l'edizione del commento di Francesco Patrizi da Siena al *Canzoniere* di Petrarca', *Nuova rivista di letteratura italiana*, 2.1 (1999), 153–311; Laura Paolino, 'Il fratello di Madonna Laura. Spigolature di biografia petrarchesca dal commento di Francesco Patrizi ai *Rerum vulgarium fragmenta*', *Studi Petrarcheschi*, 13 (2000), 243–306.

12   A facsimile edition is available: Francesco Petrarca, *Canzoniere, Trionfi. Edizione in fac-simile* (Rome: Salerno, 2016). See also the essays by Ennio Sandal, Giordana Mariani Canova, and Giuseppe

speaking, we can say that fifteenth-century commentators examined more or less the same aspects as their sixteenth-century colleagues, such as the literal meaning, the parallels and sources, the order of the poems, and the connotation of Petrarch's love for Laura. Nonetheless, they were far less accurate and knowledgeable than them. Leaving aside the commentaries, scholars have also pointed out the relevance of the academic course on Petrarch's *Canzoniere* held in Florence in 1467 by Cristoforo Landino, better known for a collection of Latin elegies entitled *Xandra*, the dialogue *Disputationes camaldulenses*, and his commentary on Dante's *Divine Comedy*, which makes extensive use of Petrarch's vernacular verse.[13] Recent studies on Petrarch's readership in the fifteenth century are also worth mentioning.[14]

Pietro Bembo's edition of the *Canzoniere*, published by Aldo Manuzio in 1501, marked a turning point in the exegetical tradition of Petrarch's masterpiece.[15] Bembo did not annotate the poems. Nonetheless, his edition can be defined 'in itself as a commentary, a grammatical commentary',[16] because of its philological approach (Bembo also had at his disposal the *Canzoniere*'s autograph-idiograph manuscript Vat.lat.3195) and the orthographical interventions. The novelty of Bembo's approach scandalized the most conservative readers. For example, the Venetian Antonio da Canal, in his unpublished commentary (1510–17) now at the Biblioteca Marciana of Venice, complained about the multitude of apostrophes and punctuation marks newly-introduced by Bembo. In his opinion, they made Petrarch's text more difficult to read than in the old 1470 edition published by Wendelin of Speyer.[17] The 1501 Aldine edition needs to be considered as the first

Frasso in Francesco Petrarca, *Canzoniere, Trionfi. Commentario all'edizione in fac-simile* (Rome: Salerno, 2016); the afterword by Giuseppe Frasso mentions the previous bibliography on Antonio Grifo and the Incunabulum Queriniano.

13   Landino's inaugural lecture of the course still survives, and can be read in Cristoforo Landino, *Scritti critici e teorici*, ed. by Roberto Cardini (Rome: Bulzoni, 1974), pp. 29–55. See Roberto Cardini, *La critica del Landino* (Florence: Sansoni, 1973); Giuliano Tanturli, 'Proposta e risposta. La prolusione petrarchesca del Landino e il codice cavalcantiano di Antonio Manetti', *Rinascimento*, 32 (1992), 213–25; Mauro De Nichilo, 'Petrarca, Salutati, Landino: *RVF* 22 e 132', *Italianistica*, 33.2 (2004), 143–61.

14   See Brambilla, pp. 185–219; Carlo Pulsoni, 'Lettori di Petrarca nel Quattrocento', in *Petrarca lettore. Pratiche e rappresentazioni della lettura nelle opere dell'umanista*, ed. by Luca Marcozzi (Florence: Franco Cesati, 2016), pp. 259–71; Francesco Davoli, '*Soneti et cantilene Petrarce*: un manoscritto petrarchesco della biblioteca di Alessandro Sforza', *Petrarchesca*, 5 (2017), 81–86.

15   On this edition, see Stefano Pillinini, 'Traguardi linguistici nel Petrarca bembino del 1501', *Studi di filologia italiana*, 39 (1981), 58–75; Giuseppe Frasso, 'Appunti sul Petrarca Aldino del 1501', in *Vestigia. Studi in onore di Giuseppe Billanovich*, ed. by Rino Avesani, Mirella Ferrari, Tino Foffano, Giuseppe Frasso, and Agostino Sottili, 2 vols (Rome: Edizioni di storia e letteratura, 1984), I, 315–35; Sandra Giarin, 'Petrarca e Bembo: l'edizione aldina del *Canzoniere*', *Studi di filologia italiana*, 62 (2004), 161–93; Kei Amano, 'Bembo e il Canzoniere aldino', *Studi Italici*, 56 (2006), 42–70; Gino Belloni and Carlo Pulsoni, 'Bembo e l'autografo di Petrarca: ancora sulla storia dell'originale del *Canzoniere*', *Studi Petrarcheschi*, 19 (2006), 149–84; Florian Mehltretter, *Kanonisierung und Medialität: Petrarcas Rime in der Frühzeit des Buchdrucks (1470–1687)*, in collaboration with Florian Neumann, preface by Gerhard Regn (Berlin-Münster: Lit, 2009), pp. 81–170; Carlo Pulsoni, 'Le fonti dell'edizione aldina di Petrarca (1501)', in *Cantares de amigos. Estudos en homenaxe a Mercedes Brea* (Santiago de Compostela: Universidade de Santiago de Compostela, 2016), pp. 733–37 (pp. 735–36); Luca Marcozzi, *Bembo* (Florence: Cesati, 2017), pp. 15, 108–09.

16   Belloni, *Laura tra Petrarca e Bembo*, p. 102. The translation is mine.

17   See Belloni, *Laura tra Petrarca e Bembo*, chap. 3.

step towards a bigger project conceived by Bembo, i.e. the canonization of Petrarch as the linguistic and poetic model *par excellence*. Later developments of such a project include his *Prose della volgar lingua* (1525), which can be also considered as a very special kind of commentary on Petrarch, and his *Rime* (1530), which conventionally mark the beginning of Renaissance Petrarchism. The Aldine edition inaugurated a new way of reading and interpreting the *Canzoniere*. Later commentators could not but deal with that edition, even if only to engage in polemics against it. That is a major theme of the fundamental book by Gino Belloni on Renaissance commentaries on the *Canzoniere*, i.e. *Laura tra Petrarca e Bembo. Studi sul commento umanistico-rinascimentale al 'Canzoniere'* (Rome-Padua: Antenore, 1992). With the exception of the already mentioned Luigi Marsili, Belloni deals with figures active in the first half of the sixteenth century and in some way related to Bembo's Venice, such as Alessandro Vellutello, Antonio da Canal, Sebastiano Fausto da Longiano and his brother Domenico Tullio, Giulio Camillo Delminio, Trifon Gabriele, Bernardino Daniello, and even the Neapolitan Giovanni Andrea Gesualdo. Notably, Belloni does not analyse Silvano da Venafro's commentary, which was published in Naples; Gesualdo symptomatically chose to publish his commentary in Venice.[18] Many of the names mentioned above also recur in another important book, *Authorizing Petrarch* by William J. Kennedy (Ithaca-London: Cornell University Press, 1994). Besides examining the ideological reasons in Bembo's canonization of Petrarch, Kennedy considers some of the most influential commentators of the *Canzoniere*, such as Antonio da Tempo, Francesco Filelfo, Girolamo Squarzafico, Alessandro Vellutello, Giovanni Andrea Gesualdo, Silvano da Venafro, Bernardino Daniello, Sebastiano Fausto da Longiano, Antonio Brucioli, and Lodovico Castelvetro. He compares their responses on several issues related to love relationships, gender roles, class differences, and national identification. While Belloni adopts a strictly historical-philological approach, Kennedy is more open to theoretical reflections inspired by, amongst other things, Freud and gender studies.[19] More recently, Florian Mehltretter has analysed the canonization process of the *Canzoniere* in his book *Kanonisierung und Medialität: Petrarcas Rime in der Frühzeit des Buchdrucks (1470–1687)* (Berlin: LIT, 2009). He dwelled extensively on Bembo's edition of the *Canzoniere*, but also considered the exegetical tradition, from the fifteenth century (Filelfo, Squarzafico, da Tempo, Grifo) to the sixteenth (Vellutello, Silvano da Venafro, Dolce, Daniello, Gesualdo, Alunno, Camillo, Castelvetro) and seventeenth (notably, Tassoni). Mehltretter's book is part of a wider project developed by a research group in Germany on Petrarch's canonization in the Italian Renaissance.[20] Scholars have also focused their attention on single commentaries,

18   See Claudio Vela, review of Belloni, *Laura tra Petrarca e Bembo* (1992), *Lettere italiane*, 45.3 (1993), 479–84 (p. 481).
19   See also William J. Kennedy, 'Versions of a Career: Petrarch and His Commentators', in *European Literary Careers: The Author from Antiquity to the Renaissance*, ed. by Patrick Cheney and Frederick A. de Armas (Toronto: Toronto University Press, 2002), pp. 146–64; William J. Kennedy, *The Site of Petrarchism. Early Modern Sentiment in Italy, France, and England* (Baltimore-London: The Johns Hopkins University Press, 2004).
20   See *Lezioni sul Petrarca. Die 'Rerum vulgarium fragmenta' in Akademievorträgen des 16. Jahrhunderts*,

such as that by Alessandro Vellutello. The latter was born in Lucca, but moved to Venice, where he played the part of the outsider (Belloni called him a 'heretic') in a Venice culturally dominated by Bembo and his circle. In addition to Petrarch, he also commented on Dante's *Comedy* (Venice: Francesco Marcolini, 1544), but with limited success.[21] His commentary on the *Canzoniere* and the *Trionfi* (Venice: Giovannantonio e fratelli da Sabbio, 1525) was instead the most popular and most reprinted of the sixteenth century, also because it was more approachable than its erudite competitors.[22] Vellutello argued that the order of the poems in the Aldine edition did not respect Petrarch's wishes. In his opinion, Bembo was wrong when he claimed that his edition was based on the original manuscript of the *Canzoniere*. Therefore, Vellutello rearranged the order of the texts, dividing them into three sections, i.e. love poems written during Laura's lifetime, those written after her death, and other occasional poems. He evaluated every clue offered by the single poems to reconstruct the chronological order of events. Indeed, Vellutello thought that the *Canzoniere* was the faithful account of Petrarch and Laura's story in real life. He corroborated such a biographistic perspective through a series of his own paratexts, that is 'Trattato de l'ordine de' sonetti e canzoni mutato', 'Vita e costumi del poeta', and 'Origine di Madonna Laura con la discrizione di Valclusa e del luogo ove il poeta di lei a principio s'innamorò', in addition to a map of Vaucluse and its surroundings. It is also worth mentioning that Vellutello even travelled to Avignon and Provence to conduct research on Laura's historical identity. All the same, Vellutello's metrical, rhetorical and linguistic annotations, as well as his explanations

ed. by Bernhard Huss, Florian Neumann, and Gerhard Regn (Münster: Lit, 2004); *Questo leggiadrissimo poeta! Autoritätskonstitution im rinascimentalen Lyrik-Kommentar*, ed. by Gerhard Regn (Münster: Lit, 2004); Bernhard Huss, Florian Mehltretter, and Gerhard Regn, *Lyriktheorie(n) der italienischen Renaissance* (Berlin-Boston: de Gruyter, 2012); Catharina Busjan, *Petrarca-Hermeneutik: Die Kommentare von Alessandro Vellutello und Giovan Andrea Gesualdo in epochalen Kontext* (Berlin-Boston: de Gruyter, 2013).

21   On this commentary, see Deborah Parker, *Commentary and Ideology: Dante in the Renaissance* (Durham, NC and London: Duke University Press, 1993), *ad indicem*; Paolo Procaccioli, 'La "nova esposizione" di Alessandro Vellutello. Un Dante per il Cinquecento', *L'Alighieri*, 27 (2006), 41–70; Donato Pirovano, 'Introduzione', in Alessandro Vellutello, *La Comedia di Dante Alighieri con la nova esposizione*, ed. by Donato Pirovano, 3 vols (Rome: Salerno, 2006); Massimiliano Rossi, 'Alessandro Vellutello e Giovanni Britto che "per sé fuoro". Sul corredo grafico della *Nova esposizione*', *Studi rinascimentali*, 5 (2007), 127–44; Simon Gilson, *Reading Dante in Renaissance Italy: Florence, Venice and the 'Divine Poet'* (Cambridge: Cambridge University Press, 2018), pp. 175–94, and the bibliography there available. It is also worth mentioning that in the 1520s an interesting *Vita del Petrarca* was written in Rome by Antonio Lelli (1465–1527/30). This work, transmitted in four manuscripts, offers a vernacular commentary on Petrarch's oeuvre (both in vernacular and in Latin). Valeria Guarna is currently working toward a critical edition of Lelli's *Vita*.

22   See Luigi Baldacci, *Il petrarchismo italiano nel Cinquecento*, 2nd edn (Padua: Liviana, 1974), pp. 61–65; Daniel Maira, 'Éclatement biographique à la base du mythe de la Laure de Petrarque: à propos des biographies d'A. Vellutello, Fausto da Longiano, Silvano da Venafro et G.A. Gesualdo', *Cenobio*, 53 (2004), 342–53; Simone Albonico, 'Osservazioni sul commento di Vellutello a Petrarca', in *Il poeta e il suo pubblico. Lettura e commento dei testi lirici nel Cinquecento*, ed. by Massimo Danzi and Roberto Leporatti (Genève: Droz, 2012), pp. 63–100; Busjan, *Petrarca-Hermeneutik*; Andrea Severi, 'Alessandro Vellutello', in *The Oregon Petrarch Open Book*, <https://petrarch.uoregon.edu/sites/petrarch1.uoregon.edu/files/andrea-severi-essay.pdf> [accessed 16 July 2019].

of historical and mythological references, are disappointing. With regard to the sources, Vellutello often quoted Latin authors, but neglected the vernacular tradition and Petrarch's Latin works. A few years later, in 1532, Sebastiano Fausto da Longiano published his commentary on the *Canzoniere* and the *Trionfi*, which however was not able to rival Vellutello's edition in popularity. Fausto seems to address a readership that is more cultivated than Vellutello's, as is suggested by his parallels with Petrarch's Latin works. Fausto's commentary is also remarkable for its many references to the vernacular literature of the thirteenth and fourteenth centuries (not only Dante and Boccaccio, but also the poets included in the *Giuntina di rime antiche* of 1527). Silvano da Venafro's commentary on the *Canzoniere* and the *Trionfi* was released the following year, in 1533 (Naples: Antonio Iovino e Mattia Canzer). This commentary stands out especially for its references to Aristotle and Petrarch's Latin works (in particular the *Secretum*, *De remediis utriusque fortune*, and *Sine nomine*). The ponderous commentary on the *Canzoniere* and the *Trionfi* by Giovanni Andrea Gesualdo, also published in 1533 (Venice: Giovanni Antonio di Nicolini e fratelli da Sabbio), was still commercially more successful than Fausto's and Silvano's.[23] Indeed, it was the only sixteenth-century commentary able to compete at least partially with Vellutello's. Gesualdo, a disciple of Antonio Minturno in Naples, devoted much attention to the grammatical, rhetorical, and metrical aspects. His commentary is also innovative for quotations from Greek authors (such as Homer, Musaeus, Aeschylus, Sophocles, Euripides, Aeschines, Nonnus of Panopolis, and even Paul the Silentiary). Another important commentary on the *Canzoniere* and the *Trionfi* was published by Bernardino Daniello, first in 1541 and then — substantially revised and augmented — in 1549 (Venice: Nicolini da Sabio).[24] Daniello is also the author of a dialogue *Della poetica* (1536) and a posthumous commentary on Dante's *Comedy* (1568). He belonged to the literary circle around Pietro Bembo and Trifon Gabriele, the so-called 'Venetian Socrates'. The latter, although he wrote almost nothing, was a key figure in the Venetian culture of the first half of the sixteenth century through his oral teachings on philological and interpretative issues concerning both ancient and modern authors.[25] Daniello's commentary is very much indebted to Bembo's and above all Gabriele's teachings, to such an extent that many rumoured that Gabriele should be considered the real author of the commentary. Especially in the 1549 edition, Daniello suggested some new sources and precedents from the Bible, as well as from Greek, Latin, and vernacular authors, in addition to new parallels with Petrarch's Latin works. More importantly, by benefiting from some Petrarchan autographs (especially those nowadays collected in the ms. Vat.lat.3196, the so-called 'Codice

---

23   See Francesca D'Alessandro, 'Il Petrarca di Minturno e Gesualdo: preistoria del pensiero poetico tassiano', *Aevum*, 79.3 (2005), 615–37; Busjan, *Petrarca-Hermeneutik*.
24   See Ezio Raimondi, 'Bernardino Daniello e le varianti petrarchesche', *Studi Petrarcheschi*, 5 (1952), 95–130, reprinted in Ezio Raimondi, *Rinascimento Inquieto* (Turin: Einaudi, 1994), pp. 19–56.
25   On Gabriele's Petrarchan teachings, see Lino Pertile, 'A lezione da Trifon Gabriele: Il sonetto "Anima, che diverse cose tante" del Petrarca', in *Studies for Dante: Essays in Honor of Dante Della Terza*, ed. by Franco Fido, Rena-Anna Syska-Lamparska, and Pamela D. Stewart (Fiesole: Cadmo, 1998), pp. 145–52.

degli abbozzi'), Daniello transcribed and discussed many corrections and glosses by Petrarch, anticipating modern genetic criticism. In the same direction, a few years later (1563/64) Ludovico Beccadelli wrote a 'speech' on Petrarch's corrections to some of his poems.[26] The handwritten annotations in Petrarch's 1514 Aldine edition owned by the Biblioteca Civica of Padua are also related to the Bembian environment. Their author is the Friulian Giulio Camillo Delminio, commonly known for his visionary and mysterious project of the 'Theatre of Memory'.[27] The erudition of such glosses is remarkable, in particular for the references to Provençal poetry. Camillo is also the author of an *Espositione* on the first two poems of the *Canzoniere*.[28] In the same years as Daniello's editions, Ludovico Castelvetro wrote his commentary on the *Canzoniere*. Indeed, even if it was published posthumously only in 1582 (Basel: Pietro de Sedabonis), its first version dates back to 1545. Castelvetro, condemned for heresy by the Inquisition and protagonist of a celebrated literary quarrel with the poet Annibal Caro, is commonly considered the most important and original critic of the sixteenth century. His commentary is very different from the previous ones, because he examined and judged Petrarch's poems from a very strict philological and grammatical perspective, leaving aside any moral and philosophical interpretation. On such a basis, he did not hesitate to express highly polemical views regarding Petrarch's linguistic choices.[29] Among the shorter annotations and the partial commentaries published in the sixteenth century, it is worth mentioning Giovan Battista Castiglione's *I luoghi difficili del Petrarcha* (Venice: Giovanni Antonio Nicolini, 1532) and Antonio Brucioli's 'Dichiarazioni e

26   Beccadelli's 'speech' was published in *Le rime di Francesco Petrarca tratte da' migliori esemplari con illustrazioni inedite di Ludovico Beccadelli*, 2 vols (Verona: Stamperia Giuliari, 1799), and, more recently, in Giuseppe Frasso, *Studi su i 'Rerum vulgarium fragmenta' e i 'Triumphi'*, 1: *Francesco Petrarca e Ludovico Beccadelli* (Padua: Antenore, 1983). See also Maria Chiara Tarsi, 'Beccadelli e Della Casa alla scuola di Bembo', *Aevum*, 87.3 (2013), 759–81 (pp. 779–81).
27   See Giulio Camillo, *L'idea del theatro. Con 'L'idea dell'eloquenza', il 'De transmutatione' e altri testi inediti*, ed. by Lina Bolzoni (Milan: Adelphi, 2015).
28   See Giulio Camillo, *Chiose al Petrarca*, ed. by Paolo Zaja (Rome-Padua: Antenore, 2009). See also: Corrado Bologna, 'Giulio Camillo, il canzoniere provenzale N2 e un inedito commento al Petrarca', in *Miscellanea di studi in onore di Aurelio Roncaglia a cinquant'anni dalla sua laurea*, ed. by Roberto Antonelli, 4 vols (Modena: Mucchi, 1989), 1, 187–213; Valentina Grohovaz, 'Prime note sul commento al Petrarca attribuito a Giulio Camillo Delminio', in *Filologia ed esegesi petrarchesca fra Tre e Cinquecento. Atti del convegno internazionale di studi (Trieste, 19–21 settembre 1986)*, ed. by Laura Casarsa, Special issue of *Studi Petrarcheschi*, 4 (1987), 339–47; Valentina Grohovaz, 'A proposito di alcuni frammenti manoscritti di opere di Giulio Camillo Delminio e Lodovico Castelvetro', *Aevum*, 67.3 (1993), 519–32.
29   See Ezio Raimondi, 'Gli scrupoli di un filologo. Ludovico Castelvetro e il Petrarca' [1952], in Ezio Raimondi, *Rinascimento Inquieto* (Turin: Einaudi, 1994), pp. 57–142; Valentina Grohovaz, 'Francesco Melchiori e Lodovico Castelvetro: frammenti di un dibattito cinquecentesco. A proposito di *Rerum Vulgarium Fragmenta* CCCLXI', *Studi petrarcheschi*, 10 (1993), 251–80; Valentina Grohovaz, 'Gli esordi di Lodovico Castelvetro nel commento a Petrarca: la lettera a Giovanni Falloppia (ms. Ambr. D 246 inf)', in *Omaggio a Lodovico Castelvetro (1505–1571). Atti del seminario di Helsinki, 14 ottobre 2005*, ed. by Enrico Garavelli (Helsinki: Publications du Département des Langues Romanes, 2006), pp. 7–25; Alberto Roncaccia, *Il metodo critico di Ludovico Castelvetro* (Rome: Bulzoni, 2006); Alberto Roncaccia, 'Castelvetro lettore di Petrarca: "Mai non vo' più cantar com'io soleva" (*RVF* 105)', in *Il poeta e il suo pubblico*, pp. 133–43.

annotazioni' in *Sonetti, canzoni, et triomphi di m. Francesco Petrarca* (Venice: Alessandro Brucioli e fratelli, 1548). Besides, many editions of the *Canzoniere* — like the ones by Lodovico Dolce (Venice: Giolito, 1554) and Girolamo Ruscelli (Venice: Pietrasanta, 1554) examined in this volume[30] — were provided with biographies, glossaries, rhyming dictionaries, etc. In this context, the glossary of the *Canzoniere* offered by Francesco Alunno's 'Osservazioni' in *Il Petrarca* (Venice: Francesco Marcolini, 1539, reprinted in a new and expanded version in Venice: Paolo Gherardo, 1550) is especially successful. Another mode of exegesis that attracted the interest of scholars, especially in recent years, is the 'lecture' on single poems from the *Canzoniere* (and some 'capitoli' in the *Trionfi*). Renaissance academies were an ideal environment for such a genre. Scholars have particularly focused their attention on the Accademia degli Infiammati of Padua (founded in 1540) and the Accademia Fiorentina (founded in 1541), with special regard to the lectures held by Benedetto Varchi and Giovan Battista Gelli.[31] However, the phenomenon of lectures on Petrarch's poems was widespread.[32]

The sixteenth century (especially the first half) was the golden age of Petrarch's exegesis in the Early Modern period. In the seventeenth century, the number of editions of the *Canzoniere* and commentaries decreased (nonetheless, it must be mentioned that over fifty editions of the *Canzoniere* were published in the first half

---

30   See Cristina Acucella's essay in this volume. See also Amedeo Quondam, *Petrarchismo mediato: Per una critica della forma "antologia"* (Rome: Bulzoni, 1974); Michele Caro Marino, 'Il paratesto nelle edizioni rinascimentali italiane del *Canzoniere* e dei *Trionfi*', in *Dante, Petrarca, Boccaccio e il paratesto. Le edizioni rinascimentali delle 'tre corone'*, ed. by Marco Santoro, Michele Caro Marino, and Marco Pacioni (Rome: Edizioni dell'Ateneo, 2006), pp. 51–76.

31   Cf. *Lezioni sul Petrarca*, ed. by Huss, Neumann, Regn; Maria Teresa Girardi, 'La lezione su "Verdi panni, sanguigni, oscuri o persi" (*RVF* XXIX) di Benedetto Varchi Accademico Infiammato', *Aevum*, 79.3 (2005), 677–718; Carlo Alberto Girotto, 'Una riscrittura accademica (Gelli-Doni)', *Studi rinascimentali*, 3 (2005), 45–63; Franco Tomasi, 'Le letture di poesia e il Petrarchismo nell'Accademia degli Infiammati', in *Il Petrarchismo. Un modello di poesia per l'Europa*, ed. by Floriana Calitti and Roberto Gigliucci, 2 vols (Rome: Bulzoni, 2006), 2, 229–50; Laura Paolino, 'All'origine della tradizione esegetica delle *disperse*: il commento di Giovan Battista Gelli alla ballata "Donna mi vene spesso nella mente"', in *Estravaganti, disperse, apocrifi petrarcheschi. Gargnano del Garda (25–27 settembre 2006)*, ed. by Claudia Berra and Paola Vecchi Galli (Milan: Cisalpino-Monduzzi, 2007), pp. 249–86; Annalisa Andreoni, *La via della dottrina. Le lezioni accademiche di Benedetto Varchi* (Pisa: ETS, 2012), pp. 43–92, 239–316; Federica Pich, 'Dante and Petrarch in Giovan Battista Gelli's Lectures at the Florentine Academy', in *Remembering the Middle Ages in Early Modern Italy*, ed. by Lorenzo Pericolo and Jessica N. Richardson (Turnhout: Brepols, [2015]), pp. 169–91; Bernhard Huss, 'Aristotelismus und Petrarkismus in der Accademia Fiorentina des *Cinquecento*: Das Beispiel von G.B. Gellis Interpretation zu Petrarca, *Canzoniere* no. 78', *Philosophical Readings*, 7.3 (2015), 23–42; Selene Maria Vatteroni, 'Le lezioni petrarchesche e i *Sonetti*. *Parte prima* di Benedetto Varchi', *Nuova Rivista di Letteratura Italiana*, 22.2 (2019), 41-64; Bernhard Huss, 'La lezione di Benedetto Varchi sul *Triumphus Cupidinis* e la raffigurazione rinascimentale di *Amor*', *Petrarchesca*, 7 (2019), 67–94; *La cultura poetica di Benedetto Varchi. Atti della Giornata di Studi (Freie Universität Berlin, 9 novembre 2018)*, ed. by Selene Maria Vatteroni, *Schriften des Italienzentrums der Freien Universität Berlin*, 3 (2019).

32   See for example Anna Laura Puliafito, 'Petrarca filosofo platonico. Francesco Patrizi commentatore di un sonetto petrarchesco (*RVF* VII)', in *Para/Textuelle Verhandlungen zwischen Dichtung und Philosophie in der Frühen Neuzeit*, ed. by Bernhard Huss, Patrizia Marzillo, and Thomas Ricklin (Berlin-New York: De Gruyter, 2011), pp. 379–98; Lorenzo Sacchini, *Identità, lettere e virtù. Le lezioni accademiche degli Insensati di Perugia (1561–1608)* (Bologna: I libri di Emil, 2016).

of the century). It is no wonder that the Baroque period devoted less attention to Petrarch's interpretation, considering its opposition to the principle of imitation. Petrarch was no more the model *par excellence* for poetic writing. Indeed, the real polemical objective of Alessandro Tassoni's *Considerazioni sopra le Rime del Petrarca* (Modena: Giuliano Cassiani, 1609) is the principle of imitation, more than the *Canzoniere* in itself. Tassoni, who is also the author of the mock-heroic poem *La secchia rapita*, blamed the many Petrarchists who uncritically followed the model of Petrarch. Like Castelvetro, he dwelled above all on technical aspects, such as tropes, rhythm, cacophonies, etc. In the seventeenth century, there was also an ideological reason for the feeling of distance from the *Canzoniere*. Petrarch had been considered a 'model of life' in the sixteenth century.[33] That is particularly evident in the commentaries by Vellutello, Gesualdo, and Daniello, who emphasized the psychological and romantic aspects of the *Canzoniere*. In the seventeenth century, instead, the attitude towards love was generally less idealistic, but rather ironic and detached (however, some prefiguration of such an approach had been already offered in satirical modes by the anti-Petrarchist writers of the sixteenth century, like Francesco Berni, Pietro Aretino, Anton Francesco Doni, Niccolò Franco, etc.). That explains the negative remarks about Petrarch in several lectures, dialogues, treatises, etc., such as Lodovico Zuccolo's *Il Gradenico [...] Nel quale si discorre contra l'amor platonico, & a longo si ragiona di quello del Petrarca* (Bologna: Gio. Battista Bellagamba, 1608)[34] and Ansaldo Cebà's lectures on the sonnets 'Solo e pensoso i più diserti campi' (*RVF*, 35) and 'Vidi fra mille donne una già tale' (*RVF*, 335), included in his *Essercitii accademici* (Genova: Giuseppe Pavoni, 1621, but written in the 1590s).[35]

The situation changed starting from the late seventeenth century. In 1690, the Academy of Arcadia was founded in Rome to oppose Marinism. While the latter aimed at virtuosity and surprise to achieve a sense of awe, the Arcadian age extolled clarity, simplicity, and measure as supreme values. Thanks to such a perspective, Petrarch once again became a paradigm of poetic excellence. In particular, Giovan Mario Crescimbeni's *L'istoria della volgar poesia* (Rome: Luca Antonio Chracas, 1698) and Lodovico Antonio Muratori's *Della perfetta poesia italiana* (Modena: Soliani, 1706) were very influential in giving Petrarch a dominant role in the literary canon. Muratori, the greatest erudite scholar of the eighteenth century, is also the author of an important commentary on the *Canzoniere*, published together with Tassoni's *Considerazioni* and some annotations by the sixteenth century writer Girolamo Muzio (Modena: Bartolomeo Soliani, 1711).[36] Most of Muratori's observations

33   See Baldacci, *Il petrarchismo italiano*.

34   A second version of this dialogue was published with the title 'Il Carrara overo Squittino dell'Amor de' Platonici et del Petrarca', in Lodovico Zuccolo, *Dialoghi* (Perugia: Annibale Aluigi e fratelli, 1615), pp. 83–147.

35   See Luigia Tassoni, 'Dante e Petrarca nel Seicento', in *Storia della letteratura italiana*, XI: *La critica letteraria dal Due al Novecento*, pp. 485–505; *Petrarca in Barocco: cantieri petrarcheschi. Due seminari romani*, ed. by Amedeo Quondam (Rome: Bulzoni, 2004); Simona Morando, 'Petrarca al vaglio degli affetti. Su alcuni commenti primo-secenteschi', *Lettere italiane*, 63.4 (2011), 505–34.

36   Muzio's annotations were taken from Girolamo Nuzio, *Battaglie [...] per diffesa dell'italica lingua [...] Et alcune bellissime annotationi sopra il Petrarca* (Venice: Dusinelli, 1582).

are psychological, but he also paid attention to some formal issues. The approach of his commentary reminds one in some way of those of Castelvetro and Tassoni because he used his own critical judgement instead of tradition to evaluate the *Canzoniere*. Even if he was a great admirer of Petrarch, he often criticized single poems of the *Canzoniere*. Indeed, he praised Tassoni because he was brave enough to occasionally blame Petrarch's poems for their flaws, instead of repeating uncritically the appreciative remarks of previous commentators.[37]

2. An Overview of the Book

This succinct overview of the commentary tradition on Petrarch's *Canzoniere* from the fifteenth to the eighteenth century has attempted to trace and highlight the works and aspects scholarship has considered most closely. The nine essays collected in this volume build on this critical literature and widen our knowledge on the subject in some distinctive ways. The majority of them focus on the sixteenth century, which is, as our overview has indicated, the age of Petrarchism *par excellence*. While the contours of Petrarch's exegetical reception in the fifteenth century are relatively clear, matters become far more complicated in the sixteenth century, despite the valuable guidance provided by Gino Belloni and William J. Kennedy.[38] Indeed, in the sixteenth century, as we have suggested, the interpretative debate on Petrarch involved not only commentaries, but also a rich variety of other genres of discourse, such as lectures, treatises, dialogues, letters, paratexts of editions, etc. While the main regular commentaries have already been analysed in some detail, as shown above, there is still much to do about other types of writing that offer some interesting observations about the interpretation and the evaluation of the *Canzoniere*. For this reason and in order to address these omissions, the present volume concentrates its attention on some (often little-known) works of the sixteenth century that cannot be considered as commentaries on the *Canzoniere* in the strict sense, but have clear exegetical functions. The works include: love dialogues and treatises; two editions of the *Canzoniere* provided with a wide array of paratexts; a lecture and a speech dealing with the figure of Madonna Laura; a theoretical text on poetry and the lyrical genre that acts as a prologue to an academic lecture on Petrarch; a prosimetrum consisting of devices, speeches, and poems that gives emphasis to the moral and philosophical connotations of the *Canzoniere*; a series of academic lectures in different forms, ranging from the 'spositione' to the narrative dialogue and that offer a basic interpretation of Petrarch's poetry and its

---

37   See Mario Fubini, 'Le *Osservazioni* del Muratori al Petrarca e la critica letteraria nell'età dell'Arcadia', in *Dal Muratori al Baretti. Studi sulla critica e sulla cultura del Settecento* (Rome-Bari: Laterza, 1975), I, 49–173; Alfredo Cottignoli, *Muratori teorico* (Bologna: CLUEB, 1987); Roberto Tissoni, *Il commento ai classici italiani nel Sette e nell'Ottocento (Dante e Petrarca)*, revised edition (Padua: Antenore, 1993), pp. 11–30; Corrado Viola, *Tradizioni letterarie a confronto. Italia e Francia nella polemica Orsi-Bouhours* (Verona: Fiorini, 2001), pp. 391–417; *Il petrarchismo nel Settecento e nell'Ottocento*, ed. by Sandro Gentili and Luigi Trenti (Rome: Bulzoni, 2006); Rossella Bonfatti, *L'"erario" della modernità. Muratori tra etica ed estetica* (Bologna: Clueb, 2010); Michele Mari, *La critica letteraria nel Settecento* (Milan: Ledizioni, 2013); *Petrarca, l'Italia, l'Europa*, ed. by Tinelli (in particular, the essays by Grazia Distaso, Giovanna Scianatico, and Francesco Saverio Minervini).
38   See Belloni, *Laura tra Petrarca e Bembo*; Kennedy, *Authorizing Petrarch*.

grammatical, linguistic, rhetorical, and semantic aspects. In addition, this volume also offers some insights on the interpretation and evaluation of the *Canzoniere* in the seventeenth and eighteenth centuries, a phase that has been more neglected than the Renaissance period by scholars of Petrarch's reception. In particular, two essays consider the aforementioned *Considerazioni sul Petrarca* by Alessandro Tassoni and the consequent literary quarrel between the latter and Giuseppe degli Aromatari. The final essay in the volume examines the eighteenth-century debate on Petrarch (and the Petrarchists) from a privileged observatory, namely the influential *Giornale de' letterati italiani*.

The first essay by Maiko Favaro ('A Problematic and Contradictory Authority: Petrarch in the Love Treatises of the Sixteenth and Early Seventeenth Centuries') draws attention to the reception of the *Canzoniere* in the love treatises of the sixteenth and early seventeenth centuries. Petrarch's verses are often quoted therein in order to solve some of the most controversial issues about love theory. Nonetheless, as Favaro shows, Petrarch appears as a problematic and ambiguous authority. The ideas expressed in his poems are frequently in contrast with common sense and/or the opinions of other well-reputed authors. In several cases, he even seems to contradict himself. This essay aims to analyse how the authors of love treatises deal with such difficulties in order to identify some recurring patterns in their argumentations.

One of the most well-known editorial rivalries of the Renaissance is at the centre of the essay in Chapter 2 by Cristina Acucella ('Editing Petrarch in Venice: The *Canzoniere* in the Dispute between Ruscelli and Dolce'). Girolamo Ruscelli and Ludovico Dolce were two of the main editors in mid-sixteenth-century Venice. In 1553, Ruscelli addressed a bitter pamphlet to his rival, entitled *Tre discorsi a M. Lodovico Dolce* (Venice: Pietrasanta, 1553). Even if their editorial war was fought mainly on the front of the illustrated prints of the *Orlando Furioso*, it is interesting that just a year after the *Tre discorsi*, in 1554, both Dolce (Venice: Giolito, 1554) and Ruscelli (Venice: Pietrasanta, 1554) edited Petrarch's *Canzoniere*. Acucella compares the two editions, highlighting their differences regarding editorial choices, paratexts, and philological aspects. She also considers their relationship with the 1501 Aldine edition. In addition, she focuses on the idea of Petrarch that the reader can obtain from the letters and the paratexts in the two editions.

Renaissance readers were very interested in the figure of Laura. The following essay in Chapter 3 by Guglielmo Barucci ('Laura's Nobility and Greatness in Two Sixteenth-Century Florentine Speeches by Simone della Barba (1554) and Francesco de' Vieri (1580)') demonstrates that not only does Madonna Laura assume a biographical identity through commentaries and paratexts, she also represents a model of behaviours, values, and virtues. Barucci analyses this new role on the basis of two texts: the *Nuova spositione del sonetto che comincia 'In nobil sangue uita humile, e queta' ne la quale si dichiara qual sia stata la vera nobiltà di madonna Laura* by Simone della Barba, a lecture held before the Florentine Academy and published in 1554; and the *Discorso della grandezza, et felice fortuna d'una gentilissima, & graziosiss. donna, qual fù m. Laura* by Francesco de' Vieri Jr., printed in 1580. The former, recalling the frame of the classical and medieval discussion on nobility (Cicero, Dante, Bartolo), elaborates a series of systematic reflections on political and ethical matters that is based on *RVF*, 215 and other quotations on Laura. The latter recalls the main stages of Laura's existence, until her ascent to Heaven. Vieri proposes Laura as a model for contemporary women.

The text analysed by Giacomo Comiati in Chapter 4 ('Judging Petrarch in the Venetian Accademia della Fama: Celio Magno and his *Prefatione sopra il Petrarca* (c. 1558)') reflects on Petrarch from a more general and theoretical point of view. Comiati dwells on the *Prefazione al Petrarca* written in the late 1550s by the Venetian Celio Magno. The *Prefazione* was first delivered as a speech during a meeting of the Venetian Accademia della Fama, one of Venice's best-known, if relatively short-lived, academies. Magno's analysis of Petrarch enables us to widen our knowledge of the discussions on poetics and rhetoric in that academy, one of the liveliest and most stimulating of the Cinquecento. Comiati also compares the *Prefazione* with Bernardo Tasso's *Ragionamento de la poesia*. The *Prefazione* represents the theoretical elaboration of many poetical concepts that Magno later applied in his lyrical production. Therefore, this preface also helps us to better understand his poetry.

The academic environment and the theoretical, philosophical concerns are also at the centre of the following essay in Chapter 5 by Simona Oberto ('Anthological *Discorsi* as Means of 'Doctrinization' of Petrarchism in the *Rime degli Accademici Occulti* (1568)'). Oberto examines the *Rime* (1568) of an important Brescian academy, the Accademia degli Occulti. The *Rime* consist of a prosimetrum with devices, speeches, and poems. The speeches are specifically used to transmit doctrinal, especially philosophical, knowledge, and thus to create a poetics of *gravitas*. With this aim in mind, not only do the Occulti emphasize the moral value of Petrarch's poems, but they also disclose what they believe is a philosophical intention in the *Canzoniere*.

The linguistic aspect in exegetical writing on Petrarch is instead prevalent in the academic lectures on Petrarch by Gregorio Anastagi from Perugia, analysed by Lorenzo Sacchini in Chapter 6 ('Reading Petrarch: Gregorio Anastagi's (1536/39–1601) Manuscript Writings on Petrarch's *Canzoniere*'). Anastagi's lectures are unpublished: they can be read on a manuscript of the Biblioteca Civica 'Attilio Hortis' in Trieste. Anastagi's interest in Petrarch's language is well exemplified in the first lecture by the list of words it is deemed legitimate to use in prose and poetry. Sacchini carefully takes into consideration Anastagi's intended audience and the influence it might have played in shaping his lectures. He also focuses on the different forms of the lectures (from the traditional 'spositione' to the fairly unusual narrative dialogue) and considers the marked preference for classical theorists and authors over contemporaneous literary critics.

The following two essays, Chapters 7 and 8, are both devoted to the *Considerazioni sul Petrarca* (1609) by Alessandro Tassoni. Andrea Lazzarini ('Deconstructing Petrarch: Alessandro Tassoni's *Considerazioni sopra le Rime del Petrarca*') discusses the textual history of this work and shows its main traits. As we noted in our earlier overview, the *Considerazioni* testify to a transformed attitude towards Petrarch's poems. Indeed, Tassoni openly criticizes many passages and features of the *Canzoniere*. While not a supporter of the 'Ancients', Tassoni is one of the harshest critics of 'modern' baroque tendencies, attacking the use of excessive and extravagant metaphors. The following chapter by Laura Benedetti ('Petrarch, Aristotle, and the Inquisition: The Controversy between Giuseppe degli Aromatari and Alessandro Tassoni') dwells on the quarrel between Tassoni and Giuseppe degli Aromatari. The latter was outraged by Tassoni's criticism of Petrarch and especially of Petrarchists. In his response (1611), Aromatari examined the first ten poems of the *Canzoniere* and defended Petrarch on the basis of Aristotelian principles.

The last essay in our volume (Chapter 9) is that by Giacomo Vagni ('"Nobiltà dello stile" and "grandezza e rarità del pensiero": Petrarch and the Petrarchists in Apostolo Zeno's *Giornale de' letterati italiani* (1710–18)'), and it explores an important example of Petrarch's reception in the eighteenth century. Vagni analyses how the *Giornale de' letterati italiani* (published from 1710 to 1740) dealt with freshly published books on Petrarch and his imitators. Following the path of Ludovico Antonio Muratori and Giovan Mario Crescimbeni, the *Giornale* sought to canonize the Italian lyrical tradition from Petrarch to Tasso as a way to restore the nobility and credibility of Italian poetry after the 'eccessi' of the Baroque. In this light, the *Giornale* can be considered one of the last examples of critical reflection on Petrarchism that is coherent with Renaissance tradition, before the Romantic revolution radically changed the approach towards Petrarch's poems.

The present volume appears at a propitious moment for research on Petrarch's reception in the Early Modern period. In addition to the bibliography already mentioned in the first part of the introduction, we would like to mention in particular the recent UK project *Petrarch Commentary and Exegesis in Renaissance Italy, c. 1350–c. 1650*, which provides both a searchable online catalogue of print and manuscript copies of exegetical works related to Petrarch's *Canzoniere* and *Trionfi*, and an online digital library encompassing full digitizations of many early printed Petrarch editions and commentary material.[39] In such a flourishing context, this book aims to offer orientation and insight into the diversity of ways Petrarch's *Canzoniere* was read, judged and interpreted across a broad chronological span, from the sixteenth to the eighteenth centuries, drawing attention at the same time to some neglected but stimulating works that deserve scholarly attention.

---

39   See <https://petrarch.mml.ox.ac.uk/> [accessed 16 July 2019]. The project was funded by the Arts and Humanities Research Council (January 2017–December 2019). The online searchable catalogue PERI (Petrarch Exegesis in Renaissance Italy Database) contains information collated by Drs. Giacomo Comiati, Lorenzo Sacchini, and Francesco Venturi and has been overseen by Prof. Simon Gilson and Dr. Federica Pich. The online digital library has been overseen by Dr. Guyda Armstrong and Julianne Simpson.

CHAPTER 1

A Problematic and Contradictory Authority: Petrarch in the Love Treatises of the Sixteenth and Early Seventeenth Centuries

Maiko Favaro

1. Introduction

In the Italian Renaissance, the popularity of love treatises was due to the diffusion of Neoplatonism and Petrarchism, which gave a positive significance to love and fostered interest in debate regarding its various aspects. It is not by chance that two of the foundational works of Renaissance love theory were written by the fathers of Renaissance Neoplatonism and Petrarchism, namely Marsilio Ficino and Pietro Bembo respectively. The former is the author of the *Commentarium in Convivium Platonis de amore* (written in 1468/69, but printed in 1484), based on Plato's *Symposium*. The latter wrote *Gli Asolani* (first edition: 1505, published in a new version in 1530), a dialogue that aims to establish if love is something positive or negative. During the sixteenth and the early seventeenth centuries, love theory was discussed in a wide range of works. Indeed, by the expression 'love treatises', I here refer not only to treatises in the strict sense, but also to dialogues, speeches, lectures, collections of novellas, book of games, 'dubbi', and 'conclusioni'.[1]

One of the most interesting aspects in this kind of production is that Petrarch's verses (especially from the *Canzoniere*, but sometimes also from the *Trionfi*) are often quoted in order to discuss some of the most controversial issues about love theory. Petrarch is a problematic and ambiguous authority when used in these works,

---

1   For an overview on this production, see Paolo Lorenzetti, *La bellezza e l'amore nei trattati del Cinquecento* (Pisa: Nistri, 1917); Ruth Kelso, *The Doctrine of the English Gentleman in the Sixteenth Century* (Urbana: University of Illinois Press, 1929); Ruth Kelso, *Doctrine for the Lady of the Renaissance* (Urbana: University of Illinois Press, 1956); John Charles Nelson, *Renaissance Theory of Love* (New York: Columbia University Press, 1958); Mario Pozzi, 'Aspetti della trattatistica d'amore', in Mario Pozzi, *Lingua, cultura, società. Saggi sulla letteratura italiana del Cinquecento* (Alessandria: Edizioni dell'Orso, 1989), pp. 57–100; Stefano Prandi, *Il 'Cortegiano' ferrarese. I 'Discorsi' di Annibale Romei e la cultura nobiliare nel Cinquecento* (Florence: Olschki, 1990), pp. 212–18; Sabrina Ebbersmeyer, *Sinnlichkeit und Vernunft. Studien zur Rezeption und Transformation der Liebestheorie Platons in der Renaissance* (München: Fink, 2002); Maiko Favaro, *'L'ospite preziosa'. Presenze della lirica nei trattati d'amore del Cinquecento e del primo Seicento* (Lucca: Pacini Fazzi, 2012). A more extensive account of the results discussed in the present chapter is given in a recent book of mine: *Ambiguità del petrarchismo. Un percorso fra trattati d'amore, lettere e templi di rime* (Milan: FrancoAngeli, 2021), chaps. 1 and 3.

because at times the ideas expressed in his poems are in contrast with common sense and/or the opinions of other well-reputed authors and because he even seems to contradict himself.

In the first part of this essay, we will examine how Petrarch is used to defend opposite points of view on the same question in a little-known but interesting love dialogue by Cornelio Frangipane. In the second part, we will dwell on the aspects of love theory on which Petrarch's authority appears most problematic to Renaissance authors. In particular, we would like to analyse how they deal with such difficulties, in order to identify some recurring patterns in their argumentations.

2. An Authority for Opposite Perspectives: Petrarch in Cornelio Frangipane's *Dialogo d'amore*

Cornelio Frangipane (1508–1588) was a Friulian nobleman and a brilliant lawyer. He was a pupil of Giulio Camillo Delminio and a friend of Pier Paolo Vergerio, the bishop of Capodistria (Koper) who became a Protestant reformer and polemist. Indeed, Frangipane's orthodoxy has been questioned. He was in contact with intellectuals like Sperone Speroni, Trifon Gabriele, Pietro Aretino, Girolamo Fracastoro, and Benedetto Varchi. In addition to the *Dialogo d'amore*, he wrote many other works, including love poems, letters, philosophical and religious writings, a rhetorical treatise (*Del parlar senatorio*), and a *Lettera overo discorso che sia meglio governare li popoli con timore che con amore*. Many of his texts are still unpublished.[2]

The work by Frangipane analysed here was published posthumously under the title of *Dialogo d'amore* in 1588 (Venice: Guerra), but its first manuscript version dates back to August 1541.[3] Properly speaking, this work is a dialogue included in a letter. Indeed, Frangipane writes to his friend Mario Savorgnan, one of the most powerful Friulian noblemen of the period, who was also a cultivated man and an expert of military art.[4] He wants to give him a detailed account of an interesting conversation he witnessed shortly before in Venice, during one of his missions as an ambassador of the 'Patria del Friuli'. In particular, the dialogue takes place at the salon of 'Signora Tullia', who is described as eloquent and cultivated in a way unusual for women. It is easy to assume that Frangipane is speaking of the celebrated courtesan Tullia d'Aragona.[5] A lover of Tullia, a certain Geri from Siena, has to leave from

2   For more information on Frangipane's life and works, see: Gian Giuseppe Liruti, *Notizie delle vite ed opere scritte da letterati del Friuli*, 4 vols (Venice-Udine-Venice: Modesto Fenzo-fratelli Gallici-Alvisopoli), II (Venice: Modesto Fenzo, 1762), pp. 161–80; Prospero Antonini, 'Cornelio Frangipane di Castello. Giureconsulto, oratore e poeta del secolo XVI', *Archivio storico italiano*, s. IV, 8 (1881), 19–64 and 335–65; 9 (1882), 20–60 and 296–335; Silvano Cavazza, 'Frangipane, Cornelio', in *Dizionario biografico degli italiani* (Rome: Istituto dell'Enciclopedia italiana, 1960–2020), L (1998), 227–30; Silvano Cavazza, 'Frangipane, Cornelio', in *Nuovo Liruti. Dizionario biografico dei friulani*, vol. II, *L'età veneta*, part 2, ed. by Cesare Scalon, Claudio Griggio, and Ugo Rozzo (Udine: Forum, 2009), pp. 1188–93.
3   For a more detailed analysis of this work and its chronology, see: Maiko Favaro, 'L'*auctoritas* di Petrarca e la lontananza dell'amante: il caso del *Dialogo d'amore* (1588) di Cornelio Frangipane', in *Interdisciplinarità del petrarchismo. Prospettive di ricerca fra Italia e Germania*, ed. by Maiko Favaro and Bernhard Huss (Florence: Olschki, 2018), pp. 17–34.
4   On Mario Savorgnan, see Roberto Norbedo, 'Savorgnan Del Monte (D'Osoppo, Dello Scaglione), Mario Aurelio detto Mario il Vecchio', in *Nuovo Liruti*, vol. II, part 3, 2283–88.
5   It is worth noting that, on the basis of the information at our disposal, Frangipane's dialogue

Venice on request of his old father. Geri promises that he will come back after his father's death. Tullia claims that she, the lover who remains, will suffer more than Geri, the lover who leaves, whereas Geri supports the opposite opinion. Therefore, Tullia proposes to discuss this question. Firstly, Tullia explains in a speech the reasons why the lover who remains suffers more than the lover who leaves. Here below, I outline her arguments, together with her quotations:

Arguments	Quotation(s)
1) The lover who leaves does not truly love, otherwise he/she would prioritize love over any other duty	Virgil, *Aeneid*, IV. 307–08 (Dido)
2) The lover who leaves takes with him/her the heart of the lover who remains	Petrarch, *Rerum vulgarium fragmenta* (hereafter *RVF*), 268. 4; 313. 7–8; Bembo, *Rime*, 160. 1
3) The lover who remains suffers because he/she is afraid that his/her beloved can be hurt or even killed while travelling	
4) The lover who remains suffers while seeing the places connected to his/her love story	Petrarch, *RVF*, 112. 5, 9–11; 301. 1, 7; Ovid, *Epist.*, XV. 137–38, 143–46 (Sappho to Phaon)
5) The lover who remains is overwhelmed by fear if his/her beloved does not come back at the planned date	Ovid, *Epist.*, II. 2 ff. (Phyllis to Demophon); Ariosto, *Orlando Furioso*, XXXII. 18–25 (Bradamante)
6) Men are unfaithful	Catullus, LXIV. 143–44 (Ariadne); *exempla*: Oenone, Hypsipyle, Sappho, Penelope, Laodamia, and other Greek women (cf. Ovid, *Epist.*, I, V, VI, XIII, XV); Virgil, *Aeneid*, IV. 309–10 (Dido)
	Tullia sings a madrigal (text without attribution, inc. *Qual fia il dolor de la crudel partita*)

As we can see, Tullia quotes from Petrarch in several cases. Despite the gender difference between Petrarch and Tullia, the latter can rely on the *Canzoniere*, because she considers it as an essential 'document' in order to understand love's phenomenology and psychology, with no need to consider the lover's gender. However, Tullia also has recourse to some other authorities, with special regard to

could be actually based on a real life experience. Indeed, in Frangipane's personal diary we can read that he was in Venice as an ambassador for the 'Patria del Friuli' from 8 June to 7 July 1541 (see Antonini, 'Cornelio Frangipane', 8 (1881), 30). The manuscript version of the *Dialogo d'amore* is explicitly dated 20 August 1541. At the same time, we do not know where Tullia was in June–July 1541 (see Salvatore Bongi, *Annali di Gabriel Giolito De' Ferrari [...]*, I (Rome: presso i principali librai, 1890), 172).

6   This madrigal is attested as starting in 1542, with music attributed to Hubert Naich. It was reprinted several times in the following years, mainly attributed to Hubert Naich (1546, 1547, 1548, 1567), even if once attributed to Leonardo Meldert (1578) and in two cases the author is declared anonymous (1543, 1558): see *RePIM — Repertorio della Poesia Italiana in Musica (1500–1700)*, ed. by Angelo Pompilio, <http://repim.muspe.unibo.it/repim> [accessed 3 August 2019]. The text of the madrigal is also published — in a version slightly different from that by Frangipane — in *Poesie italiane inedite di dugento autori — dall'origine della lingua infino al secolo decimosettimo*, ed. by Francesco Trucchi, III (Prato: Guasti, 1847), 303: it is copied from a manuscript 'Magliabechiano 371' and attributed to an unknown author of the sixteenth century.

Ovid's *Heroides*. The latter are particularly useful for her argumentation, since they consist of letters of women abandoned by their lovers.[7] It is less easy to explain why Tullia never mentions Boccaccio's *Elegia di Madonna Fiammetta*, which was very popular and reprinted in the sixteenth century.[8]

After Tullia's speech, Geri takes the floor in order to prove that the lover who leaves suffers more than the one who remains. In particular, his arguments and quotations are as follows:

Arguments	*Quotation(s)*
1) The lover who leaves suffers even more than the one who remains because he/she is eradicated from the source of nourishment for his/her spirits	Tibullus (Sulpicia), III. 14 7; Petrarch, *RVF*, 37. 1–4; Cino da Pistoia, III. 5–9, 14–20, 34–35, 41–45[9]
2) It is true that the lover who leaves takes with him/her the heart of the one who remains, but he/she also gives his/her own heart as a pledge	Petrarch, *RVF*, 180; 243; 242. 13–14; 209. 1–2; 249. 1–3; 129. 71–72; *Tr. Cup.*, III. 161–62; *RVF*, 23. 38–39; 51. 5–6; 94; 176. 6; 129. 46–48, 60–61; 127. 12–14; 130. 9–11; 228. 1–2; 96. 5–6
3) Being afraid of the travel risks is not so peculiar, because fears and hopes are typical of every lover	Petrarch, *RVF*, 182. 1–4; 134. 2
4) The lover gets pleasure from objects and places connected to his/her love story	Petrarch, *RVF*, 301; 321; 125. 53–78, 109; 126. 64–65; 85. 1–4; 162; 165; 108; 188. 13; 192. 9–14; 320. 5–7; 280; 201. 3–4; 233. 11; 127. 102–06; 129. 38–39; Propertius, II. 15 1–2; *Lydia (Appendix Vergiliana)*, 1–2, 9–10, 20–24 Catullus, 107. 1–2; Tibullus, I. 3 89–90
5) The lover who remains feels a special joy if his/her beloved comes back before the expected date	
6) Infidelity is natural for women	*Exempla*: Helen of Troy, Clytemnestra and many other Greek women, maybe even Penelope; Tibullus (Lygdamus), III. 4 61–62; 6 45–48; Aeneas, Phaon and many other Greek men were not true lovers
	Geri sings a madrigal based on a poem by Petrarch (*RVF*, 14)[10]

---

7   On the reception of the *Heroides* in the Early Modern period, see Lorenzo Geri, 'L'epistola eroica nell'Europa Barocca (1590–1717)', <http://www.enbach.eu/content/lepistola-eroica-nelleuropa-barocca-1590–1717> [accessed 3 August 2019].

8   On the reception of the *Elegia di Madonna Fiammetta* in the sixteenth century, see Elisa Curti, '"Per certo Donna Fiammetta veggio voi non havere letto gli Asolani del Bembo". Lettere di dedica e postille nelle edizioni del primo Cinquecento dell'*Elegia di Madonna Fiammetta*', *Studi sul Boccaccio*, 36 (2008), 39–61; Elisa Curti, 'L'*Elegia di Madonna Fiammetta* nella seconda metà del Cinquecento: storia di un monopolio', *Studi sul Boccaccio*, 37 (2009), 127–54.

9   For the poems by Cino da Pistoia, see the edition in: *Poeti del Dolce stil nuovo*, ed. by Mario Marti (Florence: Le Monnier, 1969), pp. 423–923.

10   This poem was set to music several times during the sixteenth century (see *RePIM*). In particular, it is worth mentioning the version by Jacob Arcadelt, which was repeatedly published over the century, starting from 1539.

In Geri's speech, the quotations from Petrarch are even more frequent than in Tullia's. Geri tries to demonstrate that Tullia has quoted from Petrarch in a partial way. In his opinion, a more comprehensive and objective approach shows that, according to Petrarch, the lover who leaves suffers more than the one who remains. For example, Tullia quotes from Petrarch to argue that the lover who leaves takes with him/her the heart of the lover who remains. Geri replies that this is true, but the lover who leaves also gives his/her own heart as a pledge to the lover who remains, as other passages from Petrarch testify. In the same way, Tullia uses Petrarch as an authority to prove that the lover who remains suffers while seeing the places connected to his/her love story. By contrast, Geri refers to Petrarch to show that the lover gets pleasure from objects and places connected to his/her love story.

Geri underlines that the *Canzoniere* shows all various and contradictory emotions felt by lovers. Indeed, Petrarch both hoped and feared, sang and cried, froze and burned, suffered because of his love desire and rejoiced because of Laura's beauty, longed to see and ran from her, was proud and regretted loving her, craved and lamented being free. In conclusion, he experienced both misery and happiness, sometimes even simultaneously, because Love is masterful at joining and blending those two opposites together.[11] Like Tullia, Geri also mentions Latin elegiac poetry, even if he refers to Tibullus and Propertius instead of Ovid's *Heroides*. In addition, Geri praises the stilnovist poet Cino da Pistoia, whose canzone 'La dolce vista e 'l bel guardo soave' expresses with marvellous sweetness the grief after leaving his own beloved.

Although Petrarch is considered a fundamental model for his refined description of love's phenomenology and its various nuances and emotions, the love relationship between Tullia and Geri is profoundly different from that of the *Canzoniere*, because their love is mutual. In addition, carnal intercourse is an important part of their relationship (this is no wonder, since Tullia was a courtesan). This helps to explain why Geri mentions Propertius's elegy II. 15, which was also imitated by Ariosto.[12] Geri says that, in his opinion, Petrarch could never personally experience the situation depicted in Propertius' elegy.[13] On the other hand, Tullia underlines the importance of sexual intercourse also as a character of Sperone Speroni's *Dialogo d'amore* and, later, of her own *Dialogo della infinità di amore*.[14] In addition, Frangipane's

11   See Cornelio Frangipane, *Dialogo d'amore* (Venice: Fratelli Guerra, 1588), p. 38.
12   On the reception of this elegy by Propertius in Renaissance literature, see Massimo Malinverni, 'Per una notte luminosa: fortuna di un *topos* da Properzio ad Ariosto', in *Fra satire e rime ariostesche*, ed. by Claudia Berra (Milan: Cisalpino, 2000), pp. 499–514; Maiko Favaro, 'Giochi di prospettive: le *Rime* dell'Ariosto fra petrarchismo e classicismo', *Hvmanistica*, 5.2 (2010), 123–32 (pp. 126–28).
13   Frangipane, *Dialogo*, p. 29.
14   See Sperone Speroni, 'Dialogo d'amore' [1542], in *Trattatisti del Cinquecento*, ed. by Mario Pozzi, I (Milan-Naples: Ricciardi, 1978), pp. 511–63; Tullia d'Aragona, 'Dialogo della infinità di amore' [1547], in *Trattati d'amore del '500*, ed. by Giuseppe Zonta (Bari: Laterza, 1912), pp. 185–248. It is worth noting also that Sperone's *Dialogo*, which was so important for the success of love dialogue in mid-century Venice, was set in Tullia's Venetian salon, where she discusses with the poet Bernardo Tasso and the Aristotelian Niccolò Grassi (known as Grazia). However, that was surely a fiction, because we know that Speroni initially wrote the dialogue without thinking about those characters, whose names he introduced only later. It is also remarkable that, like in Frangipane, the dialogue starts with the forced separation of Tullia and one of her lovers, in this case Bernardo Tasso. The latter

Dialogo devotes much attention to infidelity and jealousy, which, also in this case, are not themes typical of Petrarch, but rather of Latin poetry.[15] In the final verdict, the judges establish that separation causes some serious sufferings above all because of jealousy, namely the suspicion that the beloved will fall in love with someone else during the separation. As a confirmation, an ode by Horace (*Carm.*, III. 7) is mentioned.[16]

After a shorter dialogic exchange between Tullia and Geri, the referees deliver their verdict. Significantly, there is no winner: two judges vote for Tullia, but the other two for Geri. This balancing out of judgments fits very well with the characterization of Renaissance dialogue as an expression of a plurality of truths, each one supported by plausible reasons. In such a context, rhetorical ability can be more important than truth.[17] In this respect, it is notable that Frangipane was particularly interested in rhetoric, since he was a celebrated lawyer. It is worth remembering, too, that he was also the author of a treatise *Del parlar senatorio*, which teaches how to prepare an effective deliberative oration.[18] In that work, in order to exemplify the concepts explained in the previous chapters, Frangipane does not make use of an oration, but instead refers to a canzone by Petrarch, 'O aspectata in Ciel beata e bella' (*RVF*, 28), in which the latter urged a Crusade to be undertaken.[19] While discussing Petrarch's canzone, Frangipane underlines that it is very important to mention authorities in the oration. In the same way, Tullia and Geri repeatedly quote from Petrarch and other authors in their speeches.

has to leave because he has been recalled by his lord, the prince Ferrante Sanseverino. Therefore, the characters discuss whether separation reinforces or destroys love. Nonetheless, Speroni's dialogue is never mentioned in Frangipane's work, perhaps because the Friulian author did not know it. In 1541, Speroni's dialogue had already been written and the manuscript circulated (it was read at Pietro Aretino's home in 1537), though had not yet been published. It was printed the following year.

15   On the interest of Petrarchists (above all the Neapolitan ones) on the topic of jealousy, see Ezio Raimondi, 'Il petrarchismo nell'Italia meridionale', in *Atti del convegno internazionale sul tema 'premarinismo' e 'pregongorismo'* (Rome: Accademia dei Lincei, 1973), pp. 95–123 (pp. 105–07). See also: Paolo Cherchi, 'A Dossier for the Study of Jealousy', in *Eros and Anteros: The Medical Traditions of Love in the Renaissance*, ed. by Donald A. Beecher and Massimo Ciavolella (Ottawa: Dovehouse, 1992), pp. 123–34; Werner Gundersheimer, '"The Green-Eyed Monster": Renaissance Conceptions of Jealousy', *Proceedings of the American Philosophical Society*, 137.3 (1993), 321–31; Stefano Prandi, '"Ne le tenebre ancor vivrò beato": variazioni tassiane sul tema della gelosia', in *Mappe e letture. Studi in onore di Ezio Raimondi*, ed. by Andrea Battistini (Bologna: Il Mulino, 1994), pp. 67–83; Erika Milburn, *Luigi Tansillo and Lyric Poetry in Sixteenth-century Naples* (Leeds: Maney Publishing for the Modern Humanities Research Association, 2003).

16   See Frangipane, *Dialogo*, p. 41.

17   See Klaus W. Hempfer, *Testi e contesti. Saggi post-ermeneutici sul Cinquecento* (Naples: Liguori, 1998), pp. 25–36; Klaus W. Hempfer, 'Lektüren von Dialogen', in *Möglichkeiten des Dialogs. Struktur und Funktion einer literarischen Gattung zwischen Mittelalter und Renaissance in Italien*, ed. by Klaus W. Hempfer (Stuttgart: Steiner, 2002), pp. 1–38; Klaus W. Hempfer, 'Die Poetik des Dialogs im Cinquecento und die neuere Dialogtheorie: zum historischen Fundament aktueller Theorie', in *Poetik des Dialogs. Aktuelle Theorie und rinascimentales Selbstverständnis*, ed. by Klaus W. Hempfer (Stuttgart: Steiner, 2004), pp. 67–96.

18   See Cornelio Frangipane, *Del parlar senatorio*, ed. by Girolamo Canini (Venice: Ciotti, 1619).

19   See Cornelio Frangipane, *Del parlar senatorio*, pp. 12–16.

3. Justifying Petrarch's Controversial Passages in the Love Treatises of the Sixteenth and Early Seventeenth Centuries

By examining Frangipane's *Dialogo d'amore*, we have seen an interesting case study of how Petrarch can be used to support opposite points of view on the same question. However, as mentioned at the outset, the *Canzoniere* also appeared as a problematic and ambiguous authority because the ideas there expressed are sometimes in contrast with common sense, or other renowned authorities, or even other passages of Petrarch's masterpiece. In this section, we will discuss the aspects on which the *Canzoniere* appeared most problematic. At the same time, we will highlight the most frequent types of argument by which Renaissance love treatises overcame such difficulties.

Before we begin our enquiry, it may be useful to offer some information about the authors and the works we will mention, since most of them are not well-known. One of the liveliest environments for love treatises was Venice between the 1540s and 1550s. In that period, several editorial collaborators (Venice was, as is well known, the publishing capital of the Renaissance) wrote love dialogues following the celebrated models of Alessandro Piccolomini's *Raffaella* (1539) and Sperone Speroni's *Dialogo d'amore* (1542). One of those authors was Giuseppe Betussi, whose dialogue *Il Raverta* (1544), set in a Venetian salon, first of all examines love from a Platonic and Christian perspective, and then debates with lightness some particular aspects of love theory. Florence was also an important centre. In particular, it is worth mentioning the lectures on love and on Petrarch's poems held at the Accademia Fiorentina from the 1540s. A leading figure of such an academy was Benedetto Varchi, who left us several lectures and other writings on love theory. One of his favourite disciples was Lucantonio Ridolfi, a Florentine gentleman who moved to Lyon, but remained in contact with the Accademia Fiorentina. He wrote the dialogue *Aretefila* (1560) on love by hearsay. The academies were ideal environments for the debate on love: in 1561, Alessandro Farra delivered his *Discorso de' miracoli d'Amore* at the Accademia degli Affidati of Pavia. Some of the most renowned philosophers of the second half of the sixteenth century also wrote on love, such as Flaminio de' Nobili from Lucca and Francesco Patrizi from Cherso. The former published the *Trattato dell'amor umano* (1556), which was much appreciated by Torquato Tasso. The latter is the author of a *Discorso* on Luca Contile's *Rime* (1560), in which he also dealt with some aspects of love theory. The works by Pietro Cresci, Vitale Zuccolo, and Melchiorre Zoppio were published at the end of the century. Pietro Cresci, a poet from Ancona, wrote a *Discorso sopra le qualità di amore del Petrarca* (1585). The Paduan Vitale Zuccolo, an abbott in the monastery of San Michele in Isola (Venice), is the author of *Discorsi sopra le cinquanta conclusioni del sig. T. Tasso* (1588), in which he examined the 'conclusioni amorose' by Torquato Tasso on the basis of Platonic and Aristotelian theories. Melchiorre Zoppio, the founder of the Accademia dei Gelati in Bologna, wrote the treatise *Psafone*, which was first published in 1590 and then — in a second, much longer version — in 1617. Finally, the works by Ludovico Zuccolo and Anton Francesco Andreini date back to the early seventeenth century. The former, an important political writer whose treatise *Della ragion di stato* was appreciated by Benedetto

Croce, was the author of the dialogue *Il Gradenico. Nel quale si discorre contra l'amor platonico, et a longo si ragiona di quello del Petrarca* (1608). The latter delivered his lecture on Petrarch's sonnet 'S'Amor non è, che dunque è quel ch'io sento?' (*RVF*, 132) at the Accademia Fiorentina in 1617.

At the most general level, Renaissance authors even disagree about how to evaluate Petrarch's love for Laura. They often seem puzzled by some passages where Petrarch expresses his love in a sensual way, especially when he wishes to be with his beloved for an endless night or when he envies Pygmalion:

> Con lei foss'io da che si parte il sole,
> et non ci vedess'altri che le stelle,
> sol una nocte, et mai non fosse l'alba;
> et non se transformasse in verde selva
> per uscirmi di braccia, come il giorno
> ch'Apollo la seguia qua giù per terra.[20]

> Deh or foss'io col vago de la luna
> adormentato in qua' che verdi boschi,
> et questa ch'anzi vespro a me fa sera,
> con essa et con Amor in quella piaggia
> sola venisse a starsi ivi una notte;
> e 'l dì si stesse e 'l sol sempre ne l'onde.[21]

> Pigmalïon, quanto lodar ti dêi
> de l'imagine tua, se mille volte
> n'avesti quel ch'i' sol una vorrei.[22]

These passages could be considered as 'proofs' that Petrarch's love was physical. The commentary on the *Canzoniere* by Francesco Filelfo already stressed the sexualized connotation of Petrarch's love desire.[23] After all, in 1536 the friar Girolamo Malipiero published a famous rewriting of the *Canzoniere* in order to spiritualize it.[24] Not everybody charges Petrarch with lasciviousness, however. Cresci and Ludovico Zuccolo even state that, because carnal love is natural, there is no reason to feel ashamed about it.[25] Andreini, instead, interprets Petrarch's sensual passages

---

20   *RVF*, 22. 31–36. My reference edition is: Francesco Petrarca, *Canzoniere*, ed. by Marco Santagata (Milan: Mondadori, 2004).

21   *RVF*, 237. 31–36.

22   *RVF*, 78. 12–14.

23   See Carlo Dionisotti, 'Fortuna del Petrarca nel Quattrocento' [1974], in Carlo Dionisotti, *Scritti di storia della letteratura italiana*, ed. by Tania Basile, Vincenzo Fera, and Susanna Villari, 5 vols (Rome: Edizioni di Storia e Letteratura, 2008–), III (2010), 93–136 (pp. 106–13).

24   Girolamo Malipiero, *Il Petrarcha spirituale* (Venice: Marcolini, 1536). On this work, see Amedeo Quondam, 'Riscrittura, citazione e parodia. Il *Petrarca spirituale* di Girolamo Malipiero', in Amedeo Quondam, *Il naso di Laura. Lingua e poesia lirica nella tradizione del Classicismo* (Modena: Panini, 1991), pp. 203–62; Marc Föcking, 'Correggere il Petrarca. Tre modi di riscritture teologiche del *Canzoniere* (Bembo, Malipiero, Salvatorino)', in *Interdisciplinarità del petrarchismo*, ed. by M. Favaro and B. Huss, pp. 35–54.

25   See Pietro Cresci, 'Discorso sopra la qualità dell'amore del Petrarca', in *Il Petrarca nuovamente ridotto alla vera lettione [...]* (Venice: Eredi di Alessandro Griffio, 1588), fols b6ʳ–[12ᵛ]; Ludovico Zuccolo, *Il Gradenico. Nel quale si discorre contra l'amor platonico, et a longo si ragiona di quello del Petrarca* (Bologna: Giovan Battista Bellagamba, 1608).

as allegorical in order to acquit the poet from the charge of lasciviousness.[26] Others minimize the importance of such verses. For example, Patrizi praises Petrarch because he expressed desire for sexual intercourse only twice and, even in those cases, he did it in a very poetic and modest manner. Patrizi underlines the fact that Petrarch's focus is on the pleasures of the mind, sight, and hearing, not on those of the taste and touch. Therefore, the Italian poet is much more commendable than his Latin counterparts, who were not so chaste (Patrizi is particularly harsh against Catullus).[27] Ridolfi and Farra even consider Petrarch as a perfect model of the Platonic lover.[28]

Dwelling now upon some specific aspects of love theory, Renaissance authors use various types of argumentations to overcome the difficulties posed by Petrarch's assertions. One of the most common is that Petrarch is consciously lying for different reasons. For example, it is not clear if Petrarch was affected by jealousy or not. Although he explicitly writes that he is exempt from jealousy (*RVF*, 182. 9–10 and 12–13: 'Di queste pene è mia propia la prima, / arder dì et notte [...] / l'altra [jealousy] non già: ché 'l mio bel foco è tale, / ch'ogni uom pareggia [...]'), some other passages seem to contradict such a statement (*RVF*, 105. 69: 'Amor et Gelosia m'ànno il cor tolto'; *RVF*, 115. 9–11: 'Sùbito in allegrezza si converse / la gelosia che 'n su la prima vista / per sì alto adversario [i.e. the Sun] al cor mi nacque'). Varchi argues that Petrarch is lying: the assumption is that he is not afraid that Laura will fall in love with anybody else because she is so chaste that she refuses every potential lover.

Another example is offered by the question of free will in love. In this case, too, Petrarch seems to offer contradictory assessments. In some verses, the poet states that his love depends on fate (*RVF*, 22. 24: 'lo mio fermo desir vien da le stelle'; *RVF*, 331. 3: 'non mio voler, ma mia stella seguendo'). In other verses, he declares that love is a matter of free will (*RVF*, 70. 33–37: 'Già s'i' trascorro il ciel di cerchio in cerchio, / nessun pianeta a pianger mi condanna. / Se mortal velo il mio veder appanna, / che colpa è de le stelle, / o de le cose belle?'; *RVF*, 264. 32–34: 'Mentre che 'l corpo è vivo, / ài tu 'l freno in bailia de' penser' tuoi: / deh stringilo or che pôi'). In Flaminio Nobili's opinion, poets (and therefore also Petrarch) write that their love depends on fate for reasons of self-interest. In this way, they can appear humble: they know that they are unworthy of their beloved ones, therefore they would like to avoid loving them. Nonetheless, they cannot help but do it because of fate. That makes them excusable and worthy of mercy. In addition, fate gives their love a venerable beginning. The poet's beloved is led to think that it is not wise

---

26   See Antonfrancesco Andreini, 'Lezione di Antonfrancesco Andreini academico [...] letta da lui publicamente nell'Accademia [...] l'anno 1617 sopra il sonetto di M. Franc. Petr. il quale incomincia "S'Amor non è, che dunque è quel ch'io sento?"', in *Prose fiorentine raccolte*, vol. II, part 4 (Florence: Stamperia di Sua Altezza Reale, 1728), pp. 191–211.

27   See Francesco Patrizi, 'Discorso', in Luca Contile, *Le rime, con discorsi et argomenti di M. Francesco Patritio, et M. Antonio Borghesi* (Venice: Francesco Sansovino e compagni, 1560), fols 14ʳ–24ʳ (fol. 23ʳ).

28   See Lucantonio Ridolfi, *Aretefila* (Lyon: Guillaume Rouillé, 1562), p. 106; Alessandro Farra, *Tre discorsi. Il primo de' miracoli d'Amore. Il secondo della divinità dell'huomo. L'ultimo dell'ufficio del capitano* (Pavia: Girolamo Bartoli, 1564), fol. 12ʳ.

to despise a love of supernatural origin.[29] According to Zoppio, instead, Petrarch does not really believe that love is caused by fate. He just echoes a common view, as seems to be proven by a passage of the *Canzoniere* (*RVF*, 174. 1–2: 'Fera stella (se 'l cielo à forza in noi / quant'alcun crede) fu sotto ch'io nacqui').[30]

In other cases, Renaissance authors argue that Petrarch is wrong, but they think that he does not lie on purpose. For example, in some passages of the *Canzoniere* the poet seems to believe that it is possible to love without hope of being loved in return (*RVF*, 73. 76–78: 'Lasso, che disiando / vo quel ch'esser non puote in alcun modo, / et vivo del desir fuor di speranza'; *RVF*, 277. 4: 'che 'l desir vive, et la speranza è morta'). Varchi explains that perhaps Petrarch really thought so, but he was wrong, because it is impossible to love without hope. Petrarch wrote as a poet and as a lover, not as a rigorous, truthful philosopher like Varchi himself.[31]

However, when the ideas expressed in Petrarch's verses seem erroneous, it does not necessarily mean that they are actually wrong, but only that they need a careful interpretation. Petrarch's ostensible mistakes can be simply due to the use of an ambiguous terminology. An example is the question about the existence of love by hearsay, i.e. if it is possible to love a woman never seen, only by hearing her description and praises, as in the case of Jaufrè Rudel's *amor de lohn*.[32] Together with Boccaccio's *Decameron*,[33] Petrarch's *Canzoniere* is one of the authorities more frequently mentioned to prove that love by hearsay is possible (in particular, because of *RVF*, 53. 102–03: '[...] Un che non ti vide anchor da presso, / se non come per fama huom s'innamora'. In a dialogue entirely devoted to the question of love by hearsay, Ridolfi's *Aretefila*, a character explains that Petrarch was not properly referring to love, but instead to benevolence. In order to become love, benevolence needs confirmation from sight.[34]

Another example is given by the problem of Petrarch's jealousy. As already mentioned, in some places the poet writes that he is jealous, but in other passages he states that his love is exempt from that feeling. Betussi and Vitale Zuccolo resolve the contradiction by saying that when Petrarch declares himself to be jealous, he is properly referring to awe, rather than jealousy.[35]

In conclusion, and as the cluster of examples and quotations studied in this chapter has shown, Petrarch is one of the most important sources for the authors

---

29   See Flaminio Nobili, *Il trattato dell'Amor Humano* (Lucca: Vincenzo Busdraghi, 1567), fol. 42[r–v].

30   See Melchiorre Zoppio, 'Psafone', in *Ricreationi amorose de gli Academici Gelati di Bologna* (Bologna: Giovanni Rossi, 1590), p. 32.

31   See Varchi, 'Sopra alcune quistioni d'amore', p. 544.

32   On this subject, see Leo Spitzer, 'L'amour lontain de Jaufré Rudel et le sens de la poésie des troubadours', *North Carolina Studies in the Romance Languages and Literatures*, 5 (1944), 1–74; Brittany Asaro, 'The Unseen Beloved: Love by Hearsay in Medieval and Early Modern Italian Literature' (unpublished doctoral thesis, UCLA, 2013).

33   See in particular the novellas I. 5, IV. 4, and VII. 7.

34   See Ridolfi, *Aretefila*, p. 93.

35   See Giuseppe Betussi, 'Il Raverta, dialogo nel quale si ragiona d'amore e degli effetti suoi', in *Trattati d'amore del Cinquecento*, ed. by Giuseppe Zonta (Bari: Laterza, 1912), pp. 1–150 (p. 101); Vitale Zuccolo, *Discorsi [...] sopra le cinquanta conclusioni del Sig. Torquato Tasso* (Bergamo: Comin Ventura, 1588), fol. 100[r].

of love treatises. In the Renaissance, it was customary to use a literary work like the *Canzoniere* as an authority in theoretical contexts, even if already at that time the ideas expressed therein were sometimes rejected because 'Petrarch wrote as a poet'. The role of Petrarch in such contexts should not be a surprise. It is, after all, well known that in the Renaissance the *Canzoniere* was considered as a truthful biographical account of Petrarch's love story, especially following Vellutello's influential commentary. Petrarchism was not only a matter of a thematic and stylistic imitation of Petrarch, but it was extended to matters of morality, religion and personal conduct: Petrarch was also and often an object of *imitatio vitae*.[36] At the same time, and as we have seen, Petrarch was often regarded by authors of love treatises as an ambiguous and contradictory authority, but as we have shown, such complexity was by no means a negative fact. On the contrary, it led Renaissance authors to enrich and problematize their reflections on love.

36 See Luigi Baldacci, *Il petrarchismo italiano nel Cinquecento* (Padua: Liviana, 1974), p. 50–51; Gerhard Regn, *Torquato Tassos zyklische Liebeslyrik und die petrarkistiche Tradition* (Tübingen: Gunter Narr, 1987), p. 36; Klaus W. Hempfer, 'Per una definizione del petrarchismo', in Klaus W. Hempfer, *Testi e contesti*, pp. 147–76; Catharina Busjan, *Petrarca-Hermeneutik: Die Kommentare von Alessandro Vellutello und Giovan Andrea Gesualdo im epochalen Kontext* (Berlin: De Gruyter, 2013).

CHAPTER 2

Editing Petrarch in Venice:
The *Canzoniere* in the
Dispute between Ruscelli and Dolce

Cristina Acucella[1]

Distendersi nelle lodi dell'autore, et parimente chi con più et chi con meno modestia in quelle della diligenza di sé medesimi et vagar poi a lungo nelle lodi et ne' meriti di coloro a chi si scrive sogliono essere i fondamenti principali di quasi tutti quei che indirizzano, o dedicano, o consacrano, che s'abbia a dire, qualche libro d'altrui a Signore, o amico loro. Di queste tre cose, io, nel mandare a Vostra Signoria o più tosto al mondo sotto il nome suo questo libro delle Rime di M. Francesco Petrarca, mi truovo sì fattamente o privato o libero che se il costume de' moderni non mi ritraesse a fare il contrario, io sarei stato d'animo di non farvi altra epistola a Vostra Signoria se non porre semplicemente nel principio dell'opera 'Al S. FRANCESCO MELCHIORI', sì come così semplicemente veggiamo avere indrizzate le cose loro i Greci, et principalmente Aristotele, il quale tra l'altre cose nella sua Retorica non fa altra manifattura di dedicazione ad Alessandro che quelle sole parole πρὸς Ἀλέξανδρον, et così quasi d'ogni altra cosa sua ad ogn'altro. Et veramente, se io togliessi a lodare ora le cose del Petrarca, sarebbe non altrimenti che l'affaticarsi con molte parole a provare che la terra sia grave, o che il Sole sia lustro.[2]

1   I am currently carrying out my research activity with funding from the AIM-PON 'Ricerca e Innovazione' — Linea 1 of the Università degli Studi della Basilicata.

2   *Il Petrarca, nuovamente con la perfetta ortografia della lingua volgare, corretto da Girolamo Ruscelli. Con alcune annotationi, et un pieno vocabolario del medesimo, sopra tutte le voci, che nel libro si contengono, bisognose di dichiaratione, d'avvertimento, et di regola. Et con uno utilissimo rimario di m. Lanfranco Parmegiano, et un raccolto di tutti gli epiteti usati dall'autore* (Venice: Pietrasanta, 1554), fols ii[r]–ii[v]: 'Dwelling on praise for the Author, and likewise, some with more modesty than others, on praise for our diligence, as well as lingering on praise and the merits of those to whom we write, are the fundamental principles of almost all who address, dedicate or devote someone else's book to a Lordship or any friend of theirs. Of such three things, as I am sending this edition of Sir Francesco Petrarca's rhymes to and through your Lordship — or rather — to the world under his name, I feel deprived of or freed from these three things to the extent that, had the custom of moderns not established the opposite, I would have preferred not to write any dedicatory epistle to your Lordship, by putting only "To Sir Francesco Melchiori" at the beginning of the editorial work in accordance with the tradition of the Greeks and mainly Aristotle who, amongst other things, does not insert any words other than πρὸς Ἀλέξανδρον in the dedication to Alexander in his *Rhetoric*, as happens in his works and with those of others. And honestly, if I were now to praise the works of Petrarch, I would not do anything different but dwell on many words only to demonstrate that the earth is solid or the sun is bright'. The texts of

With these words, Girolamo Ruscelli opens his dedication on the *Canzoniere* of Petrarch, dated 21 October 1554, published by the Venetian Pietrasanta. The commentator, born in Viterbo, was a member and founder of the Accademia dello Sdegno [Academy of Disdain];[3] he subsequently relocated to Venice, the centre for the Italian printing industry at the time, where he worked prolifically as a freelance polygraph in collaboration with several publishers.[4]

No sooner did Ruscelli arrive in Venice than he had to launch a self-promotional campaign in order to put himself forward as a preferred alternative to the existing partnership between the Venetian Ludovico Dolce and the Giolito Company,[5] the latter being one of the most important publishers at the time. Ruscelli's distinctive features, such as entrepreneurship, autonomy, self-initiative and other skills in editorial promotion distinguished him as a remarkable figure within the world of contemporary publishing. His editorial works were deemed exemplary in Venice in many ways; for example, in terms of his linguistic knowledge — essential for correcting original texts — and his editorial role in arranging contents in published books. It is possible to broadly summarize some key aspects that are characteristic of the work Ruscelli carried out on the texts he edited. Following the fourteenth-century Tuscan model — albeit with a critical stance — and the canons of Pietro Bembo, the curator sought 'classical' normalization, which was characterized by the elimination of the main significant Florentine traits, namely the regularization of spelling and the polymorphism of nouns and verbs; some stylistic interventions were made, in particular, concerning some imperfect rhymes.[6] The other feature of Ruscelli's work was the strong influence of his role as a curator of published books. As he did in many other dedications, in the edition of the *Canzoniere* he called into question the 'mondo sotto il nome suo' [the world under his name] along with the recipient of the letter, who will soon play a marginal role: this formula is actually

the sixteenth century mentioned in this essay have been transcribed by partially modernizing both graphics and punctuation. All translations are my own unless otherwise stated.

3   For Ruscelli's work as a polygraph and academic, see Claudia Di Filippo Bareggi, *Il mestiere di scrivere. Lavoro intellettuale e mercato librario a Venezia nel Cinquecento* (Rome: Bulzoni, 1988), pp. 33–34, 78–80, 124–26, 148–50; Paolo Trovato, *Con ogni diligenza corretto. La stampa e le revisioni editoriali dei testi letterari italiani* (Bologna: Il Mulino, 1991), pp. 241–97; and Paolo Procaccioli, '"Costui chi è si sia". Appunti per la biografia, il profilo professionale, la fortuna di Girolamo Ruscelli', in *Girolamo Ruscelli. Dall'accademia di corte alla tipografia. Atti del Convegno internazionale di studi (Viterbo, 6–8 ottobre 2011)*, ed. by Paolo Marini and Paolo Procaccioli, 2 vols (Manziana: Vecchiarelli, 2012), I, 13–75.

4   See Antonella Iacono, *Bibliografia di Girolamo Ruscelli: le edizioni del Cinquecento* (Manziana: Vecchiarelli, 2011), pp. 76–79.

5   See Renzo Bragantini, '"Poligrafi" e umanisti volgari', in *Storia della letteratura italiana*, ed. by Enrico Malato, IV: *Il primo Cinquecento* (Roma: Salerno, 1996), pp. 681–754 (pp. 689–90). For the philological and linguistic aspects of the collaboration between Dolce and Giolito see Trovato, pp. 221–24 and 232–35. For the literary and editorial activity of Ludovico Dolce see at least Ronnie H. Terpening, *Lodovico Dolce, Renaissance Man of Letters* (Toronto: University of Toronto Press, 1997) and *Per Lodovico Dolce. Miscellanea di studi*, ed. by Paolo Marini and Paolo Procaccioli (Manziana: Vecchiarelli, 2016).

6   See Stefano Telve, 'Ruscelli e Dolce curatori editoriali dell'*Orlando Furioso*: la stabilizzazione linguistica di un modello poetico', in *Girolamo Ruscelli. Dall'accademia di corte alla tipografia*, I, 227–55 (p. 232).

a consolidated 'praxis' of Ruscelli. In this manner, he implicitly suggested that the practice of dedicating a book to a famous person — by following the typical fashion of publishing works during the courtly age — was turning into a new way of addressing the reading public, which was understood to be the true addressee of the publishing industry's outputs: Ruscelli, therefore, addressed that public as a new, modern 'Lord'.[7] Regarding this issue, Marini says:

> La contorsione retorica prodotta nella formula 'a Vostra Signoria, o più tosto al mondo sotto il suo nome' [...] è emblematica di una visione avanzata, intrinsecamente moderna, della diffusione e della circolazione della cultura scritta. Resta, e non poteva essere altrimenti, il paradosso umanistico dell'innovazione nella tradizione, che per consuetudine imponeva la sistemazione dell'oggetto librario sotto l'ombrello protettivo (sub nomine) di un personaggio illustre. Ma è proprio l'espediente retorico della correzione introdotta dalla locuzione comparativa che marca in maniera ancora più netta il vero obiettivo del discorso ruscelliano. L'opera e il 'mondo' sono i due poli di attrazione che calamitano gli interessi culturali ed economici dell'editore. La figura del *patronus* non viene esclusa dal gioco, ma del suo prestigioso ministero si sottolineano con maggiore insistenza le componenti ancillari che lo impegnano alla diffusione e alla difesa della composizione tipografica sul mercato.[8]

This practice, as Marini points out, was the result of a gradual transformation of the curator's role due to the typographical revolution which had long been ongoing. With regard to this, Ruscelli seems to establish a 'regola fissa' [fixed rule].[9] The paratext thus is the place where the dedication's purpose changes, becoming a critical essay on the text, and where the curator's involvement was becoming increasingly important,[10] acquiring a parallel and almost concurrent role with that of the original author. In a highly competitive atmosphere such as that of the Venetian publishing industry at the time, the paratext tended to be not only a place dedicated to the self-fashioning of the curator, but also a ground designed to give space to a series of disputes between 'rival' publishers in the market, because of its 'promotional'

7   See Paolo Marini, *Introduzione*, in *Girolamo Ruscelli: dediche e avvisi ai lettori*, ed. by Paolo Marini and Antonella Iacono (Manziana: Vecchiarelli, 2011), pp. i–xlv (p. ix).

8   Paolo Marini, '"A vostra signoria, o più tosto al mondo sotto il suo nome". La pratica prefatoria di Ruscelli', in *Girolamo Ruscelli. Dall'accademia di corte alla tipografia*, II, pp. 803–40 (pp. 807–08): 'The rhetorical contortion produced in the formula "to your Lordship — or rather — to the world under His name" [...] is emblematic of an advanced vision — intrinsically modern — of the diffusion and circulation of written culture. What remains — and it could not have been otherwise — is the humanistic paradox of innovation within tradition which, by force of habit, imposed the collocation of the book item under the protective umbrella (*sub nomine*) of an illustrious personality. But the rhetorical device of the correlation introduced by the comparative locution is exactly what emphasizes the true objective of Ruscelli's discourse even more clearly. The editorial work and "the world" are two magnets which attract the editor's cultural and economic interests. The figure of the *patronus* is not excluded from the game, but what is more insistently underlined about his prestigious office are the ancillary components that commit him to the circulation and to the defence of typesetting on the market'.

9   Marini, '"A vostra signoria, o più tosto al mondo sotto il suo nome"', p. 808.

10   On this topic see Brian Richardson, *Print Culture in Renaissance Italy: The Editor and the Vernacular Text, 1400–1600* (Cambridge: Cambridge University Press, 1994), pp. 1–18.

function. In fact, it is necessary to examine the paratexts in order to reconstruct the stages of controversy between Ludovico Dolce, affirmed curator of the Giolito Company, and Girolamo Ruscelli, the 'newcomer' in the publishing industry. The harsh 'battle' between these two is marked by nearly concomitant curatorships of the same works, interspersed over the course of a few months.[11] Everything originated from the public accusations in which the two men exchanged dedicatory letters to readers in the first pages of Boccaccio's masterpiece.[12] In particular, between late April and early May 1552, the *Decameron*, edited by Lodovico Dolce, was published by Giolito. Dolce received a copy of Ruscelli's draft work before its publication. Noting that his rival had based his text on that of Giunti edition (1527), correcting and modernizing many passages, he decided to give life to a fundamentally different edition: driven by a desire for polemic, he chose the trivialized version of Delfino, and the text which had until that point appeared in Giolito's edition was relocated to the margin.[13] In this way Dolce inveighed against 'those who' had made the opposite choice, without naming names:

> Nella nostra lingua, per diligenza del Bembo le Rime del Petrarca corrette e puntate si leggono. Il che, se egli medesimamente avesse fatto nel Boccaccio, sarebbe per avventura a molti levata la noia et ad alcuni l'ambizione di più oltre affaticarsi. E certo non è stato infino a qui libro al quale abbia fatto, e faccia più mestiero di emendazione, di quello che fa al suo *Decamerone*, sì per esser libro più letto dagli studiosi di essa lingua, e dal quale si cavano le regole e la forma del ben scrivere, e sì ancora perché fra tante migliaia d'impressi non ve n'è niuno (il che sia detto con pace di ciascheduno) che comportevolmente si possa leggere: et a punto la impressione fiorentina è peggiore di ciascun'altra. Il che tanto più è da riprendere, quanto più essendo questa la lingua loro, que' fiorentini che a tale impressione attesero, meno degli altri italiani mostrano di averla intesa.[14]

11   For the dispute between the two polygraphs see Di Filippo Bareggi, pp. 295–300; Trovato, pp. 241–68; Stefano Telve, *Ruscelli grammatico e polemista. I 'Tre discorsi' a Lodovico Dolce* (Manziana: Vecchiarelli, 2011), pp. 9–134; Bodo Guthmüller, '"De' tre discorsi di Girolamo Ruscelli, a M. Lodovico Dolce, discorso terzo"', in *Girolamo Ruscelli. Dall'accademia di corte alla tipografia*, I, pp. 257–82; and Chiara Gizzi, 'Girolamo Ruscelli editore del *Decameron*: polemiche editoriali e linguistiche', *Studi sul Boccaccio*, 31 (2003), 327–48.

12   The sixteenth-century prints of the *Decameron*, as stated by Vittore Branca, *Tradizione delle opere di Giovanni Boccaccio* (Rome: Edizioni di Storia e Letteratura, 1991), pp. 305–06, are irrelevant for the construction of the critical text, but at the same time very significant for the debate about language, starting from the model indicated by Bembo for prose. On this topic, see Gizzi, pp. 327–29.

13   The dispute over *Decameron*'s language was at the origin of the opposition between the Florentines, linked to the idea of the primacy in the treatment of the text, and the Venetians, in view of their supremacy in the publishing market. We must remember that the edition printed by Giunti in 1527, corrected by Francesco Sansovino and Ludovico Dolce, became a best seller of Giolito's catalogue since 1546: see *Il Decamerone [...] con gli epitheti dell'autore, espositione de prouerbi et luoghi difficili* (Venice: Giolito, 1546). This monopoly would have been broken right since the print edited by Ruscelli for Valgrisi in 1552: see Gizzi, p. 329; and Trovato, p. 251.

14   *Il Decamerone, di M. Giovanni Boccaccio. Nuovamente alla sua vera lettione ridotto da M. Lod. Dolce. Con tutte quelle allegorie, annotationi, tavole, e dichiarationi de vocaboli, che nelle altre nostre impressioni si contengono* (Venice: Giolito, 1552), fol. *iv^v: 'In our language, in the care of Bembo, we are able to read the adjusted and dotted Petrarch's rhymes. And if he had done likewise with Boccaccio, he would have relieved some of the vexation and others of the ambition to tire themselves any longer.

Building on the curatorship under Pietro Bembo, Petrarch's 'monolingualism' therefore serves as an argument justifying Dolce's editorial decision to eliminate archaisms and municipal expressions due to Boccaccio's variety of registers, after it was declared not in compliance with the will of the author.[15] The elements that were removed, through a reversal of hierarchy, were placed in the margins of the set text, which was presented as the result of a choice between the best syntactic solutions and lessons deduced from the collation of several ancient texts.[16] About a

And surely, there is no other book which needs to be corrected more than this one, either because it is read by students to learn the rules and the forms of good writing, or because — among the many thousands of print editions — there is none (no offence intended) worthy of being read. In this respect, Florentine publishing is the worst of them all, and all the more to blame, as those Florentines who have committed themselves with that edition have shown a lesser understanding of it than other Italians'.

15   *Il Decamerone, di M. Giovanni Boccaccio. Nuovamente alla sua vera lettione ridotto da M. Lod. Dolce*, fols ★v^v–★vi^r: 'Dicono costoro che 'l Boccaccio, per servar la convenevolezza delle persone che intervengono nelle novelle, ha voluto usar vocaboli fiorentini popolari, i quali noi, per non intendergli, gli abbiamo rimossi e posti in quella vece diversi altri che fiorentini non sono. [...] Accomodò adunque le parole alle materie et alle persone. E, perché il suo intendimento fu (come egli stesso afferma) di scriver queste novelle in stilo umile e chiaro quanto si potesse il più, non è verisimile che egli volesse empir le carte di parole antiche, che sogliono rendere oscurità, o abiette e vili, le quali si usarono nella età sopra lui: come *stea* in vece di *stia*, che veggiamo avere usato Dante, e non il Petrarca; e così quegli altri poeti e prosatori rozzi che furono nella età inanzi, i quali sono citati dal Sansovino, *amenduni* in cambio di *amendue*, usato dal Bembo alcuna volta nelle sue lettere, come da quello che molte altre voci antichissime usò: *atare*, per *aitare*, *fedire* per *ferire*, *vuogli* per *vuoi*, *boce* per *voce* [...] e diverse altre parole che in quel secolo non si usavano, e come non usò ancora il Petrarca' [Those people say that Boccaccio, in order to conform to the characters who take part in the tales, may have wanted to use popular Florentine words which we, for lack of understanding, have eliminated by substituting them with other non-Florentine ones. [...] He then arranged the words according to subjects and types of people. And since his intent (as he himself asserts) was to write these tales in a style as close to clear and humble as possible, it is not likely that he wanted to fill in the writings with ancient, obscure, foul or coarse words that had been used in earlier times, like *stea* in the place of *stia*, which we see being used by Dante but not by Petrarch. And equally, those other poets and coarse prose writers of the previous age cited by Sansovino used *amenduni* at the place of *amendue*, used by Bembo in some instances in his writings, as that one who used many other ancient words: *atare*, in the place of *aitare*, *fedire* in the place of *ferire*, *vuogli* in the place of *vuoi*, *boce* in the place of *voce* [...] and many other words neither in use in that century, nor used by Petrarch].

16   *Il Decamerone, di M. Giovanni Boccaccio. Nuovamente alla sua vera lettione ridotto da M. Lod. Dolce*, fol. ★vi^v: 'Noi non senza grandissima fatica avendo affrontati insieme molti antichissimi volumi, e quelle parti eleggendo per migliori [...] a esprimere il concetto dell'autore, la diversità abbiamo poste nel margine per soddisfacimento di ciascuno, non porco eziandio valendoci della diligenza già usata dal Delfino, il quale trovammo per la maggior parte conforme ai più antichi esemplari. Delle voci ancora abbiamo riposte ai luoghi loro le più belle e le più comuni; e se gli antichi usavano *atare*, *defire*, e le dette di sopra, non vogliamo ciò attribuire al Boccaccio, come anco, se da Terenzio o da Plauto fu usato *lachruma*, *scribundi*, e sì fatti termini, non li veggiamo negli scritti di Cicerone, né fu mai alcuno che ve gli mettesse' [It is not without great effort that we have compared many ancient volumes, and we have chosen the best and most proper parts best suited to express the author's will by stating in the margins the variants to everyone's benefit, to such extent that by no small degree has Delfino's working diligence been worthwhile, and we have found it to comply with the most ancient models. Among the words, we have furthermore put in the text those which were the most beautiful and common; and if the ancients would use *atare*, *defire*, as well as the others that have already been mentioned, they are not to be attributed to Boccaccio, in the same way when Plauto had used terms such as *lachruma*, *scribundi*, neither can we find them in Cicero's writings, nor has there ever been

couple of weeks after Dolce's edition appeared, Ruscelli's *Decameron* was published by Valgrisi.[17] After reading his rival's dedicatory letter, Ruscelli decided to waste no time readjusting his own. Therefore, in his own dedicatory letter, he responded to the competitor's allegations through a systematic dismantling of Dolce's weak argument with regard to the language of Petrarch, the ancient men of letters, and the municipal way of speaking, which was considered unsuitable for storytellers:

> Le parole *boto, boce, ameduni* [...], et qualch'altra tale antica, noi le abbiamo lasciate per più ragioni. Percioché se alcuno dirà essere impossibile che il Boccaccio usasse altra lingua da quella che usò il Petrarca, essendo stati ambedue in un tempo, averà torto alla fé, poiché oltre a molt'altre ragioni, sappiamo che altro è lo scrivere in prosa et in volgar fiorentino puro [...], et altro è lo scriver versi, come il Petrarca. [...] Et se dicono che quelle donne et uomini che recitano nelle novelle eran nobili, et non doveano usare alcuna parola popolaresca et abietta, o vile, hanno pure torto alla fé. Percioché, quanto ben quelle parole fossero popolaresche et abiette (che dico tutto il contrario), dette donne, et uomini erano pur Fiorentini da parlar la lor lingua [...]. Et però, tornando alle antiche, dico, che se costoro pur diranno che Cicerone non usasse *lacruma*, et *scribundi*, et altre tai voci usate da Terenzio et Plauto, averanno torto a mettere un comico che fa ragionare ogni razza di gente, con uno oratore.[18]

His analytical judgment, approach to the complexity of the language-registers-style issue in a work inspired by great rigour, and his philological and editorial scruples all seem to distinguish the work of Dolce's opponent right from the very beginning. Ruscelli went on to undertake a special work, *I tre discorsi*, in which he systematically attacked his competitor, stating that he had been aware right from the start of having been targeted by his rival in the foreword of Giolito's *Decameron*.[19] Ruscelli's polemical pamphlet, written in collaboration with the

anybody who has inserted them].

17   *Il Decamerone di m. Giovan Boccaccio, nuovamente alla sua intera perfettione, non meno nella scrittura, che nelle parole ridotto, per Girolamo Ruscelli. Con le dichiarationi, annotationi, et avvertimenti del medesimo, sopra tutti i luoghi difficili, regole, modi, et ornamenti della lingua volgare, et con figure nuove et bellissime, che interamente dimostrano i luoghi, ne' quali si riduceano ogni giornata a novellare. Et con un vocabolario generale* (Venice: Valgrisi, 1552).

18   See 'Lettera ai lettori', in *Il Decamerone di m. Giovan Boccaccio, nuovamente alla sua intera perfettione, non meno nella scrittura, che nelle parole ridotto, per Girolamo Ruscelli*, fols *6^r–*6^v. 'Words such as *boto, boce, ameduni* [...] and other old words have been kept for various reasons. So, anybody who considers it impossible for Boccaccio to have used a different language to Petrarch, the two being contemporaries, is wrong because, among other reasons, we are well aware that while it is one thing to write in prose and in vernacular Florentine, it is another thing to write in verse, like Petrarch did. And those who say that the women and men who play a part in the tales should not have used any popular, abject, or vile words, will be equally wrong. This is because, even if those words might have been popular, abject or vile (I disagree), the aforementioned women and men were all the same Florentines who spoke their own language [...]. Therefore, referring back to the subject of old words, I maintain that if anybody says that Cicero did not use *lacruma*, and *scribundi*, and other similar words used by Terence and Plautus, they will be wrong in comparing a comedian who let people of all walks of life speak with an orator.'

19   Girolamo Ruscelli, *Tre discorsi a m. Ludovico Dolce, l'uno intorno al Decamerone del Boccaccio, l'altro all'Osservationi della lingua volgare, et il terzo alla tradottione dell'Ovidio* (Venice: Pietrasanta, 1553), pp. 4–11: 'Prendendo un assai freddotto pretesto, entraste stranamente a voler biasimare quelle mie fatiche [...] nella vostra lettera ai lettori avevate con tanta collera et parole ingiuriose detto

publisher Pietrasanta, was a systematic critique of Dolce, whose three parts, as Telve observes, had a 'vertical dependence', based on his rival's three major works: Dolce's 'incorrect' typographical corrections (discussed in the first *Discorso* on the *Decameron*) due to his poor knowledge of Italian grammar (second speech on the *Osservationi*), which also reveal the lack of expertise shown in the translation from Latin (third speech on *Transformationi*).[20]

The study of the revision of the *Trasformationi*, re-edited in 1553, revealed that Dolce had 'incassato il colpo' [felt the blow].[21] The supremacy assumed by Ruscelli in graphic and linguistic regulation was also shown by the fact that his *Decameron* was republished in 1554, 1555 and 1557, while Giolito would no longer reprint Dolce's edition.[22] This first episode did not settle the literary controversy between them, the second round of which was indicative of the clear existence of an open and tight competition. It is sufficient to take one quick glance at the following table, which aligns their curatorships within a few years:

Dolce	Ruscelli
1552 (end of April, beginning of May)	1552 (mid-May)
Decameron (Venice: Valgrisi)	*Decameron* (Venice: Giolito)
	1553
	Tre discorsi a Ludovico Dolce (Venice: Pietrasanta)
1553 and 1554 (February?)	1554 (October)
Canzoniere (Venice: Giolito)	*Canzoniere* (Venice: Pietrasanta)
1555	1556
Orlando Furioso (Venice: Giolito)	*Orlando Furioso* (Venice: Valgrisi)

After the *Decameron*, it was the *Orlando Furioso* that established Valgrisi Company's prevalence of on the market. A letter, dated 18 April 1556 and sent to Giovan Battista Pigna, secretary of the court and the author of some paratexts of Valgrisi's edition of Ariosto's masterpiece,[23] evidently showed the idea of a 'final' work,[24] an insurmountable summit in the feverish intellectual conflict of *Furioso*'s editions.[25]

nominatamente contra le stampe di Fiorenza et compresamente contra le cose mie' [With a very flimsy pretext, you have come out to blame those efforts of mine harshly [...] in your letter to the readers you have spoken with much anger and using offensive words about the Florentine printings and my things, including my work].

20   See Telve, *Ruscelli grammatico e polemista*, p. 10. In addition to the aforementioned *Decameron* (1552), the works of Dolce to which I refer are, respectively, *Le Osservationi del Dolce da lui stesso in questa seconda editione ementate et ampliate* (Venice: Giolito, 1552) and *Le Trasformationi di M. Lodovico Dolce* (Venice: Giolito, 1553).

21   See Telve, 'Ruscelli e Dolce curatori editoriali dell'*Orlando Furioso*', p. 232.

22   See Trovato, p. 251.

23   Pigna is the author of a biography of Ariosto published in his *Romanzi* (Venice: Valgrisi, 1554) and after in the edition of the *Orlando Furioso* edited by Valgrisi (1556).

24   The major philological value on which the edition of Valgrisi (printed in 1556) is based on is also in the collation between Rosso's print of 1532 and a copy — perhaps a draft with handwritten revisions — that Ruscelli claimed to have received from Galasso Ariosto. On this topic see Francesco Sberlati, *Il genere e la disputa. La poetica tra Ariosto e Tasso* (Rome: Bulzoni, 2001), pp. 81–87; and Richardson, p. 120.

25   Girolamo Ruscelli, *Lettere*, ed. by Chiara Gizzi and Paolo Procaccioli (Manziana: Vecchiarelli,

The 'ambiziosissimo *Furioso*' [very ambitious *Furioso*],[26] arranged for publication within a highly competitive atmosphere, is part of a crucial context — well summarized by Franco Pignatti[27] — in which the curator's aspiration to achieve a position of supremacy is evident on several fronts, above all the linguistic front. After the *Tre discorsi* (1553), in which the bitter logomachy against Dolce was made explicit and public, Ruscelli, as a professional grammarian, made Ariosto's edition a professional showcase, wherein his linguistic and philological knowledge could reach its highest peak.[28] In this situation, the new 'modernist' canon put Ariosto in

---

2010), p. 67: 'Ora, Dio gratia, il libro è venuto tale, che spero in Dio che viverà sempre in questa forma et che non si compieranno, se non da qualche sciocco, altri *Furiosi* che questi sempre, et tanto più che ogni volta che si ristamperanno si verranno migliorando' [Now, thanks be to God, the book has turned out in such a way that I hope to God it will live forever in this form, and no other *Furiosi* will be made — other than by some inexperienced ones — and that these will be improved each and every time they are printed]. On this topic see also Daniel Javitch, *Proclaiming a Classic: The Canonization of 'Orlando Furioso'* (Princeton: Princeton University Press, 1991) and Klaus W. Hempfer, *Diskrepante Lektüren. Die Orlando-Furioso-Rezeption im Cinquecento: Historische Rezeptionsforschung als Heuristik der Interpretation* (Stuttgart-Wiesbaden: Franz Steiner, 1987).

26   Trovato, p. 282.

27   Franco Pignatti, '"Confesso d'aver letto et considerato questo poema almeno 113 volte". Ruscelli filologo ariostesco', in *Girolamo Ruscelli. Dall'accademia di corte alla tipografia*, I, 287: 'Per quanto concerne la storia di Ruscelli come editore e commentatore di testi, l'edizione del *Furioso* ha una posizione di rilievo per un insieme di ragioni [...]: 1) è l'opera al momento più importante della letteratura volgare contemporanea; 2) è in corso la sua canonizzazione come classico moderno accanto ai poemi antichi; 3) si colloca in una fase dell'evoluzione del volgare nella quale aveva cominciato ad affermarsi la formazione grammaticale, perciò la sua storia interna testimonia l'accoglimento dei modelli trecenteschi teorizzati da Bembo e insieme, implicitamente, la tensione verso uno stadio più avanzato; 4) è al centro della polemica che oppose Ruscelli a Ludovico Dolce, editore, oltre che del *Furioso*, del *Decameron*, traduttore delle *Metamorfosi* e grammatico con le *Osservationi*; perciò partecipa di un confronto condotto su più livelli: l'edizione di un testo antico, quella di un testo contemporaneo, la produzione di un testo creativo, l'elaborazione di una grammatica, strumento indispensabile per giudicare la correttezza dei testi; 5) è parte di un cantiere in cui trovano posto in breve volgere di anni, cruciali nella storia di Ruscelli, anche i *Tre discorsi* e i *Commentarii*; il confronto delle tre opere evidenzia, nella diversità di impostazione, una sostanziale unità, ma è rivelatore del metodo di Ruscelli, del suo modo di ragionare, di attuare la critica del testo' [As regards Ruscelli's career as an editor and text commentator, the edition of the *Furioso* has a prominent position for a number of reasons [...]: 1) It is the most important work within the contemporary vernacular literature; 2) its canonization as a modern classic alongside the classic poems is currently underway; 3) it takes its place inside a phase of evolution of vernacular Italian within which grammatical formation had begun to establish itself; therefore the internal editorial history (of the *Furioso*) testifies the acceptance of the fourteenth-century models theorized by Bembo and also, implicitly, the driving force towards a more advanced stage; 4) it is at the heart of the controversy that opposed Ruscelli to Ludovico Dolce, the editor of the *Decameron* as well as *Furioso*, in his role of translator of the *Metamorfosi* and grammarian with the *Osservationi*; therefore it takes part in a multilevelled comparison: the edition of an ancient text, that of a contemporary text, the production of a creative text and the elaboration of a grammar, an essential instrument to pass judgement on the correctness of texts; 5) it is part of a work in progress where, in a few years' time, crucial to Ruscelli's story, also *Tre discorsi* and the *Commentarii* find their place; the comparison of the three works highlight, in their diversity of approach, a substantial unity, but that is the revealer of Ruscelli's method, of his way of reasoning and carrying out textual criticism].

28   See Trovato, p. 286; and Telve, 'Ruscelli e Dolce curatori editoriali dell'*Orlando Furioso*', pp. 227–55.

a position of 'surpassing' even Petrarch himself, as the curators had said on many occasions. For example, in the laudatory sonnet included in the edition of *Orlando Furioso* printed by Giolito, Dolce began with the following lines:

> Spirto Divin, ne le cui dotte carte
> fra bei concetti al gran Virgilio eguali [...]²⁹

Here the writer considered Ariosto the 'new Virgil', and this idea was also connected to the 'Brieve dimostratione di molte comparationi et sentenze dall'Ariosto in diversi autori imitate', where the curator created a direct parallel between Ariosto and illustrious models of ancient literature. Similarly, in the opening letter of his *Furioso,* Ruscelli declared that the epic poem of Ariosto surpassed the same lyric poetry of Petrarch in terms of the dignity of imitation:

> in quanto alla poesia (che è la più importante per dimostrar la perfezion d'una lingua) ho proposto et nominato sempre il Petrarca et il *Furioso*; et questo poi tanto più quanto è più importante in sé stesso il poema eroico, che il lirico.³⁰

These will undoubtedly be some of the reasons why, even among modern critics, there is an important link missing in this battle fought from a distance via synchronized publications: Petrarch's *Canzoniere,* to be printed within only a few months. This publication was in many respects an important 'intermediate link', considering that Ruscelli worked on this issue simultaneously with that of the *Orlando Furioso,* which had been in the works at least since 1552–53.³¹ An essential point relates to the paratexts. While Giolito and Valgrisi's *Decameron* was already characterized by the presence of unusually large apparatuses, Petrarch represented a change in this regard. The title of Ruscelli's version, which came out from the printing presses of Vagrisi in 1554, was in fact:

> Il Petrarca, nuovamente con la perfetta ortografia della lingua volgare, corretto da Girolamo Ruscelli. Con alcune annotationi, et un pieno vocabolario del medesimo, sopra tutte le voci, che nel libro si contengono, bisognose di dichiaratione, d'avvertimento, et di regola. Et con uno utilissimo rimario di m. Lanfranco Parmegiano, et un raccolto di tutti gli epiteti usati dall'autore.

This echoed with the significant evolution of Giolito's titles, in which a growing and careful celebration of excellence is evident. The two parts of these editions (dated respectively 1553 and 1554) bore the following titles:

29   *Orlando furioso di m. Ludovico Ariosto novissimamente alla sua integrità ridotto et ornato di varie figure. Con alcune stanze del S. Aluigi Gonzaga in lode del medesimo. Aggiuntovi per ciascun canto alcune allegorie et nel fine una breve espositione et tavola di tutto quello, che nell'opera si contiene* (Venice: Giolito, 1542), fol. KK4ᵛ: 'Divine Spirit, who in the learned writings | do, through fine conceptions, equal the great Virgil'. See Javitch, *Proclaiming a classic,* pp. 21–47.
30   'Lettera ad Alfonso d'Este', in *Orlando furioso di m. Lodovico Ariosto, tutto ricorretto, et di nuove figure adornato. Al quale sono di nuovo aggiunte le Annotationi, gli avvertimenti, et le dichiarationi, di Girolamo Ruscelli, la vita dell'autore, descritta dal signor Giovan Battista Pigna, gli scontri de' luoghi mutati dall'autore dopo la sua prima impressione, la dichiaratione di tutte le favole, il vocabolario di tutte le parole oscure, et altre cose utili et necessarie* (Venice: Valgrisi, 1556), fol. ★2ᵛ: 'With regard to poetry (from which the perfection of a language is demonstrable to a better extent), I have proposed and mentioned Petrarch and the *Furioso,* and the latter all the more so, as the heroic poem is more relevant than lyric poetry'.
31   Trovato, p. 282.

> Il Petrarca novissimamente revisto, e corretto da m. Lodovico Dolce. Con alcuni dottiss. avertimenti di m. Giulio Camillo et indici del Dolce utiliss. di tutti i concetti, e delle parole, che nel poeta si trovano.

> Annotationi di M. Giulio Camillo sopra le rime del Petrarca. Tavola di M. Lodovico Dolce de i concetti et estratti di molte belle et affigurate forme di dire, e di altre cose pertinenti a moralità et all'arte. Tavola di tutti i vocaboli con le sposition loro e de gli epiteti usati da esso Petrarca e di tutte le desinenze dei Sonetti e Canzoni del medesimo secondo l'ordine delle cinque vocali.

The following year's edition (1554) also highlighted the 'novelty' of Camillo's notes[32] and the 'new' and correct spelling according to a revision of the text:

> Il Petrarca novissimamente revisto, e corretto da m. Lodovico Dolce. Con alcuni dottiss. avertimenti di m. Giulio Camillo et indici del Dolce utiliss. di tutti i concetti, e delle parole, che nel poeta si trovano, et in ultimo degli epiteti; et un utile raccoglimento delle desinenze delle Rime di tutto il Canzoniere di esso Poeta.

> Annotationi di M. Giulio Camillo sopra le rime del Petrarca. Tavola di M. Lodovico Dolce dei concetti et estratti di molte belle et affigurate forme di dire, e di altre cose pertinenti a moralità et all'arte. Tavola di tutti i vocaboli con le sposition loro e de gli epiteti usati da esso Petrarca e di tutte le desinenze dei Sonetti e Canzoni del medesimo secondo l'ordine delle cinque vocali.

Ruscelli's and Dolce's publishing operations, which had in common a tendency to use amplification in paratexts,[33] differed significantly in two main aspects: the presentation of the text and the relationship between the editor, author and publisher. Regarding the first one, it is noteworthy that Ruscelli stood in the front line, almost as a 'second author' alongside Petrarch. His role as a corrector appeared in the title, and the introductory paratexts stress the formal care taken over the text. After his opening lines, in the dedication to Francesco Melchiori, with the 'meta-textual' considerations on the function of the dedicatory epistle (as already highlighted in the quotation that opens this essay), the editor gives serious attention — in the whole body of his letter to readers — to a number of considerations and clarifications of the text yield that is based on the print of Aldo Manuzio (1501), although he changes it according to the order established by Vellutello.

> Dell'ordinare, et ricorreggere queste rime del Petrarca seguiremo in quanto alle parole il testo d'Aldo, il qual veramente è il più sincero di tutti gli altri, et fu quello, ch'egli raffrontò con uno a penna del Reverendissimo Bembo, il quale è ancora in mano dell'Illustre, et molto Reverendissimo Signor mio, Monsignor Torquato Bembo, et per molte ragioni si crede da molti, che sia di mano stessa del Petrarca; quantunque io [...] per molt'altre ne sono in dubbio, come, piacendo a Dio, per l'una, et per l'altra parte ne ragionerò più a lungo sopra una esposizione che spero di dar poi a luce sopra tutto il libro. [...] Seguiremo,

---

32   For the complex philological history of this comment see Paolo Zaja, *Introduzione*, in Giulio Camillo, *Chiose al Petrarca* (Padua: Antenore, 2009), pp. ix–lxxxviii.
33   See Daniel Javitch, *Gabriele Giolito's 'Packaging' of Ariosto, Boccaccio and Petrarch in Mid-Cinquecento*, in *Studies for Dante. Essays in Honor of Dante Della Terza*, ed. by Franco Fido, Rena A. Syska-Lamparska and Pamela D. Stewart (Fiesole: Cadmo, 1998), pp. 123–33 (p. 130).

adunque, in quanto all'ordine, quello che esso M. Alessandro Vellutello tenne nell'esposizion sua, che veramente so di poter dir con consentimento comune di tutti i dotti, che il Vellutello fu il primo che, così in quanto all'istoria, come in quanto alla dichiarazione, fosse il primo che cavasse il Petrarca dalle tenebre et che aprisse la via a tutti gli altri che dapoi han seguito.[34]

While still addressing readers, Ruscelli goes as far as to focus on a detailed explanation of his spelling choices, which are characterized by a modernism that is never uncritically obsequious towards tradition, but rather always in step with contemporary graphic modernization and rationalization. This aspect marked an important evolution with respect to the canonical edition of Aldo Manuzio, also printed in 1501.

Dell'ortografia, o modo di scrivere convien poi far altro giudizio, cioè, che quello d'Aldo et tutti i più antichi sieno veramente di molto mala ortografia et da non seguirsi per via veruna [...]. Ma con tutto ciò direi [...] quello che et sopra il *Decamerone* et ne' nostri *Commentarii della lingua Italiana*, et altrove ho detto, cio che a' tempi così del Petrarca, come di Dante, et come ancora d'ogn'altro autore che in quei tempi scrivesse in volgare, non aveano alcuna buona, né regolata, né ragionevole maniera di scrivere. [...] Servavano adunque ne' tempi del Petrarca, di Dante, et del Boccaccio un modo di scrivere non solamente senza alcuno ornamento d'accenti, ma ancora senza apostrofo [...]. Et che questo apostrofo, il quale per certo è importantissimo nella lingua nostra, non si usasse da loro ce ne fa chiarissimo testimonio il leggersi tante volte nel Petrarca quella allusione, et molte volte ambiguo fatto a studio della parola 'l'aura', cioè 'la aura', vento, con 'Laura', nome della donna sua [...]. Ma di tutto questo oltre a quanto ne abbiamo detto nelle annotazioni dell'ottava giornata del *Decamerone*, s'è ancor discorso a lungo nel 4° libro de' nostri *Commentarii*, et quanto da quegli ho ora tolto con diverse parole per metter qui, è stato per non lasciar manica ai maligni di cavillar col poco saper loro nelle cose fatte ragionevolissimamente a beneficio degli studiosi.[35]

34   Girolamo Ruscelli, 'Ai lettori', in *Il Petrarca, nuovamente con la perfetta ortografia della lingua volgare, corretto da Girolamo Ruscelli. Con alcune annotationi, et un pieno vocabulario del medesimo, sopra tutte le voci, che nel libro si contengono, bisognose di dichiaratione, d'avvertimento, et di regola. Et con uno utilissimo rimario di m. Lanfranco Parmegiano, et un raccolto di tutti gli epiteti usati dall'autore* (Venice: Pietrasanta, 1554), fols v[r]–v[v]: 'In ordering and correcting these Petrarch's rhymes we will follow, as far as the text is concerned, Aldo's version, which is the most reliable among them all since it was compared with a manuscript by the Most Reverend Bembo, still in the hands of the illustrious and my Most Reverend Lordship, Monsignor Torquato Bembo, and which is deemed to be of the very Petrarch's hand. Still [...] I am in doubt about many other rhymes as, God willing, I shall discuss them at great length and more extensively throughout the exposition on this book that I hope I will soon be able to bring out. Therefore, we will follow — with regard to the order — that which was observed by Sir Alessandro Vellutello in his exposition, as I am bold enough to say that, with the general assent of all scholars, Vellutello was the first ever to bring out Petrarch from the darkness in terms of arrangement and commentary, paving the way to all those who were later to come'.

35   Girolamo Ruscelli, 'Ai lettori', in *Il Petrarca, nuovamente con la perfetta ortografia della lingua volgare, corretto da Girolamo Ruscelli*, fols vi[r]–viii[r]: 'With regard to orthography, or the correct way to write, it is worth carrying out a different evaluation, namely to bear in mind that Aldo and the ancients used poor orthography, not ever to be adopted in any way. But with this I would say what I have already said about the *Decameron* and about my *Commentarii della lingua Italiana*, that is, during Petrarch's and Dante's times as well as those when any other author wrote, no such thing as a proper, regulated or

The quoted passage is indicative of a number of characteristics of the work of
Ruscelli: most of all the modernist perspective that was recognizable in the idea
of non-slavish, 'critical' and selective imitation of the classics, which was inclined
to the rationalization and standardization of graphic principles, such as spelling
choices, as demonstrated in the present case, although they reached their apex in the
curatorship of Ariosto's text. The professionalism and the figure of the curator also
clearly emerged from this text, as we can see by the end of the letter to Francesco
Melchiori, which preceded the letter to the readers:

> così aggradisca che io [...] abbia dato di mano alla prima occasione che mi s'è
> offerta per intero stendimento di questa mia contentezza in fare io stesso noto
> et perpetuo ai presenti et a' posteri questo splendor mio. Di Venezia, il dì XXI.
> d'ottobre MDLIIII.[36]

Here, the 'splendor mio' [my splendour] seemed to be the ultimate goal of this work
by the curator, and it was only the pinnacle of a self-fashioning which, in addition
to the content, is also evident from the frequent references to the sender's self. Even
the number of allusions Ruscelli makes to his work, which help to 'complete' a
perfect mosaic of knowledge and 'professional instruments' ('quello che sopra il
Decamerone, et ne' nostri *Commentarii della lingua italiana* et altrove ho detto'),[37] must
be connected to the same goal. In this way, the letter constituted a promotional
'showcase' of Ruscelli's catalogue rather than Pietrasanta's. It is now appropriate to
make a comparison between this 'triumphant' opening and the text that Giolito
devoted to his readers in the edition of Petrarch curated by Dolce:

> Tra le diverse cagioni che non lasciano gli studiosi pervenire a quel termine di
> laude che nello scrivere è disiderato da ciascuno, pare a me che sia senza alcun
> dubbio la presonzione che alcuni si prendono di scriver licenziosamente, come
> lor piace, o per non voler durar fatica, ovvero per non sapere intender la via di
> osservar ne' buoni scrittori i concetti, l'artificio, le figure, le forme del dire, e
> le parole da loro giudiziosamente usate. Senza che non pochi si trovano i quali,
> come che dotti siano nelle lingue e nelle scienze degli antichi, sono cotanto
> superbi, o di sì delicato gusto, che non si degnano di leggere le cose toscane
> [...]. Ora, perché a voi prudenti e studiosi giovani non manchi verun comodo
> da potere ascendere ad ogni perfezione nelle volgari cose, oltre alcune brievi,

reasonable way to write ever existed. [...] At the time of Petrarch, Dante and Boccaccio, a writing
style with no accents or apostrophes was being followed. And the fact that the apostrophe, of the
utmost importance in our language, was not used by them is witnessed by the vast presence of the
allusion — in Petrarch's work — of the word 'l'aura', namely 'la aura' (the wind) with 'Laura', his
mistress's name. But all of this, besides what has already been said in the annotations to the eighth day
of the *Decameron*, has already been extensively debated in in the fourth book of my *Commentarii*, and
the present resumption of some of those excerpts has taken place so as to leave malevolent people no
room for raising objections with their lesser knowledge about things done with much reasonableness
for the benefit of scholars'.
36   Girolamo Ruscelli, 'Lettera' to Francesco Melchiori, in *Il Petrarca, nuovamente con la perfetta
ortografia della lingua volgare, corretto da Girolamo Ruscelli*, fol. iv[v]: 'So be pleased that I [...] have been
able to fully express my satisfaction by bringing out this splendour of mine at my earliest opportunity
and to make it known to those present and to those that follows. Venice, 21 October 1554'.
37   Girolamo Ruscelli, 'Ai lettori', in *Il Petrarca, nuovamente con la perfetta ortografia della lingua volgare,
corretto da Girolamo Ruscelli*, fol. vi[r].

ma dotte annotazioni di M. Giulio Camillo sopra le Rime del Petrarca, vi do
ancora alcune fatiche del Dolce sopra i concetti, le forme del dire e le parole,
le quali quanto utile vi possano in ciò apportare lo potete giudicar da quello
c'ho sopra detto. Et ancoraché per le sue molte occupazioni lo istesso non le
abbia potute condurre a quella pienezza che egli et io desideravamo, nondimeno
serviranno elle per la maggior parte al bisogno di ciascuno, promettendovi
nelle altre impressioni di supplire per avventura in questo et in altro a quanto
si ricerca.[38]

A macroscopic point is precisely the 'disappearance' of the printer's right-hand man.
Giolito, in fact, signed the letter of dedication in person and spoke of Dolce as a
contributor who had many occupations, thus making it impossible for him to carry
out a piece of work that met their expectations. A 'complete' work was postponed
and 'promised' to readers in the future. Hence, the name of the publisher was
presented at the forefront as part of a ranked list of employees; Camillo and Dolce
stood out on this list.[39] While the former was the author of the brief notes, the
latter was associated with a task relating to 'i concetti, le forme del dire, e le parole'
[concepts, forms of speech and words], which then took on the connotations that
went more towards aesthetic forms of language rather than grammatical rigour.
Ruscelli's rival was depicted in this case as an experienced professional, who was so
busy dealing with myriad editorial chores that he was not able either to oversee the
preface of the text or give his best. At any rate, Dolce was, above all, a grammarian
who — almost concurrently with the *Tre discorsi* — preferred to differentiate
his work from that of others by opening his texts up to different perspectives,
principally that of literary criticism. Bragantini rightly noted that in the *Modi
affigurati* (1564), which is centered on a less problematic author from a grammatical
point of view (namely Ariosto), Dolce tried to move away from the 'fuoco della
contesa' [heat of the dispute].[40] It is also significant, as Bragantini notes yet again,
that, in this curatorship, Dolce seemed to be well aware that he was no match for
his opponent in the field of spelling. Even though Ruscelli was never mentioned,
he was certainly considered the most influential defamer, who the editor lashes out

38   Gabriel Giolito, 'Ai lettori', in *Il Petrarca novissimamente revisto, e corretto da m. Lodovico Dolce,
Annotationi di M. Giulio Camillo sopra le rime del Petrarca*, II fols a1^r–a1^v: 'Among the various reasons
lying at the origin of the purpose of praise, which is the wish of every writer, is undoubtedly the
presumption that some have to write lewdly at will, neither to toil nor to understand what steps must
be taken to imitate good writers as to forms of concepts, craft, using figurative language, and forms
of expressions and words accurately chosen by them. This disregarding the fact that more than a few,
no matter how erudite in classical languages and science they are, do not deign to read the Tuscan
works [...]. Now, my purpose being to provide all of you scholars with the instruments to access to
the total perfection of vulgar writing, as well as some brief remarks by Giulio Camillo on Petrarch's
rhymes, I also give you some of Dolce's works on concepts, forms of expression and words that you
will put to good use, something that you could judge by what I have just said. Also, even though I
have not been able to bring such toil to my desired completion, owing to his many engagements, it
will be useful for the most part to each and everyone's need, and I promise you that I will fill these
gaps in the following editions'.
39   Dolce, who was not only an editor of the classics, was also involved in editing various
contemporary works, including that of Delminio: see Di Filippo Bareggi, p. 59.
40   Bragantini, p. 690.

at in the dedication to Marcantonio Rezzonico, remembering 'di non aver posta la falce nelle biade di altrui' [that he would not put a sickle in another's man corn; he would not meddle in others' affairs].[41] Here Dolce seemed to 'annaspare alla ricerca di ossigeno [...] di cambiare territorio' [be gasping for breath [...] to change the field of action],[42] moving from spelling and vocabulary to syntax and the art of *dispositio*.[43] The 'disappearance' of the curator of Petrarch's *Canzoniere* in the light of all the above, is to be considered anticipatory in this regard, whereas Dolce was still trying to extract the 'forms of speech' and 'words' from Petrarch's model rather than a technical repertoire of corrections and errors. A further confirmation in this sense is traceable in Ariosto's work. Ruscelli, promoter of his texts and of his own professionalism, takes advantage of his curatorship of the very valuable Valgrisi edition to display a list-catalogue of his guardianships based on spelling:

> Nelle *Annotationi sopra il Decamerone di Boccaccio*, et così nel principio del Petrarca, ne' *Commentari della lingua italiana* et nel volume delle *Lettere de' tredici autori illustri* con altre lettere e due altri libri da me nuovamente aggiuntivi, io ho renduta piena ragione dell'ortografia.[44]

Dolce, in his following book, the *Modi affigurati*, also based on Ariosto's exemplarity, opted instead for a change of 'sector', bypassing the field of spelling and grammar:

> Ho adunque voluto pubblicare alcuni miei avvertimenti intorno alla proprietà et eleganza di così fatta lingua [...]. Abbiamo dunque noi preso il carico di ragionare ora in questo libro [...] dello scrivere ornatamente [...] raccogliendo con quell'ordine che ci parrà migliore le forme e i modi eleganti di scrivere usati dai sovra detti autori (il Petrarca, e 'l Boccaccio e da qualche moderno ancora) [...]. Percioché non basta osservar le voci che si trovano ne' buoni scrittori, ma bisogna saper disporle con quelle vie e maniere che da essi furono usate. Et in questo è riposta al mio parere la maggiore e la più importante virtù dell'imitare.[45]

The heated dispute that began with the *Decameron* was not ideological but 'entre-preneurial' and constituted a challenge from which Dolce did not emerge victorious

---

41 'Lettera' to Marcantonio Rezzonico, in Lodovico Dolce, *Modi affigurati e voci scelte et eleganti della volgar lingua, con un discorso sopra a mutamenti e diversi ornamenti dell'Ariosto* (Venice: Gio. Battista e Marchio Sessa, 1564), fol. ★3ᵛ.

42 Bragantini, p. 690.

43 Bragantini, p. 691.

44 'Della ortografia [...]', in *Orlando furioso di m. Lodovico Ariosto, tutto ricorretto, et di nuove figure adornato. Al quale sono di nuovo aggiunte le Annotationi, gli avvertimenti, et le dichiarationi, di Girolamo Ruscelli*, fol. ★★★1ʳ. 'In the *Annotationi sopra il Decamerone di Boccaccio*, at the beginning of Petrarch, in the *Commentari della lingua italiana* and in the volume of *Lettere de' tredici autori illustri* with other letters and two other books added by me, I have fully done justice to the orthography.'

45 Dolce, *Modi affigurati*, fols ★3ʳ–A1ᵛ: 'I have therefore sought to publish some of my observations on the property and the elegance of such language [...]. We have therefore made the commitment to presently discuss in this book on writing in an ornate manner [...] by collecting the elegant forms and ways to write that we deem best through the ways and forms adopted by the aforementioned authors (Petrarch, Boccaccio and some other modern author). [...] Therefore, it is not enough to observe the words that are to be found in good writers' books; in fact, one has to be conversant with their arrangement according to the ways and manners previously adopted by them. And in this lies, in my opinion, the best and most important virtue of imitation.'

in terms of grammatical competency, thus making it necessary for him to seek an alternative 'market area' in which he would attain new status in the field of eloquence, as already predicted by 'his' Petrarch ten years earlier.

CHAPTER 3

Laura's Nobility and Greatness in Two Sixteenth-Century Florentine Speeches by Simone della Barba (1554) and Francesco de' Vieri (1580)

Guglielmo Barucci

1. Simone della Barba's *Spositione*

In the cultural system of Cosimo de' Medici's regime, pivoting on Accademia Fiorentina and on Ducalis Typographus Lorenzo Torrentino, a minor but quite particular role is played by Simone della Barba.[1] In 1554, as an 'Academico Fiorentino', he published for Torrentino the *Nuova spositione del sonetto che comincia 'In nobil sangue vita humile, e queta'*, a commentary to sonnet 215 of Petrarch's *Canzoniere*.[2] Simone della Barba had previously read his *Spositione* in the Accademia (in March 1552, according to the inscription, dated 28 April 1554). The transition of academy conferences to the press was, of course, definitely (though not necessarily) routine; nevertheless, della Barba's commentary is worth some attention, both for the social network to which it is connected, and for its specific key theme, which was quite unusual, as well as consistent with the political ideology of Cosimo's Florence.

Simone della Barba is, from many points of view, ancillary to his much more famous brother, Pompeo,[3] and the little information we have about him leads to an

1   On the cultural agenda of Cosimo I, see Michel Plaisance, *L'accademia e il suo principe. Cultura e politica a Firenze al tempo di Cosimo I e di Francesco de' Medici* (Manziana: Vecchiarelli, 2004). Furthermore, Leandro Perini, 'Editori e potere in Italia dalla fine del secolo XV all'Unità', in *Storia d'Italia. Annali 4. Intellettuali e potere*, ed. by Corrado Vivanti (Turin: Einaudi, 1971), pp. 765–853 (pp. 788–800); Claudia Di Filippo Bareggi, 'Tre tipografie fiorentine fra repubblica e principato', *Nuova rivista storica*, 58 (1974), 318–48; Antonio Ricci, 'Lorenzo Torrentino and the Cultural Programme of Cosimo I de' Medici', in *The Cultural Politics of Duke Cosimo I de' Medici*, ed. by Konrad Eisenbichler (Aldershot: Ashgate, 2001), pp. 103–19.
2   Simone della Barba, *Nuova spositione del sonetto che comincia 'In nobile sangue vita humile, et queta', ne la quale si dichiara qual sia stata la vera nobiltà di Madonna Laura* (Florence: [Lorenzo Torrentino], 1554). The only modern edition is in *Lezioni sul Petrarca. Die Rerum vulgarium fragmenta in Akademievorträgen des 16. Jahrhunderts*, ed. by Bernhard Huss, Florian Neumann, and Gerhard Regn (Münster: Lit, 2004), with a short introduction by Gerhard Regn, pp. 121–25.
3   Franco A. Meschini, 'Della Barba, Pompeo', in *Dizionario biografico degli italiani* (Rome: Istituto dell'Enciclopedia Italiana, 1960–), 36 (1998), 673–76.

easily recognisable milieu:[4] in 1554 three sonnets were published in *Il Paragone della Vergine, et del Martire, e una Oratione di Erasmo Roterodamo a Giesù Christo, tradotti per M. Lodovico Domenichi* [...] by Torrentino; in 1555 a few of his sonnets were published in the paratext to Giovanni Pico's *Heptaplus*, edited by his brother, still for the official Florentine printer; and, again, a sonnet was published in Varchi's *Sonetti* [...]. *Parte seconda*, for the same publishing house.[5] Notwithstanding, his most important work, this time for Giolito, was probably the edition of Cicero's *Topica*, published in 1556 but with a letter dated 1550, at the very beginning of Simone's career. It was in some ways a collective work, with Pompeo providing a commentary on Cicero's work and the translation of Boethius's *De topicis differentiis*, and Simone supplying the translation of *Topica* and the dedication of Boethius's work.[6] Quite interestingly, the volume is opened by Pompeo's dedication to Francesco Torelli, son of Lelio (first secretary of Cosimo and instrumental in the 'normalization' of the Accademia degli Umidi) and one of the five Accademici (along with Giambullari, Varchi, Lenzoni and Gelli) called to 'far le regole del parlar toschano, et fiorentino'.[7] The letter testifies how the volume also aimed at introducing the youngest (and still inexperienced) brother to Florence's cultural high society.[8] In addition one should note that in 1554–55 Torrentino had moved to Pescia (where the two brothers were born and were still prominent)[9] and that the *Nuova Spositione* is dedicated to Giulio de' Medici, the cousin of Cosimo, and this short bio-bibliography is enough to understand how Simone, when his lecture was eventually published in 1554, was very close to the core of the Cosmian cultural system.

Simone's lecture, as already said, was just one of many held at the Accademia, roughly half of them on Petrarch. Quite surprising, nonetheless, is the text on which he chooses to comment. Sonnet 215 has never attracted much attention from critics, due mainly to its similarity to the much more famous 'Gratie ch'a pochi il

4   See Giuseppe Ansaldi, *Cenni biografici dei personaggi illustri della città di Pescia e suoi dintorni [...]* (Pescia: Vannini, 1872), pp. 289–95, and Giammaria Mazzucchelli, *Gli scrittori d'Italia [...]* (Brescia: Bossini, 1758), II, 237–38. See, *passim*, as well *Annali della tipografia fiorentina di Lorenzo Torrentino impressore ducale*, 2nd edn (Florence: Francesco Daddi, 1819). Furthermore, Simone della Barba was somehow on the fringes of the plot against Pope Pius IV in 1564; in fact, he was the man who gave the stiletto to one of the conspirators. Although he was never accused, the fact that his brother, Pompeo, was the doctor of Pius IV raised some questions. The political-religious breeding ground of the plot is too uncertain to assess any implication on Simone's side; on the plot, see Elena Bonora, *Roma 1564. La congiura contro il papa* (Rome-Bari: Laterza, 2011).

5   Two more sonnets were in the *Tempio fabbricato a Giovanna d'Aragona* (Venice: Plinio Pietrasanta, 1554), pp. 323–24.

6   On this peculiar miscellaneous work, which in any case had nearly no critical fortune, see Guglielmo Barucci, '"Chiosar con altro testo". Le Tre Corone per un commento rinascimentale ai *Topica* di Cicerone', *Parole rubate/Purloined Letters*, 1 (2010), 37–67, <http://www.parolerubate.unipr.it/issues.php> [accessed 28 April 2019]. A recent edition is *La Topica di Cicerone, col comento [...]*, ed. by Tobias Reinhardt (Oxford: Oxford University Press, 2003). By the way, the *Nuova spositione del sonetto* hints at the forthcoming book for Giolito (p. 16).

7   See Plaisance, p. 217.

8   '[...] e pregola, che accetti mio fratello ancora nel numero de' Servitori fedeli di casa sua, la quale del continuo Dio feliciti e conservi', in *Nuova spositione*, fol. [ii^r].

9   Carlo Fedeli, 'Lorenzo Torrentino e la sua dimora a Pescia', in *Miscellanea storico-letteraria a Francesco Mariotti [...]* (Pisa: Mariotti, 1907) pp. 73–87.

ciel largo destina' as a catalogue of Laura's virtues; even Vellutello's commentary is rather brisk in his comparison with *Rerum vulgarium fragmenta* (hereafter RVF), 213, thus making the forty-four pages of della Barba's *Spositione* even more surprising:

> Seguita il Poe. nel presente So. come ha nel precedente fatto, nelle singulari et divine doti che dalla natura erano state a M.L. concedute, et quantunque sia in sé ingegnosissimo, non però giudichiamo che altra esposizione li sia di bisogno.[10]

As typical of Accademici Fiorentini, his lecture becomes an opportunity to thoroughly explore a cultural and philosophical issue; nevertheless, Simone della Barba handles an element usually unresearched, as its core is exquisitely political: nobility.[11]

In some ways, the lecture reflects the importance and role of nobility in Renaissance society, as a multifaceted prism of different, even conflicting, meanings, values and forms.[12] The ambiguous complexity of the idea of nobility (an idea never devoid of clear and tangible implications) is recognizable in *La civil conversazione* by Stefano Guazzo, the most extensive Renaissance treaty on good manners and social relations. Here, the need to thoroughly represent the many perspectives on nobility leads to a cascade of forms, species, subspecies, levels, distinctions, opinions, mixtures and hybrids, with multiple implicit references (and one explicit). This digression is closed by Guazzo (twenty-four years after Simone's proposal) with his own formula, distinguishing half nobles, nobles, and very nobles:

> ANNIBALE   [...] io così in fretta vi dico che alcuni, venendo a definire la nobiltà, hanno detto ch'ella è degnità de' padri e predecessori; altri ch'ella è ricchezza antica; altri ch'ella è ricchezza congiunta con virtù: altri che è sola virtù. Oltre a ciò allegava l'altro giorno in un suo discorso l'onorato signor Giorgio Carretto, academico, l'autorità, se ben mi ricorda, di Baldo, il qual vuole che 'l nobile si dica in tre modi: il primo per sangue, come intende il volgo; il secondo per virtù, come intende il filosofo; il terzo per l'uno e per l'altro, e questi chiama perfettamente nobile.
> CAVALIERE   Vi si potrebbe aggiungere quell'altra sorte di nobiltà, che s'acquista per privilegio de' principi.
> ANNIBALE   Questa per avventura egli la incorporava con la nobiltà de' filosofi, percioché si può dire che 'l prencipe con quel privilegio venga ad approvare la virtù e i meriti di colui ch'egli ingentilisce e nobilita. Ma l'eccellenza della

---

10   *Il Petrarcha con l'espositione d'Alessandro Vellutello di novo ristampato [...]* (Venice: Giolito, 1560), fol. 60ᵛ. Even Gesualdo, though lengthy explaining the sonnet, somehow subordinates RVF, 215, to RVF, 213; the former is a 'grande e meravigliosa laude' of Laura, while the latter is just not 'minore'; see *Il Petrarcha con la spositione di M. Giovanni Andrea Gesualdo [...]* (Venice: Domenico Giglio, 1553), p. 242. It must also be noted that, in the note to sonnet 215, the whole section on nobility amounts to just twenty-seven lines.

11   See Regn, p. 121: 'Mit seinem Thema weicht Simone von den Präferenzen der *accademici* ab, die bevorzugt liebestheoretische *quistioni*, kunstphilosophische Fragen oder Probleme des Stils behandeln'. On the lectures by the Accademici, see Franco Tomasi, '"*Cose nel vero tutte misteriose e belle*": le *forme dell'esegesi petrarchesca nell'Accademia Fiorentina*', in *Dissonanze concordi. Temi, questioni, personaggi intorno ad Anton Francesco Doni*, ed. by Giovanna Rizzarelli (Bologna: Il Mulino, 2013), pp. 149–69.

12   See Regn, p. 121: 'ein Komplex von herausragender lebensweltlicher Bedeutsamkeit'.

nobiltà fu molto più ristretta da Diogene, il quale dimandato quali fra tutti gli uomini fossero nobilissimi, rispose: — Gli sprezzatori delle ricchezze, della gloria, de' piaceri e della vita, e i vincitori de' contrari, cioè della povertà, dell'ignominia, della fatica e della morte — .

[...]

ANNIBALE   Or perché si trovano scritte molte distinzioni della nobiltà, secondo la diversità delle opinioni, io nonostante che qualche filosofo assegni quattro sorti di nobiltà e che qualche altro vi aggiunga la quinta, piglierò ardire [...] di farne io ancora un'altra a mio modo, se ben mi discostassi qualche poco dalle opinioni loro. Io adunque pongo tre gradi di nobiltà, dai quali deduco tre sorti di nobili: cioè nobili del primo grado, nobili del secondo e nobili del terzo. A quelli del primo grado, non avendo per ora altro termine più proprio, darò nome di seminobili. Quelli del secondo chiamerò nobili, quelli del terzo nobilissimi.[13]

Perhaps inevitably, in Simone's lecture, the sonnet is completely detached from its original context or aim, namely framing and softening (along with sonnet 213 itself) the religious stance of sestina 214.[14] The subtitle 'ne la quale si dichiara qual sia stata la vera nobiltà di madonna Laura' alludes, on the contrary, to the Renaissance 'concretization' of Laura, probably seeking a wider and easier audience.

The topic of her nobility was in any case well debated, as proved by Fausto da Longiano who, recalling 'certe novellaccie né vere, né al vero simili' and the many discrepancies in circulation, states in Laura's biography: 'Molti credeno ch'ella fosse o villanella, o di bassa conditione; altri d'assai horrevole parentado, ma povera'. On the basis of *Epistolae metricae*, I. 6 ('Est michi post animi mulier clarissima tergum | Et virtute suis, et sanguine nota vetusto'),[15] Fausto vibrantly supports the idea of Laura's nobility[16] but, again, pays little attention to sonnet 215, considering it just a catalogue of her internal and external beauties.[17] Vellutello himself, in the 'Origine di Madonna Laura', tackles the problem of Laura's family, status and place of birth, debunking the legend of a Laura belonging to the de Sade family. Although he challenges the commonplace of the birth in Avignon, insisting on the many references in the *Canzoniere* and *Triumphs* to the 'humile e basso luogo' where she was born, he does not deny her noble origins and, piling up circumstantial evidence from the *Canzoniere*, postulates that her father 'fosse stato povero Signore', thus accepting an idea of nobility without money.[18] And Gesualdo, to cut a long

13   Stefano Guazzo, *La civil conversazione*, ed. by Amedeo Quondam (Rome: Bulzoni, 2009), II, 124–25. See also II, 244–45, nn. 431–33; and Amedeo Quondam, 'La virtù dipinta. Noterelle (e divagazioni) guazziane intorno a Classicismo e *Institutio* in Antico regime', in *Stefano Guazzo e la civil conversazione*, ed. by Giorgio Patrizi (Rome: Bulzoni, 1990), pp. 227–395 (p. 312).

14   See Marco Santagata, *I frammenti dell'anima* (Bologna: Il Mulino, 1992), pp. 310–11.

15   Francesco Petrarca, *Le epistole metriche*, ed. by Raffaele Argenio (Rome: Cicinelli, [1984]), I. 6 37–38.

16   *Il Petrarcha col commento di M.S. Fausto da Longiano, con rimario et epiteti in ordine d'alphabeto. Nuovamente stampato* (Venice: Francesco di Alessandro Bindoni, e Mapheo Pasini, compagni, 1532), fol. iiii[r].

17   See *Il Petrarcha col commento di M.S. Fausto da Longiano*, fol. 80[v]: 'Questo e quel di sopra narrano le bellezze interiori et esteriori della sua donna'.

18   *Il Petrarcha con l'espositione d'Alessandro Vellutello*, fol. [viii[r]].

story short, after mentioning in 'La vita di Madonna Laura' the erroneous opinions that saw in Laura 'una de le Contadine', states that in 'In nobil sangue' the poet 'apertamente significato egli n'habbia la nobilità di lei';[19] likewise, in the note to the sonnet Gesualdo rewords 'In nobil sangue'[20] with 'in sangue di nobilissime tempre senza veruna macchia', a paraphrase open to multiple interpretations summarized in a single sentence ('In M. L. anchor che la chiarezza de li antiqui avoli non splendesse sì come da vero in lei splendea, senza dubbio veruno ella era dal cielo di rara nobilitate ornata'),[21] stressing much more individual than inherited nobility.

Nevertheless, a lecture supposed to focus on a current issue like the 'vera nobiltà di Madonna Laura' turns mostly to an analysis of the idea of 'vera Nobiltà de gl'huomini' according to the most authoritative scholars (p. 6). Actually, the topic of Laura's 'vera nobiltà' would be touched on only at the end of the lecture, as the third and last point (in only seven pages out of forty-four). Previously Simone, in order to prepare the field by uprooting errors and 'male opinioni' (p. 5), had to analyse what 'Nobiltà' and 'degna Nobiltà' were (pp. 6–7), as two logical premises for the definition of the issue of the *Spositione*. Indeed, nobility had been a matter of controversy since the Middle Ages, given the absence of any legal definition and the wide range of interpretations. Of course, della Barba benefited extensively from classical (mainly Aristotle and Cicero) and medieval theories (mainly Bartolus de Saxoferrato), but he preceded — and it is one of the reasons of interest for his *Nuova Spositione* — many of the most famous treatises on the subject (Muzio's *Il Gentiluomo* by in 1571; the wide specific section in Stefano Guazzo's *La civil conversazione* in 1574; Tasso's *Forno* in 1581).

One of the most important peculiarities of Simone's lecture, then, is the application of a socio-political issue to a sonnet, which comes indirectly to be seen as a case study. Emphasis should be given not only to the substantial indifference, on Simone's side, to the formal and aesthetical elements, much to the advantage of the cultural and philosophical core, but also the overall Florentine and Tuscan profile of the cultural background on which the lecture is built. Not only, as typical of Verino and Varchi, is the lecture structured into proposal, problem and solution, but Simone della Barba — and it is an element common to most Academy lectures — resorts to different methodologies and critical instruments. As first, Simone deploys the traditional methodology of universities, made up of a discussion of common ideas, definition, distinction, and classification; nevertheless, his approach backs up scholastic argumentation[22] by use of many quotations from the classics (Justin, Plinius, Virgil, Varro, Diodorus Siculus, and Solinus, but also Giovio and, the only one in the vernacular, Dante) to the point that this very first section is a mosaic of

---

19   *Il Petrarcha con la spositione di M. Giovanni Andrea Gesualdo* [...] (Venice: Domenico Giglio, 1553), fol. [bb 7ʳ].
20   The translations from Petrarch are from *Petrarch's Lyric Poems. The 'Rime sparse' and Other Lyrics*, translated and edited by Robert M. Durling (Cambridge, MA: Harvard University Press, 1976).
21   *Il Petrarcha con la spositione di M. Giovanni Andrea Gesualdo* [...] (Venice: Domenico Giglio, 1553), fol. 242ᵛ.
22   According to Regn, p. 122, we could speak of Neo-scholastic argumentation: 'Im Einklang mit dieser 'neoscholastischen' Orientierung steht der Aufbau der Argumentation'.

philosophy, prose, and poetry. It is a facet that will shape the *Nuova Spositione* as a whole so that it comes to be a sort of digression on nobility in the literary tradition and not just a philosophical (even less juridical) treatise.

Nobility, as Simone points out, has indeed been recognized in all elements of life and nature. Simone della Barba thus tracks nobility from classical elements upwards to composites, plants, animals and up to arts, where, of course, the liberal arts are nobler than the practical ones. For men, at the summit of the hierarchy, nobility can imply wealth, ancestry, virtue, and manners, and such polisemy is evident in *Decameron*'s Guiscardo (pp. 14–15). Consequently, after proving how much the concept of nobility is polysemic and deceptive, Simone turns from erudition to linguistics and dialectic ('per servar la regola che si tiene ne' vocaboli che [...] son detti Equivoci', p. 15) and to the tripartition by the most important modern jurist, Bartolus de Saxoferrato. Bartolus, discussing the section 'De dignitatibus' of the *Codex Justinianus*, had divided nobility into theological, natural (itself divided into one related to every natural form and one only related to virtuous and moral men, as defined by Aristotle), and 'civile' (that is, nobility granted by a prince to a commoner).[23]

The peculiarity is that the reference to Bartolus goes well beyond the analysis of the most important and influential jurist on nobility. Given that the Latin treatise opens with a commentary on Dante's canzone 'Le dolci rime d'amor ch'i' solia', Simone della Barba, with his lecture on Petrarch's sonnet, aims to somehow recreate the Dante-Bartolus relationship, that is, a 'political' poem and its juridical commentary, of course in an innovative way. 'Le dolci rime d'amor ch'i' solia' is not, anyway, the only work by Dante that influenced Simone, since the fourth book of Dante's *Convivio*, though probably unknown to Bartolus, also offers Simone some ideas, problems, and examples. In general, the Dante-Bartolus influence on Simone's methodology and structure is clear: all of them start with the rebuttal of the most common ideas; both *Convivio* and the Latin treatise present, though with some differences, the same progression through biological kingdoms, species, and arts (often using the same examples); and Simone dismisses theological nobility with the same words as Bartolus and quotes Dante's metaphor of weed (*Cv*, IV. vii 3). It has furthermore to be stressed that the presence of Dante, unlike the quotations from the classics, is in no way just an erudite element; indeed, the poet is also the founder of the real cultural and ideological horizon of the discussion of nobility, so that della Barba takes full part in the archaeological recovery of the ancient Florentine culture fostered by Cosimo's propaganda.

At the same time, Simone considers improper both Dante's and Bartolus's concept of nobility. Dante's 'Le dolci rime d'amor ch'i' solia', indeed, with its idea that nobility is everywhere there is virtue, is considered insufficient to cope with the multiplicity of nobility. On the other hand, if Bartolus is the most important judicial reference on the subject, Simone — and here his judicial training is evident — points out how his work does not address the most important form of nobility in

---

23   By the way, one of the titles under which Bartolus' treatise was known (although improperly) was *Tractatus de nobilitate mulierum*, possibly easing the idea of a lecture handling Laura's nobility.

the past and in his own time: 'quella che consiste ne la stirpe generosa, e chiara, e ne la nobiltà del sangue' (p. 17). It is an idea of nobility as clearly aristocratic, consistent with the social and cultural transformations underway in Western society, and particularly in Cosmian Tuscany, where, according to Plaisance, 's'assiste à la liquidation des valeurs culturelles marchandes'[24] and where the Academy itself was instrumental in the diffusion of the new values.[25]

In this regard, Simone references Cicero, specifically with *Topics*, VI. 29,[26] and Aristotle, with his fifth book of *Politics*,[27] as his authorities on nobility. The former mentions, as necessary conditions for nobility, a common surname, birth from free men, no ancestors ever enslaved and continuity of economic status; the latter, ancestors beautified by wealth and virtues (p. 20). It is interesting that if the quotation from Cicero begins with 'Gentiles sunt qui', Simone's translation reads 'Nobili son quelli', allowing him — on the basis of the identity of 'gentilezza' and 'nobilitade', stated in Dante's *Convivio* (IV. xiv 5) — to connect to early Italian poetry, mainly that of Dante and Petrarch himself (pp. 25–26). Francesco Alunno's gloss on the same sonnet 'In nobil sangue uita humile, e queta', however, reads the Italian adjective 'nobil' as 'gentile, cortese', consequently confirming the connection and at the same time showing how the 'political' reading by della Barba was somehow overstated.[28] On the other hand, Simone sides with Aristotle, refusing Dante's criticism of Frederick II's concept of nobility and his position that richness is unnecessary to nobility, first because it helps protect the state, and second because largesse, without it, is impossible (p. 20). Simone's idea of nobility is thus completely detached from any metaphysical or strictly moral dimension (as in Dante), while it is definitely the expression of a new specific social milieu.

Simone then proposes his own theory of nobility, aimed at including all options and forms (pp. 27–38). Dismissing, in the wake of Bartolus, the theological nobility, Simone recognizes a natural nobility (that is, as asserted by Dante, the natural perfection of a being or of a disposition), plus three forms of civic nobility (that is, nobility of wealthy and virtuous ancestors; nobility granted by a prince; and nobility consisting of personal virtue):

> La nobiltà civile, poi, è di tre sorti: una è (come dice Aristotile nel primo libro de la *Retorica*) che consiste nella virtù, o nelle ricchezze, o in tutte quelle cose, che puon fare gl'antecessori chiari e famosi in cose honorate, e desiderate [...]. La seconda spetie di nobiltà civile è quella che è data dal Principe, o da chi tiene il principato [...]. La terza et ultima è la nobiltà causata da la virtù di colui che l'ha, et anch'ella è nobiltà civile, perché la virtù fa l'huom degno degl'honori civili [...]. (pp. 27–29)

---

24   Plaisance, p. 218.

25   It is not by chance that Simone evokes the importance of *Stemmata* in ancient Roman aristocracy, connecting them, doubtless improperly, with contemporary coats of arms; see Della Barba, *Nuova Spositione*, pp. 18–19.

26   Della Barba, *Nuova Spositione*, p. 17.

27   Della Barba, *Nuova Spositione*, p. 20.

28   *Le osservazioni di M. Francesco Alunno da Ferrara sopra il Petrarca* (Venice: Pavolo Gherardo, 1550), p. 295.

The three forms of civic nobility can occur alone or in combination with one or two of the others. Their different conjunctions are structured by the author in a clear hierarchy: the highest form happens with the concurrence of all of them; this is followed by the union of personal virtue and a title conferred by the prince, then by the union of ancestors with bestowal by the prince and, lastly, by personal virtue with inherited aristocracy:

> E questa nobiltà composta di tutte tre precede tutte l'altre, e tiene il primo grado; nel secondo luogo è quella causata da le proprie virtù, unita con la nobiltà data dal Principe; nel tertio la nobiltà data dal Principe con quella della stirpe chiara; e nel quarto è la nobiltà di sangue con quella delle virtù proprie. (pp. 30–31)

From this complicated system, the prevalence of nobility conferred by a prince is clear, as well as the priority of personal virtue over ancient ancestors. Della Barba's idea of nobility reflects, then, the politics of Cosimo and his curbing of the traditional Florentine aristocracy, much to the advantage of a new loyal élite. This is confirmed by the model proposed for the highest form of nobility overall, namely, the combination of all three forms of civic nobility plus natural nobility: inevitably, the real example of this nobility can be only Duke Cosimo I de' Medici (p. 31), as the real centre of the lecture, paralleled to Madonna Laura.

It is when only one form of civic nobility is present in a man that personal virtue prevails over a title granted by a prince, and then over ancestors, in the same way that the soul is nobler than the body or luck. In addition, della Barba proves the superiority of nobility grounded on personal virtues through multiple quotations from ancient authors and Dante (*Paradise*, XVI. 1–3), all of whom insist on the error of overestimating the importance of lineage, hence confirming a general consistency with the social and cultural programme of Cosimo's regime. Significantly, the last, long and conclusive quotation is, indeed, from Boethius's *Consolatio*,[29] with his idea that ancestry is just 'vento, e nebbia' (p. 37), well reflected in l. 7 ('Quid genus et proavos strepitis?') as the summary of the digression on nobility.

It is notable that della Barba, surprisingly, juxtaposes the quotation from Boethius with his own translation, in two mediocre stanzas:

> Tutto l'human legnaggio in terra sorge
> da una radice stessa; e un Padre è solo
> che reggie il tutto, il tutto guida e scorge.
> Egli già diede al Sole i raggi e 'l volo.
> Diede e' i corni, onde i crin la Luna avvolge.
> Ei l'huom diede a la terra, i lumi al Polo.
> Questi ne i corpi human gl'animi infuse
> da l'alto soglio, e dentro a quei gli chiuse.
>
> Se i mortai dunque tutti un nobil germe
> produsse, a che la stirpe e gl'avi alzate?
> Se 'l prio vostro natale, o menti inferme,
> e Dio, di quello autor, talor mirate,

---

29 Boeth., *Cons.*, III. carm. 6.

> non è più questo o quel vile human germe
> s'oltraggio e danno a voi da voi non fate
> co 'l mandar in oblio sì bel natale
> e sommerger l'eterno col mortale. (pp. 37–38)

The translation into Italian works somehow as a bridge to the last section of the *Spositione*, that is, that part of the lecture dedicated to the analysis of the nobility of Madonna Laura. The anomaly of the presence of Italian verses is confirmed, just two pages later, by the translation (again in ottava rima) of a few lines of one of Ovid's *Tristia*[30] (by the way, for a clearly minor and fringe element as the difference between nobility and 'generosity'). The Italian ottavas, indeed, introduce the core of the lesson, that is the commentary to sonnet 215, somehow easing the transition from ancient to modern poetry and culture:

> In nobil sangue vita humile et queta
> et in alto intellecto un puro core,
> frutto senile in sul giovenil fiore
> e 'n aspetto pensoso anima lieta
>
> raccolto à 'n questa donna il suo pianeta,
> anzi 'l re dele stelle; e 'l vero honore,
> le degne lode, e 'l gran pregio, e 'l valore,
> ch'è da stanchar ogni divin poeta.
>
> Amor s'è in lei con Honestate aggiunto,
> con beltà naturale habito adorno,
> et un atto che parla con silentio,
>
> et non so che nelli occhi, che 'n un punto
> pò far chiara la notte, oscuro il giorno,
> e 'l mèl amaro, et adolcir l'assentio.[31] (*RVF*, 215)

In light of the foregoing ethical-political part of the lecture, Laura's nobility is connected to all three forms of civic nobility (recognized in the first quatrain) and, altogether, to natural nobility (in the first two lines of the second quatrain) (p. 40). Henceforth, della Barba detaches from the sonnet 'In nobil sangue', to reshape the nobility of Laura through tesseras extracted from other texts of the *Canzoniere*, so complying with the method typical of the Accademici, that is, analysing a poet through his other texts (according to Gelli, 'non si trovando o possendo trovare modo alcuno migliore nello esporre gli autori che esporgli con le loro parole medesime').[32] As usual for the biographies of Laura in Renaissance editions of the

---

30 Ovid, *Tristia*, III. 5 31–36.

31 [In noble blood a humble and quiet life, with a high intellect a pure heart, the fruit of age in the flower of youth, and with thoughtful aspect a happy soul, have all been gathered together in this lady by her planet — rather by the King of the stars — and the true honour, the deserved praises, and the great worth that would weary any divine poet. Love has joined himself with chastity in her, with natural beauty gracious habit, and gestures that speak in silence, and I know not what in her eyes, which in an instant can make bright the night, darken the day, embitter honey, and sweeten wormwood].

32 Giambattista Gelli, *Lezioni petrarchesche*, ed. by Carlo Negroni (Bologna: Romagnoli, 1884), p. 127.

Canzoniere, della Barba recalls sonnet 4, 'Que' ch'infinita providentia et arte', as evidence that the woman was born in an obscure hamlet ('Et hor di picciol borgo un sol n'ha dato', l. 12). Nevertheless, Simone disputes the idea of Laura as a humble shepherdess, siding with the commentators who attribute an ancient heritage to her:

> Ma non però di vile, et oscuro legnaggio come mostra sì in questo presente, come in altri luoghi, il Poeta, dicendo che in quella sorte di nobiltà che è posta ne la chiarezza de gl'Antecessori, di che sogliono comunemente insuperbire gli sciocchi, il vero Principe Dio ottimo grandissimo havea raccolta una vita humile e modesta, la quale non la lassava insuperbire, né gonfiare, anchor che fusse di sangue nobile. (p. 40)

The first line itself of the sonnet 'In nobil sangue' and the aforementioned metric epistle to Cardinal Colonna prove, according to Simone, the ancient heritage of Laura (pp. 40–41). Nevertheless, God, the 're delle stelle', that is the greatest prince of all, has bestowed on Laura a modest nature that allows her to neglect the kind of nobility only stupid people boast about. The 'alto intelletto' and 'puro core' mentioned in the second line lead her to disregard what is incidental and fortuitous, such as affluence and lineage. The latter, furthermore, is defined by Simone as the most despicable of all the forms of nobility ('fra le altre nobiltà è la più infima', p. 41), consistently with what had previously been assumed about the different levels of nobility. The same disdain for hereditary nobility is even traced by Simone in sonnet 263, 'Arbor victorïosa triumphale', whose first tercet mentions Laura's indifference towards earthly and fleeting possessions (p. 41):

> Gentileza di sangue, et l'altre care
> cose tra noi, perle et robini et oro,
> quasi vil soma egualmente dispregi.[33] (*RVF*, 263. 9–11)

Although dismissing a line-by-line commentary of the sonnet ('le cose tocche a sufficienza da gli ispositori io le passo leggermente, perché ogn'uno se le può leggier da sé', p. 42), Simone specifies — probably over-intellectualizing the text — that l. 2 'et in alto intelletto un puro cuore' proposes a metonymy and should be read 'high intellect in sincere heart', given that Petrarch is here following Aristotelianism and its idea that the seat of the soul is the heart (p. 42). More importantly, Simone makes clear that the nouns in ll. 6–7 ('e 'l vero honore | le degne lode, e 'l gran pregio, e 'l valore')[34] are not just a case of *enumeratio*, but rather imply different meanings. Honour, indeed, is higher than praise, and the two apply to different objects: while the former is concerned with deeds, the latter is concerned with virtues, which are just the prerequisite for any virtuous deed to be performed (pp. 42–43). Consequently — as della Barba concludes — Laura has all three forms of civic nobility: ancient ancestry (again, disregarded, but still necessary for a full idea of nobility), that bestowed by a prince (in this case God, the king of the stars, and consequently she has this kind of nobility to the highest degree) and personal virtue, as proved by the presence of both virtues and deeds (as she has both praise

33   [Nobility of blood and the other things prized among us — pearls and rubies and gold — like a vile burden, you equally despise].
34   [and the true honor, the deserved praises, and the great worth].

and honour). Abruptly, then, Simone concludes his lecture by pointing out that the last five lines of the sonnet also prove the presence of natural nobility in Laura.

If Laura, consequently, stands out as a perfect example of nobility, comparable only to Duke Cosimo I, the abrupt, not to say brisk, conclusion of the lecture (and the sheer number of pages dedicated to Laura in comparison to the whole) is enough to assert that the sonnet is just an opportunity for a wider analysis of an issue central to Renaissance culture, and to integrate, as well and at the same time, not only Petrarch in sixteenth-century political culture, but also Laura's imaginary profile in contemporary society.

2. Francesco de' Vieri's *Discorso*

Quite surprisingly, a sonnet deemed important enough to be the basis for a lecture on Laura's nobility is not even mentioned, twenty-six years later and in the same cultural milieu of the Accademia Fiorentina, in a speech on Laura's greatness. Francesco de' Vieri, known as Verino Secondo, did indeed propose his own lesson on Laura's nature in the *Discorso della grandezza, et felice fortuna d'una gentilissima, et graziosiss. Donna qual fu M. Laura*, published by Giorgio Marescotti in 1580.[35] The work is dedicated to Pellegrina Cappello Bentivoglio, the young daughter of the first marriage of Bianca Cappello, wife of Francesco I de' Medici since 1579.[36] The name Pellegrina offers the chance for a weak play on words: as life is a pilgrimage on Earth until the soul is back in Heaven, Verino presents Pellegrina with the best model for her peregrination, that is, the portrait of the life of Madonna Laura, wishing her the same 'felice grandezza'[37] or, rather, an even greater 'grandezza', given her superiority as regards place of birth, parents and relatives:

> Le bacio le mani, e le disidero dalla D.M. quella felice grandezza, la quale io qui ho riconosciuta in M. Laura, et tanto maggiore, quanto V. Eccell. Illustriss. di maggior luogo quaggiù in terra, et di maggiori persone è nata, et con i parenti di maggiore splendore è imparentata. (fol. [A3ʳ])

It is clear that Verino is considering, with those elements, some pillars of the traditional idea of nobility on which, in 1574, he had published an essay, *Il primo libro*

---

35   On Verino, aside from Alessandra Gibba, 'Francesco de' Vieri Known as Il Verino Secondo, some Literary and Philosophical Themes in His Work' (unpublished doctoral thesis, University of London, 1993), the critical bibliography is quite scarce: Simone Fellina, 'Platone a scuola: l'insegnamento di Francesco de' Vieri detto il Verino Secondo', *Noctua*, 2 (2015), 97–181; and Alessandra Gibba, 'Francesco de' Vieri (1524–1591) and his Teaching at the University of Pisa', *History of Universities*, 14 (1995–96), 143–55. Of some interest is Rosario Pintaudi, 'Il Platone di Francesco Verino Secondo (Laur. Acquisti e doni 706)', *Rinascimento*, 16 (1976), 241–44, on his handwritten annotations in a volume of *Opere di Platone* (1548) translated by Marsilius Ficinus. His *Lezzioni d'amore* have been published by John Colaneri (München: Wilhelm Fink, 1973).

36   Pellegrina was also the dedicatee of the third part of Cesare Rinaldi's *Rime*, while Verino dedicated to Ulisse Bentivoglio, husband of Pellegrina, his *Lezione dove si ragiona delle idee e delle bellezze*. Cfr. Emanuele Cicogna, *Bianca Cappello. Cenni storico-critici* (Venice: Picotti, 1828), p. 43, n. 34.

37   *Discorso della grandezza, et felice fortuna d'una gentilissima, et graziosiss. Donna qual fu M. Laura, di M. Francesco de' Vieri, detto il Verino Secondo [...]* (Florence: Giorgio Marescotti, 1580), fol. [A3ʳ].

della nobiltà, dedicated to Eleonora di Garzia di Toledo, wife of Pietro de' Medici. It is a systematic treatise on nobility, in the wake of the best-known political theories, in some ways like the first part of della Barba's *Nuova spositione*; a peculiar aspect, nonetheless, is its strong and clear Platonic background (with many elements to be found again in the *Discorso della grandezza, et felice fortuna*), that leads Verino Secondo to identify nobility with virtue. In spite of that, the political dimension is still clear, and not only because of the many examples of the treatise derive from the ancient or, more frequently, the modern Italian aristocracy, but because the definition itself implies respect for the current social hierarchy:

> [...] in poche parole diffinirò la Nobiltà, dicendo che ella è una inclinatione alla vertù et agli atti vertuosi, acquistata primieramente da cagioni naturali e da Dio in quelli che si chiamano e sono nobili, per la quale con facilità diventono felici, et la loro felicità via più illustre, et chiara diviene.[38]

On the other hand, Verino's *Discorso della grandezza, et felice fortuna* is structured on the image of pilgrimage; the five chapters, indeed, handle five phases of Laura's life, seen as a pilgrimage on earth from heaven: prior to her birth ('innanzi che venisse al mondo'), the condition of her birth ('lo stato della nascita'), her earthly life ('mentre ella visse quaggiù in terra'), her death ('nel tempo che ella morì'), and her afterlife ('poi che l'anima sua è gita al Cielo'). Too many women, nevertheless, forget that life is just transient and that one day they will head to heaven, possibly taking with them the noblest and most distinguished things they found in their life:

> Ricordatevi, ricordatevi, gentilissime donne, che voi siate venute dal Cielo come pellegrine per dovere al Cielo ritornare, e portarne tutto quello che qua troverete, che habbia del nobile, et del pellegrino. (p. 9)

If for Hebrews, Greeks, and Romans, Judith, Aspasia, Diotima, and Lucretia could work, separately, as female models for prudence, fortitude, chastity, doctrine, and temperance, for modern women Laura will be the best, indeed a unique, example of all the virtues necessary for a fully accomplished Christian life. Studying her life, women will find, assembled in one person alone, what is necessary to help them perfecting themselves and enhancing their souls in order to return one day to heaven: 'E acciocché in una sol donna famosa, e con nobil piacere possino far questo, riguardino a tutto il progresso della graziosissima, et onestissima Madonna Laura' (p. 10).

Verino's *Discorso* comes to be in some ways a Book of Manners (to be constantly read, by the way)[39] for noblewomen. At first, the author identifies his interlocutors as the 'graziosissime, et accortissime donne' (p. 7); furthermore, the preface clearly dialogues with the best-known literature on female dignity, polemicizing against both the idea that women have been created only for male pleasure and the even more misogynistic stance that they should do nothing but sew, spin and weave, but also questioning the 'sophistry' (spreading in contemporary treatises) of a natural

---

38   Francesco de' Veri detto il Verino secondo, *Il primo libro della nobiltà* (Florence: Giorgio Marescotti, 1574), pp. 72–73.
39   See *Discorso della grandezza*, p. 10.

female superiority (pp. 7–8). In the Platonic perspective typical of the author, women must instead emulate Laura and her search for that perfection for which God and Nature had prepared her: '[...] con atti di tanta virtù a quanta innanzi si generasse era da Dio eletta, et a quanta i cieli, et l'altre cagioni naturali nel nascere l'haveano disposta' (p. 10).

This handbook to learn perfection benefits, as optimistically specified by Verino, from pleasure ('vi doverrà dilettare') and brilliance ('harà dell'ingegno'). The *Discorso*, indeed, not only contains many quotations from Petrarch ('molte belle autorità del leggiadrissimo M. Francesco Petrarca'), but also tackles and answers many difficult questions and doubts ('molte, e molte sottili dubitazioni che si muoveranno, e si risolveranno chiaramente', pp. 10–11). The structure of every chapter is similar: first the definition of a specific kind of greatness, then the recognition of it in Petrarch's poems and, lastly, the answer to the philosophical questions that arise from some passages of the texts, so that the treatise comes to be a sort of unsystematic philosophical commentary on the *Canzoniere*. In many cases, anyway, and mostly in the third chapter, questions stem from each other on multiple levels, creating an elaborate tree of poetical, critical, and philosophical problems.

As a whole, the *Discorso* aspires, then, to be a spiritual biography of Laura as well as a worldly encyclopedia of philosophical questions 'for ladies'. If, for the former, Verino's work is indubitably of some cultural interest, for the latter it sometimes amasses otiose and hair-splitting curiosities. A clear specimen of such oddity, for example, is the question — while analysing l. 5 of sonnet 77 'Per mirar Policleto a prova fiso' ('Ma certo il mio Simon fu in Paradiso') — as to how Simone Martini could actually paint Laura in heaven while he was on earth (p. 18). Although the question might seem superfluous, the answer is — although unforeseen — illuminating as to the pervasive Platonism of the *Discorso*. Simone Martini, indeed, could go beyond matter and portray Laura's beauty in the real form it has in God's mind: 'Simone fu in Paradiso [...] per modo di similitudine quanto all'atto di ritrarla più a punto di quello che nella sensibile materia non è, come ancora a punto si ritrova nella mente di Dio'.[40]

This is just a hint at the role played by Platonism (along with Plotinus, Hermes Trismegistus, Pico, Porphyry, and others) in the *Discorso*. Francesco de' Vieri, in the wake of Florentine Ficinism, was actually a committed proponent of the re-introduction of Plato in the University of Pisa, and in 1576 had been allowed to teach, on feast days, a special course on Platonism to complement his lectures on Aristotelian logic and natural philosophy. Verino aimed at reconciling Aristotle and Plato, as proved by his *Vere conclusioni di Platone conformi alla dottrina Christiana et a quella di Aristotile* (1589); in Verino's opinion, if Platonic dialogues lacked in orderliness (and Verino's goal was to provide them with recaps and a distribution in

---

40   Of course, all the lectures of the Accademici are steeped in Platonism (as well as in Aristotelianism); nevertheless, in his lecture (1549) on the two sonnets on Simone Martini's portrait, Gelli stresses in particular the importance of Aristotle for the comprehension of *RVF*, 78, and of Plato for *RVF*, 77 (analysing for example the problem, already summarized in Gesualdo's commentary, of the presence in God only of the universals, and not of the particulars, as Laura is): see Gelli, pp. 246–47 and 259–60.

chapters), they were better suited to popularization. It is therefore probably not by chance that the *Discorso* was published only two years after that de' Vieri, because of the harsh hostility of his colleagues, had been forced to abandon the course on Plato. In some ways, the lecture on Laura's greatness could be seen, then, as a continuation of the Plato-agenda outside university.

Platonism is undeniably already in the first chapter, on Laura's life prior to her birth. This opens with a preamble that is, in fact, a description of Neoplatonic cosmology, with a phenomenal world deriving, through ideas, from God. Consequently, mundane greatness and happiness are already in God's mind and are instrumental in guaranteeing a well-functioning society where the importance of aristocracy is undeniable: not only 'Chi dee essere grande e felice è prima tale nella mente divina, e per divino beneplacito a tanta altezza è eletto e disposto, perché imiti la D. Bontà, così nell'essere benefico a bisognosi, et a buoni', but also 'Ogni potestà e grandezza è da Dio' (pp. 16–17).

This Platonic system (and the role of nobility it implies) is proved, according to Verino Secondo, not only by the sonnet 'Per mirar Policleto in Paradiso', where Petrarch asserts that Simone Martini could portray Laura in paradise, but also by the first quatrain of sonnet 159 'In qual parte del cielo, in quale idea', where Petrarch wonders in which part of heaven or in which idea nature could find the model from which to craft Laura's visage:

> In qual parte del Cielo, in quale Idea
> Era l'esempio, onde natura tolse
> Quel bel viso leggiadro in ch'ella volse
> Mostrar quaggiù, quanto lassù potea?[41]

This chapter, so filled with Platonism, ends by properly and inevitably recommending Laura as a symbol of an innate and ontological nobility to women:

> Vedete. Vedete gentilissime Donne, quale si fusse il principio della grandezza, et della grazia di M. Laura, poiché hebbe origine dalla Divina Essenza, dove come in un lucidissimo specchio ella molto più bella è conosciuta da Dio, che quaggiù in terra, et dove rimirò la natura per mostrare quanto lassù potea, et come da più eccellenti Pittori, et Poeti ella è espressa, et ritratta in carte. (p. 20)

The second chapter handles the next step of Laura's pilgrimage, her birth, which can be considered as the implementation of the form in God's mind through excellent tools and pure matter. In the creation of Laura, the tools were angels, spheres, and planets, as well as the place where she was born; matter, instead, were the four classical elements, which derived in turn from the four bodily fluids of her parents. This is a position that opens not only to, again, Platonism (and Aristotelianism), but also to a Christianized astrology: the position and influence of planets and stars, and consequently the nature and status of men and women, are because of God's loving providence. A propitious influence of the stars at Laura's birth is proved through the fifth stanza of canzone 325 'Tacer non posso' (p. 22):

---

41   [In what part of Heaven, in what Idea was the pattern from which Nature copied that lovely face, in which she has shown down here all that she is capable of doing up there].

Il dì che costei nacque, eran le stelle
che producon fra voi felici effetti
in luoghi alti et electi.[42]

Again, Petrarch himself, with sonnet 154, is quoted to state that not only 'le stelle, e 'l cielo', but as well 'gli elementi a prova' were excellent in Laura while, on the popularization side, Verino has the chance to better explain the four classical elements, some aspects of Aristotelian physics (on which he had previously written a book in Italian, the *Trattato delle metheore*), and Hippocrates's humoral theory. Laura, thus, was happy in her birth because matter and spheres cooperated so that men could recognize God's role in her beauty. Furthermore, her birth, according to the second chapter of *Triumphus mortis*, in 'troppo humil terren'[43] is actually just further evidence of her greatness, because God always glorifies humility ('humiltate exaltar sempre gli piacque'),[44] and, of course, it is not by chance that the chapter on Laura's birth ends by mentioning Jesus's birth in a humble little town of Judea, a comparison authorized by the tercets of sonnet 4 'Que' ch'infinita providentia et arte'.

The third chapter, about Laura's life, is by far the longest and richest in quotations from the *Canzoniere*. It handles three specific issues: her beauties (of soul, body, and voice, which is a combination of them); the effects she produced in her lover; and the natural similes used by the poet to describe her. The three beauties, obviously, are easily recognizable in Laura, as stated by sonnet 213 'Grazie ch'a pochi il ciel largo destina'. Of striking interest, nevertheless, is the first question raised by the sonnet, namely why God, despite loving everybody in the same way, bestows his gifts upon few people. Verino's answer is that the different distribution of qualities is instrumental in structuring the world, so that those who are void of God's gifts recognize, love and imitate them in those who have instead been lavished with them, thus making their way to heaven. Again, it is a clear hint at Platonism; however, Platonism is also clear in the idea that a beautiful voice is important because melodious singing can lead to detachment from matter and contemplation of the beauty of the universe (and a few lines later, Verino adds as similar instruments mathematics and philosophy, syncretizing Plotinus, Plato, and Socrates) (p. 31). Lastly, it has probably to be underscored that, although without any explicit political dimension, the overall idea of an *a priori* hierarchy consistent with both God's will and the contemporary social context is quite significant in the chapter.

Nevertheless, the longest part of the treatise, and its core, is the second section of the chapter. Here, for twenty-two pages (out of a total of sixty-eight), Verino Secondo exhibits the whole phenomenology of love. We are faced with an extensive survey of feelings and reactions (both physical and psychological) on the side of the lover and of the dynamics of love that are clearly derived from thirteenth- and fourteenth-century Florentine poetry, although in some ways through the filter

---

42 [The day she was born, the stars that produce among you happy effects [...], in high and noble places].
43 Petrarch, *Triumphus mortis*, II. 165.
44 *RVF*, 4. 11.

of Bembo's *Asolani* (though not expressly quoted, the dialogue emerges through the distinction of the effects of love into three categories: torment, happiness, and virtuous beatitude) (p. 32). Given that Platonism also remains clear in this section (as can be seen from the questions on how the lover can contemplate God through love for a mortal, p. 43), and that there are frequent philosophical digressions to better clarify Petrarch's difficult passages, the prominence of Florentine poetical tradition is anyway probably the element that most links Verino's *Discorso* to the Accademia Fiorentina, of which he was a member and which had been the breeding ground for della Barba's lecture. This perception could be confirmed by the fact that Verino mentions here his still unpublished commentary on 'Donna me prega' (p. 40): editorial self-promotion, doubtless, but the philosopher is also introducing himself as the heir to a tradition of philosophy applied to poetry.

The point is that such phenomenology is exemplified through fifteen extended quotations from Petrarch (plus some short references); indeed, according to Verino, Petrarch would have expressed the moods and feelings of any lover through the depiction of himself, in the same way as Laura stands for every beloved woman ('Francesco Petrarca, il quale non meno con verità et a pieno ha espresso ogni condizione degli amanti con lo esempio di se stesso, et le lodi et condizioni dell'amate donne, con l'esempio della sua M. Laura', p. 47). Peculiarly interesting is the string of excerpts from the *Canzoniere* aimed at describing the positive effects of love, from discharging every other pleasure to being incited to virtue, from the way to heaven being revealed to desiring one day to contemplate the divine beauty in paradise (pp. 47–53). One more time, these effects describe a Platonic ascension from matter to God, but the same can be said for the last section of the third chapter, where Verino Secondo analyses the similes applied to Laura with a sequence from magnet, to laurel, to phoenix, up to angels and eventually to God (with the first quatrain of sonnet 191 'Sì come eterna vita è veder Dio') (pp. 53–56).

Such a climax is the best transition to the fourth chapter (pp. 56–62), addressing the three forms of Laura's happiness in her death: the first are the astonishing signs that happened at her death, and it is quite peculiar both that Verino also mentions the signs that preceded the death of the two philosophers Plotinus and Pico, and that the six visions of 'Standomi un giorno solo alla finestra' are considered foreshadowings of Laura's death, and not just allegories; the second is the way she died, with a tranquility that, through quotations from *Triumphus mortis*, I, is compared to that of Socrates in *Phaedo*; third and last are the pain and praises of the people that loved her.

Finally, the last short chapter describes three kinds of happiness experienced by Laura in the afterlife: the first and second, unsurprisingly, are the presence of angels and the intellectual love of God; the third is, rather, fame through the centuries, naturally obtained thanks to Petrarch's poems (an earthly glory, then, fully coherent neither with Christianity nor with Platonism). In one of the latter two, Verino finds the definition of Laura's real and ontological nature and condition, thus closing the treatise in such a way that gives it a circular structure. In canzone 270, 'Amor, se vuo' ch'i' torni al giogo antico', l. 96 indeed reads: 'ma piango et grido: "Ahi nobil pellegrina"'. That phrase triggers a comment by Verino that summarizes the main topics of the *Discorso*, that is the idea of pilgrimage, Laura's virtues, and the concept of innate internal nobility:

> Et è qui da sapere che questo bel nome, che il Petrarca col suo dire le acquista non è quello, che ella hebbe alle fonte, ma il nome concernente eccellenza di natura, di luogo, et d'operazioni, quale è questo nome Pellegrina con questo cognome di Nobile, et bene se le conviene perché è divina per l'animo, viene dalla celeste patria, e poiché nel suo pellegrinaggio di quaggiù ella così nobilmente e valorosamente combatté con l'amore, prima di tutte le più potenti passioni [...]. (p. 65)

We are very far, of course and inevitably, from the nobility analysed by della Barba. Simone, after all, was a lawyer lecturing in a public context in politically crucial years, while Verino was a philosopher struggling to introduce Plato into university curricula and writing in private form to an audience of women. Nevertheless, in this peculiar Platonic treatise an aristocratic social hierarchy often surfaces: in his final address, Verino again recommends Laura to the women as the best model for their pilgrimage in order to resemble, as much as they can, God, that is the 'Principe de' principi'. In the very last words of the treatise, the platonic and philosophical hierarchy comes to superimpose itself on the political hierarchy.

CHAPTER 4

Judging Petrarch in the Venetian Accademia della Fama: Celio Magno and his *Prefatione sopra il Petrarca* (c. 1558)

Giacomo Comiati

1. Preface to a *Preface*

The *Prefatione sopra il Petrarca* [*Preface to Petrarch*] is a text on poetry composed by the Venetian author Celio Magno (1536–1602) in the late 1550s most probably intended as an introduction to an academic lecture that he wished to deliver on either the entire book of rhymes by Petrarch or a single poem of the *Canzoniere*.[1]

1   On Celio Magno, see Emanuele Antonio Cicogna, *Delle Iscrizioni Veneziane*, 6 vols (Venice: Picotti, 1824–54; repr. Bologna: Forni, 1982), v, 232; Giacomo Zanella, 'Della vita e degli scritti di Celio Magno', *Atti dell'Istituto veneto di scienze, lettere ed arti*, 7 (1880–81), 1063–75; Daniele Ghirlanda, 'Magno, Celio', in *Dizionario biografico degli italiani* (Rome: Istituto dell'Enciclopedia Italiana, 1960–), LXVII (2006), 496–98. On Magno's poetical works, see Antonio Pilot, 'Le canzoni di Celio Magno in relazione colla lirica veneta del tempo', *Ateneo veneto*, 32 (1909), 117–308; Riccardo Scrivano, 'La lirica dal Casa al Magno', in Riccardo Scrivano, *Il manierismo nella letteratura del Cinquecento* (Padua: Liviana, 1959), pp. 75–108; Edoardo Taddeo, *Il manierismo letterario e i lirici veneziani del tardo Cinquecento* (Rome: Bulzoni, 1974), pp. 139–69; Cesare Galimberti, 'Disegno petrarchesco e tradizione sapienziale in Celio Magno', in *Petrarca, Venezia e il Veneto*, ed. by Giorgio Padoan (Florence: Olschki, 1976), pp. 315–32; Giuseppina Stella Galbiati, 'Contributo per Celio Magno: una lettura della canzone "Deus", insieme ai suoi antichi commentatori', in *Studi di onomastica e letteratura offerti a Bruno Porcelli*, ed. by Davide De Camilli (Pisa-Rome: Gruppo Editoriale Internazionale, 2006), pp. 129–44; Giuseppina Stella Galbiati, 'Epilogo sacro e libro: alcune considerazioni sulle *Rime* di Celio Magno', in *Autorità, modelli e antimodelli nella cultura artistica e letteraria tra Riforma e Controriforma. Atti del seminario internazionale di studi, Urbino-Sassocorvaro, 9–11 novembre 2006*, ed. by Antonio Corsaro, Harald Hendrix, and Paolo Procaccioli (Manziana: Vecchiarelli, 2007), pp. 369–85; Giacomo Comiati, ' "Benché 'l sol decline vince un sol raggio suo tutte le stelle". La parabola amorosa nelle *Rime* di Celio Magno', *Italique*, 17 (2014), 104–40; Andrea Campana, 'Ipotesi di lettura sul macrotesto delle *Rime* (1600) di Celio Magno', *Studi e Problemi di Critica Testuale*, 89 (2014), 211–52; Giacomo Comiati, 'Presenze oraziane nelle *Rime* di Celio Magno', in *Canzonieri in Transito. Lasciti petrarcheschi e nuovi archetipi letterari tra Cinque e Seicento*, ed. by Alessandro Metlica and Franco Tomasi (Milan: Mimesis, 2015), pp. 59–76; and Giacomo Comiati, 'Componente paratestuale e didascalie nelle *Rime* di Celio Magno', in *Questioni filologiche: la critica testuale attraverso i secoli*, ed. by Pamela Arancibia, Johnny L. Bertolio, Joanne Granata, Giovanna Licata, Erika Papagni, and Matteo Ugolini (Florence: Franco Cesati, 2016), pp. 143–59.

Unfortunately, a copy of the lesson itself — if ever written — has never been found,[2] but a manuscript of the Marciana Library in Venice carries the only existing copy of the *Preface* to Magno's lecture.[3] The numerous autograph linguistic and stylistic revisions present in the Marciana manuscript signal that the text in question must have been a draft (albeit a near final one) of Magno's *Prefatione*,[4] prepared to be sent — as some scholars have argued — to a senior member (if not the secretary) of the academy for review and approval before Magno delivered the lecture itself.[5] Scholars have debated about the academy concerned.[6] Internal evidence offered by the text suggests that 1) it was an academy to which Magno belonged, since he explicitly writes 'nostra Academia' [our academy] at the beginning of his *Preface*;[7] and 2) this affiliation occurred while Magno was still young, because the author makes reference to his 'poche e giovanili forze' [limited and youthful forces] while invoking a precautionary (and rhetorical) forgiveness from his audience for his inadequacy to deal with the high task he was called to (that of discussing poetry and Petrarch).[8] Considering these aspects and aligning them with other biographical data we possess on Magno, scholars are agreed that the *Prefatione sopra il Petrarca* was most probably composed for the Accademia della Fama (or Accademia Veneziana), which flourished in Venice between November 1557 and August 1561 under the patronage of the Venetian nobleman Federico Badoer (1519–93).[9] This

2   See Taddeo, *Il manierismo letterario*, p. 219.

3   Celio Magno's *Prefatione sopra il Petrarca* can be read in Venice, Biblioteca Nazionale Marciana, MS It. IX, 171 (=6092), fols 154ʳ–59ᵛ and the two following endpapers. On this manuscript, see Taddeo, *Il manierismo letterario*, p. 217; and Cicogna, *Delle Iscrizioni Veneziane*, v, pp. 247–50. Magno's *Prefatione* has been transcribed and published in Pietro Pagan, 'Una prefazione di Celio Magno al Petrarca', *Studi petrarcheschi*, 8 (1976), 231–56 (pp. 247–56); and Taddeo, *Il manierismo letterario*, pp. 221–32. From the latter, the quotations of Magno's *Preface* present in this article are drawn. Magno's critical work, as it had been edited by Taddeo, will be hereafter referred to as *Prefatione*. On Magno's *Prefatione*, see Antonio Pilot, *Giudizi sul Petrarca del Groto e di Celio Magno* (Cividale del Friuli: Officina grafica dei fratelli Stagni, 1912); Pagan, 'Una prefazione', pp. 231–46; Taddeo, *Il manierismo letterario*, pp. 199–204 and 217–20; and Lina Bolzoni, *La stanza della memoria. Modelli letterari e iconografici nell'età della stampa* (Turin: Einaudi, 1995), p. 9.

4   See Pagan, 'Una prefazione', p. 233.

5   See Pagan, 'Una prefazione', p. 234.

6   See Taddeo, *Il manierismo letterario*, pp. 218–19; and Pagan, 'Una prefazione', pp. 233–34.

7   *Prefatione*, p. 221. See also Taddeo, *Il manierismo letterario*, p. 218.

8   *Prefatione*, p. 221.

9   On Magno's affiliation with the Accademia della Fama, see Michele Maylender, *Storia delle Accademie d'Italia*, 5 vols (Bologna; Trieste: Licinio Capelli, 1926–1930; repr. Bologna: Forni, 1976), v, 436–43; Taddeo, *Il manierismo letterario*, p. 218; Pagan, 'Una prefazione', pp. 234–35; and Stella Galbiati, 'Contributo per Celio Magno', p. 130. On the Accademia della Fama, see Paul L. Rose, 'The Accademia Venetiana: Science and Culture in Renaissance Venice', *Studi veneziani*, 11 (1969), 191–241; Pietro Pagan, 'Sulla Accademia "Venetiana" o della "Fama"', *Atti dell'Istituto veneto di scienze, lettere ed arti*, 132 (1973–74), 359–92; Paolo Ulvioni, *Accademie e cultura in Italia dalla Controriforma all'Arcadia* (Milan: Archivio Storico Civico e Biblioteca Trivulziana, 1979), pp. 21–75; Lina Bolzoni, 'L'Accademia Veneziana: splendore e decadenza di una utopia enciclopedica', in *Università, Accademie e Società scientifiche in Italia e in Germania dal Cinquecento al Settecento*, ed. by Laetitia Boehm and Ezio Raimondi (Bologna: Il Mulino, 1981), pp. 117–67; Lina Bolzoni, 'Il "Badoaro" di Francesco Patrizi e l'Accademia veneziana della Fama', *Giornale storico della letteratura italiana*, 158 (1981), 71–101; Manfredo Tafuri, *Venezia e il Rinascimento: religione, scienza, architettura* (Turin: Einaudi, 1985), pp. 172–84;

view is mainly supported by three facts: 1) the duration of the academy corresponds to Magno's statement in his *Preface* since, between 1557 and 1561, he was in his twenties; 2) the academy had strong links with the circles of Domenico Venier (1517–82) and Girolamo Molino (1500–69), to which Magno belonged;[10] and, more decisively, 3) the name of Celio Magno — as well as that of his brother Alessandro — is mentioned among the founders of the Accademia della Fama.[11]

The principal reason to explain, instead, why Magno's work lays in unfinished form is — according to scholars — related to the way its content overlaps with that of another lecture prepared and delivered by a senior member of the Venetian academy in 1559. The text in question is Bernardo Tasso's *Ragionamento de la poesia*, a short lecture on poetry that Tasso read in front of the very audience for which Magno was preparing his *Prefatione*.[12] It had been persuasively argued that Magno might have possibly been assigned the task to lecture on Petrarch before Tasso, and started writing his introductory text, where he praised and reasoned about poetry

Anna Laura Puliafito Bleuel, 'Due lettere del Pinelli e l'Accademia della Fama', *Studi veneziani*, 18 (1989), 285–98; Barbara Marx, 'Die Stadt als Buch. Anmerkungen zur Academia Venetiana und zu Francesco Sansovino', *Studi. Schriftenreihe des Deutschen Studienzentrums in Venedig*, 9 (1993), 233–60; Lina Bolzoni, '"Rendere visibile il sapere": L'Accademia Veneziana fra modernità e utopia', in *Italian Academies of the Sixteenth Century*, ed. by David S. Chambers and François Quiviger (London: The Warburg Institute, 1995), pp. 61–78; Ian Fenlon, 'Zarlino and the Accademia Venetiana', in *Italian Academies of the Sixteenth Century*, pp. 79–90; Bolzoni, *La stanza della memoria*, pp. 3–25; Shanti Graheli, 'Reading the History of the Accademia Veneziana through its Booklists', in *Documenting the Early Modern Book World: Inventories and Catalogues in Manuscript and Print*, ed. by Malcolm Walsby and Natasha Constantinidou (Leiden-Boston: Brill, 2013), pp. 283–320; Simone Testa, *Italian Academies and their Networks, 1525–1700: From Local to Global* (Houndmill; New York: Palgrave Macmillan, 2015), p. 121; Anna Laura Puliafito Bleuel, 'Somma delle opere', in *Venice and Aristotle (c. 1450–c. 1600): From Greek and Latin to the Vernacular*, ed. by Alessio Cotugno and David Lines (Venice: Marcianum Press, 2016), pp. 120–21; and Valeria Guarna, *L'Accademia Veneziana della Fama (1557–1561). Storia, cultura e editoria* (Manziana: Vecchiarelli, 2018).

10   On the link between Venier, Molino, and the Accademia della Fama, see Rose, 'The Accademia Venetiana', pp. 222–24; and Bolzoni, *La stanza della memoria*, p. 5. On Domenico Venier and his literary circle, see Giacomo Comiati, 'Venier, Domenico', in *Dizionario Biografico degli italiani* XCVIII (2020); Piero Antonio Serassi, 'La vita di Domenico Venier', in Domenico Venier, *Rime* (Bergamo: Lancellotto, 1751), pp. i–xlviii; Damaso Alonso, *Pluralità e correlazione in poesia* (Bari: Adriatica, 1971); Bodo L. O. Richter, 'Petrarchism and Antipetrarchism among the Veniers', *Forum Italicum*, 3 (1969), 20–42; Taddeo, *Il manierismo letterario*, pp. 39–70; Martha Feldman, 'The Academy of Domenico Venier. Music's Literary Muse in Middle-Renaissance', *Renaissance Quarterly*, 44 (1991), 476–512; Martha Feldman, *City Culture and the Madrigal at Venice* (Berkeley-Los Angeles-Oxford: University of California Press, 1995), pp. 87–120; and Agostino Casu, 'Sonetti "Fratelli". Caro, Venier, Tasso', *Italique*, 3 (2000), 45–87. On Girolamo Molino and his cultural milieu, see Elisa Greggio, 'Girolamo Molino', *L'ateneo veneto*, 18 (1894), 188–202 and 255–323; Taddeo, *Il manierismo letterario*, pp. 73–97; Francesco Erspamer, 'Petrarchismo e manierismo nella lirica del secondo Cinquecento', in *Storia della cultura veneta*, ed. by Girolamo Arnaldi and Manlio Pastore Stocchi, 10 vols (Vicenza: Neri Pozza, 1976), IV.1, 189–222 (pp. 207–10); and Franco Tomasi, 'Molin, Girolamo', in *Dizionario Biografico degli italiani*, LXXV (2011), pp. 359–62.

11   See Taddeo, *Il manierismo letterario*, p. 218.

12   See Taddeo, *Il manierismo letterario*, p. 219; Pagan, 'Una prefazione', pp. 234–44; and Bolzoni, *La stanza della memoria*, p. 9. Tasso's *Ragionamento* can be read in Bernardo Tasso, *Lettere*, 3 vols (Padua: Comino, 1733), II, 513–23. A modern edition of the text is in *Trattati di poetica e retorica del Cinquecento*, ed. by Bernard Weinberg, 4 vols (Bari: Laterza, 1970), II, pp. 567–84.

and the lyrical genre.[13] But, before Magno had completed his work, Tasso, as secretary of the academy, delivered his general opening speech on poetry dealing with most of the subjects taken into account by Magno in his *Preface*. In this way, Tasso's lecture would have overshadowed Magno's work and obliged him to leave it unfinished and, presumably, focus instead on the second part of his project — the lecture on Petrarch. The abrupt demise of the academy, occurring less than one year and a half after Tasso's delivery, might have put an end to Magno's projected lecture.[14] In spite of such circumstances, the relationship existing between Tasso and Magno's works can prove very useful to date the latter. By considering the similarities between the two texts and the fact that it is improbable that Magno drafted a lecture quite similar — in terms of content — to that of Tasso after that the latter was delivered, one can postulate that Magno's *Preface* was either written slightly before, or in the same moment as Tasso's speech in 1559, and, quite clearly, after November 1557, when the academy was founded.

This essay has three main sections. After having offered a detailed analysis of the content and structure of Magno's work on Petrarch (2), it will focus on the similarities between Magno's *Prefatione* and Tasso's *Ragionamento* (in section 3.3) as well as those manifold connections that link Magno's text to the cultural milieus of contemporary Venice, such as Domenico Venier's literary circle (3.1). The echo of the works and debates fostered by and produced in the Accademia della Fama is vivid in Magno's *Preface* too, and will be analysed (3.2). A closing section will be devoted to discussing the repercussions of Magno's text with respect to his own subsequent poetical production (4). Indeed, while working his entire life as a diplomat, an ambassador, and a civic secretary of the Venetian Republic, Magno never ceased to write poems, which he later collected in a book of rhymes that he edited and published in 1600.[15] Many of those aspects that, in his *Preface*, he defined as distinctive traits of lyric poetry and that he praised and presented as those that should be imitated, following Petrarch's example, form the basis for his later lyrical production. A thoroughgoing analysis of Magno's *Prefatione sopra il Petrarca* will thus help to cast new light on the interplay occurring between theoretical disputes on the leading Trecento authority on Italian vernacular poetry, on the one hand, and the concrete ways in which the teachings drawn from Petrarch were applied in authentic poetical works, on the other. Our discussion will also assist our understanding of the debates on poetry that animated the Italian and Venetian mid-sixteenth century, the contemporary discussions on and readings of Petrarch's *Canzoniere*, and the new tendencies of the lyrical genre in the mid-Cinquecento Venetian lively milieus.

---

13   See Taddeo, *Il manierismo letterario*, p. 219.
14   On the sudden demise of the Accademia della Fama, see Pagan, 'Sulla Accademia "Venetiana"'; Pagan, 'Una prefazione', p. 231; Bolzoni, *La stanza della memoria*, pp. 18–21; and Guarna, *L'Accademia Veneziana della Fama*, pp. 58–64.
15   *Rime di Celio Magno et Orsatto Giustinian* (Venice: Muschio, 1600), which will be hereafter referred to as *Rime*. On the textual history of Magno's *Canzoniere* see Francesco Erspamer, 'Per un'edizione critica delle rime di Celio Magno', *Studi di filologia italiana*, 41 (1983), 45–72; and Francesco Erspamer, 'Lo scrittoio di Celio Magno', in *Il libro di poesia dal copista al tipografo*, ed. by Marco Santagata and Amedeo Quondam (Modena: Panini, 1989), pp. 243–50.

2. Structure and Content of Magno's *Prefatione sopra il Petrarca*

Magno's *Prefatione sopra il Petrarca* is a short work — it takes up just eight manuscript folios — but, in spite of its limited originality, its content remains interesting, as does its argumentative structure. It aims to uphold the idea that poetry has primarily an ethical and religious goal, being — according to the author — the only uniquely divine art that inspires virtue into people and leads them from their human condition to a purer, spiritual one. In his text, Magno, first, lauds poetry, describes its origins, and reveals its purposes; he then exalts the lyric genre as foremost among the others (on the basis of its deeper and more intricate relationship with the divine), and, finally, he focuses on Petrarch — viewed as one of the most refined lyric poets — whom he presents as both a master of style and a champion of morality and spirituality, one whose poetical example should be followed to produce higher and worthier verses. This concluding section on Petrarch — which can be understood as an implicit call for renovating contemporary poetry — is the concluding strand of the *Preface*'s critical contribution. The treatise moves from the general to the particular, proceeding from a discussion of poetry in a broad sense (in part one), to analysis of a single poetical genre (in part two), and then to the examination of a work — Petrarch's vernacular *Canzoniere* (in part three) — belonging to that genre and seen as one of its most eminent specimens. Magno is detailed and systematic in the way in which he structures the overall pattern of his *Prefatione*, but he also meticulously plans the internal discourse of the three sections of his work, since he organizes all of them as a logical series of general statements, each of which he endeavours to validate with either logical demonstrations, or the backing of a philosophical authority (mainly Plato), or both.

The *Prefatione* is, in fact, a remarkable text that springs from the Italian mid-sixteenth century multifaceted debate on both poetics and Petrarch, bearing traces of many works that circulated at the time.[16] Although many of the topics treated by Magno are not unprecedented, the text can nevertheless be considered as a sophisticated compound of poetic theories, with an explicit predilection for those centred on an ethical strain and involving threads of influence from contemporary Neoplatonism. As will be shown below, Neoplatonic principles are building-blocs in the *Preface* and support Magno's assertions about the poet being divinely inspired, and poetry itself being capable of bringing humans to contemplate the divine via terrestrial beauties. Furthermore, notwithstanding the commonplace nature of some of Magno's viewpoints, the work presents some highly original traits too, such as an overt declaration of the predominant position of the lyrical genre. In what follows, we will investigate these points and elucidate their claims, by focusing on a close reading of the text itself and its various sections.

Magno's lesson on Petrarch begins with a short introduction (which takes up a little more than a tenth of the entire work) where the author describes the tripartite structure of his speech, after having first presented himself — in accordance to a *topos modestiae* — as inadequate for the high task he is about to start (that of

16   See Pagan, 'Una prefazione', pp. 234–35.

extolling Petrarch). In the manuscript copy, we find the first of the three parts of the *Preface* placed under the label 'Poema' [Poetry], a label which summarizes the first main topic that will be covered, and, at the same time, highlights the importance that ordering and structuring had for Magno in his work. In this section — the longest of the text (taking up half of the *Preface*) — the author starts by focusing on the origin of poetry — a word that, according to Magno, is almost a synonym for poem, even though the latter refers to a created work and the former to a poetical work in the making.[17] Magno takes his distance from the lengthy considerations about the inventor of poetry — on which other authors lingered, e.g., Boccaccio in book 14 of his *Genealogie deorum gentilium* or Bernardo Tasso in his *Ragionamento*[18] — and sharply affirms that neither Apollo nor Moses invented poetry, but it must have born with the first human beings. A demonstration of this statement follows. The author maintains that, since poetry is made of 'imitatione' and 'numero' [imitation and rhythms], and considering that both these features are intricately bound up with the nature of human beings, poetry must have appeared with mankind itself.[19] Magno maintains too that the first poetry was religious in content and aimed to praise God and celebrate his mysteries. Because of the divine topic that the first poets had to sing, a language distant from the common one was sought and invented; for this reason, beginning with the very first compositions, poets made use of refined words, rhetorical features, and rhythms.

The second point on which Magno focuses in the first section of his lecture is the main goals of poetry. He identifies two of them: an ethical and a spiritualizing one. Speaking about the former, the author remembers that poetry is a 'propriissima maestra dell'operare' and a 'guida alla virtù' [life coach of the utmost morality and guide to virtue],[20] as — he states — the myths of Orpheus and Amphion suggest. Referring to mythological episodes to exemplify the power and function of poetry was a commonplace of poetic treatises, but, on the basis of linguistic and structural analogies, it is possible to put this passage by Magno in contact with two specific works on poetics: Bernardino Daniello's *Della poetica* (1536) — many of whose expressions return in Magno's paragraph[21] — and *De Poetarum laudibus*, written in

---

17   See *Prefatione*, p. 222: 'Poema, over Poesia (che l'un nome si è quasi l'istesso che l'altro, se non in quanto Poema significa l'opera fornita, et Poesia più tosto l'opera in quel corso mentr'ella si fa)' [Poem or Poetry (since one is almost the same of the other, despite the fact that Poem refers to the completed work, while Poetry to the work in the making)].

18   See Tasso, *Ragionamento*, pp. 571–72; and Giovanni Boccaccio, *Genealogie deorum gentilium*, ed. by Vittorio Zaccaria, in Giovanni Boccaccio, *Tutte le opere*, ed. by Vittore Branca, 10 vols (Milan: Mondadori, 1967–1983), VII–VIII.1 and VIII.2, 1152–1813 (pp. 1403–11). On books 14 and 15 of Boccaccio's *Genealogie* see also Giovanni Boccaccio, *Généalogie des Dieux païens (Genealogia deorum gentilium). Livres 14 et 15. Un 'manifeste' pour la poesie*, ed. and trans. by Yves Delegue (Strasbourg: Presses Universitaires de Strasbourg, 2001).

19   See *Prefatione*, p. 223, where Magno states that 'imitatione' [imitation] is 'tanto natural all'huomo, che a pena nato quasi si diletta mirabilmente d'imitare' [so much distinctive of human beings that, as soon as they are born, they look to imitate] and that 'numero' [rhythm] is 'corrispondente et proportionato alla nostra anima' [compatible with and proportionate to our souls].

20   See *Prefatione*, p. 223.

21   See *Prefatione*, pp. 223–24 and Bernardino Daniello, *Della poetica*, in *Trattati di poetica e retorica del Cinquecento*, I, 227–318 (p. 234). See also Pagan, 'Una prefazione', p. 239.

the late 1550s by Bernardino Regazola (called Feliciano), member of the Accademia della Fama — whose passage on Orpheus and Amphion is mirrored in that of Magno.[22] The author also states that poetry is an art that has always both provided honest guidance for humankind and directed it along the path of happiness, and, after this definition, he feels the need to specify that, differently from other arts, poetry is a divine one — as Plato wrote and many maintained, echoing this view (e.g., Petrarch, Boccaccio, Salutati, and Landino) — since it requires inspiration provided by an 'influsso divino' [divine spirit].[23] Magno, then, moves to consider another very specific faculty of poetry: that of arousing human senses and souls through harmony and, going beyond the veils of fables, thereby enabling them to contemplate the divine. Thanks to this faculty, poetry is proved to have a deeply purifying aim. The author, finally, closes his praise of poetry, by defending it from the accusation of those who believe it to be a corrupting force on the basis of the affirmations of Plato's *Republic* — where it is written that poets should be excluded from the city ruled by philosophers. Following Boccaccio's accounts in his *Genealogie* 14 — recalled also, among other works, in Tasso's *Ragionamento* and Scipione Ammirato's *Il Dedalione* (1560)[24] — Magno clearly maintains that they are mistaken both from a logical and an authoritative point of view. Since poetry — as remembered above — is intimately bound up with human beings, excluding it from them would imply eliminating part of their own nature. Furthermore, in many other works, Plato praises poets (e.g., in the *Phaedrus*, the *Ion*, the *Lysis*, and the *Protagoras*, all explicitly quoted in the *Preface*), and so in the controversial passage of the *Republic* Plato cannot but have meant — says Magno, following a view shared by many other authors (e.g., Tasso, Daniello, Patrizi, and Ammirato) — to reject only those poets who lead people astray and not all of them. He concludes by declaring that, if poetry targets its noblest aims, it must be considered as the 'reina dell'altre arti' [queen of the other arts].[25]

After this opening section on poetry, Magno focuses on the lyric genre, to which the second part of his *Prefatione* is devoted — as the label 'Lirico' [Lyric] in the manuscript testifies. In this section (approximately a quarter of the entire text), the author primarily aims to affirm and demonstrate that, among the numerous poetical genres, the lyric one is both the first that has been practised and the one that has

---

22   See *Prefatione*, pp. 223–24, and Bernardino Feliciano, *Orationes quinque habitae Venetiis* (Venice: Bolognino Zalterio, 1563), pp. 55–56. See also Pagan, 'Una prefazione', pp. 239–40. On Renaissance discussion about Orpheus, Amphion, and the origin of poetry, see Eugenio Refini, 'Per via d'annotationi'. *Le glosse inedite di Alessandro Piccolomini all'*'Ars Poetica' *di Orazio* (Lucca: Pacini Fazzi, 2009), pp. 49–54; and Gustavo Costa, 'Giovanni Pontano and the Orpheus Myth: Poetry and Magic in the Age of Humanism', *Rivista di studi italiani*, 4 (1986), 1–17.

23   See *Prefatione*, p. 224.

24   See Boccaccio, *Genealogie*, VII–VIII.2, p. 738; Tasso, *Ragionamento*, pp. 577–78; and Scipione Ammirato, *Il Dedalione o ver del Poeta*, in *Trattati di poetica e retorica del Cinquecento*, II, 477–512 (p. 483). On Renaissance defence of poetry, see Vittorio Zaccaria, 'La difesa della poesia: dal Petrarca alle *Genealogie* del Boccaccio', *Atti e Memorie dell'Accademia Galileiana di Scienze, Lettere ed Arti*, III (1998–99), 1–29; and Roberto Cardini, 'Il Landino e la poesia', in Roberto Cardini, *La critica del Landino* (Florence: Sansoni, 1973), pp. 85–112.

25   See *Prefatione*, p. 228; and Pagan, 'Una prefazione', pp. 242–43.

the highest degree of nobility. The rhetorical opening of the first paragraph helps to emphasize these two points. By employing the stylistic scheme of the *Priamel*, Magno states that he wishes neither to laud lyric poetry, nor to consider the fact that it deals with the widest-ranging array of topics, nor to focus on its various other characteristic features. He rather yearns to devote this section of his *Preface* to uphold that it is the foremost genre, as it has been argued by Plato in the second book of his *Laws*, where it is affirmed that lyric poets are the noblest because they deal with divine topics. Probably perceiving the distance between the practice of the earlier lyric poets and that of contemporary ones, who — according to Magno — only seldom deal with religious topics, the author allows himself to insert in his discussion a brief peroration on how enhanced and improved the contemporary literary scene would be if poets were to deal with divine or, at least, moral matters in their compositions. After this comment, the focus of the section shifts to the origin and purpose of lyric poetry. Magno affirms that it was not invented by a specific person, as others have maintained. At the same time, since he believes that king David is the poet who offered the lyric genre the greatest dignity and nobility, he should be considered the utmost and most distinguished of its first exponents, and, as such, he can be seen as its effective creator. In his solemn compositions, David extolled God, whose glorification is — writes Magno — one of the main goals of lyric genre. Yet lyric poetry aims also to purify human beings and inspire in them moral behaviour and chaste thoughts. Magno then recalls that David's poetical voice was inspired by God. Accordingly, since one cannot but argue that God chose the lyric verse and style to be sung by his prophet, lyric poetry should be considered the divinely elected genre and, therefore, the noblest. Magno thus concludes the second section of his *Prefatione* by centring his attention back on the topic that he dealt with at the beginning of the section itself: the primacy of lyric poetry. In so doing, he structurally organizes his considerations in a chiastic scheme.

The third and final part of Magno's work is devoted to Petrarch — as the label present in the Marciana manuscript ('Petrarca' — 'Petrarch') witnesses. Yet the author does not concentrate on the whole Petrarchan corpus. He rather focuses on Petrarch's vernacular book of rhymes, the *Canzoniere*, which he wishes to praise, and whose traits are taken as a literary model to be followed. Magno seems to perceive these tasks as the most demanding ones of his work — or, at least, aims to give this impression — therefore he has recourse to the literary expedient of an invocation to superior spirits in aiding him to deal with these topics. In accordance with an argumentative structure that he had already outlined, he summarizes his main idea in one pithy sentence that he later supports with various demonstrative examples. Magno starts this last section of his *Preface* by comparing Petrarch's work to a flourishing garden, rich in 'dolcezza' and 'amenità' [sweetness and pleasantness],[26] which is neither second in lushness to the finest ones of the Greek and Roman past, nor paralleled by any in the present days. Magno pinpoints this statement with several endorsements that take into consideration the elocution, disposition, and invention rhetorical levels of Petrarchan poetry respectively. Petrarch's *Canzoniere* is

---

26   See *Prefatione*, p. 231.

not merely rich in 'ornamenti poetici', 'figure rhetoriche', and 'locutioni esquisite' [poetical embellishments, rhetorical features, and exquisite turns of phrase],[27] but it also displays a noteworthy array of 'leggiadre rime', 'varij versi', and 'ben composti numeri' [elegant rhymes, various metres, and sophisticated metrical features][28] that can all be imitated so as to polish one's own style and adorn new works. Reading Petrarch's poems — suggests Magno, echoing a rich and longstanding tradition — offers the prospective poet the finest examples of rhetorical traits and literary features. Yet — Magno continues — Petrarch's poems offer the readers also a rich variety of 'dotte sentenze', 'nobili pensieri', and 'essempi di continenza et di virtù' [learned sentences, noble thoughts, and examples of moderation and virtue][29] that can inspire similar honest feelings in the public. Nothing else but honourable topics — argues Magno — could have ever been dealt with by an author who lead a righteous and praiseworthy life, as Petrarch's biographers have asserted and as Magno himself reports, by referring in his *Preface* to some passages drawn from Alessandro Vellutello's life of Petrarch in his 1525 commentary and Giovan Pietro Capriano's treatise *Della vera poetica* (1555) that describe the pious behaviours and moral attitudes of the poet.[30] Such virtuous teachings can be found in every composition by Petrarch, including those that apparently deal only with terrestrial love. By interpreting the whole love story outlined in the *Canzoniere* in a Neoplatonic perspective — thus following the perspective developed by Vellutello in his commentary[31] (and echoing the views of Pietro Bembo's *Asolani* and, more

27   Ibid.

28   Ibid.

29   Ibid.

30   See ibid. See also Pagan, 'Una prefazione', pp. 244–45. On Capriano and his work, see Giovan Pietro Capriano, *Della vera poetica*, in *Trattati di poetica e retorica*, ed. by Weinberg, II, 239–334; and Bernard Weinberg, *A History of Literary Criticism in the Italian Renaissance*, 2 vols (Chicago: Chicago University Press, 1961), II, 737. On Vellutello's life of Petrarch, see Alessandro Vellutello, *Vita e costumi del poeta*, in Angelo Solerti, *Le vite di Dante, Petrarca e Boccaccio, scritte fino al secolo decimosesto* (Milan: Vallardi, 1904), pp. 361–67.

31   On Vellutello's commentary on Petrarch, see Luigi Baldacci, *Il petrarchismo italiano nel Cinquecento* (Milan; Naples: Ricciardi, 1957), pp. 59–62; Carlo Dionisotti, 'Vellutello, Alessandro', in *Enciclopedia Dantesca*, ed. by Giorgio Petrocchi and others, 6 vols (Rome: Istituto dell'Enciclopedia Italiana, 1970–1978), V, 905–06; Gino Belloni, 'Un eretico nella Venezia del Bembo: Alessandro Vellutello', *Giornale storico della letteratura italiana*, 157 (1980), 43–74; Gino Belloni, *Laura tra Petrarca e Bembo: Studi sul commento umanistico-rinascimentale al 'Canzoniere'* (Padua: Antenore, 1992), pp. 58–88; William Kennedy, *Authorizing Petrarch* (Ithaca; London: Cornell University Press, 1994), pp. 45–52; Catharina Busjan, *Petrarca-Hermeneutik. Die Kommentare von Alessandro Vellutello und Giovan Andrea Gesualdo im epochalen Kontext* (Berlin; Boston: De Gruyter, 2013), pp. 1–185; and Sabrina Stroppa, 'Oltre la questione dell'"ordine mutato": sul commento di Alessandro Vellutello al Petrarca volgare', Atti e memorie dell'Accademia Galileiana di scienze, lettere ed arti in Padova, 131.3 (2019-2020), in press. For a contextualization of Vellutello's commentary within the sixteenth-century phenomenon of Petrarch exegesis, see Bernard Weinberg, 'The Spositione of Petrarch in the Early Cinquecento', *Romance Philology*, 13.4 (1960), 374–86; Ettore Bonora, 'Il Classicismo dal Bembo al Guarini', in *Storia della Letteratura italiana*, ed. by Emilio Cecchi and Natalino Sapegno, 14 vols (Milan: Garzanti, 1965–2005), IV, 165–746 (pp. 259–64 and 666–67); Gino Belloni, 'Commenti petrarcheschi', in *Dizionario critico della letteratura italiana*, ed. by Vittore Branca, 4 vols (Turin: UTET, 1986), II, 22–39; Paola Vecchi Galli, 'Petrarca nel Cinquecento', in *Storia della letteratura italiana*, ed. by Enrico Malato, 14 vols (Rome: Salerno, 1996–2004), XI, 325–51; Edoardo Barbieri, 'Alessandro Vellutello: il successo

distantly, of both Ficino's *De Amore*, and some passages devoted to Petrarch in Cristoforo Landino's *Comento sopra la Comedia*),[32] but also giving substance through the Petrarchan example to the spiritualizing process described, in the previous section, as one of the constitutive traits of lyric poetry — Magno maintains that Petrarch shows in his book of rhymes how miserable are those who only care about passing and ephemeral beauties, without showing interest in them for their real and higher purposes: that of purifying and bringing humankind to the contemplation of true eternal splendours.[33] Indeed, Magno wrote:

> [Petrarca] s'affatica et mette il suo ingegno in coltivare, adornare et celebrare il suo tanto amato Lauro [...]. A l'ombra del quale lauro questo divino Poeta, hora temendo, hora sperando, hora allegrandosi, hora dolendosi, hora pregando, hora vinto dal senso, hor da la ragione, mostra et insegna quanto sia infelice lo stato degli amanti di queste fragile e caduche bellezze, quando elle non si amino per il vero e proprio loro uso, che è di salire per quelle alla contemplatione della bellezza eterna.[34]

In order to further prove his point, Magno backs this avowal up with two quotations from Petrarch's texts where the poet refers to the sublimating power of refined worldly beauties (i.e., *RVF*, 360. 139, and *RVF*, 62. 16–21).[35] In so doing, he aims to prove that his Platonizing reading of Petrarch's book of rhymes is implicit in and can be endorsed by the poet's works themselves. One direct corollary of such a vision of the poet's love as a pure, chaste, and righteous one is the final series of deliberations that Magno places at the end of his work. Considering the literary

di un petrarchista "ereticale"', in *Petrarca nel tempo. Tradizione lettori e immagini delle opere. Catalogo della mostra (Arezzo, Sottochiesa di San Francesco, 22 novembre 2003–27 gennaio 2004)*, ed. by Michele Feo (Pontedera: Bandecchi&Vivaldi, 2003), pp. 149–51; Edoardo Barbieri, 'Il "petrarchismo ereticale" di Alessandro Vellutello (Milano, Biblioteca Ambrosiana, S.C.L. VIII.47)', in *Francesco Petrarca. Manoscritti e libri a stampa della Biblioteca Ambrosiana*, ed. by Marco Ballarini, Giuseppe Frasso, and Carla Maria Monti (Milan: Scheiwiller, 2004), pp. 130–31; *Questo leggiadrissimo poeta. Autoritätskonstitution im rinascimentalen Lyrik-Kommentar*, ed. by Gerhard Regn (Munster: LIT, 2004); Donato Pirovano, 'Introduzione', in Alessandro Vellutello, *La 'Comedia' di Dante Alighieri con la nova esposizione*, ed. by Donato Pirovano, 3 vols (Rome: Salerno, 2006), I, 9–68; and Gino Belloni, 'Commenti petrarcheschi dall'Umanesimo al Daniello', in *Petrarca e il suo tempo*, ed. by Gilda Paola Mantovani (Milan: Skira, 2006), pp. 183–204. For a general overview of the phenomenon of Petrarch's exegesis in Renaissance Italy, see Giacomo Comiati and Lorenzo Sacchini with Francesco Venturi (overseen by Simon Gilson and Federica Pich), *Petrarch Exegesis in Renaissance Italy* (PERI), available online at <https://petrarch.mml.ox.ac.uk/>.

32   On the Platonic background of Landino's commentary, see Simon Gilson, 'Plato, the *platonici*, and Marsilio Ficino in Cristoforo Landino's *Comento sopra la Comedia*', *The Italianist*, 23 (2003), 5–53.

33   On the phenomenon of Renaissance Platonic readings of Petrarch, see Luca Marcozzi, *Petrarca platonico* (Rome: Aracne, 2004).

34   *Prefatione*, pp. 231–32: '[Petrarch] strains himself and aims to cultivate, adorn, and praise his beloved laurel tree [...]. In the shadows of that laurel tree, fearing, hoping, cheering himself up, suffering, praying, being conquered either by his senses, or by his wisdom, this divine poet shows and teaches how miserable is the condition of the lovers of fragile and evanescent beauties, if these beauties are not cherished for their true purpose, which is that of raising through them to the contemplation of the eternal beauty'.

35   See *Prefatione*, p. 232. Since Magno quotes the passages by heart, he makes some mistakes (in particular, the second quotation is slightly wrong). See Taddeo, *Il manierismo letterario*, p. 232 n. 10; and Pagan, 'Una prefazione', p. 245.

mastery, morality, and integrity of both Petrarch and his poetry, everyone — writes Magno — should read the *Canzoniere*, where each and every person — from the honest young girl to the austere philosopher, from the learned theologian to the experienced orator — can find useful teachings and benefits. With these reflections, and postponing a detailed analysis of Petrarch's book of rhymes to another occasion, Magno concludes his *Prefatione*.

3. Sources and Influences

As previously argued, although Magno's *Prefatione* shows some forms of distinctiveness in both its internal structural organization and some of its critical claims (such as the primacy of lyric poetry), it has a close relationship with earlier works. Within the many-sided debate on poetics and rhetoric that flourished throughout the fifteenth century and grew even more in intricacy and complexity during the first half of the Cinquecento, we should probably not expect great originality to be displayed in a work dealing with poetry, above all by a young author — as Magno was when he composed his *Preface*. It is undeniable that, in his lecture, Magno's critical voice relies on and echoes that of many others who, before him, debated about poetry and Petrarch. In this section we will consider both which theories — among the many — were chosen to be presented again and re-discussed in Magno's new composition, and which sources were employed in order to help us to investigate Magno's critical background, the major ideas and works from which he was influenced, and — more broadly — the tendencies that circulated in the cultural environs that he frequented, before and while writing his *Prefatione* (such as the Venier and Molino's Venetian circles and the Accademia della Fama).

3.1 The Venetian and Veneto Milieus

The Venetian cultural scene, in which Magno grew up, was one of the livelier milieus of the Italian mid-sixteenth century. This environment was vibrant with both lyrical experimentations and rich cultural debates on many disciplines, including poetry and poetics. Thus, for example, we witness a critical interest in Petrarch and a strong incentive to renovate the Petrarchist poetry that dominated the interests of the post-Bembian poetical school, including many circles that Magno attended.[36] We can also note a widespread and multifaceted discussion on various literary topics, including Petrarch's manifold legacy, which was at the core of both works and academic lectures composed in Venice at the time.[37] Among those

---

36   See Taddeo, *Il manierismo letterario*; Armando Balduino, 'Petrarchismo veneto e tradizione manoscritta', in *Petrarca, Venezia e il Veneto*, ed. by Padoan, pp. 243–70; Erspamer, 'Petrarchismo e manierismo'; Alessandro Duranti, 'Sulle *Rime* di Luigi Groto', *Filologia e critica*, 2 (1977), 337–88; Antonio Corsaro, 'Dionigi Atanagi e la silloge per Irene di Spilimbergo. Intorno alla formazione del giovane Tasso', *Italica*, 75 (1998), 41–61; and Riccardo Bruscagli, 'La preponderanza petrarchista', in *Storia letteraria d'Italia*, ed. by Armando Balduino, 10 vols (Padua; Milan: Piccin-Vallardi, 2007), VII.3, 1559–1615 (pp. 1586–91).

37   See Franco Tomasi, 'Esegesi di Petrarca nelle accademie del XVI secolo (1530–1550)', in Franco

who delivered a lesson specifically focused on Petrarch, it is worth remembering that there were two of the most eminent disciples of Bembo: Trifon Gabriele and Lodovico Beccadelli.[38] Many tendencies of this variegated environment either emerged in or inspired some of the traits and thoughts occurring in Magno's *Preface*.[39] By considering the two aspects of Petrarch that Magno values most in the last section of his work, it is possible to perceive some threads of influence from the Venetian milieu that inform and run through his *Prefatione*. It has been observed that Magno praises Petrarch for being, first, one of the finest examples of style, and, second, a moral and, above all, spiritual author. The first trait is typical of mid-sixteenth-century Bembian poetical culture, but the accuracy of Magno's references and minute attention to every textual aspect of Petrarch's poems in his lesson (i.e., language, style, and rhetorical ornaments) might betray a more profound and deeply-rooted interest, that could have been aroused by a twofold cultural stimulus. First, it might have been stirred and encouraged by the ever-greater attention that post-Vellutello commentaries paid to the rhetorical traits of Petrarch's poems, as the exegetical works by Giovanni Andrea Gesualdo (appeared in Venice in 1533) and Bernardino Daniello (published in Venice too, in 1541) testify.[40] Secondly, Magno's emphasis on single elements of Petrarch's language is redolent of the tendency of the post-Bembian Venetian school to employ Petrarch's lyrical *corpus* as a source from which to draw single poetical elements to be re-used and re-composed in an endless and often audacious set of possibilities. This lyrical tendency was an important poetical trend practised by and admired within the Venier circle, to which Magno

---

Tomasi, *Studi sulla lirica rinascimentale (1540–1570)* (Rome; Padua: Antenore, 2012), pp. 177–218; and Gino Benzoni, 'Le Accademie', in *Storia della cultura veneta*, ed. by Arnaldi and Pastore Stocchi, IV.1, 131–62. See also Gino Benzoni, 'Aspetti della cultura urbana nella società veneta del Cinque e Seicento. Le Accademie', *Archivio veneto*, 143 (1977), 87–159; Paolo Ulvioni, 'Accademie e cultura in Italia dalla Controriforma all'Arcadia. Il caso veneziano', in *Libri e documenti*, 5 (1979), 21–75; and Fernando Lepori, 'La scuola di Rialto dalla fondazione alla metà del Cinquecento', in *Storia della cultura veneta*, ed. by Arnaldi and Pastore Stocchi, III.2, 539–605.

38   See Carlo Dionisotti, 'Fortuna del Petrarca nel '400', *Italia medioevale e umanistica*, 17 (1974), 61–113 (p. 70); and Kennedy, *Authorizing Petrarch*, pp. 44–45.

39   On Magno's link with Venetian culture, see Cesare Galimberti, 'Celio Magno e il petrarchismo veneto', in *Crisi e rinnovamento nell'autunno del Rinascimento a Venezia*, ed. by Vittore Branca and Carlo Ossola (Florence: Olschki, 1991), pp. 359–72; and Ettore Bonora, 'Celio Magno e la lirica alla fine del secolo', in *Storia della letteratura italiana*, ed. by Cecchi and Sapegno, IV, 546–50.

40   See Kennedy, *Authorizing Petrarch*, p. 52. On Gesualdo, see Jon A. Quitslund, 'Spenser's *Amoretti* VIII and Platonic Commentaries on Petrarch', *Journal of the Warburg and Courtauld Institutes*, 36 (1973), 256–76; Gino Belloni, 'Di un parto d'elephante per Petrarca. Il commento di Gesualdo al *Canzoniere*', *Rinascimento*, 20 (1980), 359–81; Gino Belloni, *Laura tra Petrarca e Bembo*, pp. 189–225; Kennedy, *Authorizing Petrarch*, pp. 55–62; and Busjan, *Petrarca-Hermeneutik*, pp. 186–382. On Daniello, see Belloni, 'Commenti petrarcheschi dall'Umanesimo al Daniello'; Belloni, 'Sul Daniello commentatore del Canzoniere', *Lettere italiane*, 32 (1980), 172–202; Belloni, *Laura tra Petrarca e Bembo*, pp. 226–83; Carlo Dionisotti, 'Daniello, Bernardino', in *Enciclopedia Dantesca*, II, pp. 303–04; Kennedy, *Authorizing Petrarch*, pp. 62–67; Edoardo Barbieri, 'Nella selva delle varianti d'autore: l'esperienza di Bernardino Daniello', in *Petrarca nel tempo*, p. 151; and Edoardo Barbieri, 'Bernardino Daniello e le varianti d'autore (Milano, Biblioteca Ambrosiana, S.N.G. VII.58)', in *Francesco Petrarca. Manoscritti e libri a stampa*, pp. 126–27.

belonged.[41] The passage of the *Preface* in which considerable importance is given to single elements of Petrarch's compositions might, then, appear as a tribute not only to Petrarch's admirable style, but also to a specific form of Petrarchism that was familiar to and appreciated by some of his poetical guides (Domenico Venier and Girolamo Molino *in primis*), who were indirectly affiliated to the Accademia della Fama and who presumably were to be part of the audience for which he was planning to deliver his lecture.[42]

The second major reason — according to Magno — to admire and follow Petrarch lies in the fact that he was a moral and religious author. Without a doubt, the mid-*Cinquecento* Counterreformation climate played a role in Magno choice to primarily focus on spiritual themes, which he considered most significant within Petrarch's oeuvre.[43] But it cannot be ignored that a concern with these topics must also have been instigated by the stimuli that the author received from the specific Venetian context in which he operated. Throughout the two decades before Magno penned his *Preface*, there had developed a trend that saw Petrarch as the model of a new ethical and religious poetry and this had a special resonance in Venice (as well as throughout the Italian peninsula). This new spiritual strain of Petrarchism was largely influenced by the *Petrarca Spirituale* written by the Venetian poet Girolamo Malipiero — a work in which Petrarch's *Canzoniere* was re-written in religious tones (1536)[44] — and, although it nourished the practice of many Italian poets of the time (such as Vittoria Colonna and Michelangelo Buonarroti),[45] its impact was

41   See Taddeo, *Il manierismo letterario*, pp. 37–70; Erspamer, 'Petrarchismo e manierismo', pp. 192–215; and Galimberti, 'Celio Magno e il petrarchismo veneto', p. 362.

42   Venier and Molino were not among the founders of the Accademia della Fama, but almost certainly endorsed and supported it. See Bolzoni, *La stanza della memoria*, p. 5.

43   See Antonio Pilot, 'Del protestantesimo a Venezia e delle poesie religiose di Celio Magno', *Ateneo veneto*, 32 (Mar.–Apr. 1909), 199–231; and Antonio Pilot, 'Le canzoni di Celio Magno in relazione colla lirica veneta del tempo', *Ateneo veneto*, 32 (Sep.–Oct. 1909 and Nov.–Dec. 1909), 117–55 and 267–308.

44   On Malipiero, see Amedeo Quondam, 'Riscrittura, citazione, parodia. Il *Petrarca spirituale* di Girolamo Malipiero', in Amedeo Quondam, *Il naso di Laura. Lingua e poesia lirica nella tradizione del classicismo* (Modena: Panini, 1991), pp. 203–62; Taddeo, *Il manierismo letterario*, pp. 180–82; Luigi Baldacci, *Il petrarchismo italiano*, pp. 165–69; Ursula Schick, 'Malipieros *Petrarca spirituale* als Canzoniere-Allegorese', in *Interpretation. Das Paradigma der europäischen Renaissance-Literatur*, ed. by Klaus W. Hempfer and Gerhard Regn (Wiesbaden: Steiner, 1983), pp. 272–87; Roberto Fedi, 'Soli e pensosi. Censura, parodia, fortuna di un sonetto petrarchesco (*RVF* XXXV)', *Lingua e stile*, 26 (1991), 465–81; Marc Föcking, *'Rime sacre' und die Genese des barocken Stils. Untersuchungen zur Stilgeschichte geistlicher Lirik in Italien 1536–1614* (Stuttgart: Steiner, 1994), pp. 59–71; Rosalma Salina Borello, *Testo, intertesto, ipertesto. Proposte teoriche e percorsi di lettura* (Rome: Bulzoni, 1996), pp. 101–04; Christoph Hoch, *Apollo Centonarius. Studien und Texte zur Centodichtung der italienischen Renaissance* (Tübingen: Stauffenburg, 1997), pp. 155–73; Christian Mouchel, *Rome franciscaine. Essai sur l'histoire de l'éloquence dans l'Ordre des frères mineurs au XVIe siècle* (Paris: Champion, 2001), pp. 329–37; *Lirici europei del Cinquecento. Ripensando la poesia del Petrarca*, ed. by Gian Mario Anselmi, Keir Elam, Giorgio Forni, and Davide Monda (Milan: BUR, 2004), pp. 613–15; Giorgio Forni, 'Vittoria Colonna, la "Canzone alla Vergine" e la poesia spirituale', in *Rime sacre dal Petrarca al Tasso*, ed. by Maria Luisa Doglio and Carlo Delcorno (Bologna: Il Mulino, 2005), pp. 65–71; and Ginetta Auzzas, 'Notizie su una miscellanea veneta di rime spirituali', in *Rime sacre dal Petrarca al Tasso*, ed. by Doglio and Delcorno, pp. 205–20 (pp. 208–10).

45   On Colonna, see *A Companion to Vittoria Colonna*, ed. by Abigail Brundin, Tatiana Crivelli,

particularly profound and widespread in the Venetian literary scene, as it is testified by the works by Paolo Crivelli, Luca Contile, Laura Battiferri, Girolamo Muzio, Antonio Minturno, and Gabriel Fiamma.[46] Moreover, moral compositions and

and Maria Serena Sapegno (Leiden; Boston: Brill, 2016); Carlo Dionisotti, 'Appunti sul Bembo e su Vittoria Colonna', in *Miscellanea Augusto Campana*, 2 vols (Padua: Antenore, 1981), I, pp. 257–86; Giovanna Rabitti, 'Vittoria Colonna, Bembo e Firenze: un caso di ricezione e qualche postilla', *Studi e problemi di critica testuale*, 44 (1992), 127–55; Rinaldina Russell, 'The Mind's Pursuit of the Divine: A Survey of Secular and Religious Themes in Vittoria Colonna's Sonnets', *Forum Italicum*, 26.1 (1992), 14–27; Carlo Vecce, 'Petrarca, Vittoria, Michelangelo. Note di commento a testi e varianti di Vittoria Colonna e Michelangelo', *Studi e problemi di critica testuale*, 44 (1992), 101–25; Monica Bianco, 'Rinaldo Corso e il *canzoniere* di Vittoria Colonna', *Italique*, I (1998), 35–45; Alan Bullock, 'Il canzoniere di Vittoria Colonna: nuove prospettive e discussioni', *Rassegna europea di letteratura italiana*, 8 (2000), 111–29; Giovanna Rabitti, 'Vittoria Colonna as a Role Model for Cinquecento Women Poets', in *Women in Italian Renaissance Culture and Society*, ed. by Letizia Panizza (Oxford: Legenda, 2000), pp. 478–98; Giovanni Bardazzi, 'Le rime spirituali di Vittoria Colonna e Bernardino Ochino', *Italique*, 4 (2001), 60–101; Abigail Brundin, *Vittoria Colonna and the Spiritual Poetics of the Italian Reformation* (London; New York: Routledge, 2008); Virginia Cox, *Women's Writing in Italy, 1400–1650* (Baltimore: The Johns Hopkins University Press, 2008), pp. 64–76; Virginia Cox, *The Prodigious Muse: Women's Writing in Counter-Reformation Italy* (Baltimore: The Johns Hopkins University Press, 2011), pp. 56–61; Maria Musiol, *Vittoria Colonna: A Woman's Renaissance* (Berlin: Epubli, 2013); and Ambra Moroncini, 'Vittoria Colonna: Matriarch of Italian Petrarchism and *Christi ancilla* of the Italian Renaissance', in Ambra Moroncini, *Michelangelo's Poetry and Iconography in the Heart of the Reformation* (London; New York: Routledge, 2017), pp. 37–57. On Michelangelo, see Umberto Maria Milizia, *Alcune brevi note sul Canzoniere di Michelangelo Buonarroti* (Rome: Artecom, 2007); Antonio Corsaro, 'Michelangelo e la lirica spirituale del Cinquecento', in *Ludovico Castelvetro. Letterati e grammatici nella crisi religiosa del '500. Atti della XIII Giornata Luigi Firpo, Torino, 21–22 settembre 2006*, ed. by Massimo Firpo and Guido Mongini (Florence: Olschki, 2008), pp. 261–84; Ambra Moroncini, 'La poesia di Michelangelo: un cammino spirituale tra neoplatonismo e Riforma', *The Italianist*, 30.3 (2010), 352–73; Arnaldo Bruni, 'A proposito di Michelangelo poeta', in *Filologia e critica nella modernità letteraria. Studi in onore di Renzo Cremante*, ed. by Andrea Battistini, Arnaldo Bruni, and Irene Romera Pintor (Bologna: CLUEB, 2012), pp. 33–45; Ida Campeggiani, *Le varianti della poesia di Michelangelo. Scrivere per via di porre* (Lucca: Pacini Fazzi, 2012); Maiko Favaro, 'Gli occhi del cielo. Sull'interpretazione di alcune rime michelangiolesche', *Rivista di letteratura italiana*, 31.2 (2013), 185–97; and Ambra Moroncini, 'Michelangelo's poetry: A religious journey from Neo-Platonism to the credo in *sola fide*', in Ead., *Michelangelo's Poetry*, pp. 58–83. For a more detailed bibliography (up to June 2017) see <http://www.nuovorinascimento.org/cinquecento/mich-biblio.pdf> [accessed 30 October 2020].

46   On Crivelli, see Enrico Benini Clementi, *Riforma religiosa e poesia popolare a Venezia nel Cinquecento. Alessandro Caravia* (Florence: Olschki, 2000), pp. 101–12; and Massimo Firpo, *Artisti, gioiellieri, eretici. Il mondo di Lorenzo Lotto tra Riforma e Controriforma* (Rome; Bari: Laterza, 2001). On Contile, see Amedeo Quondam, 'Le *Rime cristiane* di Luca Contile', in Id., *Il naso di Laura*, pp. 263–89. On Battiferri, see Giovanna Rabitti, 'Laura Battiferri Ammannati', in *Italian Women Writers: A Bio-Bibliographical Sourcebook*, ed. by Rinaldina Russell (Wesport; London: Greenwood Press, 1994), pp. 44–49; Victoria Kirkham, 'Laura Battiferri degli Ammannati's First Book of Poetry: A Renaissance Holograph Comes out of Hiding', *Rinascimento*, 36 (1996), 351–91; and Victoria Kirkham, 'Dante's Phantom, Petrarch's Specter: Bronzino's Portrait of the Poet Laura Battiferri', *Lectura Dantis*, 13 (1998), 63–139. For a more detailed bibliography (up to January 2012) see <http://www.nuovorinascimento.org/cinquecento/battiferri.pdf> [accessed 30 October 2020]. On Muzio, see Francesco Bausi, 'Un'egloga inedita (e sconosciuta) di Girolamo Muzio', *Studi di filologia italiana*, 47 (1989), 211–54; Luciana Borsetto, 'Lettere inedite di Girolamo Muzio tratte dal codice Riccardiano 2115', *La rassegna della letteratura italiana*, 94 (1990), 99–178; Giovanni Amoretti, 'Un umanista italiano alla corte di Emanuele Filiberto: Girolamo Muzio e l'elogio di Nizza (1542)', in Giovanni Amoretti, *La città fedele. Letteratura di lingua italiana a Nizza da Emanuele Filiberto a Vittorio Emanuele II* (Bordighera: Istituto Internazionale di Studi Liguri 1998), pp. 13–44; Valentina

debates about them were sponsored and promoted by the Accademia della Fama too.[47] These poetical and critical tendencies must have deeply stimulated Magno, who not only praised honourable and religious poetry in his *Preface*, but also invited his contemporaries to compose poems inspired by religion and morality, and even followed this trend in his own verses.

A further sign of the influence of the Venetian milieu on Magno's *Preface* can be identified in the Neoplatonic readings that the author displays in his work and, specifically, in his interpretation of Petrarch's *Canzoniere* as a series of compositions showing how humankind can be elevated from a terrestrial condition to the contemplation of celestial beauties. Neoplatonic interpretations of love in vernacular literary texts had already been legitimized by and had found validation in various influential theories developed, for instance, by Landino in his *Comento sopra la Comedia* (1481), and by Bembo in his dialogue *Gli Asolani* (1505). Similar explanatory principles were applied to the poetical love story of Petrarch's book of rhymes by Alessandro Vellutello in his successful commentary to Petrarch (1525) — some of whose viewpoints had been suggested to Vellutello by Bembo himself.[48] This text had a powerful influence on the ways in which Petrarch was read in early- and mid-sixteenth-century Italy (a Platonized Petrarch, for example, was a diffused model in the Florentine Academy),[49] but, particularly, in the Veneto cultural environments, where Vellutello's work was conceived and published and where Bembo's authoritative voice kept being more prominent than in other parts of Italy.[50] For example, in the early 1540s critical analysis that investigated literary

Grohovaz, 'Girolamo Muzio e la sua "battaglia" contro Pietro Paolo Vergerio', in *Pier Paolo Vergerio il giovane, un polemista attraverso l'Europa del Cinquecento. Atti del Convegno internazionale di studi, Cividale del Friuli, 15–16 ottobre 1998*, ed. by Ugo Rozzo (Udine: Forum, 2000), pp. 179–206; Luciana Borsetto, 'L'ufficio di scrivere "in suggetto di honore". Girolamo Muzio duellante, duellista', in Luciana Borsetto, *Riscrivere gli antichi, riscrivere i moderni e altri studi di letteratura comparata tra Quattro e Ottocento* (Alessandria: Edizioni dell'Orso, 2002), pp. 343–63; Luciana Borsetto, 'L'egloga in sciolti nella prima metà del Cinquecento. Appunti sul *liber* di Girolamo Muzio', in *Miscellanea di studi in onore di Giovanni da Pozzo*, ed. by Donatella Rasi (Rome; Padua: Antenore 2004), pp. 123–61; and Marco Faini, 'Muzio, Girolamo', in *Dizionario storico dell'Inquisizione*, ed. by Adriano Prosperi, Vincenzo Lavenia, and John Tedeschi, 4 vols (Pisa: Edizioni della Normale, 2010), II, 1093. For a more detailed bibliography (up to March 2011) see <http://www.nuovorinascimento.org/cinquecento/muzio.pdf> [accessed 30 October 2020]. On Minturno, see Stefano Carrai, 'Sulle rime del Minturno. Preliminari d'indagine', in *Il libro di poesia dal copista al tipografo*, ed. by Marco Santagata and Amedeo Quondam (Modena: Panini, 1989), pp. 215–30; Giulio Ferroni and Amedeo Quondam, *La 'locuzione artificiosa'. Teoria ed esperienza della lirica a Napoli nell'età del manierismo* (Rome: Bulzoni, 1973), pp. 299–314; and Stefano Carrai, 'Classicismo latino e volgare nelle rime del Minturno', in Stefano Carrai, *I precetti di Parnaso: metrica e generi poetici nel Rinascimento italiano* (Rome: Bulzoni, 1999), pp. 167–92. On Fiamma, see Carlo Ossola, 'Il "queto travaglio" di Gabriel Fiamma', in *Letteratura e critica. Studi in onore di Natalino Sapegno*, ed. by Walter Binni, 5 vols (Rome: Bulzoni, 1974), III, 239–86; and Taddeo, *Il manierismo letterario*, pp. 141–69.

47   See Bolzoni, *La stanza della memoria*, p. 12.
48   See Belloni, *Laura tra Petrarca e Bembo*, pp. 71–85; and Kennedy, *Authorizing Petrarch*, p. 46.
49   In the Accademia Fiorentina, Petrarch was interpreted in an Aristotelian perspective too. See, for instance, Alfredo Bonfatti, 'Il Petrarca peripatetico di Giovan Battita Gelli', *Aevum*, 27 (1953), 359–69.
50   See Kennedy, *Authorizing Petrarch*, pp. 51–52.

texts (and, specifically, Petrarch's) through the Neoplatonic lens were developed in Padua, such as Francesco Patrizi's lecture on Petrarch's sonnet 'La gola, e 'l sonno, e l'ociose piume' (*RVF*, 7),[51] and Bernardino Tomitano's interpretation of Petrarch's madrigal 'Perch'al viso d'Amor portava insegna' (*RVF*, 54), that can be read in the second book of Tomitano's *Quattro libri della lingua Thoscana*, written to depict the activity of the Paduan Accademia degli Infiammati.[52] In front of the same academy, two other authors (Benedetto Varchi and Ugolino Martelli) delivered two lectures

51   See Anna Laura Puliafito Bleuel, 'Petrarca filosofo platonico. Francesco Patrizi commentatore di un sonetto petrarchesco (*RVF* VII)', in *Para/Textuelle Verhandlungen. Zwischen Dichtung und Philosophie in der frühen Neuzeit*, ed. by Bernhard Huss, Patrizia Marzillo, and Thomas Ricklin (Berlin-New York: De Gruyter, 2011), pp. 379–98. On Patrizi, see Lina Bolzoni, *L'universo dei poemi possibili. Studi su Francesco Patrizi da Cherso* (Rome: Bolzoni, 1980), pp. 26–38; Maria Muccillo, 'Marsilio Ficino e Francesco Patrizi da Cherso', in *Marsilio Ficino e il ritorno di Platone*, 2 vols (Florence: Olschki, 1986), II, 615–79; Anna Laura Puliafito Bleuel, 'Il *Liber de principiis* di Francesco Patrizi', *Rinascimento*, 17 (1987), 141–45; Anna Laura Puliafito Bleuel, 'Per uno studio della *Nova de Universis Philosophia* di F. Patrizi da Cherso: note alla *Panaugia*', *Atti e memorie dell'Accademia toscana di scienze e lettere La Colombaria*, 52 (1987), 161–99; Anna Laura Puliafito Bleuel, '"Principio primo" e "principi principiati" nella *Nova de Universis Philosophia* di Francesco Patrizi', *Giornale critico della filosofia italiana*, 2 (1988), 154–201; Cesare Vasoli, *Francesco Patrizi da Cherso* (Rome: Bulzoni, 1989); Cesare Vasoli, '*L'Amorosa filosofia* di Francesco Patrizi', *Rivista di filosofia*, 43.3 (1998), 419–41; Anna Laura Puliafito Bleuel, 'Hermetische Texte in Francesco Patrizis *Nova de Universis Philosophia*', in *Das Ende des Hermetismus*, ed. by Martin Mulsow (Tübingen: Morh-Siebeck, 2002), pp. 237–51; Anna Laura Puliafito Bleuel, 'Francesco Patrizi e la ragione degli animali', *Bruniana e campanelliana*, 17.1 (2011), 129–36; Anna Laura Puliafito Bleuel, 'L'uomo, gli animali, il linguaggio. Alcuni aspetti della riflessione patriziana su ragione, anima umana e anima dei brutai', in *The Animal Soul and the Human Mind: Renaissance Debates*, ed. by Cecilia Muratori (Pisa; Rome: Serra, 2013), pp. 113–30; Ester Pietrobon, 'Gli "Argomenti" di Francesco Patrizi come teatro ermeneutico del testo', in *Canzonieri in transito*, pp. 37–58; and Anna Laura Puliafito Bleuel, '"Donec expurgentur": Francesco Patrizi correttore di se stesso', *Bruniana e campanelliana*, 22.2 (2016), 429–41.

52   On the lectures on poetry and Petrarch at the Paduan Accademia degli Infiammati, see Franco Tomasi, 'Le letture di poesia e il petrarchismo nell'Accademia degli Infiammati', in *Il Petrarchismo. Un modello di poesia per l'Europa*, ed. by Loredana Chines, Floriana Calitti, and Roberto Gigliucci, 2 vols (Rome: Bulzoni, 2006), II, 229–50; and Tomasi, 'Esegesi di Petrarca', pp. 189–209. On Tomitano's work, see Piero Floriani, 'Grammatici e teorici della letteratura volgare', in *Storia della cultura veneta*, ed. by Arnaldi and Pastore Stocchi, III.2, 139–81; Antonio Daniele, 'Bernardino Tomitano: dai *Ragionamenti* ai *Quattro libri della lingua toscana*', *Museum patavinum*, 1 (1983), 67–85; Marco Pecoraro, 'Tomitano, Bernardino', in *Dizionario critico della letteratura italiana*, ed. by Branca, IV, pp. 313–18; Maria Teresa Girardi, 'Il contributo di Bernardino Tomitano alla riflessione sulla letteratura volgare del XVI secolo', *Rendiconti dell'Istituto Lombardo*, 124 (1990), 51–77; Maria Rosa Davi, *Bernardino Tomitano filosofo, medico e letterato (1517–1576). Profilo biografico e critico* (Trieste: Lint, 1995); Maria Teresa Girardi, *Il sapere e le lettere in Bernardino Tomitano* (Milan: Vita e Pensiero, 1995); and Tomasi, 'Le letture di poesia', p. 235. On the Accademia degli Infiammati, see, at least, Florindo Cerreta, *Alessandro Piccolomini. Letterato e filosofo senese del Cinquecento* (Siena: Accademia senese degli Intronati, 1960), pp. 19–41 and 263–78; Francesco Bruni, 'Sperone Speroni e l'Accademia degli Infiammati', *Filologia e letteratura*, 13.1 (1967), 24–71; Richard S. Samuels, 'Benedetto Varchi, the Accademia degli Infiammati, and the Origins of the Italian Academic Movement', *Renaissance Quarterly*, 29.4 (1976), 599–634; Antonio Daniele, 'Sperone Speroni, Bernardino Tomitano e l'Accademia degli Infiammati', *Filologia veneta*, 2 (1989), 1–53; Valerio Vianello, *Il letterato, l'Accademia, il libro. Contributi sulla cultura veneta del Cinquecento* (Padua: Antenore, 1989); and Jill Kraye, 'La filosofia nelle università italiane del XVI secolo', in *Le filosofie del Rinascimento*, ed. by Cesare Vasoli (Milan: Mondadori, 2002), pp. 350–73.

where vernacular poems were read in accordance with a Neoplatonic perspective.[53] Their focus were not Petrarch's texts, but those of his most eminent follower, Pietro Bembo. Varchi devoted his academic lesson to Bembo's sonnet 'A questa fredda tema, a questo ardente', whereas Martelli to 'Piansi e cantai lo strazio e l'aspra guerra'. Both employ Neoplatonic categories to investigate the two vernacular love poems. Yet the latter makes use of the philosophical reference to Neoplatonic theories not only to justify his reading of Bembo's composition, but also interpret the whole genre of love poetry. In his discourse, Martelli presents love poets as those who dealt with terrestrial feelings as a means to reach the contemplation of God.[54] Among the authors he lists, he offers a prominent position to Petrarch.[55] Though these precise works by Tomitano, Varchi, and Martelli might not have been read by Magno himself, they nonetheless reveal and influence the contemporary critical practice of reading vernacular poetical texts (and, in particular, those of Petrarch's) through a Platonizing lens. Set in this wider context, Magno's philosophical reading of Petrarch's book of rhymes in his *Prefatione* appears, then, as a sign of an ongoing interest in this exegetical approach in the Veneto region.

3.2 The *Accademia della Fama*

Where Magno might have experienced an environment in which Neoplatonic theories were actively discussed and tangibly influenced literary and critical works was the Accademia della Fama. Neoplatonism — combined with Hermeticism — occupied a central position within the wide-ranging array of the Academy's cultural interests.[56] The Academy intended to present itself as an heir of Italian humanism, by aiming to recover, translate, and re-elaborate the Platonic and Hermetic traditions.[57] This ambitious plan involved and encompassed many disciplines and arts, including poetry, perceived as a depositary of ancient knowledge.[58] This way of interpreting and decoding poetry was dear to Federico Badoer even before he founded the Accademia della Fama, as is shown from the fact that, in the mid-1540s, Antonio Brucioli presented Badoer in his *Dialoghi della naturale philosophia humana* as a character supporting the idea of poetry as a custodian of ancient knowledge.[59] This theory was also explicitly employed in some of the works produced for and under the patronage of the Academy, such as the *Primo discorso sopra il Dante poeta* (c. 1557–61) by Giacomo Tiepolo, dedicated to Badoer himself.[60] If — as it is highly possible — Magno's *Preface* was written for and meant to be read in front of the Accademia della Fama, the Neoplatonic theories that lay at the centre of Magno's

53   See Tomasi, 'Le letture di poesia', pp. 237–40.
54   See Tomasi, 'Le letture di poesia', p. 240 n. 29.
55   See Tomasi, 'Le letture di poesia', p. 240.
56   See Rose, 'The Accademia Venetiana', p. 193; Taddeo, *Il manierismo letterario*, p. 203; and Bolzoni, *La stanza della memoria*, p. 6.
57   See Bolzoni, *La stanza della memoria*, p. 8.
58   See Bolzoni, *La stanza della memoria*, pp. 7–9.
59   On the interlocutors of Brucioli's dialogue, see Carlo Dionisotti, 'Tiziano e la letteratura', *Lettere italiane*, 28 (1976), 401–09; and Bolzoni, *La stanza della memoria*, pp. 4–5.
60   See Bolzoni, *La stanza della memoria*, pp. 8–9, and p. 24 n. 28.

interpretations of Petrarch's book of rhymes must not have merely been encouraged by the philosophical ideas underpinning in the Venetian exegetical tradition, but also actively and vigorously inspired by Badoer's circle.

The Academia della Fama was probably also the environment that stimulated and in which Magno found an incentive to develop other concepts dear to him in his lecture, such as, for instance, the importance of ethics and morality within the poetical domain. This subject — which was strictly intertwined with that of spiritual Petrarchism — was highly significant for Magno, as the references to it in his *Preface* indicate. The Accademia della Fama was deeply engaged with ethics, too. Two critical works — both dealing with the moral principles that can be drawn from Aristotle's *Ethics* — were composed under the sponsorship of the Academy. What is more the Academy did not simply look for moral teaching in philosophical works, but — on the basis of the principle of poetry as a repository of wisdom — believed it to be disseminated in literary texts.[61] Thanks to this perspective, a work on the moral beauties of Ariosto's *Orlando Furioso* was conceived.[62] It seems likely that the Academy's rich debate on moral topics further stirred and shaped Magno's pre-existing interests for moral poetry.

There are other doctrines that were cultivated by the Accademia della Fama and whose signs can be observed in some aspects of Magno's *Preface*. First, Magno's insistence on lyric poetry's possibility to deal with every subject recalls the encyclopaedic approach that pinpointed both specific disciplines cultivated in Badoer's circle (including poetry itself) and, in a broader perspective, the whole cultural programme of the Academy. Second, the dignity of vernacular poetry — whose self-aware and proactive status in contemporary literature was briefly maintained in Magno's *Prefatione* — was strongly extolled in the Accademia della Fama's philosophy too, because contemporary poetry was kept in high esteem by its members and vernacular language was given a core functional role in the literary and editorial plans of the Academy.[63] Finally, the primary importance that, in his work, Magno bestowed to a didactic approach and educational attitude significantly echoed the propensity to didacticism that laid at the centre of the Accademia della Fama's cultural programme.[64] Although the general-to-specific logical order followed in the *Prefatione* and the tripartite-scheme of the lecture — designated with labels for each of its sections — might be simply referred to Magno's general inclination for an orderly designed discourse, the author's demonstrative approach — according to which most of his sentences are followed by either a demonstrative example, or a quotation from an authoritative work meant to support them — and his interest in conveying a clear and validated messages should be taken as two more probable signs of Magno's desire to show his presumed audience how he

61   See Bolzoni, *La stanza della memoria*, p. 12, and p. 24 n. 41.

62   Discourse 'delle bellezze dell'Ariosto, sotto 'l quale titolo s'intendono le allegorie morali, e naturali di quel poeta, paragonandolo con Homero, e con Virgilio ne gli offici poetici'. See Bolzoni, *La stanza della memoria*, p. 8, and p. 23 n. 27.

63   See Bolzoni, *La stanza della memoria*, pp. 7–8.

64   See Bolzoni, *La stanza della memoria*, pp. 10–13; and Stella Galbiati, 'Contributo per Celio Magno', p. 131.

valued a didactic approach in practical terms. Furthermore, from the general point of view of educational attitude, the significance that Badoer's Academy conferred to the instructive power of literature finds an even stronger correspondence in the didactic approach treasured by Magno, as is shown by his explicit assertion about the usefulness that everyone can derive from reading Petrarch's *Canzoniere* remarks.

3.3 Bernardo Tasso's *Ragionamento de la poesia*

The Accademia della Fama regarded poetry and poetics not only as the leading arts by which to convey and disseminate its cultural programme, but also considered them as subjects worthy to be accurately discussed in critical investigations. They were the core topics of some of the lectures delivered in Badoer's Academy, such as those by Bernardo Tasso and Giovan Mario Verdizzotti.[65] The former is one of the works that mainly influenced Magno's *Prefatione*, as we have noted above and may well have also led to its state of non-completion. Magno must have known Tasso's lecture because he either attended the session in which it was delivered (in 1559), or read it in a manuscript copy (certainly before that it was published by Giolito in 1562).[66] The parallels between the two works are many: several formulas, features, and themes of Tasso's *Ragionamento* recur in Magno's *Prefatione*. Yet, since Tasso's text deals with poetry in a broad sense, but does not focus on specific case studies (as Magno, instead, does in his third section), the overlaps between the two works are exclusively evident in the first and second part of Magno's *Preface*. Although it cannot be excluded that — given that some of the topics discussed are commonplaces of the genre — Magno might have derived some of them from other sources (e.g. Boccaccio, Daniello, Feliciano, Ammirato), a strong link between the two lectures persists and is undeniable in linguistic, stylistic, and thematic similarities, as we will detail below.

Formal correspondences can be observed in some rhetorical aspects of the two lectures' discourses. Both Tasso and Magno pretend to be unable to deal with the subjects they wanted to focus on, by having recourse to a *topos modestiae*, and then including an invocation to receive poetical support to face their goals, as if their texts were poetical compositions. Still more significant structural parallels can also be established between the two works. These links concern the conclusions reached by both authors about the origin and scopes of poetry. As Magno would have later done, Tasso stated in his *Ragionamento* that the real inventor of poetry is unknown and unidentifiable. Tasso also connected poetry's primary purpose with its religious function, by affirming — exactly as Magno wrote in his *Prefatione* — that poetry must have been firstly conceived to praise God. This is certainly a *topos* (to which previous other works on poetry referred, as, for example, Boccaccio's *Genealogie*

---

65   On Tasso's lecture, see n. 12. On Verdizzotti's lecture, see Giuseppe Venturini, *Saggi critici: Cinquecento minore: O. Ariosti, G. M. Verdizzotti e il loro influsso nella vita e nell'opera del Tasso* (Ravenna: Longo, 1970); Lina Bolzoni, 'Variazioni tardocinquecentesche sull'*ut pictura poesis*: la *Topica* del Camillo, il Verdizzotti e l'Accademia Veneziana', in *Scritti in onore di Eugenio Garin* (Pisa: Scuola Normale Superiore, 1987), pp. 85–115; and Lina Bolzoni, *La stanza della memoria*, pp. 34–36.
66   *Ragionamento della poesia di M. Bernardo Tasso* (Venice: Giolito, 1562).

and Salutati's *De laboribus*), but the linguistic expressions employed by Magno and the connection that he establishes between the purpose of the first forms of poetry and the consequent invention of a new stylistic register to sing divine topics recall Tasso's *Ragionamento*, which can thus be seen as a reference point for Magno's passage. In Tasso's work, one can read:

> e perché non parve loro, che le cerimonie, e i sacrificii de la loro religione fossero taciti, e muti, vollero, che da sacerdoti s'incominciassero a cantar le lodi del loro falso Iddio. Né contenti di ciò istimando non convenirsi, che la gloria, e grandezza di tanta maestà con modo, e con parole plebee, e comuni si cantassero; commisero a sacerdoti, che una nuova maniera, et un vago ordine di parole; che al merito di tanta divinità fosse conforme, s'imaginassero e cosi fu da loro trovata la poesia.[67]

Echoing Tasso, Magno stated:

> i primi versi fatti dagli huomini fossero per lodare et celebrare Dio [...]. Questo instinto di religione da principio è da creder che movesse la mente humana a conoscere che le cose divine doveano meritamente esser trattate con la forma di parlare lontana et estratta dalla volgare et commune usanza, et che tenesse in sé del divino, onde scegliendo le parole più nobili, le sentenze più esquisite, i numeri et gli ornamenti più dolci et rari, ne cominciava a comporre quell'eccellente parlare, di cui si compone il Poema.[68]

Furthermore, Magno found that Tasso's work stressed the importance of another key objective of poetry: that of presenting people with moral examples in order to invite them to behave in accordance with the same principles. This belief was at the heart of Magno's line of reasoning too. With regard to this last analogy, it should be remembered that the ethical strain of poetry was a theme that was not only developed in Tasso's *Ragionamento*, but was common to many other contemporary works. There is, therefore, no univocally direct link between Tasso and Magno's considerations about the moral value of poetry. Nonetheless, it is interesting to underline that both authors included sections on this aspect in their works, possibly being stimulated by and finding an interested audience in the cultural milieu of the Accademia della Fama that valued this subject.

Other elements link together the *Ragionamento* and the *Prefatione*. First, in referring to Plato's invitation to expel poets from the ideal city, both do not merely interpret the passage — as others had done (e.g., Boccaccio, Bernardino Daniello,

---

67   Tasso, *Ragionamento*, p. 572: 'In order not to celebrate in silence their rituals and religious sacrifices, the first humans ordered their ministers to sing the praises of their false God. Yet, being unsatisfied of this decision — since they believed that it was not convenient for the glory and splendour of the divine Majesty to be celebrated with common and plebeian words — they also commanded their ministers to invent a new set of words more appropriate to sing God's magnificence; and so, they invented poetry'.

68   *Prefatione*, p. 223: 'The first verses were composed by the humans to celebrate God. It ought to believe that the first religious instincts encouraged human minds to deem that divine topics should be expressed in a register that was distant from the common and vulgar language and that partakes of the divine; thus, choosing the noblest words, the most exquisite sentences, the sweetest and rarest rhythms and turns of phrase, they invented that excellent form of speaking by which poetry is composed'.

Giovan Pietro Capriano, and Scipione Ammirato)[69] — as a condemnation of bad and corrupted poets, rather than an attack addressed towards poetry in general, but they also employ to support their interpretations a suggestive simile: that of the incompetent doctors who, like immoral poets, do not deprive their art (medicine and poetry, respectively) of its inner value, despite their being inept. This parallel was not completely unprecedented — it had been briefly referred to, for instance, in Ammirato's *Il Dedalione*[70] — yet, in Tasso and Magno's passages, it is developed more extensively. Moreover, the latter recall the former in the expressions used and images put forward. Indeed, as Tasso, who affirmed that 'né questo è difetto della poesia ma del poeta, il quale a guisa di malvagio medico dà il veleno invece de la medicina' [this (i.e., the existence of corrupted poems) is not a flaw of poetry, but of the poet (who wrote them), who, as a wicked doctor, gives (patients) poison rather than medicine], Magno wrote 'Non s'escludono tutti i Medici perché ve ne siano d'ignoranti, et che in luogo di salute diano morte agli infermi' [one cannot blame every doctor because there are some ignorant ones who kill their patients rather than cure them].[71] The similarities between the two sentences can be seen as a proof of Magno's following (or, at least, being aware of) Tasso's reading of Plato's passage.

A further correspondence is evident in the way in which Tasso and Magno dealt with the theme of the poets' divine inspiration. It is undeniable that the theory of the poets' *enthousiasmos* was a *topos* of Renaissance debates on poetry and poetics,[72] and that — in the mid-sixteenth-century Veneto cultural scene — it had been not only discussed by Tasso, but also, among the others, by one of the most eminent representatives of Renaissance Platonism, Francesco Patrizi, in his work *Discorso della diversità dei furori poetici* (1552). Magno could have certainly based his account on Patrizi's examination, without necessarily referring to Tasso's statement.[73] Yet, what connects Tasso and Magno's texts is the fact that, in his *Ragionamento*, Tasso intertwined this topic with that of poetry's primacy among the arts, exactly as Magno would have later done in his *Preface*. Indeed, after having asserted that all the arts and sciences share a part of divine inspiration to be performed, Tasso

---

69   See Pagan, 'Una prefazione', pp. 242–43.

70   See Ammirato, *Il Dedalione*, p. 483 ('Molte altre e quasi infinite sono le somiglianze tra il poeta e il medico' [there are many more, if not endless, similarities between the poet and the doctor]).

71   See Tasso, *Ragionamento*, p. 577; and *Prefatione*, p. 227.

72   See William Scott, 'Perotti, Ficino and "Furor platonicus"', *Res Publica Litterarum*, 4 (1981), 273–84; Salvatore Cerasuolo, 'Storia critica dell'*Ars Poetica* dal Landino al Maggi', in *Letture oraziane*, ed. by Marcello Gigante and Salvatore Cerasuolo (Naples: Arte Tipografica, 1995), pp. 267–89; Donatella Coppini, 'L'ispirazione per contagio: "furor", e "remota lectio" nella poesia latina del Poliziano', in *Agnolo Poliziano poeta scrittore filologo. Atti del convegno internazionale di studi (Montepulciano, novembre 1994)*, ed. by Vincenzo Fera and Mario Martelli (Florence: Le Lettere, 1998), pp. 127–64; Liane Nebes, *Der Furor poeticus im italienischen Renaissanceplatonismus. Studien zu Kommentar und Literaturtheorie bei Ficino, Landino und Patrizi* (Marburg, Tectum, 2001); Simon Gilson, *Dante and Renaissance Florence* (Cambridge: Cambridge University Press, 2005), pp. 186–93; and Christopher Pieper, '"Horatius praeceptor eloquentiae". The *Ars Poetica* in Cristoforo Landino's Commentary', in *Neo-Latin Commentaries and The Management of Knowledge in the Late Middle Ages and the Early Modern Period (1400–1700)*, ed. by Karl Enenkel and Henk Nellen (Leuven: Leuven University Press, 2013), pp. 221–40.

73   On Patrizi's influence on Magno, see Galimberti, 'Celio Magno e il petrarchismo veneto', p. 369.

affirms that poetry is the more inspired one and, consequently, it is the most divine. Therefore, because poetry has a nature more partaking of that of God, it must be considered — concludes the author — as the first of the arts:

> S'egli è vero ciò che dice Platone nel *Fedro*, che chi senza il favor delle muse, confidandosi con l'aiuto e con la industria dell'arte di poter divenire gran poeta, a qualche poema comporre si dispone, et egli è vano e vana e degna di poca laude la sua poesia da tutti sarà giudicata, a lato a quella che dal furor poetico sarà aiutata. [...] S'egli è vero, dico che senza questo singolar dono di natura, ancor che altri di tutte le dottrine abbia cognizione, ancor che con lungo studio abbia imparata la legge e l'arte del perfettamente scrivere, ancor che lunga esperienza abbia delle cose del mondo, impossibil tuttavia sarà che riesca buon poeta. Non è dubbio alcuno che la perfezione di questa scienza non partecipi di divinità e che per questo anco non sia da essere antiposta a tutte l'altre. La filosofia, la retorica, l'aritmetica e l'altre scienze et arti liberali con lungo studio e con continua essercitazione s'imparano, ma questa senza quel dono infuso e conceduto dalla benignità e liberalità di Dio non si può in alcun modo sì fattamente imparare che s'aggiunga non dico al sommo ma al più basso grado di questa perfezione.[74]

The same concept is stressed by Magno with use of the parallel *auctoritas* from *Phaedrus*:

> chiamando la Poesia facultà et Arte, viene a farla di natura commune con le altre arti e facultà, che dipendono solamente dallo studio e poter nostro. La Poesia adunque quasi Reina di tutte l'altre si trahe fuor della loro conditione, et si riduce a più alto e nobil principio, al quale per sé non arrivano le forze nostre ordinarie. [...] Qual la causa di effetti così maravigliosi? Certo questa causa è fuor di noi, fuor della nostra possibilità. Dal cielo viene, da spirito et influsso divino [...] Né è dubbio alcuno che, se ben debbiamo dire che tutte le arti e dottrine ordinarie in noi vengono da Dio, come quello che ci ha prodotti atti ad acquistarle, e che ci aiuta insieme a conseguirle quando le procuriamo ad honesto fine, nondimeno in tutte le altre usando più la nostra volontà et studio, ci mettiamo più del nostro, e ci habbiamo più parte che in questa, la quale par che miracolosamente discenda in noi, et che senza molta nostra fatica la riceviamo in dono dalla propria e benigna man di Dio. Il che vien confermato da Platone nel suo Fedro, dove dice che niuno benché eruditissimo e studiosissimo diviene Poeta, se non è desto e sospinto dal divino furore.[75]

---

74 Tasso, *Ragionamento*, p. 580: 'If it is true what Plato wrote in his *Phaedrus*, i.e. that if, aiming to become a great poet, someone decides to compose a poem without the support of the Muses but only relying on the help provided by the poetical art, he does so in vain, and his poetry will be considered frivolous and unworthy of any praises by everyone else, once compared to that inspired by poetic *furor*. [...] If this is true, I affirm that without this unique gift of nature, he will not become a good poet, even though he was expert in every existing discipline, had studied at length the rules and art of good writing, and had long experienced the world. There is no doubt that this science [i.e. poetry] partakes of a divine nature, and that, for this reason, it must be put before every other science. Philosophy, rhetoric, arithmetic and the other sciences as well as liberal arts can be learnt thanks to long studies and constant exercise, while this one [i.e., poetry] cannot be practiced, not only at the utmost level but also at the lower one, without that gift instilled and offered by God's benignity and generosity'.

75 *Prefatione*, pp. 224–25: 'if Poetry is referred to as a discipline and an art, then it seems that it shares the same nature and status with the other arts and disciplines, which are only supported by

Despite the similarities between the two lectures, in some of his affirmations Magno marks his distance from Tasso's text, such as, for example, when he emphasizes the theological role of poetry, or when he implicitly draws parallels between the status of the ancient poetry of the Psalms and that of modern religious verses on the basis of their being equally godly inspired.[76] This second notion seems to stem from an original idea developed by Magno, who — among the many echoes that occur in his discussion of poetical *enthousiasmos* — distinctively upholds that godly inspiration, common to all poets, should be considered as the unifying principle informing every kind of spiritual composition (but also lay and religious poetry), because both the Psalms and modern religious verses partake in the same divine *furor*, and so there must be no difference between them.[77] The other difference with Tasso (concerning the theological role of poetry that only Magno explicitly stresses) derives either from Magno's agreeing with the principles of the Accademia della Fama, or from his possible harking back to other sources that, sharing analogous beliefs, underlined and lingered on the spiritual and mystical nature of poetry and its moral disposition, such as Alessandro Piccolomini's preface to his book of rhymes, *Cento Sonetti* (1549).[78] This work — conceived at the margins of the Paduan Accademia degli Infiammati[79] — can be put in contact with Magno's *Prefatione*

study and our will. Poetry, instead, almost as the queen of every other art, differs from them, and aims to a higher and nobler scope, which cannot be reached by merely employing our ordinary forces. [...] What is the cause of such extraordinary effects? Certainly this cause is external to us, beyond our potentialities. It comes from Heavens, from divine spirit and inspiration [...]. And there is no doubt that, even though every art and ordinary discipline comes from God — since he both created us as apt to acquire them, and helps us to practise them when we address them toward a right goal — we take more part to practise the other disciplines, rather than this one [i.e., Poetry], which seems to descend miraculously onto us and is received as a gift, without much effort, from the generous hand of God. This is confirmed by Plato in his *Phaedrus*, where he states that no one — no matter his education and skills — becomes poet, if he is not awoken and inspired by the divine *furor*'.

76   See Stella Galbiati, 'Contributo per Celio Magno', pp. 129–30.

77   See Campana, 'Ipotesi di lettura', p. 224 n. 1.

78   See *Cento Sonetti di Messer Alessandro Piccolomini* (Rome: Valgrisi, 1549). There is a modern edition of this *Canzoniere*: Alessandro Piccolomini, *I cento sonetti*, ed. by Franco Tomasi (Geneva: Droz, 2015). On Piccolomini's poetical work, see Giambattista Pellizzaro, 'I sonetti di Alessandro Piccolomini', *Rassegna critica della letteratura italiana*, 8 (1903), 97–111; Paolo Zaja, 'Intorno alle antologie. Testi e paratesti in alcune raccolte di lirica cinquecentesche', in *'I più vaghi e più soavi fiori'. Studi sulle antologie di lirica del Cinquecento*, ed. by Monica Bianco and Elena Strada (Alessandria: Edizioni dell'Orso, 2001), pp. 113–45 (pp. 124–25); Agostino Casu, '*Romana difficultas*. I *Cento sonetti* e la tradizione epigrammatica', in *La lirica del Cinquecento. Seminario di studi in memoria di Cesare Bozzetti* (Alessandria: Edizioni dell'Orso, 2004), pp. 123–54; Klaus Ley, 'Alessandro Piccolominis *Cento sonetti* zwischen Zensur und Selbstzensur. Zur Aktualität von Petrarcas "poesia civile" in der Krise der Renaissance', *Italienisch*, 26 (2004), 2–18; Eugenio Refini, 'Le "gioconde favole" e il "numeroso concetto": Alessandro Piccolomini interprete e imitatore di Orazio nei *Cento Sonetti*, 1549', *Italique*, 10 (2007), 17–57; Eugenio Refini, *'Per via d'annotationi'*, pp. 62–68; and Franco Tomasi, 'L'accademia degli Intronati e Alessandro Piccolomini: strategie culturali e itinerari biografici', in *Alessandro Piccolomini (1508–1579). Un siennois à la croisée des genres et des savoirs. Actes du colloque international (Paris 23–25 septembre 2010)*, ed. by Marie-Françoise Piéjus, Michel Plaisance, and Matteo Residori (Paris: Université Sorbonne Nouvelle Paris 3, 2012), pp. 23–38.

79   On Piccolimoni's link with the Accademia degli Infiammati, see Andrea Baldi, 'Piccolomini e l'Accademia degli Infiammati', *Italian Culture*, 9 (1992), 115–27; Livia Vendruscolo, 'Il problema

not simply because key aspects of the latter reverberate with some of the critical pillars of Piccolomini's introduction, such as the ethical value of poetical works and the profound relationship existing between theology and poetry (even though the latter — according to Piccolomini — has the primary position, because poets show the truth beyond appearance).[80] One further correspondence links together the two texts. In his preface, Piccolomini maintains that Italian contemporary poetry (and the lyric one, in particular) has a superior status over all the other ones.[81] He does not go further declaring the primacy of lyric poetry in general, as Magno did. Yet his affirmation can be seen as an authoritative basis from which Magno could have developed his sharp assertion about the pre-eminence of lyric genre, which is another unique trait of his lecture.

4. The Legacy of the *Prefatione* in Magno's Following Poetical Production

Throughout his life, Magno adhered to many of the theories, lyric elements, and features he focused on and presented as crucial in his *Prefatione*. They were later applied in his own lyrical works too.[82] At the centre of Magno's literary production lay the ethical and religious topics which he praised as the sources and the original driving forces of poetry and that he wished that, following the model of Petrarch, were to invigorate every poetical composition. It seems as if, through his verses, Magno himself answered the call for a renovation of poetry that he formulated in his *Preface*. Moral themes are kept in so high esteem by the author that he does not simply deal with them in many poems of his collection, but he also innovatively positions a series of texts devoted to these topics at the beginning of his book of rhymes (poems 1–10).[83] Through his opening compositions, Magno invites his readers to meditate on the fragility of life, human happiness, and the overpowering force of death. The moral strain of Magno's poetry not only propounds the topics to be dealt with in the various poems, but — being conceived as an ordering force too — it also provides the gathered texts with a structure and a rational arrangement. Indeed, in his book of rhymes Magno does not merely juxtapose short series of poems devoted to similar topics. He rather structures his first section in accordance with a logical order meant to invite readers to ponder human mortal fate and the gifts offered to humankind to dignify and face its condition. The first moral series is followed by other three sections in which the poet deals with the sufferings of human life and the protection against these offered by either friendship (poems 11–18) or civic virtues (poems 19–26), and funereal subjects (poems 27–42),

---

filologico dell'*Institutione* di Alessandro Piccolomini', *Filologia e critica*, 8.2 (1983), 161–77; Marie-Françoise Piéjus, 'L'*Orazione in lode delle donne* di Alessandro Piccolomini, con una *Postilla* di A. Di Benedetto', *Giornale storico della letteratura italiana*, 170 (1993), 524–51; and Refini, 'Per via d'annotationi', pp. 55–62.

80   See Refini, 'Le "gioconde favole"', pp. 20–23.
81   See Refini, 'Le "gioconde favole"', pp. 21 and 25 (and p. 50 n. 32).
82   On Magno's poetical works, see n. 1 and n. 15.
83   See Comiati, 'Presenze oraziane', pp. 59–68; and Comiati, 'Componente paratestuale', p. 151.

respectively.[84] In these sections, too, the rhymes convey their moral themes in a twofold perspective: as both single texts dealing with a specific topic, and as part of a wider poetical discourse. Only after these set of series does Magno start including love texts in his *corpus*.[85] The organizational structure of the poet's book of rhymes can be interpreted as a clear sign of the importance that he attributed to moral subjects. Yet he even more clearly stresses the centrality of these topics in another critical writing of his: a short analytical work where he stated that contemporary poets should stop focusing on trite subjects such as love, and devote their efforts instead to ethical ones, by following the example of Horace.[86] These statements echo and corroborate those maintained throughout his *Prefatione* and put into practice in his lyrical production.

Religious themes also have a core position in Magno's *Canzoniere*.[87] Following the Petrarchan model, he devotes the closing section of his *corpus* (poems 125 to 137) to spiritual matters, dealing with repentance, doubts of faith, Christian mysteries, and contemplation of the divine. In this case, too, the poet attributes prominence to single spiritual topics by dealing with them in specific poems or else in small groups of poems. Yet he also builds this section as the last movement of a longer progressive pathway that — moving from previous texts about earthly love, to others devoted to purer and spiritual feelings — passes through those of pious contrition, and, finally, reaches those dealing with holy sublimation. In some compositions, Magno's interest for religious topics is also merged with Neoplatonic elements — whose key role in the author's critical considerations and whose poetical implications had been pointed out in his *Prefatione*. This combination notably occurs in the last poem of his book, the *canzone* 'Deus', an allegorical text in which the personified Christian Faith appears to the poet, unveils and explains some of her mysteries, and invites him to join her in a glorification of God.[88] 'Deus' is a work so complex, sophisticated, and rich in mystical, biblical, and religious connotations and references, that in 1597 — three years before its publication at the end of Magno's poetical *corpus* — it had been printed as a single text, accompanied by three philosophical and theological commentaries (written by Ottavio Menini, Valerio Marcellini, and Teodoro Angelucci).[89] The readings of the three exegetes precisely aimed at elucidating the mystical and allegorical meanings of the text, and perceived in its verses a symbolic representation of the journey of the human soul towards God. The *canzone* also represents a tangible example of how Petrarch's language

---

84   See Galimberti, 'Celio Magno e il petrarchismo veneto', p. 364; Galimberti, 'Disegno petrarchesco', p. 318; Stella Galbiati, 'Epilogo sacro e libro', pp. 369–71; and Campana, 'Ipotesi di lettura', pp. 211–23.

85   On the Magno's section of love texts, see Comiati, '"Benché 'l sol decline"'.

86   See Comiati, 'Presenze oraziane'.

87   See Taddeo, *Il manierismo letterario*, p. 169; Galimberti, 'Disegno petrarchesco'; Stella Galbiati, 'Epilogo sacro e libro'; and Stella Galbiati, 'Contributo per Celio Magno'.

88   See Pilot, 'Le canzoni di Celio Magno', pp. 292–308; Stella Galbiati, 'Epilogo sacro e libro'; Stella Galbiati, 'Contributo per Celio Magno'; and Campana, 'Ipotesi di lettura', pp. 238–50.

89   *Deus, canzone spirituale di Celio Magno. Con vn discorso sopra di quella dell'eccellentissimo signor Ottauio Menini. Vn commento dell'eccellentissimo signor Valerio Marcellini, & due lettioni dell'eccellentissimo signor Theodoro Angelucci* (Venice: Domenico Farri, 1597).

could be bent and reworked to provide the model not only for love poetry, but for theological verses too — as Magno planned and recommended in his *Preface*.[90]

Another poem written by Magno in which religious and Neoplatonic theories are combined — and where the spiritualized reading of Petrarch's work, presented in the *Preface*, is also put into practice — is a sonnet of correspondence — published at the end of Magno's *Canzoniere* — 'Non creò Dio bellezza, acciocché spento', addressed to one of the commentators of the *canzone* 'Deus', Valerio Marcellini.[91] In this text, Magno invites his addressee to prize the terrestrial beauties because through their pure contemplation it is possible to reach God,[92] exactly as Petrarch — according to the interpretation offered in the *Prefatione* — had aimed to show through his poems. Magno valued so profoundly a poetical pathway that moved from earthly to refined loves and then, through a progressive purifying journey, towards the divine, that he did not limit himself to put it into effect in his production and invite others (such as Marcellini) to follow his and Petrarch's example. He also openly celebrated some of those who applied this feature in their literary work. In particular, in his *canzone* 'Dunque rea morte ha spente', a eulogy of Girolamo Molino — after having praised his friend's patriotic deeds and virtuous behaviours — Magno exalts Molino's poems for having gracefully sung of God and love, and shown how, by only cherishing the latter as a symbol of a purer reality, human beings can be raised towards the former.[93] In his homage, Magno openly states that Molino 'altrui portò salute | [...] mostrando a quanto mal s'apprende | chi 'l senso in guida prende: | et, che, mortal beltà tanto s'apprezza, | quanto ella è scala a l'immortal bellezza' [provided others with safety, by showing how dangerous is the way of those who follow their senses, and by demonstrating that terrestrial beauties are much more truly appreciated if taken as a way to reach the divine beauties].[94] It is noteworthy that, like select other parts of the *canzone*, the last two lines of Magno's quoted passage were slightly different in the first version of the poem (printed at the end of Molino's book of rhymes, posthumously published in 1573).[95] Although — by always dealing with the salutary power of Molino's love poetry — the two lines convey in both versions almost the same content, in their first draft they enunciated it less clearly and focused more on a comparison between earthly and divine splendours, rather than on the former's implicit potential to achieve contemplation of the latter. Indeed, in the first version of his *canzone*, Magno wrote that Molino's poems revealed 'c'humana beltà, che tanto apprezza, | par notte al Sol de l'immortal bellezza' [that human beauty, so much appreciated, is nothing but a dark night in front of the bright sun of immortal beauty', *canzone* 'Deh; se dal tristo core', ll. 63–64]. The shift from the earlier to the final version of this passage could have been dictated by the author's intention either to make

---

90   See Stella Galbiati, 'Epilogo sacro e libro', p. 372.
91   See *Rime*, p. 145.
92   See Stella Galbiati, 'Contributo per Celio Magno', p. 130.
93   See poem 70 (*Rime*, pp. 72–75).
94   Poem 70. 44–48 (*Rime*, p. 73).
95   See *Rime di Girolamo Molino* (Venice, 1573), fol. 120ᵛ. On the two versions of Magno's *canzone* to Molino, see Taddeo, *Il manierismo letterario*, pp. 127–37.

more explicit the interest that Molino had for a purifying poetry marked by Neoplatonic tones (and to which Magno's first statement only vaguely alluded), or more to openly present him as a poet who, materializing his appeal for this subject through his works, gave his pupil (i.e. Magno) a tangible model to imitate, in the light of Petrarch's previous ideal paradigm (already remarked upon in the *Preface*). In either case, Magno seems intent on showing that he is proud to have treasured and followed Molino's example.

As well as being an important work where voicing thoughts on poetry and theories about the lyric genre, Petrarch's teachings, and the importance of Neoplatonic and spiritual strains in a poetical discourse, Magno's *Prefatione sopra il Petrarca* can rightly also be seen as a literary training ground where the author aimed to exhibit the wide-ranging and multifaceted potentialities of his prose, experiment with its stylistic possibilities, and test his rhetorical skills. The logical and demonstrative focus of Magno's style has already been pointed out. The author's controlled yet expressive use of rhetorical questions, for instance, was employed in the first section of the *Preface*.[96] But there are other interesting characteristics of his discourse that are worth considering in the light of their being re-employed in the following literary production of Magno. A feature of Magno's early eloquence that kept being appreciated and used by the author in his later poetical compositions was the *Priamel*.[97] This feature appears at the beginning of the section on lyric poetry of Magno's *Prefatione* and was later re-employed, for example, in the opening sonnet of his book of rhymes, 'Non di porfido tomba eletto e duro'.[98] Another rhetorical element that, after having appeared in the critical work on Petrarch, was retained by Magno and — even though partially transformed — finds its place in one of the last love poems of his *Canzoniere* is a potent simile that compares the brightness of the last sunbeams and that of the other stars, by aiming to reveal that, even at dusk, the former exceeds the latter. Its first occurrence is at the end of the second section of the *Preface*, when the author stated that, if God wanted David to sing in lyric verses, then it is right to deduce that 'la sua divina Maestà' [God's divine majesty] chose that specific poetical genre among many others as the noblest, worthiest, and most appropriate to celebrate his glories, and convey to the world the heavenly thoughts

---

96   See *Prefatione*, pp. 223 and 227.

97   The *Priamel* pattern is a rhetorical structure and consists of listing a series of elements explicitly presented as opposed to what the poet wishes to say, before the author says it (e.g., the poet will not deal either with A, or B, or C, but he will deal with D). The trope was often employed by Horace in his works and, specifically, in prominent texts, such as the opening ode of his first book of the *Carmina*. For a general overview of the phenomenon in the ancient literature, see William H. Race, *The Classical Priamel from Homer to Boethius* (Leiden: Brill, 1982). For the Horatian use of the *Priamel*, see Gian Franco Gianotti, 'Priamel', in *Enciclopedia Oraziana*, ed. by Scevola Mariotti, 3 vols (Rome: Istituto della Enciclopedia Italiana Treccani, 1996–1998), II, 726–27; and Henry D. Jocelyn, 'Carm. I, 12 and the Notion of "Pindarising" Horace', *Sileno*, 19 (1993), 101–29.

98   See *Rime*, p. 1. On this sonnet, see Galimberti, 'Disegno petrarchesco', pp. 318–20; and Comiati, 'Presenze oraziane', pp. 61–62. On the Italian *Canzonieri* that have an opening poem structured in accordance to the *Priamel* scheme, see Stefano Carrai, 'Minturno, Marino e un modulo oraziano', *Italique*, I (1998), 96–101; and Refini, 'Le "gioconde favole"', pp. 30–32.

of his eternal mind.[99] After this statement — affirms the author — he could not put forward any more eloquent reason to prove the superiority of the lyric genre, because 'dopo che l'authorità di Dio ha reso chiaro il nostro intelletto, ogni altra ragione, che sopraggiunge, riman come stella, che tenti far vedere il suo lume dove risplende il sole, anzi ella sparisce come tenebra dinanzi al sole' [after that God's authority cleared our mind, every other explanation that could be added would either appear as a star that aims to have its brightness admired while the sun still shines, or which would even disappear like darkness in the light of the sun].[100] This comparison must have been prized by Magno, who decided to employ it — many years later — in his lyrical farewell to the woman he loved, as a last tribute to both her and their affection, before setting aside his terrestrial feelings and devoting his poems to spiritual topics.[101] In his valediction — sonnet 121, 'Quand'ergo al ciel le tante grazie ond'io' — the poet sings the last praises of his beloved, by upholding that, even though the age could partially lessen her graces, she would, nevertheless, be the most divine creature on earth, exactly as the sun would — even at twilight — overcome with its brightness that of all the other stars; or — as Magno wrote — 'E se sue doti eccelse e pellegrine | si fan per gli anni a par di sé men belle, | a par de l'altre son rare e divine. || Ché non ponno oscurar l'ore rubelle | celeste lume: e benché 'l sol decline, | vince un sol raggio suo tutte le stelle' [and if, for the passing of time, her heavenly beauties diminish in comparison to how they previously were, they would still exceed in rarity and splendour those of every other woman, since flying time cannot obscure the light [of his beloved], exactly as a single ray of the setting sun overcomes the glare of the whole firmament].[102]

5. Conclusions

Although Magno wrote the *Prefatione sopra il Petrarca* in his youth, the work is an important document that illustrates his ideas about poetry and Petrarch, and how he develops some theories that demonstrate his understanding and knowledge of contemporary debates on poetics and literature. The author was certainly sensitive to many influences that came from the various Venetian cultural environments that he frequented — in particular, those of Venier's circle and the Accademia della Fama. From these contexts, Magno derived his interests for — or was, at least, invited to ponder over and consider more attentively — the spiritual strain of poetry and the Neoplatonic principles of love. The stimuli that Magno received inclined him to concentrate his investigation on the repercussions that these principles had and could keep having on lyrical compositions. Furthermore, the debates that arose

99   *Prefatione*, p. 230: 'Non possiamo noi [...] mantenere che la eleggesse tra gli altri questa sorte di verso e di stile, come più nobile, degno et atto a cantar le sue glorie, et a spiegar in terra i concetti del cielo e della sua mente eterna?' [How could we not maintain that (God's divine majesty) chose that specific poetical and stylistic genre among many others as the noblest, worthiest, and most apt to celebrate his glories, and convey to the Earth the thoughts of the Heavens and his eternal mind?].
100   *Prefatione*, p. 230.
101   On this sonnet, see Comiati, '"Benché 'l sol decline"', pp. 130–31.
102   Sonnet 121. 9–14 (*Rime*, p. 119).

in the Venetian circles encouraged the author to intensively focus on the ethical and moral components of poetical writing, as well as on the idea that lyrical verses were invented to give expression (and explore) human religiosity. Yet Magno was not slavish in the way he relied on previous notions and concepts upheld by others. He, in fact, combined these various ideas and beliefs in original forms, and merged them with other ones — such as the debated question of the divine inspiration of poets — derived from a variety of other writings that were diffused throughout the Italian peninsula at the time. As a result, he wrote a critical work that was nourished with contemporary arguments on poetics and rhetoric, but also gave space to new views, as is shown, for instance, in Magno's claim regarding the superiority of lyric genre. The author also put forward a corollary proposal and explicitly called on poets to appreciate lyric poetry as the worthiest to be written. Consequently, the subjects that lay at the core of this genre — such as spiritual and religious matters — should be treasured most in new compositions. In line with this perspective, in his *Preface*, Petrarch was exalted by Magno as one of the most eminent representatives of lyric poetry, not only for his having dealt extensively with moral and spiritual subjects (even when he devoted himself to terrestrial forms of love — infers Magno — he had always approached them in a spiritualizing and Neoplatonic perspective), but also because he employed the most polished and refined style. As a consequence, Petrarch was judged — both from a content and a rhetorical viewpoint — as the most authoritative literary model to be followed and imitated in lyric works. Magno himself, as a poet, applied this rule and respected what he believed were the core elements of lyric poetry — exemplified in Petrarch's *Canzoniere* — in his own poetical production.

CHAPTER 5

Anthological *Discorsi* as Means of 'Doctrinization' of Petrarchism in the *Rime degli Accademici Occulti* (1568)[1]

Simona Oberto

During the sixteenth century, the phenomenon of Petrarchism reached its literary and poetological peak. Originating in the Trecento, Petrarchism is defined as the practice of imitating the works of Francesco Petrarca (1304–74); more precisely his vernacular works and, above all, his *Canzoniere*. Far from being a homogeneous movement, over the course of the next two centuries Petrarchism developed into a spectrum of different genres and themes, including the epos at the Ferrarese court, the courtesan poetry of the *strambottisti*, Lorenzo de' Medici's (1449–92) philosophical poetry, the tragedies and comedies of the Cinquecento, pastoral dramas and erotic epistolography, as well as the so-called *rime sacre* and *spirituali*.[2]

Meanwhile an ever-increasing number of academic publications contributed significantly to the diversification of the phenomenon; in fact, at least twenty academic anthologies appeared from the 1520s onward. One of these, the *Rime degli Academici Occulti con le imprese et discorsi* (1568), which will be the focus of this chapter, can present and reflect Petrarchism on up to three different levels: on the level of the *impresa*, the image-motto combination that precedes the literary sections, on the level of the *discorsi*, the prose explanations, and on the level of the poetry. Their activities will result in what I call the 'doctrinization' of Petrarchism, that is, a doctrinal charging of Petrarchist semantics. Before focusing on this particular

---

1   The present chapter is an extract from the 'Introduction' and chapter '2.4 Die *Rime degli Academici Occulti con le loro imprese et discorsi* (Brescia 1568)' of my doctoral thesis: Simona Oberto, *Poetik und Programmatik der akademischen Lyrik des Cinquecento* (Heidelberg: Winter, 2016), pp. 7–28 and 256–96. The images derive from the *Rime degli Academici Occulti* at the Biblioteca Marciana of Venice (shelfmark: D 063 D 078). They have been reproduced by courtesy of the Ministero dei Beni e delle Attività Culturali e del Turismo — Biblioteca Nazionale Marciana. Reproduction is strictly prohibited.
2   See Gerhard Regn, 'Petrarkismus', in *Historisches Wörterbuch der Rhetorik*, ed. by Gert Ueding (Tübingen: Niemeyer, 2003), VI, columns 911–21; Marc Föcking, *'Rime sacre' und die Genese des barocken Stils. Untersuchungen zur Stilgeschichte geistlicher Lyrik in Italien 1536–1614* (Stuttgart: Steiner, 1994); Bernhard Huss, *Lorenzo de'Medicis 'Canzoniere' und der Ficinianismus. Philosophica facere quae sunt amatoria* (Tübingen: Narr, 2007).

approach to the movement, it is necessary to briefly outline the poetological framework before which the academics operate.

1. Petrarchism and Bembism

The succinct, above-mentioned summary of Petrarchism's diverse manifestations underlines, on the one hand, its adaptability. On the other hand, it underlines the fact that Petrarchism represents only one among many contemporarily available literary discourses and moreover only one erotic discourse among others of philosophical, classic, or even burlesque descent.[3]

With this background in mind, it is clear that the general definition of Petrarchism as an imitative practice is insufficient, because it does not specify what exactly is being imitated: is it Petrarch's conception of love, *Petrarca modello di poesia amorosa*, or his style and language, *Petrarca modello di lingua*, or maybe even both? Furthermore, it becomes necessary to distinguish different types of Petrarchism arising from the imitated field or fields and to establish whether they can be considered more or less 'faithful' ('orthodox') to Petrarch's model.

One further factor must then be taken into consideration for the sixteenth century: in the light of the extremely authoritative efforts made by the influential cardinal Pietro Bembo (1470–1547) in his grammar and poetology from 1525, the *Prose della volgar lingua*, that sought to give the Petrarchist discourse one consistent and homogeneous shape, this progression of Petrarchism is by no means self-evident. Explicitly allowing only Petrarch as a linguistic and stylistic model for poetry, the Venetian cardinal succeeds in directing literary production by offering very precise formal and euphonic-aesthetic rules for the *scriver bene*. Additionally, he establishes Petrarch as the authority for the erotic discourse in his *Rime* from 1530 by recreating topical elements of the *Canzoniere* therein. His imitation of Petrarch's language and content has led Bembo to be considered the most devoted of Petrarch's paladins. Nonetheless, a closer look at Bembo's two works also reveals his detachment from the model. While the *Prose della volgar lingua* accentuate a certain stylistic fallibility of Petrarch's writing, which Bembo immediately justifies and relativizes in order to not compromise the model on the whole, one of the most prominent features of the *Rime* is the substitution of Petrarch's poetics of critical, spiritual self-concern ('Poetik der Selbstsorge') for a poetics of *gloria*, which, below the Petrarchist textual surface, returns to, among other things, the ancient epic discourse in order to assure its lyrical subject fame in the afterlife.[4] Therefore Bembo's works not only establish

---

3   See Ulrike Schneider, *Der weibliche Petrarkismus im Cinquecento. Transformationen des lyrischen Diskurses bei Vittoria Colonna und Gaspara Stampa* (Stuttgart: Steiner, 2007), p. 19.

4   See Alfred Noyer-Weidner, 'Lyrische Grundform und episch-didaktischer Überbietungsanspruch in Bembos Einleitungsgedicht', *Romanische Forschungen*, 86 (1974), 314–58; Andreas Kablitz, 'Lyrische Rede als Kommentar. Anmerkungen zur Petrarca-Imitatio in Bembos *Rime*', in *Der petrarkistische Diskurs. Spielräume und Grenzen. Akten des Kolloquiums an der Freien Universität Berlin 23.10.–27.10.1991*, ed. by Klaus W. Hempfer and Gerhard Regn (Stuttgart: Steiner, 1993), pp. 29–79; Gerhard Regn, 'Petrarkische Selbstsorge und petrarkistische Selbstrepräsentation: Bembos Poetik der *gloria*', in *Autobiographisches Schreiben und philosophische Selbstsorge*, ed. by Maria Moog-Grünewald (Heidelberg: Winter, 2004), pp. 95–125.

Petrarch as a model, they also signal the boundaries beyond which that model can be surpassed, and establish a unique discourse known as 'Bembism'.[5]

With respect to these developments, the German scholars Klaus Hempfer and Gerhard Regn have advanced the notion of Petrarchism as a 'dynamic system', which can be classified according to the criteria of 'core' and 'periphery', and which disposes of 'system–constitutive', 'system–possible' and 'system–incompatible' elements.[6] This approach, the essentials of which shall be outlined here, offers several useful categories for the classification of the discourse.

The core of this system is achieved by an 'integral' imitation of the so-called 'system–constitutive elements', in other words the employment of a love-concept going back to Petrarch as well as the use of Petrarchan expressional modes (topics, rhetorical figures, genres) related to the *Canzoniere*. The integration of 'system–compatible' or 'system–incompatible elements' then directs the system towards its 'periphery'; they distance it from its core elements and in the most radical cases trigger its transgression. While 'system–compatible elements' can be integrated into the framework without automatically impeding the overall function of the system (for example the integration of Platonic elements, which to a certain extent are present in Petrarch's *Canzoniere*), 'system–incompatible elements', for instance the integration of modules or elements of sensual eroticism from the Latin elegiacs, strain the system's tolerance. The decisive factor in determining the dynamism of the system is its capacity for 'assimilation of the unfamiliar or new Petrarchist elements whilst creating a contextual compatibility with the semantic core of the system'.[7] This means that whenever a writer attempts to integrate a novel or different item into the dominant literary system, he does so by seeking a (possible, at times feeble) connection to items that are already present in Petrarchism. This strategy avoids exposure to criticism and permits innovation within the chosen framework, which is exactly the path chosen by the academies.

2. Implicit Criticism of Bembism

Unlike Bembo's primarily formal and aesthetic approach to Petrarchism, the academic anthologies are evidence of the need for a discourse in which the semantic dimension is not merely subordinated. In fact, a very large number of academic anthologies not only insist on displaying beautiful poetry but also on pointing out the *dottrina*, knowledge of a philosophical, scientific, or religious character, which reinvigorates the aesthetic composition. As we will see in the case of the Occulti, the aim is to create a literary product that merges the elegance of Petrarchist diction with the *gravitas* of philosophical *dottrina*.

---

5   See Kablitz, 'Petrarca-Imitatio in Bembos *Rime*', p. 33; and Schneider, *Weiblicher Petrarkismus*, p. 33.
6   See Regn, 'Petrarkismus'; and Klaus W. Hempfer, 'Probleme der traditionellen Bestimmung des Petrarkismus. Überlegungen zum Forschungsstand', in *Die Pluralität der Welten. Aspekte der Renaissance in der Romania*, ed. by Wolf-Dieter Stempel und Karlheinz Stierle (München: Fink, 1987), pp. 253–77.
7   Schneider, *Weiblicher Petrarkismus*, p. 105 (our translation).

Taking into account the statements in the second book of Bembo's *Prose* on the 'generali [parti]'[8] [general parts] of the *scrittura*, however, these requirements become somewhat problematic. According to the author, the *materia* is a negligible 'part' of the writing process, which is excluded from theorization:

> [N]on della materia, dintorno alla quale alcuno scrive; ma del modo col quale si scrive [...] ragionasi hoggi tra noi. [...] Percioche il suggetto è ben quello; che fa il poema, o puollo almen fare, o alto o humile o mezzano di stile: ma buono in se o non buono non giamai: [...] Non dico gia tuttavia, che un suggetto piu che un'altro non possa piacere. Ma questo rispetto non è di necessita: dove quegli altri, de quali s'è hoggi detto, sono molti, et ciascuno per se necessariissimo a doverne essere il componente lodato et pregiato compiutamente.[9]

This exclusion of the *materia* as a relevant category in the writing process makes Bembo and his version of Petrarchism vulnerable to criticism from the academies. Nonetheless, at the height of the late 1560s this criticism was not made explicit. Rather the authors faced the dilemma of either dedicating themselves to a semantically 'lightweight' literature of *pura forma* or of composing works that had doctrinal aspirations, but which prevented their authors from profiting from the success of Petrarchism. The road chosen by the academies lies in between these options. First of all, they do not completely abandon Petrarchist semantics; instead doctrinal elements are 'imposed' onto those semantics, as well as onto Petrarch's own works. Second, this has an effect on the Petrarchist *verba* and expressional modes as well as its genres, which are re-functionalized to transmit the new *res*. A concrete example of this modified approach towards the discourse can be found in the *Rime degli Academici Occulti*.

3. The *Rime degli Academici Occulti*

As in the case of many other contemporary institutions, we only have a limited amount of information about the members and exact activities of the Occulti. Founded in the city of Brescia in the year 1563 by the mathematician Alfonso Cavriolo (or Capriolo; birthdate unknown), the man of letters Girolamo Bornato (birthdate unknown), and the poet Giulio Martinengo (1541–1614), the academy very soon (1564) started holding lectures on moral philosophy, logics, mathematics, and poetry.

Among these disciplines the priority is assigned to philosophy, as we can infer from the *Ragionamento* held by the secretary of the academy, the Academico Selvaggio

---

8   Pietro Bembo, *Prose della volgar lingua. L'editio princeps del 1525 riscontrata con l'autografo Vaticano Latino 3210*, ed. by Claudio Vela (Bologna: CLUEB, 2001). Hereafter *PVL*; here, *PVL*, II. 4, p. 61.
9   *PVL*, II. 4 p. 61, and II. 20, pp. 101–02: 'Today we will not be reasoning about the subject-matter, of which one writes, but rather about the manner, which is used in writing. [...] For, the subject certainly is, or at least can be, of such nature as to place the composition either in the high or humble or medium style; but it can never make the composition good or not good in itself [...] I will however not deny that one subject may please more than another. But this consideration is not necessary: whereas the other aspects, of which we have spoken today, are numerous, and each one of them in itself very necessary if the composer is to be praised and valued completely'. Unless indicated differently, all the Italian texts throughout the present chapter have been translated by us.

(presumably Cosimo Lauro, birthdate unknown), in honor of its foundation. The academy's principal purpose is thus to serve 'quella singolare, & valorosa donna eßempio di gratia, & di bellezza [...] ch'à nome Filosofia'[10] through 'ingeniose, & dotte compositioni, [...] secondo ò la diversità de'soggetti, ò la varietà de'concetti'.[11] The academics shall behave like lovers towards her: 'Questa donna [...] tratteremo [...] come veri, & gentilißimi innamorati [...] speßißime volte visitandola [...] & con ogni diligenza, & amore servendola'.[12] The reward for the upright service of this lady, who will fill the academics' souls with the splendor of her light, is nothing less than the elevation to a higher form of existence and the access to the highest knowledge, the vision of the 'causa delle cause' [cause of causes].[13] Based on ll. 10–11 of Petrarch's sonnet 'La gola e'l sonno e l'otiose piume' (*RVF*, 7), 'Povera, e nuda vai Filosofia, | Dice la turba al vil guadagno intesa',[14] the Selvaggio points out that unfortunately nowadays *donna Filosofia* (a theme that goes back to Dante's *Convivio*) has fallen into oblivion.[15] In this sense it is the Occulti's chore to bring her back to life and to restore her dignity: 'debbono essere impiegati gli animi vostri à render vita, & splendore à quelle scienze, che sono [...] hoggimai dal mondo spente, & morte'.[16] The *Ragionamento* then proceeds to specify how this *servitium amoris* directs its disciples towards the love of virtue in private life and in public affairs. This commitment to philosophy, however, is not free from counter-reformatory preoccupations, as becomes clear towards the end of the text. After offering a list of about ten ancient philosophers, among which are Plato and Aristotle, whose path the Occulti are not to follow, the Selvaggio exhorts the academics to seek the 'vera somma della Filosofia' [the true ends of Philosophy], which is 'l'unirsi delli huomini con Dio per lo sapere; per più sicuro, & fedel camino [...] nell'unica virtù accompagnata dal dono di quella gratia, ch'à Dio ne rende grati [...] nella patria del

---

10   C. L. [Cosimo Lauro], *Ragionamento fatto dal Selvaggio Academico. Nel Nascimento dell'Accademia Delli Occolti* (Brescia: Giovan Francesco Marchetti, 1565), fol. [a7] (hereafter *Ragionamento*): 'that unique and valorous lady example of grace, and beauty [...] whose name is Philosophy.'

11   *Ragionamento*, fol. b4: 'ingenious, and erudite compositions [...] according to either the diversity of subjects, or the variety of concepts.'

12   *Ragionamento*, fols a7–b: 'This woman [...] we will treat [...] as would the true, and most gentle lovers [...] visiting her very often [...] and serving her with all due diligence, and love.'

13   *Ragionamento*, fol. b.

14   *Ragionamento*, fol. b1: 'Poor, and naked you proceed Philosophy | Says the crowd aiming to the vile profit'. See *RVF*, 7. The reference edition is: Francesco Petrarca, *Canzoniere*, ed. by Marco Santagata (Milan: Mondadori, 1996).

15   For the image of a *Petrarca morale* in the Renaissance, see Catharina Busjan, ' "Sotto leggiadro et mirifico velamento poetico". Bernardo Ilicino und Petrarcas *Trionfi*', in *Para/Textuelle Verhandlungen zwischen Dichtung und Philosophie in der Frühen Neuzeit*, ed. by Bernhard Huss, Patrizia Marzillo, and Thomas Ricklin (Berlin: De Gruyter, 2011), pp. 91–116; Catharina Busjan, *Petrarca-Hermeneutik. Die Kommentare von Alessandro Vellutello und Giovan Andrea Gesualdo im epochalen Kontext* (Berlin: De Gruyter, 2013); *Lezioni sul Petrarca. Die 'Rerum vulgarium fragmenta' in Akademievorträgen des 16. Jahrhunderts*, ed. by Bernhard Huss, Florian Neumann, and Gerhard Regn (Münster: LIT, 2004); Bernhard Huss, ' "Il Petrarca, che ordinariamente suole essere Platonico". Die Petrarca-Exegese in Benedetto Varchis Florentiner Akademievorträgen', in *Questo leggiadrissimo poeta! Autoritätskonstitution im rinascimentalen Lyrik-Kommentar*, ed. by Gerhard Regn (Münster: LIT, 2005), pp. 297–332.

16   *Ragionamento*, fol. b1: 'your souls are to be employed to restore life, and splendor to those sciences, which have [...] nowadays faded, and died from the earth.'

cielo'.[17] The *renovatio* of ancient philosophy is linked to a Neoplatonic elevation process, in which the love of a superior female entity is a means and an end that leads to the final union with the Christian God.

These key topics, with slight modifications in accordance with the main subject, are discussed in the *discorsi* of the Occulti's first collection of vernacular poetry, the *Rime*. The latter appeared in 1568, three years after the *Ragionamento*, and they resume its topics in the dedication's opening statement:

> Fu sempre la vera Bellezza nelle Donne [...] forte & soave catena a trarre [...] gli animi [...] ad operar bene & virtuosamente: [...] Quanti animi nobili [...] [hanno] poi lasciato il particolar'amore, d'una in altra bellezza trascendendo, con l'ali dell'Intelletto & della Volontà son'iti a riporsi alla fine nel grembo a Dio?[18]

In the *Rime* the philosophical topic is additionally subject to the dictate of secrecy, displayed in the name of the academy, 'gli Occulti', and in that of several academics, for example Arcano, Oscuro, and Sepolto. Unfortunately there is not sufficient space to explore here the numerous connections to the various forms of Occultism in the Renaissance, which will have to be the object of future scholarly investigation. It is worth pointing out, however, that on the most elementary level the programmatic issue of 'occultism' refers to keeping precious philosophical notions hidden from profane and vulgar minds so as to protect them from decay:

> però v'aggiungiamo, qual sia il fine nostro [...] il coprir & occultare lo splendore de gli alti misterij della Verità à gli occhi de'plebei & minuti huomini, perche le pretiosißime gemme della philosophia non s'aviliscano nella lordura [...] dimostriamo, che sotto velo di favole, parabole, od amori sempre sarà nostra mente d'occultare cose remote dal cieco & storto giudizio delle turbe.[19]

In this sense, the first *discorso* 'intorno al Sileno' explains that the Occulti have chosen the Platonic analogy of the satyr from the *Symposion* as a symbol of their endeavour, a creature that on the outside seems 'vile, sozzo & negletto' [vile, dirty, neglected] but on the inside carries the light of divinity: 'la divina particella, che IDDIO benedetto, à guise di scintilla di fuoco ne' penetrali de' corpi nostri ci ha

---

17   *Ragionamento*, fol. b5: 'the uniting of men with God for knowledge; through a safer, and more faithful path [...] in the only virtue accompanied by the gift of that grace, which makes us pleasant to God [...] in the homeland of heaven.' This condemnation of the ancient philosophers will be revoked in the *Rime degli Occulti*.

18   'Alla Valorosissima et Illustre Sig. La Signora Barbara Calina', in *Rime de gli Academici Occulti con le loro imprese et discorsi* (Brescia: Vincenzo di Sabbio, 1568), fols 2ʳ–3ᵛ: 'The true Beauty of Women has always been [...] a strong and sweet chain to draw [...] the souls [...] to operate well, and virtuously: [...] How many noble souls [...] [have] then left behind the particular love, transcending from the one to the other beauty, with the wings of the Intellect and the Will have gone to finally place themselves in God's womb?'. The poems will be cited hereafter as *Rime*.

19   'Discorso intorno al Sileno: Impresa de gli Academici Occulti', in *Rime de gli Academici Occulti con le loro imprese et discorsi* (Brescia: Vincenzo di Sabbio, 1568), no page number indicated: 'thus we add, what is our end [...] to cover and to conceal the splendor of the high mysteries of Truth to the eyes of the vile and low men, in order to avoid degrading the very precious gems of philosophy in the filth [...] we prove, that underneath the veil of fables, parables, or loves it will always be our intention to conceal remote things from the blind and deviant judgement of the crowds.'

occultato' [the divine particle, that the blessed GOD has concealed, like a spark of fire in the innermost part of our bodies]. The same satyr is displayed on the cover of the *Rime* as their *impresa* [fig. 5.1].[20]

Philosophy is thus concealed under the fictional or amorous 'narratives' of the anthology, which are to be considered as nothing but the external 'shell'. These quotations indicate a clear functional separation between the 'outside' and the 'inside' of the Occulti's production, between a façade accessible to all but unsubstantial in itself and a semantic core transmitting the highest knowledge — a separation in which the explicitly mentioned 'amori' fall into the first category. As we will see very soon, though, the topic of love is not dismissed. These observations on a functional separation between the 'outside' and the 'inside' of the Occulti's production, between 'fiction' and philosophy, are corroborated by the particular structure of the anthology and its metapoetic observations.

The *Rime* can be considered an unprecedented anthological creation made of three features, *imprese*, *discorsi*, and poems. More precisely, it contains sixteen *imprese* — the *impresa generale* of the academy and the fifteen *imprese particolari* of the academics — sixteen *discorsi* in prose, and fourteen lyrical sections (making a total of 231 poems). The features of this iconic prosimetrum build upon and engage in functional relationships with one another, contributing to the creation of 'micro-poetics' embedded into the academic 'macro-poetic'. Even though the title directs the attention towards the poetry (*Rime*), the pivotal role is played by the *discorsi*, which on the one hand refer to the preceding *imprese* and on the other hand offer exegetic suggestions for the lyrical creations that follow.

Moreover, the *discorsi* are of great relevance with regard to the above-mentioned functional separation of 'outside' and 'inside' as the dedication of the *Rime* to Barbara Calina (or Callina; birthdate unknown) illustrates. Apart from informing us that all the *discorsi*, except his own, were written by the lecturer and poet Bartolomeo Arnigio (1523–77), who is to be considered the creator of the *imprese*, the dedication raises awareness of a very important aspect of the relationship between the lyrics and the *discorsi*: 'Parerà [...] che da i sentimenti d'i Discorsi siano alquanto lontane le Rime: ma cio pensi esser fatto a bello studio, perche la dolce leggiadria di queste sia temperata dalla severa gravità di quelli'.[21] Hence the verse compositions cannot implement the philosophical programme of the Occulti. With the indication that they privilege a 'dolce leggiadria', i.e. love poetry on a medium stylistic level, the discourse of Petrarchism is implied and at the same time characterized as a phenomenon of style, with its function reduced to a mere 'shell'. In contrast to this, the task of 'tempering', or raising the anthology up to the semantic *gravitas*, is assigned to the *discorsi*, which hereby become the 'carriers' of doctrinal knowledge, of the actual 'substance' of the anthology.

---

20   For details on the programmatic function of imprese in sixteenth-century academies, see Simona Oberto, 'Die Impresa als Ausdruck literarischer Programmatik in den italienischen Akademien des 16. Jahrhunderts', *Germanisch-Romanische Monatsschrift*, 66.2 (2016), pp. 141–62.

21   *Rime*, fol. 3ᵛ: 'It might seem [...] that the Poems are somewhat far from the sentiments of the Discorsi: but consider this done intentionally, so that the sweet gracefulness of the former be tempered by the severe gravity of the latter.'

FIG. 5.1. Cover of *Rime de gli Academici Occulti con le loro imprese et discorsi*. Venice, Biblioteca Nazionale Marciana, D 063 D 078. Reproduced by courtesy of the Ministero dei Beni e delle Attività Culturali e del Turismo–Biblioteca Nazionale Marciana.

This passage from the dedication not only addresses a clear functional distinction between poetry and *discorsi* though; it also reveals a 'strategic move' to prevent possible criticism of the anthology by advocates of the *dottrina* before it could even arise. To understand why this manoeuver is so important to the Occulti, it is necessary to take a closer look at individual sections of the *Rime*. For this purpose, I have chosen to scrutinize the section by the Adombrato, the academic with the strongest ties to Petrarchism in the anthology.

4. The *Discorso* of the Accademico Adombrato

On a general level all the *discorsi* reveal a very similar structure. At first the specific symbolic complex of *impresa*, *motto*, and academic pseudonym are 'de-crypted' and the allegorical meaning of each element is explained with the help of literary, mythological, philosophical, religious, and scientific sources (*espositione*). Furthermore, the information about single elements is sometimes extended. Subsequently a short biography gives readers hints about the author and suggestions for how to interpret his poetry. At the end, a synthetic general interpretation of the *impresa* is found, containing further recommendations for the exegesis of the poetry. Nonetheless, it is very important to point out that not all the meanings unfolded in the *discorsi* actually apply to the academic's lyrical compositions. The work of Pietro Antonio Soncino (birthdate unknown), alias L'Adombrato, is the second to appear in the *Rime* and the best example of this phenomenon.[22] Beyond this it is symptomatic of the difficulties, or rather the strong tensions, which can arise in the attempt to harmonize Petrarchism with *dottrina*.

The *impresa* of the Adombrato depicts a swan under a laurel tree surrounded by the *motto* 'Non come soglio il folgorar pavento', a quotation from l. 6 of Petrarch's sonnet 'Qui, dove mezzo son, Sennuccio mio' (*RVF*, 113) [fig. 5.2].[23] The affiliation to Petrarchism could hardly be expressed more ostentatiously. Nonetheless the argumentation of the Adombrato's *discorso* is extremely striking, because it demonstrates the systematic, but at the same time very precarious, mediation of the Petrarchist discourse with philosophical and religious elements: its 'doctrinization'.

The *discorso* comprises three steps: first it concentrates on the swan and its meanings, second on the laurel tree, and finally on the name 'Adombrato'. Each step attempts to solidify the doctrinal background of the element in question through philosophical references. However, the doctrinal foundation is *de facto* relativized through the concentration on the specific poetic and poetological credentials of the three elements.

The swan is introduced by a rather conventional selection of mythological figures named 'Cygnus', among other things from Ovid's *Metamorphoses*. Its purity, the beauty of its singing, and its generous and excellent nature are also pointed out.

---

22   *Rime*, fols 8^r–18^v; the *discorso* is to be found in fols 8^v–11^r.
23   *RVF*, 113: 'I do not, as I used to, fear the thunder.' The lyrical speaker expresses the topic of glory through the proximity to Laura.

FIG. 5.2. *Rime de gli Academici Occulti con le loro imprese et discorsi.* Venice, Biblioteca Nazionale Marciana, D 063 D 078, fol. 8ʳ. Reproduced by courtesy of the Ministero dei Beni e delle Attività Culturali e del Turismo–Biblioteca Nazionale Marciana.

Hereafter the 'literal sense' of the *impresa* is explained: the swan seeks and finds protection from lightning under the laurel tree and has nothing more to fear. At this point, the allegorical meaning of the swan is unfolded with reference to the academic, who is symbolized by the bird. Against all expectations, though, instead of explaining the poetological meaning of the swan as a symbol of the poet, the *discorso* sets it out in terms of ethical categories:

> Et primieramente veggiamo, come intende sotto il Cigno se stesso; non tanto, perche si persuada (come alcuni improvisamente potrebbero pensare) di essere uno di que'Cigni che portano i nomi degli huomini valorosi in bocca al Tempio sublime dell'Immortalitade [...] ma sotto il Cigno si conosce haver più tosto voluto dimostrar l'integrità, la piacevolezza, la candidezza, la modestia & bontà dell'animo suo.[24]

The subsequent allegorical meaning assigned to the laurel, which is no longer a symbol of poetical fame, but rather of virtue, reinforces this interpretation:

> niun più certo ò più sicuro riparo [...] nelle fortunose revolutioni di questo mondo, che l'appoggiarsi alla Virtù [...] [intesa con il] corpo [...] del Lauro. Percioche come 'l Lauro è pianta favorita da GIOVE, & amata da Apolline Rè della luce corporea; cosi la Virtù è amata & favorita da DIO Padre.[25]

Hence two of the most influential poetic symbols, the swan and the laurel, poet and glory, are alienated from their original semantic area and assigned new meanings, indicating the purity of the soul and the salvation offered by virtue, that comply with the program of moral philosophy pursued by the Occulti. Furthermore, this semantic reallocation changes the mythological premises of the laurel, almost as if the academics wanted to distance the plant even more from its 'glorious' poetic-poetological background. The tree is no longer the main attribute of Apollo but of Zeus and, what is more, the divinities themselves correspond respectively to God the Father and intellectual illumination ('intellettual illuminatione'). Beyond this, the classic literary properties of the laurel as an evergreen, a bitter tasting plant, and the fact that it is not struck by lightning[26] are used to enforce its image as 'Albero della Virtù':

> La onde sicuramente possiamo affermare [...] il suo dilettarsi estremamente nella Virtù, cosi morale come intellettiva; che voglia dimostrare, come veramente ADOMBRATO dall'Albero della Virtù non teme più adversità, persecutioni,

---

24   *Rime*, fol. 9ʳ: 'And first of all we see, how by the Swan he intends himself; not as much, because he is persuaded (as some might believe at first glance) to be one of those Swans, who in their mouths carry the names of the valorous men to the sublime Temple of Immortality [...] rather by the Swan one recognizes his will to demonstrate the integrity, the pleasantness, the purity, the modesty and the bounty of his soul'.

25   Ibid.: '[There is] no safer or more certain shelter [...] in the eventful revolutions of this world, than to lean upon Virtue [...] [intended by] the body [...] of the laurel. For the Laurel is the plant favored by JUPITER, and loved by Apollon King of bodily light; in this way Virtue is loved and favored by GOD the Father.'

26   These attributes can be found, among other things, in Petrarca's *Collatio laureationis*; see Francesco Petrarca, 'Collatio laureationis, Orazione per la laurea', in Francesco Petrarca, *Opere latine*, ed. by Antonietta Bufano (Turin: UTET, 1975), pp. 1256–83.

insidie, tentationi, calunnie [...] havendo l'animo munito di quella: overo s'intenda questa Virtù poi per habito acquisito, o per l'infuso da DIO.[27]

However suggestive this association may seem, the subsequent remark reveals the precariousness of the enterprise:

> Oltre che non negherei, che per compiacersi più che mezanamente ne' componimenti Poetici volgari [...] et l'uno et l'altro corpo, del Lauro, come Arbore triomphale, di cui si coronano gl'Imperadori, & i Poeti, & del Cigno come sacro à Phebo [...] [ha posto].[28]

By these means, the classic poetic symbolism of the two elements is restored and, what is more, this happens specifically through the authority of Petrarch, who, unlike his 'philosophical' presence in the *Ragionamento*, is quoted as the poet of the *Canzoniere*.

The explicit introduction of Petrarch directs the *discorso* away from philosophy and towards the topics of immortality and love, even more so because the conventional function of the laurel as the tree of glory, as a woman named Laura, and as soft lovely breeze in accordance with the *Canzoniere*, are pointed out. While discussing the properties of the Adombrato's *donna Laura*, on the one hand, and of the wind, on the other hand, the *discorso* is again (briefly) able to insert them into a doctrinal context. Thus the female entity belongs to the Neoplatonic elevation scheme, in which her virtues purify each soul and inspire to 'pellegrine operationi' [pilgrim operations], while semi-medical terms are used to declare the breeze as 'terrestrial exhalations' or as 'exhalations' from Laura's heart ('aere piacevolmente mosso ò dall'essalationi terrestri, ò da quelle del cuore di Laura'), that also make the poet fall in love.[29] Nonetheless, the *discorso* at the end of this second step lapses into the predominantly poetic (amorous) explanation for the academic and his *donna*:

> Dico dunque, che da questa Impresa accompagnata da quel Verso del Petrarca per Motto, si può trarre questa interpretatione: ch'essendo l'Autor suo in età giovanile, è probabil cosa, che come il Petrarca si trovò fieramente innamorato di Laura, che allegoricamente intese sotto la voce del Lauro; cosi ancor'egli, per esser di cuor gentile, sia preso dall'Amore di qualche giovane Donna di tal nome. Et come 'l Petrarca nella sua Canzone detta la picciola Metamorphosi, dice; che si trasformò in Cigno, & che [...] in vece di ragionare mandava fuori un canto querulo & lagrimevole [...] cosi questo nostro Academico converso in Cigno per le molte Poesie, che per amor, & virtù di questa Laura và tessendo; & aßicuratosi nell'honesto & casto intendimento dell'Amor suo, significato per lo colore & tranquillità natia di questo Vccello, si stia sicuro all'ombra del Lauro suo de' folgori & tempeste, riputando esser di tanta forza il favore inteso per l'ombra, della Donna sua.[30]

27 *Rime*, fol. 9[v]: 'Hence we can surely affirm [...] his extreme delight in Virtue, moral as well as intellectual; that as truly OVERSHADOWED by the Tree of Virtue he wants to demonstrate how he does not fear any adversity, persecution, snare, temptation, slander [...] having his soul fortified by it: that is to be intended as this Virtue acquired by habit, or instilled by GOD.'
28 *Rime*, fol. 9[v]: 'Besides I would not deny that in his great delight of vernacular Poetic compositions [...] [he has used] the one and the other body, the Laurel as triumphal Tree, of which the Emperors, and the Poets crown themselves, and the Swan as sacred to Phoebus.'
29 *Rime*, fol. 10[r].
30 *Rime*, fol. 10[r-v]: 'Thus I say that from this Impresa accompanied by that Verse of Petrarca as a

Finally, the last element to be clarified, the name 'Adombrato', is also expounded by returning to Petrarch, specifically to nine quotations from the *Canzoniere*[31] and one from the *Triumphus Cupidinis*.[32] In this ambience, the aim is to underline how the academic pseudonym is not only faithful to Petrarchist language but also respects the academic name and programme, for the Adombrato is 'covered'/'hidden' by the tree of virtue. The very last lines of the *discorso* sum up the academic's poetics. At the same time they evidence the failure to successfully merge the Petrarchist with the philosophical discourse, confirming the adherence to the 'poetics of *gloria*' initiated by Bembo and not the 'poetics of *dottrina*' proclaimed by the academy:

> Perilche conchiudendo dico, che l'ADOMBRATO nostro rappresentandosi sotto 'l Cigno Vccello innocentißimo, & magnanimo non teme più per l'ombra et protettione della Virtù, ò della sua Donna detta LAVRA, il folgorar del Cielo, cioè avversità alcuna di maligna Fortuna, over danno alcuno, che la Morte e 'l Tempo suole recar à Mortali.[33]

Even though the attempt to 'doctrinize' Petrarchism in order to align it with the academic programme in the case of the Adombrato seems to struggle, and this impression is confirmed by an analysis of his very conventionally Petrarchist lyrical section, this does not mean that the *Rime* of the Occulti fail on the whole. The great part of the other *discorsi* in fact can be considered successful in this respect. The section of the Trasformato for instance, which shall be mentioned by way of comparison, is a particularly fitting example, allowing us to visualize how Petrarchist premises can instead be adapted to doctrinal expectations with positive results.

The *discorso* of the Trasformato (Giulio Martinengo) and his poetry close the *Rime* of the Occulti. His *impresa* shows a sun shining on a crescent moon, surrounded by the motto 'VNIVS ASPECTV' [fig. 5.3]. The latter is explained by referring to the 'anagogiche proportioni',[34] more precisely the fourfold exegesis. The interesting fact about the Trasformato's *discorso* is that it does not force a new semantic onto Petrarchist elements but rather keeps them as functional entities and includes them as an inferior step of the programmatic elevation scheme. As the author of this

---

Motto we can draw this interpretation: that being its Author of young age, it is probable, that he like Petrarca found himself fiercely in love with Laura, whom he allegorically intended with the word Lauro; in the same way, further, being of gentle heart, he has been taken by the Love of some young Lady with the same name. And just like Petrarca in the Canzone called the little Metamorphosis he says; that he turned into a Swan, and that [...] instead of speaking he produced a querulous and tearful song [...] thus our Academician converted into a Swan due to the many Poems woven for the love and virtue of this Laura, and having assured himself of the honest and chaste intention of his Love, signified by the color and native tranquility of this Bird, in the shadow of his laurel he is safe from the thunders and the storms, considering the force of the favor of his Lady intended by the shadow.'

31   *Rime*, fols 10ʳ–11ʳ: *RVF*, 30. 16; 142. 1–3; 337. 7–8; 56. 5; 340. 14; 264. 72; 129. 27; 212. 1–2; 269. 1–2.
32   *Rime*, fol. 10ᵛ; and see *Triumphus Cupidinis*, I. 40. The reference edition is: Francesco Petrarca, *Trionfi, Rime estravaganti, Codice degli Abbozzi*, ed. by Vinicio Pacca and Laura Paolino (Milan: Mondadori, 1996).
33   *Rime*, fol. 11ʳ: 'Thus in conclusion I say, that our ADOMBRATO representing himself as the Swan, most innocent and magnanimous Bird, due to the shadow and the protection of Virtue, or else his Lady called LAVRA, does not fear the thunders of Heaven, that is adversities caused by malign Fortune, or else any harm, that Death and Time bestow upon Mortals, any longer'.
34   The impresa of the Trasformato is on fol. 119ʳ, while the *discorso* is on the fols 119ᵛ–25ʳ of the *Rime*, from which all the following quotes are taken.

FIG. 5.3. *Rime de gli Academici Occulti con le loro imprese et discorsi*. Venice, Biblioteca Nazionale Marciana, D 063 D 078, fol. 119ʳ. Reproduced by courtesy of the Ministero dei Beni e delle Attività Culturali e del Turismo–Biblioteca Nazionale Marciana.

discorso explains, on the level of the *sensus literalis* the sun and moon are two celestial bodies, of which the one is dependent on the other for its light, and hopes to unite with it ('la Luna [...] non hà luce da se stessa, senon quanto dal lume del Sole viene più o meno percossa [...] così poi dando volta per ricongiungersi con essolui');[35] on an allegorical level the sun and moon stand for the *donna* and her lover, who receives her light and is dependent on her for elevation to God ('la Luna riceve lume & splendore dall'aspetto d'un sol corpo, ch'è il Sole; così anch'egli riceve dallo sguardo d'una bellißima Donna splendore & virtù');[36] according to the *sensus moralis* the moon represents the human soul, which is directed towards God for its enlightenment ('ella [la Luna] è simulacro dell'Anima nostra: la quale quando tutta s'occupa & si volge alla parte intellettiva superiore, come à Sole, allhor si fà luminosa nella parte, che alla contemplatione appartiensi')[37] and finally according to the *sensus anagogicus* the sun stands for God himself, with whom the soul seeks to be reunited:

> come la Luna, quasi fatta Emula del Sole, girando intorno lo vagheggia, et d'accoppiarsi con lui si gode; così egli per ciò TRASFORMATO chiamandosi, IDDIO Sol di giustitia contemplando, studi di seco unirsi, & di trasformarsi in lui totalmente: over desideri almeno di ricever cotal habilità & illustratione nell'anima sua, che sia rapito un dì & collegato con quello inacceßibil lume di tutti i lumi.[38]

Petrarchism is thus the second of the four levels and one key for the reading of the poems. Unlike the Adombrato's, the lyrical section of the Trasformato reflects and applies this doctrinal approach right from the first poem:

> Se volgo gli occhi à rimirar intenti
> De le rote superne il moto eterno,
> E i lumi, che nel ciel splendon lucenti,
> E 'l lor mirabil magistero interno;
>
> Io dico; o Mente mia, perche paventi?
> Non vedi (se dal falso il ver discerno)
> Miracoli maggior tra noi presenti?
> Et questi regge ancor l'alto governo.
>
> Raro moto nell'alma vostra io scorgo,
> BARBARA, di valor, di cortesia,
> E in aspetto Real vaga figura,

---

35 'the Moon [...] has no light in herself, unless she is more or less struck by the light of the Sun [...] thus revolving to reunite with him.'
36 'the Moon receives light and splendor from the appearance of a single body, which is the sun; in the same way he [the academic] receives splendor and virtue from the look of a beautiful Lady.'
37 'she [the moon] is a symbol of our Soul: which becomes enlightened in the part belonging to contemplation when it [the soul] entirely dedicates and directs itself to the superior intellectual part, as if it were looking at the Sun.'
38 'just as the Moon, almost becoming an Imitator of the Sun, by revolving around him expresses her desire and enjoys uniting with him; in the same way, calling himself TRASFORMATO, contemplating GOD Sun of justice, he [the academic] studies to unite with him [i.e. God] and to completely turn into him: that is, he at least hopes to gain the ability and insight in his soul, to be rapt one day and connected with that inaccessible light of all lights.'

(Meraviglie del Mondo) ond'io m'accorgo,
Che'l mirar voi al sommo ben m'invia,
O del primo motor nobil fattura.[39]

The sonnet presents and merges several of the previously described elements of the *impresa*. The lyrical speaker is contemplating the celestial bodies, overwhelmed by the greatness of their design, when he makes the reader aware of the fact that on earth there is an even greater 'miracle' (l. 7). The virtues in the soul of the *donna*, Barbara Calina, to whom the *Rime* are dedicated, are of such power that, by contemplating her, the lover and poet is directed to the highest good ('sommo ben', l. 13). As can easily be observed, the ascension from the *donna* to God and from earth to heaven implies the Neoplatonic elevation scheme, which is programmatic for the *Rime* of the Occulti on the whole.

5. Conclusions

The *discorsi* of the Adombrato and the Trasformato thus present opposite solutions for the enactment of the doctrinal academic programme in combination with the dominant lyrical discourse of Petrarchism. The first of these initially marginalizes and disparages classic Petrarchist elements (the swan and the laurel) by recurring to a different poetological meaning and by 'surcharging' their semantics with an ethical, philosophical meaning. Nonetheless, the *discorso* is incapable of keeping up a systematic development of this 'doctrinization', so that its final lines evidence a certain failure to unite Petrarchism and *dottrina*.

The *discorso* of the Trasformato instead maintains the functional integrity of the Petrarchist elements and includes them in the programmatic academic (Neoplatonic) elevation scheme. Even though they are placed low down in this scheme, their integration into a fourfold philosophical and religious framework ('anagogiche proportioni') gives them doctrinal dignity. In both cases, a very delicate balance of the intertwined discourses is achieved.

Despite the creation of a contextual compatibility with important Petrarchist symbols, in the case of the Adombrato, and with the prototypical love relationship in the case of the Trasformato, the 'doctrinization' of poetry distances the Occulti from the semantic core of Petrarchism, pushing it towards its periphery. They gradually become detached, acquiring increasing critical distance from the main discourse.

---

39   *Rime*, fol. 125ᵛ: 'If I turn the eyes intended on contemplating | Of the superior spheres the eternal motion | And the lights, which shine bright in the sky | And their admirable interior mastery; || I say; oh my Mind, why do you fear? | Don't you see (if I can discern the false from the true) | Greater miracles among us? | And this [eternal motion] even more bears the high government. || In your soul I see a rare motion, | BARBARA, of valor, of courtesy, and of Royal graceful appearance, | (Wonders of the World) from which I notice, | That contemplating you sends me to the highest good, | Oh noble creation of the first mover'. See also: 'Quando fia Amor, che 'l mio Lucente Sole' (fol. 124ʳ; there is a mistake in the numbering of the pages), and 'L'Alma che pura in ciel creata fue' (fol. 128ʳ).

CHAPTER 6

Reading Petrarch:
Gregorio Anastagi's (1536/39–1601)
Manuscript Writings on
Petrarch's *Canzoniere*

Lorenzo Sacchini

1. Introduction

This essay makes accessible to scholars a hitherto unknown episode related to Petrarch's reception during the Renaissance. The core of the article is the analysis of a compact selection of manuscript writings composed in Perugia in the second half of the sixteenth century by grammarian and poet Gregorio Anastagi.

My interest in these texts arose while I was investigating the cultural environment of Perugia during my doctoral dissertation on the local Accademia degli Insensati [Academy of the Senseless]. I quickly realized that the widespread practice of reading Petrarch, established in the numerous literary academies of Perugia, took various forms and developed in different ways. Within the context of the reception of Petrarch in sixteenth-century Perugia, I will concentrate on the aforementioned selection of Anastagi's writings for two primary reasons. Firstly, they present a great richness and variety as regards the literary forms and the approaches applied by Anastagi in illustrating the works of Petrarch. On one hand, Anastagi considers and merges together in his writings grammatical, linguistic, rhetorical, and semantic aspects. On the other hand, he makes use of dramatically different forms in his literary pieces, ranging from lists of words and paraphrases to more elaborate dialogues. Secondly, Anastagi's writings differ from the mainstream exegetical tradition of *Cinquecento* commentaries and academic lectures on Petrarch: Anastagi humbly offers to the reader practical guidance, useful in the composition of lyrics or understanding Petrarch's sonnets. Anastagi's works are purely at the reader's service, accompanying him/her through different aspects of Petrarch's language. They generally limit or avoid any philosophical or moral teaching, which is a typical element of many academic lectures of the sixteenth century; and replace the 'elaborate sophistication' of the commentaries with a more basic interpretation of Petrarch's texts.[1]

---

1   Giuseppe Mazzotta, 'Petrarch (Francesco Petrarca)', in *Encyclopedia of Italian Literary Studies*, ed.

In this paper, I will analyse three out of the five writings from the MS I 55 kept in the Biblioteca Attilio Hortis in Trieste. After providing a concise overview of the historical and geographical context in which these discourses were created and delivered, I then present a short bio-bibliographical sketch of Gregorio Anastagi. In the central part of the chapter, I concentrate on the content of the three dissertations, focusing in particular on the key elements characterizing Anastagi's works. In the conclusion, I develop the central themes of the writings that might trigger a series of questions or reflections that further research on Petrarch's reception in the Renaissance might then address.

2. The Historical and Geographical Context

The city of Perugia in the second half of the sixteenth century provides an interesting case study in the still largely uncharted territory of Petrarch's reception in the Italian Renaissance. Perugia offered the author of the *Canzoniere* a particularly favorable reception. Petrarch's compositions were often recited and discussed at the meetings of Perugia's academies. The practice of reading and commenting on Petrarch's poems was well established in the Accademia degli Insensati, the Accademia degli Unisoni [Academy of the Concordants], the Accademia del Disegno [Academy of Design], and the Accademia degli Eccentrici [Academy of the Eccentrics] — that is, in four of the seven academies then active in Perugia.[2] The members of the city's main academy, the Insensati (active at various times from 1561 to the beginning of the eighteenth century), composed the most extensive corpus of academic lectures on Petrarch's sonnets. The literary output of the Insensati dedicated to Petrarch amounts to nineteen lectures composed between 1565 and 1594, with the greatest concentration between the 1560s and 1570s. The Insensati's lectures consist of two types. A first set of lectures mainly focuses on the linguistic and rhetorical aspects of Petrarch's sonnets, providing only occasionally any philosophical considerations. A second series of lectures concentrates, instead, on the philosophical and ethical concerns lying beyond the primary intended meaning of the sonnets. This more philosophically informed approach developed especially in the later period, when the Insensati became more familiar with and adopted the

by Gaetana Marrone, Paolo Puppa, and Luca Somigli (New York; London: Routledge, 2007), p. 1413.

2   For an overview of the academies based in Perugia see Giuliano Innamorati, 'Memorandum per la storia delle Accademie Umbre', in *La funzione delle accademie nella cultura odierna. Atti del Convegno organizzato per il 5° centenario della fondazione dell'Accademia (1477–1977)* (Spoleto: Edizioni dell'Accademia spoletina, 1979), pp. 33–53; Erminia Irace, 'Le Accademie letterarie nella società perugina tra Cinquecento e Seicento', *Bollettino della Deputazione di storia patria per l'Umbria*, 87 (1990), 155–78; Lorenzo Sacchini, *Identità, lettere e virtù. Le lezioni accademiche degli Insensati di Perugia (1561–1608)* (Bologna: I libri di Emil, 2016), pp. 29–32. Relying on the data provided by Michele Maylender in his dated *Storia delle accademie d'Italia*, 5 vols (Bologna: Cappelli, 1926–30), Amedeo Quondam lists eight academies active in Perugia in the sixteenth century ('L'Accademia', in *Letteratura italiana*, ed. by Alberto Asor Rosa, 12 vols (Turin: Einaudi, 1982), I: *Il letterato e le istituzioni*, pp. 823–98). There is no clear evidence, however, of the existence in Perugia of the Accademia degli Alessi. It may be therefore safer to limit the number of academies to the seven listed in *Perugia Augusta* (Perugia: eredi di Tomassi e Zecchini, 1648, pp. 50–52) by Cesare Crispolti, who was one of the leading men of culture in the second half of the sixteenth century and a member of more than one academy.

approach seen in the lectures from the Accademia degli Infiammati [Academy of the Enflamed] of Padua.[3] Analogously, their literary canon widened to gradually include in their lectures, in addition to Petrarch's poems, expositions of the lyrics of other *Cinquecento* poets.[4]

3. Gregorio Anastagi and the Accademia degli Eccentrici

Compared to the output of the Insensati, the literary activity of the Accademia degli Eccentrici is less known. The extant corpus of its writings has never been appraised or analyzed by scholars. The characters of the members of the academy therefore still remain obscure.[5] Founded in 1567, it adopted the orbit of the moon as its general *impresa* or emblem. By the motto 'retardat non rethahit' [it delays, it does not withdraw], the members of the academy, largely students at the local university, intended to claim that their common theoretical activity would have delayed, but not ultimately frustrated, the progress of their studies (mostly in law). Among the members of the Eccentrici was Florentine Giuliano De' Ricci (1543–1606), nephew of Niccolò Machiavelli, who gave three lectures in the academy between 1567 and 1568.[6] In the most relevant of these discourses, the *Letione in biasimo delle stampe* (*Lecture in condemnation of printing*), Ricci inveighs against contemporary printed culture, which can corrupt young people. On the contrary, classical works, which are instilled with morals and educational purposes, never benefit from printing. Therefore, Ricci exhorts the other members to follow the teaching and the example of the Classics, distrusting and keeping away from printing. This admonition proved to be formidably efficient as the Eccentrici's literary production circulated almost entirely in manuscript form.

Gregorio Anastagi's literary output is no exception, including the five pieces kept in the MS I 55 of the Biblioteca Attilio Hortis in Trieste. The following is a concise description of the manuscript and its contents:

3   Their series of academic lectures, composed in the 1540s, have been recently studied by Franco Tomasi, who defined them as a model for other similar academies: 'Le letture di poesie e il petrarchismo nell'Accademia degli Infiammati [2006]' and 'Esegesi di Petrarca nelle accademie del XVI secolo (1530–50)', in Franco Tomasi, *Studi sulla lirica rinascimentale (1540–1570)* (Rome-Padua: Antenore, 2012), pp. 148–76, 177–218.
4   On the Insensati's lectures on Petrarch see Lorenzo Sacchini, 'Scritti inediti dell'Accademia degli Insensati nella Perugia del secondo Cinquecento', *Lettere italiane*, 63.3 (2013), 376–413; Lorenzo Sacchini, *Identità, lettere e virtù*, pp. 89–104.
5   An overview of the academy is provided by Abdelkader Salza, *L'Accademia degli Eccentrici di Perugia* (Perugia: Tipografia Umbra, 1898) and by Maylender, *Storia delle accademie*, II, 228–31. A very interesting source regarding the literary production of the academy is a manuscript collection of poems entitled *Rime degli Accademici Eccentrici di Perugia*; it is kept in the Biblioteca Nazionale Centrale of Florence (MS Magl. VII. 1177).
6   Recently these three lectures have been analysed and edited by Luca Sartorello, 'Una lezione accademica di Giuliano De' Ricci, nipote di Machiavelli, sull'invidia (1568)', *Atti e memorie dell'Accademia Galileiana di Scienze, Lettere ed Arti già dei Ricovrati e Patavina*, 120 (2007–08), 69–113; Luca Sartorello, 'In biasimo delle stampe. Censura e modernità in una inedita orazione di Giuliano De' Ricci', *Giornale storico della letteratura italiana*, 190 (2013), 67–93; a first transcript of the lecture on 'scienza legale' [forensics] is available in Luca Sartorello, 'Tra diritto politica e morale: la modernità di Machiavelli' (unpublished doctoral thesis, Università degli Studi di Padova, 2005), pp. 303–27.

Trieste, Biblioteca Attilio Hortis, MS I 55.
Paper. Second half of the sixteenth century; internal references to 1570s and
1580s. 203 x 135 mm. 98 fols. No Binding. Folios numbered in pencil but not
consistently.
The manuscript is autograph. The order of the five writings listed below does
not correspond to their actual composition dates (see, for instance, footnote 19).
Contents:

·   fols 1ʳ–40ᵛ: Gregorio Anastagi, *Diversità del Petrarca e del Boccaccio nell'uso di
    molte voci* (*Differences Between Petrarch and Boccaccio in the Usage of Many Words*);
    <inc> 'Terentio Varrone scrivendo a Marco Tullio'; <exp> 'crederei di me
    ritorni honore almeno di fronde se non di frutti. Il fine. Gregorio Anastagi';
·   fols 41ʳ–62ᵛ: Gregorio Anastagi, *Dialogo sopra il primo sonetto del Petrarca*
    (*Dialogue on Petrarch's First Sonnet*); <inc> 'Molte e diverse le maniere sono';
    <exp> 'ciascuno se ne tornò alle sue case. Il fine. Gregorio Anastagi';
·   fols 63ʳ–83ʳ: Gregorio Anastagi, *Lettione sopra quel sonetto del Petrarca 'Passa
    la nave mia colma d'oblio'* (*Lecture on Petrarch's Sonnet 'Passa la nave mia colma
    d'oblio'*); <inc> 'Mentre che io mi sedeva fra me stesso'; <exp> 'finir qui,
    senza andar più oltre, questa nostra lettione. Il fine. Gregorio Anastagi';
·   fols 83ᵛ–84ᵛ: blank;
·   fol. 85ʳ: inscription to 'Monsignor Francesco Maria del Monte';
·   fol. 85ᵛ: blank;
·   fols 86ʳ–88ᵛ: Gregorio Anastagi, *Discorso sopra la canzone del Petrarca 'Ne la
    stagion che 'l ciel rapido inchina'* (*Discourse on Petrarch's Canzone 'Ne la stagion
    che 'l ciel rapido inchina'*); <inc> 'Poiché humana cosa dicono'; <exp> 'solo al
    mondo miserissimo sono. Il fine. Gregorio Anastagi';
·   fol. 89ʳ: inscription to 'Monsignor Francesco Maria del Monte';
·   fol. 89ᵛ: blank;
·   fols 90ʳ–97ʳ: Gregorio Anastagi, *Discorso sopra quel sonetto del Petrarca 'Se
    Virgilio e Homero havessin visto'* (*Discourse on Petrarch's Sonnet 'Se Virgilio
    e Homero havessin visto'*); <inc> 'Poiché niuna cosa veggiamo ritrovarsi';
    <exp> 'ascoltarono tutti insieme attentamente il lettore che già in ringhiera
    era salito. Il fine. Gregorio Anastagi';
·   fols 97ᵛ–98ᵛ: blank.
Bibliography: a full description of the manuscript is given by Stefano Zamponi,
I manoscritti petrarcheschi della Biblioteca Civica di Trieste. Storia e catalogo (Padua:
Antenore, 1984), pp. 127–29.

The manuscript was transferred from Perugia to Trieste at the beginning of the
nineteenth century at the request of Domenico Rossetti (1774–1842). Patriot,
nobleman, and jurist, Rossetti was collecting bibliographic material from across
the Italian peninsula, specifically on Petrarch and Enea Silvio Piccolomini. He
regarded, in fact, the author of the *Canzoniere* and Pope Pius II as two unparalleled
models of civic virtue. Anastagi's manuscript writings were gathered together with
a group of four other manuscripts of academic lectures on Petrarch's poems from
the Insensati. The resulting five manuscripts (I 49, I 50, I 53, I 55, I 60) made a
significant and cohesive addition of Perugian documents to the Museo Petrarchesco
that Rossetti was setting up in Trieste.[7] They were grouped together by Rossetti

7   On Rossetti and the establishment of his Museo in Trieste see Stefano Zamponi, 'Introduzione',
in *I manoscritti petrarcheschi*, pp. 3–37; Carlo Dionisotti, *Petrarca, Rossetti e Hortis* [1987], in Carlo

under the incorrect label 'Manoscritti degli Accademici Insensati' [Manuscripts of the members of the Insensati].

Based on what is known to date, there is in fact no evidence of Anastagi's admission to this academy. Rossetti's mistake can be, however, easily explained by his — and our — lack of knowledge about Anastagi's life. Born in Perugia in 1536 or in 1539,[8] Anastagi was a productive man of letters. However, as his literary output is almost exclusively in manuscript form, his name remains largely obscure today. During his lifetime he only published the *Proverbi toscani* in 1590, a collection of proverbs that illustrate practical matters of ethics.[9] The most important piece of information about his life is the donation of books to the nascent public library that he arranged for in 1590. Amounting to twenty-four volumes, this collection includes the works of Plato and Aristotle, the comedies of Aristophanes and Terence, the orations of Demosthenes and Isocrates and other classical works.[10] He died in Perugia in 1601.

4. The First Writing: *Diversità del Petrarca e del Boccaccio*

The title of the first writing, *Diversità del Petrarca e del Boccaccio nell'uso di molte voci*, can be translated as *Differences between Petrarch and Boccaccio in the Usage of Many Words*. Despite the lack of a specific date for its composition, scattered references to Girolamo Ruscelli's *De' commentarii della lingua italiana* allow us to consider the *Diversità* posterior to the posthumous publication in 1581 of Ruscelli's work.[11] As

Dionisotti, *Ricordi della scuola italiana* (Rome: Edizioni di Storia e Letteratura, 1998), pp. 165–78; Simone Volpato, *Petrarca, Winckelmann, Trieste e la Patria del Friuli. La biblioteca di Domenico Rossetti* (Udine: Del Bianco, 2010).

8   In the nineteenth century Arrigo Arrighi records Anastagi's name among the baptized of the church of Santa Maria della Misericordia of Perugia in 1536. This piece of information, for which I thank Francesca Grauso, is found in Arrigo Arrighi and Antonio Brizi, *Memorie delle famiglie perugine*, Perugia, Biblioteca Augusta, MS 1548, fol. 136[v]. At fol. 141[r] of the same MS, though, Anastagi is said to be born in 1539 on the basis of a sixteenth-century manuscript *Libro di memorie* by Pompeo Barzi. Similarly, Giovan Battista Vermiglioli sets Anastagi's date of birth in 1539 without declaring his source: *Biografia degli scrittori perugini e notizia delle opere loro*, 2 vols (Perugia: Bartelli e Constantini, 1828–29), I, 40.

9   The only available information on Anastagi's life and works is provided by aforementioned Vermiglioli, *Biografia degli scrittori perugini*, I, 40–41. Anastagi's literary output includes a small series of poems published in the nineteenth century as *nuptialia* (*Agille ninfa del Trasimeno* (Perugia: Garbinesi e Santucci, 1827); *L'Endimione* (Perugia: Santucci, 1833); *Orazione in lode di Astorre Baglioni* (Perugia: Bartelli, 1848), numerous unpublished writings and an extensive commentary on Petrarch's *RVF* and *Triumphi*, entitled *I giorni estivi*, kept in manuscript form in Perugia (Biblioteca Augusta, MS B 24) and in Bologna (Biblioteca Universitaria, MS 2451). A substantial collection of his writings, entitled *Opere toscane*, deals mostly with grammar topics. It is kept in manuscript form in the Archivio Storico dell'Università di Perugia (MS PI III 37). On the Anastagi family see Erminia Irace, *La nobiltà bifronte. Identità e coscienza aristocratica a Perugia tra XVI e XVII secolo* (Milan: Unicopli, 1995), pp. 35, 135–36.

10   The list of these volumes is included in the MS 3081 of the Biblioteca Augusta of Perugia, fol. 97[r]; the act of donation is also registered in Giovanni Cecchini, *La Biblioteca Augusta del Comune di Perugia* (Rome: Edizioni di Storia e Letteratura, 1978), pp. 139, 465–66. On the shaping of the Biblioteca Augusta of Perugia see Maria Alessandra Panzanelli Fratoni, 'Prospero Podiani (1535–1615) and the Foundation of a City Library', *Italian Studies Library Group Bulletin*, 10–11 (2012), 36–42.

11   A modern edition of this work has recently been published: Girolamo Ruscelli, *De' Commentarii*

with the latter, Anastagi's piece of writing was not intended to be read aloud; on the contrary, it was designed to serve as a reference work for aspiring writers and composers. It belonged to that set of selected authors' lexicons that spread throughout the sixteenth-century Italian peninsula as a consequence of Pietro Bembo's impact on the literary canon. Following the establishment, in his 1525 *Prose della volgar lingua* (*Prose on the vernacular language*), of Petrarch and Boccaccio as the undisputed models for poetry and prose respectively, numerous linguistic and literary theorists compiled lists of words used by the aforementioned (and a few other select) authors in their works. This tradition of lexicons and vocabularies can be traced back to Niccolò Liburnio, *Le tre fontane* (*The Three Fountains*, 1526). Following the form of Bembo's solution, notwithstanding a certain degree of variation, Liburnio's work provides a clear distinction between poetic and prose-like language and expands the canon to include Dante's literary output, partially objected to by Bembo. In the twenty years following the publication of Liburnio's *Tre fontane*, a series of similar works emerged, written by authors in many different parts of Italy. Unsurprisingly, the majority of these works limited themselves to Petrarch and Boccaccio. Within this tradition of lexicons, we can cite Lucilio Minerbi's *Vocabolario boccaccesco* (*Vocabulary of Words from Boccaccio's Works*, 1535) and Francesco Alunno's works, such as the *Osservazioni sopra il Petrarca* (*Observations on Petrarch*, 1539 and 1550, second revised edition) and the *Ricchezze della lingua volgare sopra il Boccaccio* (*Treasures of vernacular language in Boccaccio*, 1543).[12] Another work, which may have influenced Anastagi's *Diversità*, is Francesco Sansovino's *Ortografia delle voci della lingua nostra* (*Spelling of the Words of our Language*, 1568), which consists of a long series of vernacular headwords taken from the 'perfetti e antichi maestri di bella scrittura' [great and ancient masters of good writing] (fol. 2ᵣ). In the dedication to his son, Sansovino celebrates the key role played by orthography in convincingly conveying ideas.[13]

Quite surprisingly, the theoretical framework provided by Anastagi in the *Diversità* for a work on the vernacular language does not include any contemporary theorists and is based instead on classical authors. Quoting Varro in a passage from Aulus Gellius's *Attic Nights*, Anastagi first establishes that 'usanza' [custom] is the principle that governs language.[14] As a consequence, aspiring writers should observe and follow the habits of the best authors, namely Petrarch and Boccaccio. Secondly, quoting Varro again, Anastagi stresses the need for amateur writers to distinguish the language of prose from that of poetry and vice versa.[15] Such a difference,

della lingua italiana, ed. by Chiara Gizzi, 2 vols (Manziana: Vecchiarelli, 2016).

12   On Italian lexicography see Valeria Della Valle, 'Lessicografia', in *Storia della lingua italiana*, ed. by Luca Serianni and Pietro Trifone, 3 vols (Turin: Einaudi, 1993), I: *I luoghi della codificazione*, pp. 29–91.

13   On the development of early modern Italian orthography see Andreas Michel, 'Italian orthographies in Early Modern times', in *Orthographies in Early Modern Europe*, ed. by Susan Baddeley and Anja Voeste (Berlin: De Gruyter Mouton, 2012), pp. 63–96.

14   'M. Varronis liber ad Ciceronem *De Lingua Latina* octavus nullam esse observationem similium docet inque omnibus paene verbis consuetudinem dominari ostendit': Gel. II. 25.

15   In the passage recalled by Anastagi, Varro as a prose writer states that one should at the same time both enjoy and avoid poetic words: 'Poeticis multis verbis magis delector quam utor'. It is again — as Anastagi himself declares — an indirect quotation: Pietro Crinito [Pietro Baldi], *De honesta*

though, does not lie in a series of stylistic preferences but rather in the choice of the most appropriate form for a word in prose and in poetry. Consideration of these two principles suggests Anastagi's debt to Bembo's *Prose*, curiously not quoted. As is well known, Bembo had not only crafted his model for prose on the example of Boccaccio and for poetry on that of Petrarch, but he had also insisted in his *Prose* on distinguishing prose from poetry.

Anastagi's writing displays a long series of variants of words taken from Petrarch's and Boccaccio's works. These selected words appear in alphabetical order, ranging from *Armelino* [*ermine*] to *Vinegia* [*Venice*] and embracing different parts of speech, such as verbs, nouns, adjectives, etc.[16] Each analysed 'voce' is signaled by a decoration similar to braces. Although the total number of flagged words amounts to 182, it is more correct to state that this number refers to the headwords which may sit above one or more derivative words. Such is the case, amongst others, for the entry *ufficio* under which is listed also *ufficiale* (fol. 23^v). All the words are presented first in the form used in poetry and are then compared to the form employed in prose. The words are subsequently followed by a few quotations, mostly from Petrarch's and Boccaccio's principal works. When quotations from their works are not available, Anastagi includes citations from, among others, Dante, Jacopo Sannazaro, Giovanni Della Casa, Domenico Venier, and Pietro Bembo himself, thus expanding his canon to include other (Petrarchist) writers.[17] Even slight differences in the form of words are emphasized, such as in the following example of the word *Occulto* [hidden/concealed]:

> *Occulto* per *o* davanti alla *l* usa il Petrarca sempre ne' testi migliori:
> 'Ch'ogni occolto pensiero tira in mezo la fronte' (Canzone 'I' vo pensando')
> *Occulto* per *u* sempre ho letto nel Boccaccio se a le scritture diamo fede:
> 'Perciò che quello ne è occulto' (Giornata I novella I).
> 'Da lei secondo il suo occulto guidicio' (Giornata I novella 3).[18] (fol. 24^r)

This pattern of comparison through pairs of quotations runs throughout Anastagi's lecture for each of the analysed terms. In the very brief concluding paragraph, Anastagi declares neither his criteria for the choice of words nor his preference as to the spelling of vernacular words. By contrast, he stresses the usefulness of this list, showing his pride in completing a work of this type.

---

disciplina libri 25 (Basel: Petri, 1532), p. 316.

16   The words on which Anastagi's attention focuses will be written, henceforth, in italics.

17   On the Petrarchist element of Sannazaro's and Della Casa's poetry see, among others, Stefano Jossa, 'Bembo and the Italian Petrarchism', in *The Cambridge Companion to Petrarch*, ed. by Albert Russell Ascoli and Unn Falkeid (Cambridge: Cambridge University Press, 2015), pp. 199–210; on Domenico Venier see Armando Balduino, 'Petrarchismo veneto e tradizione manoscritta', in *Petrarca, Venezia e il Veneto*, ed. by Giorgio Padoan (Florence: Olschki, 1976), pp. 243–70.

18   'In the best texts, Petrarch always uses *Occolto* with an *o* before the *l*: "Ch'ogni occolto pensiero tira in mezo la fronte" (*Canzone* "I' vo pensando"). I have always read *Occulto* with a *u* in Boccaccio, if we trust the texts: "Perciò che quello ne è occulto" (Day I novella 1). "Da lei secondo il suo occulto guidicio" (Day I novella 3)'. Given the importance of spelling variants in Anastagi's thought, the criteria for transcription have been conservative. I have only changed *et* to *e/ed*, simplified *j* and *ij* to *i*, and distinguished *u* from *v*. I have also modernized punctuation, accents, and capitalization to conform to modern usage. In case of multiple quotations from the same primary source, references are given in the text, in brackets, in order to limit the number of footnotes.

5. The Second Writing: *Dialogo sopra il primo sonetto*

The following *Dialogo sopra il primo sonetto del Petrarca* (*Dialogue on Petrarch's First Sonnet*) focuses on the opening poem of the *Canzoniere*. In the exordium of the dialogue, Anastagi once more makes reference to classical authorities to justify his mode of exposition. Anastagi looks for the most suitable methodological approach to apply to Petrarch among the ones adopted by Virgil's commentators. Anastagi's selection of critical models evidently stems from the implicit assumption that Petrarch is comparable (if not corresponding) to Virgil and therefore worthy to be treated as his vernacular equivalent. After rejecting Maurus Servius Honoratus's 'diviso' [order] and Tiberius Claudius Donatus's 'maniera parafrastica' [paraphrastic method],[19] Anastagi finally decides to illustrate the poem 'sotto lo stile di Prisciano' [following the style of Priscian] (fol. 41^r).

As his eighteen volume *Institutiones grammaticae* (*Grammatical Institution*) had been the standard textbook for the study of Latin grammar throughout the Middle Ages, the reference to the Latin of Priscian reveals the grammatical and linguistic focus of the *Dialogo*. Furthermore, the mention of Priscian's 'style' also suggests, more precisely, the application of a specific pedagogical approach to the Petrarchan sonnet. Quite surprisingly, Anastagi does not seem to follow the systematic exposition of the monumental *Institutiones*;[20] instead, he adopts the dialogic teaching style Priscian had employed in one of his other works, the *Partitiones*. In this grammatical treatise, Priscian analyses, in question and answer form, every word of the first few lines of each book of the *Aeneid*.[21]

In the same vein, Anastagi's second piece is structured as a dialogue. During the long conversation, developed as a master-student relationship, the elder Filoreto clears up the doubts of his younger friend Scipione concerning the grammatical aspects of the sonnet.[22] The setting is almost entirely unspecified. Only in the last scene, Anastagi informs us that the two speakers finally arrive in a central square of an unnamed city while the sun is sinking behind the mountains of Spain.

---

19   As Anastagi declares in this passage, he had already adopted the method of Servius 'già molti anni' [several years ago] at the time when he presented the sonnet 'Passa la nave mia colma d'oblio'. This sonnet is the subject of the fourth writing of the current manuscript. The time indication reveals that the order of the writings in the manuscript does not correspond to the chronological order of their composition.

20   On the *Institutiones grammaticae* see for instance Rita Copeland and Ineke Sluiter, 'Priscian, *Institutiones grammaticae* and *Institutio de Nomine Pronomine Verbo*, ca. 520', in *Medieval Grammar and Rhetoric: Language Arts and Literary Theory*, ed. by Rita Copeland and Ineke Sluiter (Oxford: Oxford University Press, 2009), pp. 376–89.

21   For an overview of *Partitiones*'s codices in the Renaissance and Middle Ages see Marina Passalacqua, 'Le *Partitiones* di Prisciano nella tradizione medievale e umanistica', in *Mousa. Scritti in onore di Giuseppe Morelli* (Bologna: Pàtron, 1997), pp. 371–80. On the revival of the dialogical form in teaching grammar after the rediscovery of Priscian during the Middle Ages, see Federica Ciccolella, '*Donati Graeci*'. *Learning Greek in the Renaissance* (Leiden; Boston: Brill, 2008), p. 15.

22   Although the name of Filareto or Philaretus, which can be linked to the homonymous academy founded in Ferrara in 1554, to the Florentine architect and sculptor Filarete, or even to the Byzantine urologist Theophilus Protospatharius, is far more evocative and meaningful than Filoreto, the handwriting does not seem to support this hypothesis.

This conversational pattern recurs throughout the entire text: Scipione keeps asking Filoreto very precise and straightforward questions about specific words or phrases in each line of Petrarch's sonnet. Most of the questions raised by Scipione, following the model of the *Partititiones*, address very basic features of the vernacular language and often introduce a comparison with Latin. With regard to the first line 'Voi ch'ascoltate in rime sparse il suono', for instance, Scipione asks '*Voi* che parte è dell'oratione?' [what part of the speech is *voi* (the second-person plural)?], and then asks '*Che* appresso che cosa è?' [what is the following *che* (that or which)]? (fol. 42ᵛ). Patiently, Filoreto explains that the former is a 'pronome primitivo' [primitive pronoun], a definition presumably derived from Gian Giorgio Trissino's *Grammatichetta*,[23] and that *che* is a relative pronoun. Addressing then the following line 'di quei sospiri ond'io nudriva 'l core', at the request of Scipione, the teacher Filoreto explains that '*di*' [of] is used to form the genitive case and that in Latin the endings of words — and not prepositions — mark the different cases.

Filoreto only occasionally illustrates the actual meaning of certain terms, generally starting from their grammatical value. Considering the word '*stile*' [style] of line 5, 'del vario stile in ch'io piango et ragiono', the teacher first specifies that it is a 'nome sostantivo' [a noun] and then that it means here 'maniera di parlare' [way of speaking], but in other contexts it can mean the 'stilo de' pittori' [painters' style] and even 'costume o usanza' [custom or habit]. The explanations provided of the meaning of the words in the on-going conversation seem to be oriented solely to facilitate the basic understanding of the sonnet. Filoreto limits himself to a strictly lexical investigation and refuses to examine in depth abstract and theoretical concepts. This is certainly the case for the term *speranze* of l. 6, 'fra le vane speranze e 'l van dolore'. Filoreto briefly defines the concept of *speranza* [hope] as 'espettatione di bene' [anticipation of good things], if intended philosophically, or, more ordinarily, as 'openione di cose future' [thought of future things]; then, he simply ends his explanation. Commenting on his own evident reluctance, Filoreto claims that he wants to avoid vainglory and that he prefers to leave philosophy to Varchi and other scholars.

On a few distinct occasions, Filoreto expands his didactic grammatical analysis to include the main figures of speech present in the sonnet. Analysing the word *mondo* in the last line, which reads 'che quanto piace al mondo è breve sogno', Filoreto explains that it is being used as a metonymy and correctly defines it as a means to access the content by using the container. So here *mondo* actually refers to its content, 'uomini' or humans, the broadest audience for Petrarch's lyrics.

6. The Fifth Writing: *Discorso sopra quel sonetto del Petrarca 'Se Virgilio e Homero havessin visto'*

The last two writings in the manuscript are dedicated to Francesco Maria del Monte (1549–1626), who is known today mainly for his early patronage of Caravaggio. Born to an aristocratic family in Venice, he embarked on a successful

---

23   Gian Giorgio Trissino, *Grammatichetta* (Vicenza: Ianiculo, 1529), fol. c5. This definition is not present anywhere in Bembo's *Prose*.

ecclesiastical career. Appointed as auditor for Cardinal Alessandro Sforza, by 1580 he was made referendary of the Tribunals of the Apostolic Signature of Justice and of Grace. On 14 December 1588, he was then created cardinal by Pope Sixtus V.[24] The two writings by Anastagi reached him before this date as in the inscription he is still called simply 'Monsignor'. The young prelate would probably have derived just a brief moment of pleasure from reading Anastagi's *Discorso sopra la canzone del Petrarca 'Ne la stagion che 'l ciel rapido inchina'* (Discourse on Petrarch's Canzone 'Ne la stagion che 'l ciel rapido inchina'). In this exposition, by far the shortest of the collection, Anastagi states that he will be arguing 'come parafrasta' [as a paraphraser] (fol. 86ʳ). Composed of only three folios, this *Discorso* does not consider any aspect of the author's language or style and turns out, in fact, to consist of an elegant paraphrase of the *canzone*. Anastagi's literary piece does not just simply clarify the literal meaning of Petrarch's poem but also rivals it to some degree by means of emulation.

Anastagi's fifth piece, the *Discorso sopra quel sonetto del Petrarca 'Se Virgilio e Homero havessin visto'* [Discourse on Petrarch's sonnet 'Se Virgilio e Homero havessin visto'] is a vast composition written in the form of a dialogue. Unlike the previous example of the second dialogue, though, the interlocutors engaged in conversation are real figures and the social setting is clearly specified, as is the occasion of the discussion. Anastagi in fact declares himself to be restaging a dispute on the sonnet *RVF* 186 that took place some months previously 'in accademia' [in the academy] between Ludovico Sensi (1509–79) and Ludovico De Torres (1551–1609). The former, born in Perugia, was a jurist and canon who took part in both the Accademia degli Insensati and the Eccentrici. The latter moved to Perugia in 1567 to study law at the local university and later served as archbishop of Monreale in Sicily. He was named cardinal in 1606 by Pope Paul V.[25] Although Anastagi does not specify the academy by name, it is safe to say that the dispute took place (or was thought by the author to have taken place) in the Accademia degli Eccentrici, to which the same Anastagi, De Torres, and Sensi all belonged. Furthermore, it is possible to date the debate and the resulting composition of the *Dialogo* to the '70s of the *Cinquecento*, in particular to the first half of that decade: De Torres left Perugia by 1574 and Sensi died in November 1579. There would have been no point in writing it after De Torres's departure since 'a mention in a dialogue brought publicity and honour' for the interlocutors and likely 'tangible rewards' for the author to enjoy.[26]

24   On the Venetian cardinal, see Victor Ivo Comparato, 'Bourbon Del Monte, Francesco Maria', in *Dizionario biografico degli italiani* (Rome: Istituto dell'Enciclopedia Treccani, 1960–), XIII (1971), 523–24; Franca Trinchieri Camiz, 'Music and Painting in Cardinal del Monte's Household', *Metropolitan Museum Journal*, 26 (1991), 213–26; Zygmunt Wazbinski, *Il cardinale Francesco Maria Del Monte (1549–1626)*, 2 vols (Florence: Olschki, 1994); Laura Teza, *Caravaggio e il frutto della virtù: il Mondafrutto e l'Accademia degli Insensati* (Milan: Electa, [2013]), pp. 17, 26, 49, 85.

25   On Sensi see Vincenzo Cavallucci, 'Vita di Ludovico Sensi', in *Rime di messer Ludovico Sensi giureconsulto Perugino*, ed. by Id. (Perugia: Constantini, 1772), pp. vii–xxvii, whose information has been partly rectified by Vermiglioli, *Biografia degli scrittori perugini*, II, 285–87. On De Torres see Pietro Messina, 'De Torres, Ludovico', in *Dizionario biografico degli italiani*, xxxix (1993), 480–83.

26   Virginia Cox, *The Renaissance Dialogue. Literary dialogue in its social and political contexts, Castiglione to Galileo* (Cambridge: Cambridge University Press, 1992), p. 35.

The discussion in the fifth *Discorso* originates from two objections that De Torres made against Petrarch. The first deals with plausibility; the second with literary style. Firstly, De Torres defines Laura's beauty as superlative and therefore not in need of, nor indeed capable of, being increased by the praise of the greatest poets, not even Homer or Virgil. Secondly, Petrarch errs in allocating to heroic poets a subject that belongs to lyric poets, namely, love. De Torres's critique is challenged by Sensi, who is willing to defend Petrarch and 'la verità' [the truth] (fol. 93ʳ). Anastagi provides a brief and vivid description of him while he is taking the floor. As would a modern novelist, Anastagi shows Sensi indulging in a contemplative moment ('un pochetto sopra di sé pensoso' [very pensive for a while]) and then starting to reply 'con lieto viso, riguardando il signor Torres' [with a halcyon face, staring at Torres] (fol. 92ᵛ). In his prolonged response, Sensi addresses the two questions of Laura's beauty and the adequacy of the literary style. With regards to the former, Sensi declares that her beauty would have remained concealed had it not been praised and celebrated by Petrarch. Even if something is flawless, it would be lost if not socially and universally recognized as such:

> Le cose, avenga che perfette sieno, se elle dalla fama divolgatrice dell'altrui grandezza illustrate e divolgate non sono, possono dirsi essere apunto come i marmi non politi, come le gioie inviluppate nel fango.[27] (fol. 93ᵛ)

Sensi then makes a parallel with the situation described in *RVF* 187, in which Alexander the Great, standing in front of the tomb of Achilles, calls the Greek hero 'fortunato' [fortunate] for having been celebrated by Homer.

He then sets about rejecting the second part of Torres's argumentation, on the basis of two main reasons. Firstly, he states that the two great poets were, in theory, more than capable of expressing lyrical subjects. This is proved by Martial's epigram 'Si tua, Cerrini, promas epigrammata vulgo' [Cerrinius if you (were to give) your epigram to the public], where Virgil is said to have been potentially superior to other Roman composers of *carmina* if he had only tried. The second reason rests on the authority of Virgil himself. Though Sensi concedes that Homer and Virgil were more inclined to heroic poetry, he reminds us — recalling a line from Virgil's tenth eclogue — that love conquers all ('omnia vincit Amor'). In this case, Sensi argues, even Virgil and Homer would have been conquered by love for Laura and would have then combined the lyric and heroic styles:

> [I due poeti] havrieno [...] mescolato l'uno stile con l'altro, ciò è la grandezza eroica e 'l decoro con la piacevolezza ed eleganza lirica, e la divina e larga abondanza di Omero con la tersa, ristretta e adorna maestà di Vergilio.[28] (fol. 95ʳ)

In light of Sensi's words, any potential reason to disapprove of Petrarch vanishes. Even De Torres declares himself 'soddisfatto' [satisfied] and 'lieto' [relieved] at

---

27 'Even when things are perfect, if they are not illustrated and made known by broadcasting their fame and others' greatness, they can be said to be like unpolished marble, like jewels coated in mud'.
28 '[The two poets] would have [...] merged one style into the other, that is, heroic greatness and decorum with lyric pleasantness and grace; the divine and broad abundance of Homer with the terse, restrained and adorned solemnity of Virgil'.

having finally learned the truth. Torres and Sensi finally fall silent, ready to listen to another academician who — in the fiction of the academic setting — was about to speak from the podium.

7. Conclusions

Three key aspects of Anastagi's writings may trigger interesting lines of enquiry for further research on Petrarch's reception in Italy and in Europe during the early modern period.

Firstly, we should consider the literary form of the writings. It will have been noted that Anastagi's collection of writings is clearly marked by a great variety of forms: the first *Diversità* is structured as a long list of words, the second and the fifth pieces are dialogues, and the fourth is a paraphrase. In the third lecture — not analysed here — Anastagi undertakes the interpretation of the sonnet 'Passa la nave mia colma d'oblio' 'sotto il diviso di una maniera non ancora da toscani [...] usata' [through an approach not yet adopted [...] by Tuscans] (fol. 64ʳ). It implies a biographical sketch of the author,[29] a brief description of the verse form, the illustration of the poet's intention, the paraphrase, and the declaration of the sonnet (which, in turn, includes the analysis of rhetorical elements and the explanation of its figurative meanings). As a matter of fact, this expository technique used by Anastagi is very commonly found in the great majority of *Cinquecento* academic lectures on Petrarch. The Insensati's and Infiammati's lectures, for instance, present similar sections dedicated to declaring the poet's intention, to paraphrasing the poetry, and to discussing obscure meanings as well as ethical and philosophical matters stemming from the sonnet. The well-established structure of this *Lettione* adds to the overall significant variation expressed in this collection of writings. Anastagi's writings explore new possibilities in the shape of expositions of Petrarch's sonnets, elaborating new forms that cross the traditional modes of academic exegesis on Petrarch.

Secondly, Anastagi's analysed writings reveal a marked preference for classical theorists and authors over contemporary literary critics. As has been shown, an early passage of the *Diversità* recalls Marcus Terentius Varro, Anastagi's second piece is structured according to Priscian's theories, and his fifth *Discorso* is centered on a sonnet that celebrates the classical poets Homer and Virgil. We may therefore conclude that Anastagi adopted methodologies from the Classics and merged ancient doctrines with the ideas of contemporary theorists (above all Bembo and Ruscelli). In the wider context of the reception of Petrarch, we may wonder what kind of influence classical grammarians and theorists had on this phenomenon and how, and to what extent, their theories interacted with modern ideas.

Lastly, we should concentrate on the audience targeted by the author and its role in the expositions of the sonnets. In the case of Anastagi, the last *Discorso* in

---

29   Surprisingly, Anastagi in this section states that Petrarch was serving Pope John XXIII instead of John XXII in the court of Avignon (*Lettione sopra quel sonetto*, fol. 64ᵛ). This statement is, of course, false as Pope (or better Antipope) John XXIII was inaugurated on 25 May 1410, well after Petrarch's death. Likely, Anastagi was still referring to John XXII, but was misled by the discrepancies in the numbering of the Popes John.

particular, reconstructing an academic debate, reveals the nature of the expected audience for his writings. It appears clear that the (actual or potential) members of the academy constituted the original and ideal recipients of Anastagi's discourses on Petrarch. All the five writings considered here are clearly reader-oriented and are heavily influenced by their expected academic audience. It is no coincidence that each of them (maybe with the exception of the third *Lettione*) shows a clear instrumental nature. Anastagi's last *Discorso*, which deals with interpretation, is oriented towards authorizing Petrarch — to paraphrase the work of William Kennedy[30] — and thereby towards defending his literary authority. The fourth *Discorso* on Petrarch's canzone aims to decipher its literal meaning in the form of paraphrase. The first and second writings intend to provide all the basic tools for aspiring writers who lacked a solid knowledge of Tuscan and Latin grammar and lexicon. The aim of these two writings is to make their recipients familiar with the orthographic and grammatical rules of the Tuscan literary language exemplified by Petrarch's poetry and suggested by Bembo.

This statement invites us to consider once more — and to better delineate — the cultural environment of Perugia that we briefly touched upon at the beginning of this chapter. Within Perugia's literary circles, in fact, in addition to the reading of Petrarch's sonnets, Pietro Bembo's theories also enjoyed wide circulation. However, in a few cases these theories were simplified versions of what Bembo had originally proposed. I am referring particularly to the (still largely unknown) work of poet and Perugian grammarian Vincenzo Menni (1517–70). His *Regole della thoscana lingua* (*Rules of the Tuscan language*, 1568) represents a summary or, rather, a gross simplification of Bembo's *Prose*.[31] Menni attempts to shrink Bembo's rules into a 'brevissimo' [very concise] volume since many people — he declares — find them 'ardue e difficilissime' [arduous and very difficult] to comprehend (fol. 2ᵛ).[32] Menni therefore simplifies them so that even those oblivious to Latin grammar could learn to speak and write 'thoscanamente' [in a Tuscan manner] (fol. 2ᵛ). In accordance with Bembo's preference for Petrarch, Menni lists examples of poetic forms and rhetorical devices almost exclusively from Petrarch's works and deduces his rules concerning poetic language, meter, and verse forms, predominantly from Petrarch's compositions.

The extent of circulation of Menni's theories within the literary circles of Perugia is still to be assessed. Yet, his role as coordinator of literary activity for the Accademia degli Unisoni,[33] as well as the quotations of his *Regole* in a couple of academic lectures delivered by the Insensati, seem to suggest a rather favorable reception.[34] It is beside the point to establish whether there is a direct connection

30   William J. Kennedy, *Authorizing Petrarch* (Ithaca: Cornell University Press, 1994).
31   In addition to the *Regole*, Menni printed a translation of Virgil's *Eclogues*: *Bucolica di Vergilio* (Perugia: Bianchini, 1544) and a partial translation of Virgil's *Aeneid*: *I sei primi libri della 'Eneide' di Virgilio detti in ottava rima da messere Vincenzo Menni perugino* (Perugia: Bresciano, 1567).
32   Vincenzo Menni, *Regole della thoscana lingua* (Perugia: Bresciano, 1568).
33   Irace, 'Le accademie letterarie', p. 174.
34   Anonymous untitled lecture on Petrarch's sonnet 'I begli occhi ond'i' fui percosso in guisa', Trieste, Biblioteca Attilio Hortis, MS I 50, fol. 9ʳ; Contolo Contoli, *Lettione [...] sopra il sonetto del Petrarca 'Amor che 'ncende il cor d'ardente zelo'*, Trieste, Biblioteca Attilio Hortis, MS I 53, fol. 92ᵛ.

between Menni's and Anastagi's works. Rather, it is important to stress and explain their similarities. Anastagi's collection of writings appears as a practical development of the principles found in Menni's volume. The two works even display some common elements, both of them, indeed, presenting a catalogue of variants used by Petrarch and Boccaccio. These similarities reveal that the two works share the same audience of aspiring writers. Their ideal recipient is, once more, a person of literary pursuits, wishing to attain the rather vague status of *literato*, and neither a prominent humanist wishing to show his/her refined erudition nor a humanist courtier. The diffusion of Anastagi's and Menni's writings and other similar works in academic milieus invites us to carefully consider (or re-consider) the actual means of dissemination in specific environments, such as the academies, of the most important works of so-called 'high' culture. In other words, when addressing the reception of Petrarch's poetry within the fragmented Italian literary society of the *Cinquecento*, we should consider the influence exerted on this phenomenon by minor, and today often overlooked, works.

CHAPTER 7

Deconstructing Petrarch:
Alessandro Tassoni's
Considerazioni sopra le Rime del Petrarca[1]

Andrea Lazzarini

When the *Considerazioni sopra le Rime del Petrarca* first appeared in print during the early days of 1609, Tassoni was nearly forty-four years old.[2] Since the end of 1607, he had resided permanently in Modena, having been detained there by the disposition of uncomfortable legal matters (first and foremost, there was the question of the validity of his son Marzio's succession).[3] Tassoni had recently moved on from an unhappy experience at court and had just one publication to his name, the *Quisiti* (1608), an early seed of a far more ambitious project: the *Pensieri*.

May of 1608 was marked by the departure of Ascanio Colonna, who Tassoni had accompanied to Spain between 1600 and 1603 (with a brief return to Italy in the course of 1602).[4] The relations between Tassoni and Colonna were interrupted during the second half of 1603, at exactly the moment when Alessandro — having definitively re-established himself in Rome after some exhausting back-and-forth travels between Spain and Italy — took on the role of 'assistant' to Costanza, the daughter of the Cardinal (who had recently become the viceroy of Aragon). Tassoni also became Costanza's 'secretary and general agent regarding all her matters in Italy'. But events soon took an entirely different turn:

> mentre che 'l Tassoni era intento a dar sodisfazioni alli creditori e già in 3
> mesi aveva pagati ventidue milia scudi di debiti e le cose cominciavano a

1   This essay offers a preview of a few of the critical results of a larger work, recently published as *'Pazza cosa sarebbe la poesia'. Alessandro Tassoni lettore del Trecento fra Barocco ed Età muratoriana* (Modena: Franco Cosimo Panini, 2020).
2   Alessandro Tassoni, *Considerazioni sopra le Rime del Petrarca [...]* (Modena: Giuliano Cassiani, 1609).
3   A special thank you goes to Grazia Biondi who, with her customary generosity, pointed me in the direction of the contents of a document at the State Archive of Modena (Archivio notarile, Busta 2552, inserto F): '1607 et 1608. Pro Illustri domino Alexandro de Tassonis, cum Illustri Domino Nicolao pariter de Tassonis, et omnibus aliis sua quomodolibet interesse putantibus. Copia processus coram Perillustri Domino Praetori Mutinae. Rogato Marcho Sighizzi, notario Mutinae'.
4   For a discussion of this period of Tassoni's life, see Girolamo de Miranda, 'Alessandro Tassoni tra Virginio Orsini e Ascanio Colonna', *Filologia e Critica*, 17 (1992), 88–99 (pp. 92–99).

pigliar qualche forma, eccoti arrivar lettere di Spagna del Cardinale, nelle quali dichiarava che non voleva più servirsi né di esso né di sua sorella, e quando era più in termine che mai di poter sperar qualche premio delle fatiche sue, lo lasciò su l'asciutto. *Così fortuna va cangiando stato!*[5]

So ended Tassoni's *Relazione sopra l'andata del cardinal Ascanio Colonna in Ispagna*, written in 1613. Ten years after the events, Tassoni was able to reflect on his own misfortunes with some sort of ironic detachment, even citing at the end of his booklet some verses from Cesare Caporali's *Capitolo della Corte*.[6] But the abrupt dismissal was still quite a blow for the ex-secretary, and he was not left without hard feelings: in 1606, in the middle of the crisis of the Venetian Interdict, Tassoni, who was by all accounts driven by an unresolved animosity, anonymously authored a polemic response to Colonna's *Contra Reip[ublicae]Venetae episcopos sententia* (the *Pro Reipublicae Venetae episcopis ad S. D. N. Paulum V apologia*).[7] It is during this turbulent span of years that the *Considerazioni sopra le Rime del Petrarca* were written.

The *Considerazioni*, which sparked one of the most famous literary debates of the early 1600s,[8] were brought to prominence again in 1711 by Ludovico Antonio Muratori along with a highly successful edition of the *Rime di Francesco Petrarca*. Muratori tacked on his own *Osservazioni*, thus ensuring Tassoni's commentary more than two centuries of popularity, as demonstrated through the widespread (though not always explicitly acknowledged) reusage of his interpretative solutions by eighteenth- and nineteenth-century commentators.[9]

But in addition to the significance of the *Considerazioni* in the history of the commentaries on Petrarch, Tassoni's notes on the *Canzoniere* and the *Trionfi* constitute — in and of themselves — a literary and critical undertaking of considerable complexity, the results of which are, at times, somewhat unsettling. Tassoni's work

---

5   Alessandro Tassoni, 'Relazione sopra l'andata del cardinal Ascanio Colonna in Ispagna' [1613], in Alessandro Tassoni, *Annali e scritti storici e politici*, ed. by Pietro Puliatti, 2 vols (Modena: Panini, 1990–1993), I, 176–200 (p. 199): 'while Tassoni was intent on satisfying creditors and, in only three months, he had paid twenty-two thousand *scudi* in debts and the situation began getting clearer, there arrived some letters sent from Spain by the Cardinal, in which he declared that he did not want to employ either him or his sister anymore; and when Tassoni was nearer than ever before to obtaining some gratification for his labors, the Cardinal left him empty-handed'.

6   Cesare Caporali, 'La Corte. Parte Prima', l. 300, in Cesare Caporali, *Capitoli*, ed. by Danilo Romei, <http://www.nuovorinascimento.org/n-rinasc/testi/pdf/caporali/capitoli.pdf> [accessed 25 April 2019]. On the importance of Caporali for Tassoni's work, see Guido Arbizzoni, '"Poema misto nuovo e secondo arte": l'eroicomico secentesco', in *Gli 'irregolari' nella letteratura. Atti del Convegno di Catania (31 ottobre–2 novembre 2005)* (Rome: Salerno, 2007), pp. 193–224 (p. 214).

7   Ascanio's pamphlet and Tassoni's response were published by Puliatti in Tassoni, *Annali e scritti storici e politici*, I, 145–64.

8   See Antonio Daniele, '"Una pura disputa di cose poetiche, senza rancore di sorte alcuna". Alessandro Tassoni, Cesare Cremonini e Giuseppe degli Aromatari', in *Cesare Cremonini. Aspetti del pensiero e scritti, I: Il pensiero. Atti del Convegno di studio (Padova, 26–27 febbraio 1999)*, ed. by Ezio Riondato and Antonino Poppi (Padua: Accademia Galileiana di Scienze, Lettere ed Arti, 2000), pp. 19–41; later in Antonio Daniele, *La memoria innamorata. Indagini e letture petrarchesche* (Rome; Padua: Antenore 2005), pp. 219–47.

9   See Mario Pazzaglia, 'Il commento ai *Rerum Vulgarium Fragmenta* petrarcheschi di Alessandro Tassoni', *Studi e problemi di critica testuale*, 64 (2007), 117–40 (pp. 117–22; addressing the influence of the *Considerazioni* on the Carducci-Ferrari edition).

does not offer a commentary on the vernacular works of Petrarch in the true or traditional sense of the word; instead, it consists of a bare series of annotations in which erudite investigations and interpretations are mixed with cutting, irreverent assessments of the *Canzoniere*'s style and content in addition to other kinds of observations that were entirely beyond the scope of traditional commentary. According to Tassoni, these critiques of Petrarch, the 'principe de' melici' [Prince of the Melic Poets], were meant to be functional in nature: they were intended, in other words, to criticize the kind of slavish imitation of the *Canzoniere* affirmed in the Petrarchist experience. As we shall soon see, however, the implications of Tassoni's critical discourse have a still more radical relevance.

1. The Three Editorial Phases

We currently possess attested versions corresponding to three distinct editorial phases of the work. These are, in order: 1) a version from a manuscript that had long been kept at the Collegio San Carlo in Modena and is now held at the Biblioteca Estense Universitaria (MS Dep. Coll. S. Carlo 3); 2) a print version, from types by Giuliano Cassiani, which dates to 1609; 3) a copy of the 1609 edition with notes by the author, which is likewise available at the Estense (α.S.2.10 = It. 1228). The conservation of these documents enables us to reconstruct much of the work's compositional process.

It is to Orazio Bacci that we owe the first historical-critical overview of the *Considerazioni*.[10] Bacci's booklet is surprising both in terms of the solid erudition that informs it, and because of its use of positive data, which is skillfully deployed to combat judgments based on critical prejudice or taste. In fact, Bacci is the first and last critic to have attempted a study of the work that maintains an awareness of its diachronic development.

The San Carlo 3 manuscript has been, until now, the object of the only preliminary survey carried out by Bacci; in the twentieth century, the only ones to interest themselves in the manuscript text of the *Considerazioni* were Bertoni and Debenedetti, two renowned scholars of Romance Philology, who were drawn by the presence of Provençal citations issuing from the codex that belonged to Giovan Maria Barbieri and later to his son Ludovico.[11]

10   Orazio Bacci, *Le Considerazioni sopra le Rime del Petrarca di Alessandro Tassoni* (Florence: Loescher and Seber, 1887).
11   Giulio Bertoni, 'Noterelle provenzali. VII. Quale manoscritto provenzale ebbe tra mano il Tassoni per la prima redazione delle "Considerazioni sul Petrarca"?', *Revue des langues romanes*, 67 (1904), 156–58; Giulio Bertoni, 'Attorno ad alcune citazioni provenzali e a una grammatichetta francese di Alessandro Tassoni', in *Miscellanea tassoniana di studi storici e letterari [...]*, ed. by Tommaso Casini and Venceslao Santi, with a preface by Giovanni Pascoli (Bologna-Modena: Formiggini, 1908), pp. 267–76 (pp. 270–71 and notes); Santorre Debenedetti, *Gli studi provenzali in Italia nel Cinquecento* (Turin: Loescher, 1911), p. 231, now reprinted in Santorre Debenedetti, *Gli studi provenzali in Italia nel Cinquecento e Tre secoli di studi provenzali*, ed. by Cesare Segre (Padua: Antenore, 1995); Marco Boni, 'Le citazioni sordelliane delle *Considerazioni sopra le rime del Petrarca* di Alessandro Tassoni', *Siculorum Gymnasium*, 8 (1955), 352–61; Maria Careri, 'Per la ricostruzione del Libre di Miquel de la Tor. Studio e presentazione delle fonti', *Cultura neolatina*, 66 (1996), 251–408 (pp. 309–19).

There is evidence that the San Carlo 3 manuscript was drafted prior to the Cassiani edition. In order to obtain a printing permit, the copy — which is not without frequent autograph corrections and additions — appeared before the Master of the Sacred Apostolic Palace (*Maestro del Sacro Palazzo*) in Rome. The signatures of Alessandro Borghi and Berlingero Gessi, which were affixed to the license, are extremely useful for the purposes of dating the document. Borghi, formerly the bishop of Borgo Sansepolcro, moved to Rome in December 1605 as a vicar of Paolo V, although he had known Tassoni since 1595 and in the course of 1605 had done everything he could to obtain a position for him with Alessandro D'Este, albeit unsuccessfully.[12] Gessi, who signed as 'Vicegerente' to Borghi, was named bishop of Rimini in November 1606, and was definitely still in that role at the beginning of 1607 because he did not establish residency in Rimini until June of that year.[13]

In light of these facts, it would not seem imprudent to propose — following Bacci's suggestion — that 1606 is the latest possible date of composition for the volume. According to Bacci, the manuscript was composed of an older nucleus, interpolated with a later revision. Although it is certain that more elaborative stages can be identified in the text of the San Carlo 3 manuscript (a fact which confirms the feverish labour of rewriting that occupied Tassoni in those years), only scant traces of these stages remain. As such, the definitive determination of an internal chronology of the manuscript remains, for the moment, rather difficult to achieve.[14]

The request for a print license for the San Carlo 3 manuscript seems to suggest that, as early as the end of 1606, Tassoni thought that the *Considerazioni* had reached a sufficient stage of development; in fact, he considered it ready for print. More than two years would be necessary before the work reached the presses (the Modenese

---

12   On Borghi see Gian Maria Mazzuchelli, *Gli scrittori d'Italia, cioè notizie storiche e critiche intorno alle vite e agli scritti dei letterati italiani*, 6 vols (Brescia: Giambattista Bossini, 1753–63), II.3, 1731–32; on his participation in the Accademia degli Umoristi, see Michele Maylender, *Storia delle Accademie d'Italia*, 5 vols (Bologna: Cappelli, 1926–30), V, 375; see also Borghi's letter of recommendation to Alfonso Fontanelli, major-domo of the Cardinale d'Este, which can be dated to 1605, published in Venceslao Santi, 'Alessandro Tassoni e il cardinal Ascanio Colonna', *Atti e Memorie della R. Deputazione di Storia Patria per le Provincie Modenesi*, 2 (1903), 197–233 (p. 205). Tassoni's epistolary features two letters to Borghi, dated 20 December 1607 and 31 May 1608 (the latter in occasion of Colonna's death): see Alessandro Tassoni, *Lettere*, ed. by Pietro Puliatti, 2 vols (Bari: Laterza, 1978), I, 54–55.

13   Simona Feci, 'Gessi, Berlingero', in *Dizionario biografico degli italiani* (Rome: Istituto della Enciclopedia Italiana, 1960–), LIII (2000), 474–77 (p. 475).

14   Bacci (*Le considerazioni*, pp. 3–9, particularly p. 3 and n. 1 at pp. 4–5) considered the MS S. Carlo 3 as evidence of at least 'due [...] redazioni dell'opera tassoniana': 'già la diversità dell'inchiostro e della carta [...] e una differenza della scrittura che in una parte del manoscritto è più dritta e più serrata, ci fanno sospettare che si tratti almeno di due manoscritti (sempre autografi del Tassoni) fusi in un solo. Abbiamo la certezza di questo fatto osservando la fine di quasi ogni *verso* in confronto del *recto* seguente: troviamo cassate le parole ultime del *verso*, che sono le prime del *recto* seguente anticipate (come s'usava allora) quando il *recto* cominci con parole diverse da quella che dovevano essere il principio del *recto* scomparso. [...] Possiamo ritenere quindi sicuramente che si tratti almeno di due redazioni diverse del lavoro, e possiamo di più stabilire quali carte ci rappresentino la datazione più antica e quali la più recente'. The interpolations between different editorial phases, however, are less frequent than Bacci, a bit peremptorily, would lead us to believe. The analysis of the internal chronology of the manuscript lies outside the scope of the present chapter, and is deferred for a deeper study of the material aspects of the codex.

imprimatur dates to July 1608). It is impossible, for the moment, to establish whether this delay was due to the internal history of the text or whether it resulted from questions linked to Tassoni's biography, but what is clear is that the transition between the manuscript and the Cassiani edition is marked by a minute operation of rewriting and expansion.

In the print copy of the *Considerazioni*, Tassoni adds an appendix containing some of the *Annotazioni* to Petrarch which could be found in the Girolamo Muzio's *Battaglie* (printed posthumously in Venice in 1582). Muzio, motivated by an anti-Bembist intent, is often criticized in terms of his slavish imitation of the Petrarchan model. Tassoni reports that the *Annotazioni* had 'fallen into his hands' when the last folio of the *Considerazioni* was 'already nearly finished printing'.[15] The noteworthy affinities between the two works (which are linked not only by similar structuring and the assonance of their titles, but also by a parallel development of the theme, which was crucial for Tassoni, of the relationship between ancients and moderns) would lead one to believe that Tassoni's first encounter with Muzio's text had been earlier.[16]

After his polemic with Aromatari (1611–13), Tassoni resumed work on the text of the *Considerazioni*, annotating a specially-prepared copy of the 1609 edition: indeed, many of his textual interventions responded directly to issues that had arisen from the pamphlets of his Paduan adversary. For the most part, Tassoni's changes represent additions, but rewritings are not uncommon. It is not easy, at the moment, to establish when (and even if) Tassoni finished working on this expansion, nor is it clear why it never appeared in print.

15   Tassoni, *Considerazioni*, p. 563.

16   Without a doubt attributable to the memory of Muzio's *Annotazioni* is the inclusion of a reference to the comparison between the genius of the ancients and the moderns in the 'Introduzione' to the *Considerazioni*, dating back to the revision of the text prior to the 1609 printing. See Tassoni, *Considerazioni*, fol. †3^{r-v}: 'Odio per certo, né maltalento contro il Petrarca re de' melici non m'ha mosso, ma la stitichezza (per così dire) d'una mano di zucche secche che non voglion che sia lecito dir cosa non detta da lui, né diversamente da quello ch'egli la disse, né che pur fra tante sue rime alcuna ve n'abbia che si possa dir meglio. Come se gli umani ingegni, in cambio di andar perfezionando e loro stessi e le cose trovate, ogni dì più s'annebbiassero, e fosse da seguitare la sacciutezza di certi barbassori che, auggiando gli usi moderni, vestono tuttavia colle berrette a taglieri e le falde del saio fino al ginocchio'. Cf. Girolamo Muzio, *Battaglie per diffesa dell'italica lingua*, ed. by Carmelo Scavuzzo (Messina: Sicania, 1995), pp. 329–31: 'volendo altri senza scelta dir tutto quello che è stato detto da lui, ed iscrivere come è stato scritto da lui, non credo che sia per satisfare ad ognuno'; 'noi veggiamo per prova che le arti e le scienze da uno ad altro secolo tuttavia si vanno avanzando: se le tavole de' dipintori, se le statue degli scultori di cento anni a dietro si metteranno a paragone con quelle della nostra età, molto perderanno di dignità; né lo stile di chi latinamente scrisse già dugento anni passati è da agguagliare a quello del nostro secolo. Il medesimo si vede nella delicatezza delle fogge de' panni di seta e de' ricami, nelle arme de' soldati, nell'edificar delle case, nel fabricar le navi e le galee, nel fortificar delle città, e così nelle altre arti, siano onorate o vili: ché le cose le quali appresso i nostri antecessori erano di ammirazione, a noi non sono di molta stima'. References to the *querelle* — on the importance of which in Tassoni's writing, see Giancarlo Mazzacurati, 'Alessandro Tassoni e l'epifania dei "moderni"', in Giancarlo Mazzacurati, *Rinascimenti in transito* (Rome: Bulzoni, 1996), pp. 159–85 — are still present in the MS S. Carlo 3, fol. 294^{v} (commentary to *Triumphus Mortis*, 1): 'Ma alle volte l'opinione dell'antichità muffata ci fa credere contra l'isperienza che sempre gli ingegni peggiorino' (Tassoni, *Considerazioni*, p. 323: 'Ma alle volte il credito che ha l'antichità muffata ne fa credere contra l'isperienza che sempre gli ingegni antichi piggiorino').

2. The Voyage to Spain and the Time of Composition

Tassoni claims to have composed the *Considerazioni* in the course of a trip 'from Rome to Spain' (MS S. Carlo 3, fol. 1^r); in the introduction to the 1609 print version, he defines it as an 'opera di viaggio': a kind of travel work. The author is referring to the final trip to Spain, with a departure in November 1602:

> Lettore, opera di viaggio è questa, tessuta nel cuor del verno; parte fra l'onde e gli scogli d'un tempestoso mare, parte fra le balze e le arene di due infecondi regni; e dopo ne' triboli e rancori d'amare liti ricorsa: stravagante stagione, siti strani e diversi, intempestiva opportunità, nuovi e bizzarri umori. E nondimeno tal novità è piacciuta ad alcuni così autorevoli ingegni che 'l gusto loro m'ha lusingato a pubblicar questi fogli. Or voglia Dio che in istampa non cangi effetto.[17]

Tassoni certainly could have brought a copy of the *Canzoniere* with him and begun his annotations during the trip. Nevertheless, various circumstances suggest that the majority of his commentary on the Petrarchan text must have been completed in Rome, and that his work began only at the end of 1603.[18] In fact, in the *Considerazioni* it is easy to discern a critical design that was coherently developed through continual recourse to a large and varied bibliography (including manuscripts): this alone suffices to show a clear distinction between the work itself and the many other annotations by Tassoni.[19] In addition, it seems hard to believe that Tassoni, who was still in the service of Cardinal Ascanio, would have been able to conceive of a work denigrating Petrarch — the Poet of the Colonnas — whose authority was unquestioned and inviolable (we have already mentioned the disagreements that led to Tassoni's abrupt dismissal).

Tassoni was well aware that the *Considerazioni* would meet with criticism: claiming that they had been written only during the short period of his travels to Spain might offer, to some degree, a justification for its often impudent tone. The passage through 'a stormy sea' and 'two infecund kingdoms' (Catalonia and Aragon) during an 'extravagant' winter would provide a kind of medical excuse, given that

---

17   Tassoni, *Considerazioni*, fol. †3: 'Reader, this is a travel work, and composed in the dead of the winter; in part between the waves and the rocks of the sea, in part between the cliffs and the sands of two barren realms; after that, it stumbled upon the pains and grudges of harsh quarrels. Extravagant season, strange and diverse locations, untimely opportunity, new and bizarre humours. Nevertheless, this novelty was well received by minds so authoritative that their approval has flattered me into publishing these pages. Now, God willing, I hope that the effect of this novelty does not change when the work is printed'. Here, instead, is the previous version of the passage for the purposes of comparison with how it is presented in the *Intenzione* of the MS S. Carlo 3, fol. 1^{r-v}: 'In un viaggio ch'io feci da Roma in Ispagna, non avendo altra compagnia che di queste sole *Rime*, sopra di esse notai le considerazioni seguenti: non per biasimare un poeta tenuto da me sempre in grandissima stima, ma con intenzione di dover giovare ai professori della poesia, separando nel prencipe de' lirici toscani e nel maestro del ben dire quello che non mi pareva da essere imitato; ed esaminando con rigore molte cose che prima forse non erano state avertite'.

18   On questions of dating, see also the reflections by Pazzaglia, *Il commento*, pp. 138–39.

19   On these, see Luca Ferraro, *Nel laboratorio di Alessandro Tassoni: lo studio del 'Furioso' e la pratica della postilla* (Firenze: Cesati, 2018).

— according to a widespread belief— the inconsistencies of the climate affected the temperament of the humours (which were in fact called 'new and bizarre').

Travel notes punctuate the entire work and, at times, clearly take on the flavor of a diary. Consider, for example, the commentary on *RVF*, 153. 1–2 ('Ite caldi sospiri al freddo core | rompete il ghiaccio, che pietà contende', p. 228 [Go, warm sighs, to her frozen heart | shatter the ice that chokes her pity]):

> Andando il poeta a dar l'assalto alla donna sua, questi erano i guastatori ch'egli rimandava inanzi ad appianar le strade e diboscare il cammino. Ma viemmi da ridere, ché mentre sto qui scrivendo nell'osteria della Fortuna, s'è gelata tutta questa marina e tutto questo stagno di Martega, di sorte ch'egli ci vorrà altro che sospiri a rompere il ghiaccio per uscirne.[20]

Here, Tassoni offers a description of his stay near the Berre lagoon, a short distance from the port of Marseille: 'Martega' corresponds to the present-day Martigues, the 'stagno' [pond] is precisely the saltwater lake still called the Étang de Berre. In fact, the passage is exactly the same as the one that appears in the San Carlo 3 manuscript.[21] Commenting on *RVF*, 194, Tassoni proclaims himself still frozen with cold:

> È sonetto che mostra appunto d'esser stato fatto per cammino, come le mie *Considerazioni*: benché a me cominci omai a parere di non essere più in cammino, essendo oggi ventitré giorni che io mi trovo gelato e confinato in questa maladetta riviera.[22]

It is worth emphasizing the fact that, in the manuscript (fol. 172^r), this passage was presented in identical form (with one noteworthy exception: in place of '*Considerazioni*' it had instead read 'notazioni').

In the handwritten version, the allusions to the voyage are more frequent than in the Cassiani edition, where they are in some cases expunged or lightened. Eliminated from the commentary on 'Zefiro torna e il bel tempo rimena' (*RVF*, 310), for example, is the passage in which Tassoni — in appreciation of the success of the Petrachan sonnet — writes:

20   'While the Poet was going to carry out the assault on his beloved, these were the saboteurs that he sent forth to flatten roads and clear-cut the path. But this makes me laugh, for as I am writing here at Fortune's Inn, this whole coast and the whole pond of Martigues froze, so that it will take a lot more than sighs to break the ice and get out of here'.

21   MS S. Carlo 3, fol. 149^v: '"Ite caldi sospiri al freddo core | rompete il ghiaccio [...]" Mi vien da ridere che mentre sto qui scrivendo nell'osteria della Fortuna, s'è gelata tutta questa marina, e tutto questo stagno di Martega, di sorte che ci vorrà altro che sospiri a rompere il ghiaccio'. A passage from Martigues, 'terra distante dal porto [of Marseille] 3 miglia, alla quale si va per un canale di mare che da mezo del porto stesso a dirittura si stende verso detta terra, o con poco volgimento' is also documented by Cassiano dal Pozzo, *Il diario del viaggio in Spagna del cardinale Francesco Barberini*, ed. by Alessandra Anselmi (Aranjuez: Doce Calles, 2004), p. 37. From Marseille (or from nearby ports, such as the Isle de Port-Cros, also known as Torre di Buccari or d'Ambucari) one attempted the crossing of the Gulf of Lion towards Barcelona (cf. Tassoni, *Relazione*, p. 188).

22   'This sonnet was evidently composed while travelling, like my *Considerations*: although I am starting to feel like I am not travelling anymore, because it's twenty-three days today that I have been frozen and confined to this damned coast' (p. 265).

È sonetto espresso leggiadramente, e che merita per la vaghezza sua d'esser connumerato fra i migliori. E fa giusto a proposito di questo soave venticello che finalm[en]te salvi ne conduce nel porto di Barcellona.[23]

In addition, the references to the voyage that had been present in the extremely brief introduction to the *Trionfi* section are attenuated in the 1609 print version; the rewriting involves, moreover, a remarkable rhetorical and linguistic expansion (emphasis mine):

> MS S. Carlo 3, fol. 274[v]:
>   Fornito il viaggio, sarei obligato, come opera di quiete, a considerare con più essattezza questi *Trionfi*; *ma essendo materia scossa e vagliata da molti, e dovendo fra quindeci giorni rimettermi in camino per Italia*, io non mi fermerò eccetto che dove i passi mi parranno fangosi.[24]

> Ed. 1609, p. 476:
>   Fornito il viaggio allo scorcio dell'altre *Rime* con più esattezza potrei bilanciare i *Trionfi* che restano; ma essendo materia digrummata e dibucciata da altri, non mi fermerò eccetto che a ma' passi, e dove le prunaie m'andranno trattenendo, per non ispicciolare innanzi agli asini la treggea ed empire i fogli d'inutili schicheramenti.[25]

Even acknowledging that a few 'travel notes' did manage to survive the various editing phases of the text, there is no doubt that the often perfect coincidence between the timing of the voyage to Spain and the timing of writing of the commentary was, on more than one occasion, created *ex post facto* by Tassoni;[26] the progressive reduction of the travel additions in the passage of the manuscript to print tends, perhaps, to make their artificiality less apparent.

3. An Example of Tassoni's Rewriting (*RVF*, 1)

The commentary on the proemial sonnet of the *Canzoniere* can serve as an example of how Tassoni worked on the text during the course of the three documented stages of revision. Unsurprisingly, it is a place where the author made changes many times during the course of the long development of the work. The most revealing differences have to do with the transition from the manuscript to the print version: in the San Carlo 3 manuscript, the commentary on *RVF*, 1 actually included much of the material later merged into the introduction for the Cassiani

---

23 'This is an exquisitely expressed sonnet, which for its beauty deserves to be numbered among the best. And it serves the purpose of this sweet breeze that finally leads us safe into the port of Barcelona' (fol. 228[r–v]).

24 'My journey being ended, I would be obliged, as a work of rest, to examine these *Triumphs* more precisely; but because this matter has been shaken and sifted by many, and because I have to head back to Italy in a fortnight, I will not stop except where passages seem muddy to me'.

25 'My journey being ended at the termination of the other *Rhymes*, I could weigh the remaining *Triumphs* with greater precision; but because this matter has been ruminated on and peeled away by others, I will not stop, except for difficult passages, and where thornbushes hold me back, in order not to serve donkeys with confectioneries and fill the pages with useless scrawls'.

26 One thinks also of the case of the arrival in Zaragoza, which supposedly occurs at exactly the same time as the commentary on *RVF*, 366 (Tassoni, *Considerazioni*, p. 460).

edition (after the dedicatory epistle 'A chi legge', the manuscript opened with just a brief 'Intenzione').[27]

The beginning of the true commentary to *RVF*, 1 was rearranged many times. This is how it was introduced in the San Carlo 3 manuscript:

> Questo sonetto che serve di proemio, sopra del quale hanno finti tanti miracoli, non pure i commentatori ma alcuni maestri della lingua e del modo di comporre, se resuscitasse Aristotele figliuolo di Nicomaco, che ci stendesse sopra tutta l'arte della poetica ch'egli lasciò ombreggiata, non sarà mai altro che un sonetto molto comune.[28]

Noteworthy here is the adhesion to Castelvetro's thesis which argued that the *Poetics* was just a collection of unfinished notes; Aristotle is invoked through the somewhat reductive epithet of 'figliuolo di Nicomaco' [son of Nicomachus]. Likewise, in the print edition (p. 20) Tassoni continues to define Aristotle's work as a kind of outline — merely an 'abbozzamento di *Poetica*' — thus predictably drawing the ire of the devoted Aristotelian Aromatari.[29] Perhaps also for reasons of preemptive censorship (note the deletion of 'miracoli', a rather dangerous word), the beginning of the commentary on *RVF*, 1 was corrected as follows for the 1609 edition:

> Questo sonetto, che serve di proemio, sopra 'l quale tant'hanno cicalato, non pure i commentatori ma i correttori delle stampe ed i maestri del ben dire, in verità che se Aristotele figliuolo di Nicomaco Stagirita mi volesse dare a credere ch'egli uscisse punto della schiera commune, l'avrei per uomo che trasognasse.[30]

A new formulation came after the polemic with Aromatari, and is included in the annotated copy of the *Considerazioni* (later published by Muratori):

> Se Aristotele figliuolo di Nicomaco Stagirita, che tanto seppe, mi volesse dare a credere che questo sonetto che serve di proemio, sopra 'l quale tant'hanno cicalato, non pure i commentatori, ma i satrapi della lingua, uscisse punto dalla schiera comune, in verità ch'io non gliel crederei.[31]

---

27   MS S. Carlo 3, fol. 1ʳ. The material later reintegrated in the introduction is found at fols 3ʳ–6ᵛ.
28   'This sonnet, that serves as a preface, about which so many have imagined miracles, not only the commentators but also the masters of language and composition, even if Aristotle son of Nichomacus were to come back from the dead and write on it all of his *Poetics*, which he left in a sketched form, it would still be nothing more than a very ordinary sonnet' (fol. 7ʳ).
29   Lodovico Castelvetro, *Poetica d'Aristotele vulgarizzata e sposta*, ed. by Werther Romani, 2 vols (Bari: Laterza, 1978), I, 3: 'conciosia cosa che io mi sia aveduto che questo libretto sia una prima forma rozza, imperfetta e non polita dell'arte poetica, la quale è verisimile che l'autore conservasse perché servisse in luogo di raccolta d'insegnamenti e di brievi memorie, per poterle avere preste quando volesse ordinare e compilare l'arte intera'. See Giuseppe degli Aromatari, *Risposte di Gioseffe degli Aromatari alle Considerazioni del Sig. Alessandro Tassoni sopra le Rime del Petrarca* (Padua: Orlando Iadra, 1611), p. 47: 'Che la *Poetica* d'Aristotele poi sia uno abbozzamento, questa è un'opinione seminata dal Castelvetri, ed è stata da tanti, e con tante e sì efficaci ragioni ributtata, che se non si sciolgono quelle, io non posso crederla per abbozzo ad un semplice detto del S. Tassoni'. On Aromatari and Tassoni, see also Laura Benedetti's chapter in this volume.
30   'This sonnet, that serves as a preface, about which so many have blabbered, not only the commentators but also print correctors and the masters of good language, if Aristotle son of Nichomacus Stagirite wanted me to believe that it was even a little better than the average, I would think he was daydreaming'.
31   'Even if Aristotle son of Nichomacus Stagirite, who knew so much, would have me believe

Particularly interesting in this last drafting is the use of the expression 'satrapi della lingua' meaning despots or 'satraps' of language, which was probably adapted from Caro's *Apologia* — 'A voler fare lo *satrapo delle lingue* ci si richiede più studio, più pratica e più cervello che non avete voi' [To be a despot of languages requires more study, more practice and more brain than you possess] — where, curiously, the insult is directed against one of the authors that Tassoni most admired: Lodovico Castelvetro.[32]

The use of expressions borrowed from sixteenth-century polemics — expressions which, in more than one case, were given new vigor by the *Considerazioni* and thus entered into lexicon of subsequent literary skirmishes — is particularly common in those moments when the work reaches the greatest heights of rhetorical zealousness.[33]

Tassoni's reading of *RVF*, 1 is somewhat biting to say the least: it has a low style and lacks syntactic order, other than a cogent link between its *quaternari* and *terzine*. The proemial sonnet was also conceptually inexact, and its content was in contradiction with other lyrics found in the *Canzoniere*. The commentary concluded with a rebuttal of Castelvetro's thesis that 'il popol tutto' in l. 9 referred to the cowardly and foolish multitudes of Italy, the 'moltitudine vile e sciocca d'Italia'.

To demonstrate the stylistic lowness of the proemial sonnet, Tassoni even goes so far as to define l. 4 ('Quand'era in parte altr'huom da quel ch'i' sono') as

> [...] piutosto prosa che verso, come quello che per essere tale manca di tutti i privilegi dell'arte e della natura. Dell'arte, non avendo egli né traslato, né figura, né formato, né metafora, né sonorità di numero, né parte alcuna di quelle che usa l'arte per fare i versi. Di natura, non avendo scelta di frasi, né vaghezza, né bontà di parole, né grazia di concetti, né lume insomma alcuno di quelli che

that this sonnet, that serves as a preface and about which so many have blabbered, not only the commentators, but also the satraps of language, was anything other than a very ordinary sonnet, I wouldn't believe him'.

32   Annibal Caro, *Apologia degli Academici di Banchi di Roma contra M. Lodovico Castelvetro da Modena [...]*, (Parma: Seth Viotto, 1558), p. 152. On the meaning of *satrapo* as 'persona superba e autoritaria', 'chi si atteggia a conoscitore esperto di un argomento o anche di tutto lo scibile', see *Grande dizionario della lingua italiana*, ed. by Salvatore Battaglia and Giorgio Bàrberi Squarotti, 21 vols (Turin: Utet, 1961–2004) [henceforward called *GDLI*], XVII, 601. Also the 'politici di Roma' that bet on the defeat of the Savoys against Spain are defined as 'satrapi della dottrina politica' in Alessandro Tassoni, 'Filippiche contra gli Spagnoli', in Alessandro Tassoni, *Annali*, I, 217–43: 227. In Alessandro Castelvetro's preface to Fulvio Testi, *Rime [...] all'invittissimo Carlo Emanuello Duca di Savoia* (Modena: Giuliano Cassiani, 1617), p. 14, there is an allusion to Marino through an accusation against the 'satrapi di Parnaso, non contenti di lacerare in voce i suoi componimenti.' On Tassoni and Castevetro, see Pazzaglia, *Il commento*, p. 135.

33   Regarding the later reusage of the expression 'satrapi della lingua', see Prospero Viani, *Dizionario di pretesi francesismi e di pretese voci e forme erronee della lingua italiana*, 2 vols (Florence: Le Monnier, 1858–60), I, 100: 'Oh! so quanto i caporioni, *i satrapi della lingua* posso incontanente opporre' (Viani read, inserting it also in the *Tavole* at the close of the volume, Muratori's edition of Tassoni's text). A suspicious affinity between the style of the *Considerazioni* and that of G. B. Marino's polemics can be identified by reading Vania de Maldé, 'Percorsi intertestuali negli scritti polemici di Giovan Battista Marino', in *Bufere e molli aurette. Polemiche letterarie dallo Stilnovo alla 'Voce'*, ed. by Maria Grazia Pensa, with a note by Silvio Ramat (Milan: Guerini, 1996), pp. 81–118; see also Emilio Russo, *Marino* (Rome: Salerno, 2008), pp. 320–25.

a' poeti nati somministra la natura, la quale l'avea partorito per una schiera di prosa, che andava scritta così: *Quand'io era in parte altr'uomo | da quello che io mi sono*. Ma coll'accorciarla e storpiarla e fare (come si dice) d'una lancia un fuso, levandone alcune sillabe, e voci intiere, èvvi stato intruso il numero, insieme con quell'equivoco '*Da quel ch'io sono*', che s'usa per maniera di giuramento. Né creda alcuno che per aver egli undici sillabe non gli si possa negare il nome di verso; perciochè nelle migliori prose del Boccaccio leggonsene molti di tali, e fra gli altri questi due nel proemio appunto della prima novella delle cento:

> *Perché dovend'io al nostro novellare,*
> *sì come primo dar cominciamento*

che però finora non sono stati presi per versi da alcuno ch'io sappia: indizio manifesto che alle undici sillabe sole non si ristrigne l'essenza de' versi, a' quali inoltre si richiede che sieno maestosi senza gonfiatura, chiari senza bassezza, figurati senza freddura.[34]

In this case, Tassoni seems to be re-invoking a critical tradition that originated with Salviati's *Avvertimenti* (which devalued both Boccaccio's versification as well as his use of prose in the *cursus*):

> verso ch'avesse verso nel verso non fece mai, o così radi che nella moltitudine de' lor contradi restano come affogati. [...] Ma nelle prose, dove non bisognava, ne fece, non accorgendosene, molti de' molto belli.[35]

This tendency of Boccaccio had also been ironically stigmatized by the aforementioned Muzio, in his *Arte poetica* (ll. 297–99):

> E 'l Certaldese molte volte sciolto
> da' numeri di rime è più poeta
> che quando a poetar si mette in rima.[36]

---

34 'more prose than verse, because it lacks all of the privileges of art and nature. Of art, not having tropes, nor figures, nor harmony, nor metaphors, nor metric musicality, nor any of those features that art employs to make verses. Of nature, not having polished phrases, nor beauty, nor good words, nor refined conceits, nor, in conclusion, any of those lights handed out to natural born poets by nature, who gave birth to it as a prose sequence that had to be written in this way: 'Quand'io era in parte altr'uomo | da quello che io mi sono'. But shortening, distorting and making — as we say — a spindle out of a spear, by removing some syllables and whole words, meter was forced into it, together with that ambiguous 'da quel ch'io sono', that is used as the formula for an oath. Nor should anyone believe that, because it has eleven syllables, it must necessarily be called a verse; in fact, you can read many such verses in Boccaccio's best prose pieces, and, among the others, these two in the beginning of the first of the one-hundred tales: 'Perché dovend'io al nostro novellare, | sì come primo dar cominciamento', which up until now have never been mistaken for verses by anyone that I know: this is clear evidence that the essence of verses cannot be reduced to eleven syllables; indeed, verses need to be majestic but not pretentious, clear but not base, rich in figures without being cold'.

35 Leonardo Salviati, *Degli Avvertimenti della lingua sopra 'l Decamerone Volume Primo* (Venice: Domenico and Giovan Battista Guerra, 1584): 'he never wrote a proper verse in his verses, or so seldom that they are somehow drowned in the multitude of their opposite [i.e. bad verses]. [...] However in his prose, where there was no need of it, he made unknowingly a lot of good verses'. On this question see Michele Bordin, 'Boccaccio versificatore. La morfologia ritmica dell'endecasillabo', *Studi sul Boccaccio*, 31 (2003), 137–201: 140–41, n. 7 (in which Salviati's passage is also cited).

36 Girolamo Muzio, *Dell'arte poetica*, in *Trattati di poetica e di retorica del Cinquecento*, ed. by Bernard Weinberg (Bari: Laterza, 1970), II, 165–209 (p. 173): 'And often Boccaccio, free | from meter is more of a poet | than when he starts composing in rhyme'. See also Bordin, *Boccaccio versificatore*.

Aromatari pointed out that the text of Boccaccio's hendecasyllables as cited by Tassoni ('Perché dovend'io al nostro novellare | sì come primo dar cominciamento') had been altered slightly so that the verses had the right number of syllables: the original *dare* had been, in effect, forcibly truncated to form *dar*.[37] Tassoni certainly took Aromatari's criticism into account, because in the postscript to the *Considerazioni*, he included — before the example offered above — an excerpt from Day Five of the *Decameron*: 'cantando per esempio nel principio della quinta giornata: *Era già 'l monte tutto bianco | e li surgenti raggi etc.*' It is noteworthy, moreover, how these two examples of Boccaccio's metrical prose were highlighted by Tassoni in his annotated copy of Salviati's *Decameron*.[38]

In the final version of the *Considerazioni*, the one including Tassoni's annotations, the commentary on the proemial sonnet was expanded by the addition of a paragraph discussing the inadmissibility of the 'absolute' vocative *Voi* that opens the composition, that had nothing to do with the following verses given the excessive distance to the conclusion of the phrase ('che legatura convenevole non pare avere con alcuna delle cose seguenti per la soverchia distanza della conchiusione'). The observation is repeated in Muzio's *Annotazioni* and had already been included in the *Scelta* placed at the end of the 1609 edition:

> Nota il Muzio in questo primo sonetto quello stesso che fu notato da me circa l'ordine e la spiegatura de' quaternari intralciata, mercé di quel *voi* quinto caso, che non s'appoggia a nulla, e va a conchiudere in *spero*, che non ha seco interesse.[39]

Tassoni thus proclaimed his position in a debate that had begun in the 1500s, aligning himself against Castelvetro (and before him Camillo) who appreciated the choice made by Petrarch.[40] In this case as well, Tassoni's inclusion of a nod in the direction of the debate concerning the initial vocative might have led to conflict with Aromatari; Aromatari had in fact criticized Muzio's disapproval of the vocative as though it had been written by Tassoni himself, in fact brilliantly using the same piece of criticism to attack his adversary:

---

37   Aromatari, *Risposte*, pp. 18–19.
38   Giovanni Boccaccio, *Il Decameron [...] di nuovo ristampato e riscontrato in Firenze con testi antichi, ed alla sua vera lezione ridotto dal Cavalier Lionardo Salviati [...] Quarta edizione* (Florence: Giunti, 1587): Florence, Biblioteca Nazionale Centrale, Fondo Postillati, 20. See also pp. 16 ('*Perché dovendo al nostro novellare | sì come primo dar cominciamento | Nota che sono due versi*') and 261 ('*Era [...] surgenti*', underlined). On Boccaccian hand-written annotations by Tassoni see Lazzarini, 'Pazza cosa sarebbe la poesia', pp. 1–76, 215–301, and Pietro Puliatti, 'Le letture e i postillati del Tassoni', *Studi secenteschi*, 18 (1977), 3–58.
39   'Muzio observes in this first sonnet the same thing that had been observed by me about the order and the bad development of the quatrains, because of that *you* in the fifth case [i.e. vocative] that does not rely on anything, and ends with *I hope*, which has no relation to it' (p. 563). See Muzio, *Battaglie*, pp. 332–34.
40   Lodovico Castelvetro, *Le Rime del Petrarca brevemente sposte per L. C. [...]* (Basel: Pietro de Sedabonis, 1582), p. 2; Valentina Grohovaz, 'L'*Esposizione sopra 'l primo et secondo sonetto del Petrarca* di Giulio Camillo Delminio', *Studi petrarcheschi*, 16 (2003), 197–244 (pp. 210–11).

> Né può negare il S. Tassoni ch'a lui non piaccia, poiché se l'adoperò nel principio delle sue *Considerazioni*, dicendo 'Lettore, opera di viaggio è questa [...]', dove la parola *Lettore* fa l'istesso effetto che *Voi* nel presente sonetto.[41]

4. Commentary and Non-Commentary, a 'Hybrid' Genre

Much like the later *Secchia rapita*, the *Considerazioni* are characterized by a blending of genres, tones, and styles: erudite remarks, textual explanations, and etymological theories are placed on the same plane alongside personal notations, witticisms, puns, and at times risqué double entendres. In this amalgam of ingredients, the boundaries between jokes and serious content are often indistinguishable. The confusion of stylistic planes is matched, so to speak, by a corresponding confusion of chronologies: at times Petrarch's text is approached through the tools of history and philology; at other times the text is attacked as though Tassoni was engaged in debate with a contemporary.

It is precisely these brusque excursions in tone that lead to suspicions about Tassoni's level of awareness regarding the final meaninglessness of the act of commentary: following a dynamic perhaps comparable to the 'non-narration' present in the *Secchia*, there are many notes in the *Considerazioni* that 'non-comment' on Petrarch's text.[42] After all, the author himself declared that he intended to approach the text of the *Canzoniere* and the *Trionfi*

> non per commentarlo (ché i commenti non mancano) ma per andar brievemente segnando quello che forse è di più momento, e che gli altri imbrigati e distratti a fettar le ciregie per imboccarle a' fanciulli tutti hanno trasandato.[43]

On the other hand, in those instances where the interpretative effort is real, Tassoni's commentary demonstrates a depth of erudition certainly comparable (and at times perhaps greater) to which is found in commentaries by Castelvetro, Gesualdo, or Daniello.

Another way in which the *Considerazioni* distance themselves from the previous Petrarch commentaries is by defining themselves as — paradoxically — not 'in service to' or dependent in any way on the Petrarchan text; the attention of the reader is distracted from the letter of the *Canzoniere* and the *Trionfi*, and held fixedly by Tassoni's own notes.

Although offering an exhaustive catalogue of the strategies of commentary and 'non-commentary' enacted in the *Considerazioni* is far beyond the scope of this chapter; I would like to point out that experiment in stylistic hybridization moves the work closer, in many respects, to the tradition of 'esegesi giocosa' [playful exegesis], which is typical of the 1500s.[44]

---

41   Aromatari, *Risposte*, pp. 19–20: 'Nor can Mr. Tassoni deny that he likes it, since he used it in the beginning of his *Considerazioni*, by saying: "*Reader*, this is a travel work [...]", where the word *Reader* has the same effect as *You* in this sonnet'.

42   Giovanni Pozzi, 'Narrazione e non narrazione nell'*Adone* e nella *Secchia rapita*', *Nuova secondaria*, 5 (1987), 24–29.

43   Tassoni, *Considerazioni*, fol. †5ʳ: 'not to comment on it (for there are plenty of commentaries) but to briefly annotate what is probably more important and that has been neglected by the others while busy and distracted slicing cherries to feed to the children [i.e. explaining the obvious]'.

44   On the tradition of burlesque commentary, see *Cum notibusse et comentaribusse. L'esegesi parodistica*

The *Considerazioni* contains explicit references to burlesque commentaries; in Tassoni's observations on *RVF*, 105, for example, there is a reference to Anton Francesco Doni's annotations on Burchiello:

> MS S. Carlo 3, fol. 117^r
> *Mai non vo' più cantar com'io soleva*
> Questa è una pistacchiata di stravagante sapore, e credo che 'l *commentator del Burchiello* non ne caverebbe succo.[45]

> Ed. 1609, p. 165
> *Mai non vo' più cantar com'io soleva*
> Questo è lavoro a grotteschi, com'io non so se Merlino o *l'interprete del Burchiello* ne traessero e' piedi.[46]

The *canzone RVF*, 105 consists of a long sequence of proverbial forms with 'rima al mezzo', a kind of internal rhyme, similar to the genre of the frottola. Notice how the difficult jumble of maxims, proverbs, and allusions ('sentenze, proverbi, allusioni a chiave') is initially equated with a 'pistacchiata', a kind of pistachio pie, and then (using a metaphor with more elevated tone) to a 'lavoro a grotteschi' [a grotesque drawing].[47]

Another way that the *Considerazioni* approaches the tradition of burlesque commentary (as well as the vivacious literary polemics of the mid-1500s, like the one between Caro and Castelvetro) is by choosing a language that is often smugly allusive, requiring a full command of the often obscure sixteenth-century comic language. In the introduction, the author defends Petrarch against the accusation that he was an imitator of the Catalan poet Ausiàs March, who lived in the 1400s. On this matter, Tassoni invokes the opinions of Juan López de Hoyos and Diego de Fuentes, which can be read at the beginning of the Castillian translation of the works of March, prepared by Jorge de Montemayor:

> MS S. Carlo 3, fol. 4^v
> Ora, che costui fosse prima del Petarca, e che 'l Petrarca togliesse da lui molte cose, oltra l'opinione dei già nominati ci sono due altri testimoni di spagnoli: l'uno di Diego di Fuentes, che scrisse la sua vita, il qual fingendosi contemporaneo del Petr[arc]a dice fra le altre cose d'Ausiás: 'Y tanto caminò per este tan honrado trabajo, que despues depor muchas excelencias suyas fue laureado por poeta, no menos affamado que lo fue el doctissimo Francisco Petrarca en nuestros tiempos'.[48]

---

e giocosa del cinquecento (Seminario di Letteratura italiana, Viterbo, 23–24 novembre 2001), ed. by Antonio Corsaro e Paolo Procaccioli (Manziana: Vecchiarelli, 2002). On Tassoni, see in particular Gian Piero Maragoni, *Prolegomeni ad uno studio dell'esegesi denigratoria in età barocca*, ibid., pp. 221–36 (pp. 226–34).

45   ' "Now I don't wish to sing as I used to do": This is a pistachio pie of extravagant taste, and I believe that Burchiello's commentator wouldn't make sense of it'.

46   ' "Now I don't wish to sing as I used to do": This is such a grotesque drawing that I don't know if Merlin or Burchiello's exegete understood it'. Doni's commentary on Burchiello is now published in Burchiello, *Rime del Burchiello commentate dal Doni*, critical edition and commentary by Carlo Alberto Girotto (Pisa: Edizioni della Normale, 2012).

47   Francesco Petrarca, *Canzoniere*, ed. by Marco Santagata (Milan: Mondadori, 1996), p. 491. See also Tassoni, *Considerazioni*, p. 289: 'che quanto a me il Poeta *parla a grotteschi* [...]'.

48   'Now, beyond the opinions of the aforementioned people, there are two other testimonies by

Ed. 1609, fol. †4^v

A questa non ricercata fede del Maestro s'aggiugne un *testimonio da Montefalco*, che fu Diego di Fuentes, il quale scrivendo la vita d'Ausiàs e volendola anch'egli contigiar di sue favole, fintosi contemporaneo del Petrarca, v'insertò fra l'altre queste parole: 'Fue Ausiàs laureado per poeta no menos affamado que lo fue el doctissimo Francisco Petrarca en nuestros tiempos.'[49]

The expression 'testimonio da Montefalco', which was absent in the first manuscript version, has just one known precedent in the *Idropica* of Guarini (the only modern author openly lauded in the *Considerazioni*), and must, in all probability amount to a kind of insult;[50] cf. *testimoni*: 'testicles'; *falcone*: 'male sexual organ'; and the analogous *Monte Gelboè, Monte Nero, Monte di Venere*: 'female sexual organ'; *Monte Morello, Monteritondo*: 'ass, anus'.[51] The low-comic insert thus functions to discredit the opinion of Fuentes. The text of the MS San Carlo 3 does not contain the expression (instead of which we find the neutral 'testimoni'), and, in effect, one

Spaniards saying that March lived before Petrarch, and that Petrarch stole a lot from him. One of these testimonies is by Diego de Fuentes, who wrote March's biography and, pretending to be a contemporary of Petrarch's, says about Ausiás, among other things: "Y tanto caminò por este tan honrado trabajo, que despues depor muchas excelencias suyas fue laureado por poeta, no menos affamado que lo fue el doctissimo Francisco Petrarca en nuestros tiempos"'.

49 'Ausiàs March, *Las obras del excelentissimo poeta Ausias Marc, cavallero valenciano. Traduzidas de lengua lemosina en castellano por el excelente poeta Jorge de Montemayor* [...] (Madrid: Francisco Sanchez, 1579), fol. A2^r. At the time of the printing of the *Considerazioni*, Tassoni only knew the Castilian translation of the works of March. In the following years, however, he came into possession of the Catalan text, and made use of it during the writing of the annotations to the *Considerazioni*. I retraced Tassoni's volume with *ex libris* and a few pen marks (for the most part coinciding with manuscript additions) in Paris (Bibliothèque Mazarine, 22136 Réserve): see Andrea Lazzarini, 'Appunti sulla ricezione italiana di Ausiàs March. Prima e dopo le *Considerazioni* di Alessandro Tassoni', in *Ausiàs March e il canone europeo*, ed. by Benedetta Aldinucci and Cèlia Nadal Pasqual (Alessandria: Edizioni dell'Orso, 2018), pp. 217–49 (pp. 230–41).

50 'Beyond this not requested declaration of the Master [i.e. López de Hoyos] there is also a *testimony from Montefalco*, that was Diego de Fuentes, who, writing Ausiàs' biography and wanting to embellish it with his own fabrications, pretending to be a contemporary of Petrarch's, inserted in it these words among the others: "Fue Ausiàs laureado per poeta no menos affamado que lo fue el doctissimo Francisco Petrarca en nuestros tiempos"'. See Battista Guarini, *Opere*, ed. by Marziano Guglielminetti (Turin: Utet, 1974), p. 450: 'PISTOFILO: Il medesimo ha detto Gostanza a me, signor sì. | Patrizio: *Testimonio di Montefalco*'. See also the *Progetto di risposta di Ant[on] M[aria] Salvini da farsi all'Anticrusca di Mess[er] Paolo Beni*, in Orazio Rucellai, *Saggio di lettere di O. R. e di testimonianze autorevoli in lode e difesa dell'Accademia della Crusca* (Florence: Magheri, 1826), p. 189: 'piglio Montefalco, perch'è terra nell'Umbria, provincia di Mess[er] Paolo, assai conosciuta, della quale è un proverbio (*testimoni da Montefalco*)'. On Tassoni's appreciation of Guarini, see Tassoni, *Considerazioni*, p. 91 (commentary on *RVF*, 43): 'Sopra la lontananza della sua donna, cantò eccellentemente il Guarino in que' tre sonetti: *Quando spiega la notte il velo intorno etc.* | *Or che 'l mio vivo sole altrove splende, etc.* | *Vedovo e fosco albergo, almo soggiorno, etc.* | Ma è da lasciare al tempo, imperoché le lodi degli uomini viventi, quelli che portano loro invidia non le possono patire. Oltra che sempre *vetera extollimus, recentium incuriosi*, come disse Cornelio'. In January 1609 Tassoni sent a copy of the *Considerazioni* to Guarini, who responded with a heartfelt letter of thanks, in which he placed him on guard with respect to the predictable polemics that the text would animate; the missive is published in Giovanni Campori, 'Appunti intorno Alessandro Tassoni', *Indicatore modenese*, 2 (1852), pp. 3–4, 9–11, 17–18, 25–27, 33–35, 41–42 (pp. 3–4).

51 Valter Boggione and Giovanni Casalegno, *Dizionario letterario del lessico amoroso. Metafore eufemismi trivialismi* (Turin: Utet, 2000) [hencefoward called *DLA*], pp. 538, 173, 336–37.

of the most significant tendencies of the rewriting process is the expansion of the literarily burlesque tone of the text.

For example, the commentary to *RVF*, 5 reads as follows:

> E se ne gli altri trascorro a notar quello ch'io ho giudicato da non imitare, non è il mio fine di tassar lui [*scil.* Petrarca], ma di levar le franchigie a certi che voglion comporre al dispetto della natura; e se le stitichezze loro non s'approvano, subito te le autorizano con *un esempio scappato dal pennaiuolo* al Petrarca in tempo di penuria; e che molte volte ancora (la Iddio grazia) non fa punto a proposito.[52]

'Scappato dal pennaiuolo' does not mean simply 'bursting forth from the pen', but rather 'bursting forth from the buttocks' (and plays on the contrast with the earlier 'stitichezze' or constipation, which boasts an ancestry tracing back to Aretino).[53] A *pennaiolo* is a small vase, cup, or other type of desk container in which one keeps pens or, in general, other things needed for writing; in a comedic register it signfies 'ass, or anus.'[54] The expression *rompere il pennaiolo* or 'sodomize' appears in Bracciolini's *Scherno*, in which Jupiter is said to have broken the *pennaiolo* of Ganymede after finding him alone in the forest ('[...] *ruppe in questi boschi, un dì che solo | trovollo, a Ganimede il pennaiuolo*').[55]

Another example of Tassoni's use of the low-comic register can be identified in the commentary to a 'Due rose fresche, et colte in paradiso' (*RVF*, 245 — the erasures present in the original manuscript have been maintained):

> MS S. Carlo 3, fol. 188^v
> *Due rose fresche e colte in paradiso*
> Li quaternarii di questo sonetto hanno sconcertatiss[im]a spiegatura, per quel passaggio di rose a bel dono che fece cangiare il viso. Io leggerei:
> A E l'uno e l'altro fe' cangiare in viso.
> ~~Che quantunque si legga altrove~~
> ~~Cangiati i volti e l'una e l'altra coma~~

---

52   'And if in the other [poems] I just highlight what I have deemed unworthy of imitation, I do not intend to levy a tax on him [i.e. Petrarch], but to remove the exemptions to those that want to compose in spite of nature; and if their constipation is not approved, they immediately authorize it with an example bursting forth from Petrarch's pen container when he was not inspired, and which often (thank God) does not even serve their purpose'.

53   See *stitichezza* 'eccessiva meticolosità, pignoleria, pedanteria [...] derivante da ristrettezza di vedute e da meschineria e angustia di pensiero': *GDLI*, xx, 203. See 'A chi legge', in Alessandro Tassoni, *La secchia rapita*, ed. by Ottavio Besomi, 2 vols (Padua: Antenore, 1987–1990), II, 435: 'La favola è una, e se non è d'una solo, Aristotele non ristrinse mai i compositori a così fatte *stitichezze* e *strettezze*'. The term is part of the lexicon of the polemics on language and can probably be traced to Aretino (Pietro Aretino, *Lettere*, ed. by Paolo Procaccioli, 6 vols [Rome: Salerno, 1997–2002], IV, 339–40 [p. 340]: 'A ciò il nostro secolo pigliasse a scherzo *la stitichezza* de le età passate, le quali mettevano in nota e in memoria non che de i servi, ma de i filosofi, cose che la cuoca del mio mangiare si vergognarebbe a notarle in le mura de la cocina').

54   *Rompere il pennaiolo* 'sodomizzare' — *GDLI*, XII, p. 1024, 'ano' (in as much as it is a container of the *penna*, with the allusion to anal sex) — *DLA*, p. 396.

55   Francesco Bracciolini, *Lo scherno de' falsi dei* (Venice: Paolo Guerigli, 1618), XIV, 33, 5–8, p. 290: 'E non sol dele femmine e pulzelle | ma de' maschi il poltron si fece amante, | e ruppe in questi boschi, un dì che solo | trovollo, a Ganimede il pennaiuolo.'

~~Là è detto per un altro termine.~~
Con sì dolce parlare e con un riso
Da fare innamorare un uom selvaggio
Di sfavillante ed amoroso raggio.
Se costui che donò le rose era amante vecchio e persona grave come lo descrive il poeta, perché parlare poi come si farebbe d'un Adone e d'un Ganimede, attribuendoli raggi sfavillanti e viso che infiamma l'alme?
Serpentes avibus geminantur, tigribus agni
disse Orazio.[56]

Ed. 1609, pp. 328–29
Due rose fresche e colte in paradiso
Grande è il viluppo di questi quaternari, per quel passaggio di rose a bel dono che fe' cangiare il viso, e per l'ordine loro intralciato di sorte che ci vorrebbe la machina. Io leggo:
Due rose fresche e colte in paradiso
L'altr'ier nascendo il dì primo di Maggio
Appositivamente.
Bel dono, e d'un amante antiquo e saggio
Tra duo minori egualmente diviso.
Con sì dolce parlare e con un riso
di sfavillante ed amoroso raggio
da far innamorar un uom selvaggio
a l'uno e l'altro fe' cangiare il viso.
Ed intendo che 'l dono delle rose fu quello che fe' cangiare il viso all'uno ed all'altro, venendo accompagnato da quel tal favellare e da quel tal riso del donatore.
Le chiama il poeta rose fresche, e non appassite, e colte in Paradiso per lo contento che portavano con essoloro: comeché, secondo il significato della parola, ogn'orto sia Paradiso.
Ma quello attribuire ad una persona vecchia e grave riso sfavillante ed amoroso da fare innamorare un uom selvaggio, mi riesce una pantalonata, e parmi vedere Amore in pelliccia colle pantofole a scaccafava. |
Serpentes avibus geminantur, tigribus agni
Direbbe qui Orazio, s'io non m'inganno.[57]

Tassoni takes note of the difficult syntax found in the first two quatrains and formulates an interpretative proposal by re-ordering the verses of the composition. In the first manuscript draft, we see that the author merely thought it unrealistic that

---

56 '*Two fresh roses, gathered in paradise*: The quatrains in this sonnet have a very disconcerted development, because of that transition from "roses" to "lovely gift" that made them "change their aspect". I would read: [...] If the one that gave the roses was, as the poet describes him, an old lover and a serious person, why then speaking as though he were an Adonis or a Ganymede, attributing to him sparkling rays and a soul-inflaming visage?'
57 '*Two fresh roses, gathered in paradise*: Great is the disconcert of these quatrains, because of that transition from "roses" to "lovely gift" that made them "change their aspect", and for their order so contorted that it would require a torture machine [to be stretched out]. I read: [...] And I mean that the gift of the roses was what made both "change their aspect", because it was accompanied by such a smile from the giver. *The poet calls them fresh roses, and not withered, and gathered in Paradise because of the enjoyment they brought with them: even though, according to the meaning of the word, every garden is Paradise.* But attributing to an old and serious person a smile so sparkling and lovely that a savage man would fall in love with it seems a *pantalonata* to me, and it is like I was seeing Love in a fur coat and slippers'.

a lover so 'antiquo e saggio' could 'far innamorare un huom selvaggio', as though he were Ganymede or Adonis, who were renowned for their ephebic beauty; this judgment was then sealed with the canonical reference to l. 13 of Horace's *Ars poetica*. In the print edition, Tassoni instead develops a playful comparison with the 'pantalonate' (comedies featuring an elderly Pantalone as protagonist) in which the plot scenarios usually had to do with his unhappy marriages to very young women. Tassoni even imagines the figure of Amore 'in pelliccia colle pantofole a scaccafava' — clothing, in other words, that characterized Pantalone (the 'pantofole a scaccafava' are in all probability a memory of Caro's burlesque *Commento* on Molza's *Ficheide*).[58]

In the re-elaborated print version, the reference to Adonis and Ganymede is replaced by a notation on the freshness of the roses picked in Paradise, which leads the author to assert, with the pretense of offering historical-etymological observation, that 'ogni orto *è* Paradiso' [every garden *is* Paradise], where the risqué double meaning deploying *orto* as a reference to 'female genitalia' is obvious.[59]

In fact, this kind of obscene allusion is quite frequent. Another case is found in the commentary on the first two quatrains of *RVF*, 148 ('Non Tesin, Po, Varo, Arno, Adige e Tebro'):

> Non Tesin, Po, Varo, Arno, Adige et Tebro,
> Eufrate, Tigre, Nilo, Hermo, Indo et Gange,
> Tana, Histro, Alpheo, Garona, e 'l mar che frange,
> Rodano, Hibero, Ren, Sena, Albia, Era, Hebro;
>
> non edra, abete, pin, faggio o ginebro
> poria 'l foco allentar che 'l cor tristo ange,
> quant'un bel rio ch'ad ognor meco piange
> co l'arboscel che 'n rime orno et celebro.
> [...][60]

Tassoni notes that this catalogue of rivers ('leggenda de' fiumi') does no honour to Petrarch and that is self-evident that no wood taken from any tree has the capacity to put out fire. Petrarch, as had been observed by the commentary tradition beginning with Vellutello, was actually referring to the shadows cast by the branches of the trees: it is possible that Tassoni's observation has a reactive and ironic undertone.[61] But still, the reader is more struck by the malicious reading

58   Annibal Caro, *Gli straccioni, comedia. La Fichieide, comento. La Nasea e La statua della foia, dicerie di A. C.* (Milan: G. Daelli e Comp., 1863), p. 135: 'Dal ginocchio in giù ha in gamba un paio di usatti ricotti a due suola con buone fibbie, ed in piedi sopr'essi un paio di *pantofole a scaccafava*'. A scaccafava indicates 'un tipo di calzature di uso popolare, con suola larga e piatta' (*GDLI*, XVII, 726).
59   *DLA*, p. 366.
60   Not Tesino, Po, Varo, Arno, Adige, or Tiber, Euphrates, Tigris, | Nile, Hermus, Indus or Ganges, Don, Danube, Alpheus, | Garonne, the sea-breaker Timavus, Rhon, Ebro, Rhine, Seine, | Elba, Loire, or Hebrus— || not ivy, fir, pine, beech, or juniper–could lessen the fire that | wearies my sad heart as much as a lovely stream that from time | to time weeps along with me, and the slender tree that in my | rhymes I beautify and celebrate'. I quote from Francesco Petrarca, *Petrarch's Lyric Poems: The 'Rime sparse' and Other Lyrics*, ed. by Robert M. Durling (Cambridge: Harvard University Press, 1979), p. 294.
61   Tassoni, *Considerazioni*, p. 224 'Io non ho mai letto né inteso dire che alcuno di questi alberi si abbia proprietà d'allentare il fuoco, ma gli ho ben veduti servire a conservarlo, ed ardere come gli

proposed for l. 7 ('Quant'un bel rio ch'ad ogn'or meco piange').

> MS S. Carlo 3, fol. [150^r]
> *Quant'un bel rio ch'ad ogn'or meco piange.*
> Tristo significato più facilmente che buono può darsi a questo verso, applicandolo non a Lumergue, ma *al rio più segreto di Laura, con tristo epiteto di lagrimoso e colante.*[62]

> Ed. 1609, p. 224
> *Quant'un bel rio ch'ad ogn'or meco piange.*
> Scandaloso significato potrebbe ricever questo verso applicandolo non a Lumergue, *ma ad un rio più segreto, con tristo epiteto di lagrimante.*[63]

I believe that the specimens proposed here are sufficient to determine the absolute singularity of Tassoni's commentary work, and to signal a strong discontinuity between the places that truly comment on the Petrarchan text and the many that, on the other hand, merely use the verses as a starting point for observations of an extemporaneous nature.

Conclusions

Just as the *Secchia rapita*, with its mixture of the serious and the burlesque, has been read as a requiem for the languishing heroic poem, the *Considerazioni* — with a ferocity equal to the outdatedness of the attack — savages the 'defunct' genre of the Petrarchan commentary. Although the disagreement with Ascanio Colonna is not negligible in terms of a personal motive, it is not easy to identify the literary motivations that led to the writing of the work: Tassoni was not particularly interested in lyric poetry, and he was even less moved by the contemporary fashion for a 'militant' Petrarchism (Tassoni, who was champion of the moderns but at the same time a critic of modernity, still connected the influence of the *Canzoniere* to some typically Baroque forms of excess).[64]

One is led to believe that the *Considerazioni*, with their systematic antidogmatism, are not so much aimed at destroying the *Canzoniere* itself as a model, so much as, in its literary variation, the very principle of authority itself. This continued exercise in 'skepticism' is perhaps one of the most fascinating aspects of Tassoni's work.

---

altri e più degli altri; perciochè il genebro arde benissimo verde e del pino si fanno facelle ch'ardono come la cera.' Cf. Alessandro Vellutello, *Le volgari opere del Petrarca con la esposizione di A. V. da Lucca*, (In Vinegia: per Giovanniantonio e fratelli da Stabbio, 1525), fol. 45^r: 'Quello che il nostro innamorato poe[ta] volse nel presente so[netto] in sentenzia significare si fu che non era in facultà del rinfrescamento di tutte le altre acque, né di tutte le altre piante (le cui foglie per se stesse e mediante la loro ombra rinfrescamento rendere) di allentare ed alquanto amorzare il fuoco.' Modern commentators are in complete agreement with Vellutello, see Petrarca, *Canzoniere* (ed. Santagata), p. 715; Francesco Petrarca, *Canzoniere. Rerum vulgarium fragmenta*, edited by Rosanna Bettarini, 2 vols (Turin: Einaudi, 2005), I, 714.

62   '*As much as the lovely river that always weeps with me*: This verse could more likely be interpreted in a scabrous sense, by referring it not to Lumergue but to *Laura's most secret river, with the sad epithet of "weeping and draining"*'.

63   '*As much as the lovely river that always weeps with me*: This verse could be interpreted in scandalous sense by referring it not to Lumergue, *but to a more secret river, with the sad epithet of "weeping"*'.

64   See Andrea Lazzarini, 'Poesia eroicomica e satira poetica: Tassoni, Bracciolini, Marino', *Nuova rivista di letteratura italiana*, 17 (2014), 107–47.

CHAPTER 8

❖

Petrarch, Aristotle, and the Inquisition: The Controversy between Giuseppe degli Aromatari and Alessandro Tassoni

Laura Benedetti

This essay aims to analyse one of the most acrimonious controversies of the seventeenth century, which involved Alessandro Tassoni (1565–1635), future author of *The Stolen Bucket* (1622), and Giuseppe degli Aromatari (1587–1660), at the time a young student at the University of Padua. The main documents of this contentious dispute are the five volumes that Tassoni and Aromatari published, either under their real names or pseudonyms, between 1609 and 1613: Alessandro Tassoni, *Considerazioni sopra le Rime del Petrarca* (1609);[1] Giuseppe degli Aromatari, *Risposte alle considerazioni del Sig. Alessandro Tassoni sopra le Rime del Petrarca* (1611);[2] Tassoni (Crescenzio Pepe), *Avvertimenti al Sig. Giuseppe Aromatari intorno alle risposte date da lui alle Considerazioni del Sig. Alessandro Tassoni sopra le Rime del Petrarca* (1611);[3] Aromatari (Falcidio Melampodio), *Dialoghi in risposta agli Avvertimenti dati sotto il nome di Crescenzio Pepe a Giuseppe Aromatari intorno alle Risposte fatte da lui alle Considerazioni del Sig. Alessandro Tassoni sopra le rime del Petrarca* (1613);[4] and, finally, Tassoni (Girolamo Nomisenti), *La tenda rossa. Risposta ai Dialoghi di Falcidio Melampodio* (1613).[5]

What began as 'una pura disputa di cose poetiche, senza rancore di sorte alcuna'[6] [a mere dispute about poetry, without any animosity whatsoever] degenerated into

1   Alessandro Tassoni, *Considerazioni sopra le Rime del Petrarca* (Modena: Cassiani, 1609). The volume also includes a discussion of some passages of Petrarch's *Trionfi* and a selection of Girolamo Muzio's notes on Petrarch's *Canzoniere*.

2   Giuseppe degli Aromatari, *Risposte alle considerazioni del Sig. Alessandro Tassoni sopra le Rime del Petrarca* (Padua: Orlando Iadra, 1611).

3   Crescenzio Pepe, *Avvertimenti al Sig. Giuseppe Aromatari intorno alle risposte date da lui alle Considerazioni del Sig. Alessandro Tassoni sopra le Rime del Petrarca* (Modena: Cassiani, 1611).

4   Falcidio Melampodio, *Dialoghi in risposta agli Avvertimenti dati sotto il nome di Crescenzio Pepe a Giuseppe Aromatari intorno alle Risposte fatte da lui alle Considerazioni del Sig. Alessandro Tassoni sopra le rime del Petrarca* (Venice: Deuchino, 1613).

5   Girolamo Nomisenti, *La tenda rossa* (Frankfurt [Modena]: [n. pub.], 1613).

6   This is how Tassoni himself described the controversy in the letter he wrote to Alfonso Molza on 27 May 1611 (Alessandro Tassoni, *Lettere*, ed. by Pietro Puliatti [Bari: Laterza, 1978], I, 70), also included in Pepe, *Avvertimenti*, p. 4. The expression is quoted in Antonio Daniele, '"Una pura disputa di cose poetiche, senza rancore di sorte alcuna". Alessandro Tassoni, Cesare Cremonini e Giuseppe degli Aromatari,' in Antonio Daniele, *La memoria innamorata. Indagini e letture petrarchesche* (Rome-Padua: Antenore, 2005), pp. 219–47.

a vehement argument that provides insights not only into Petrarch's exegesis but also into its philosophical and religious implications.

The controversy was ignited by the 1609 publication of Alessandro Tassoni's *Considerazioni sopra le Rime del Petrarca*, a work that can be considered both a culmination of the author's reflection on Petrarch and the prelude to the attacks against the Accademia della Crusca that would characterize the 1612 edition of his *Pensieri*. In a memorable *incipit*, Tassoni claims to have penned the work during his trip to Spain:

> Lettore, opera di viaggio è questa, tessuta nel cuor del verno; parte tra l'onde, e gli scogli d'un tempestoso mare; parte fra le balze, e l'arene di due infecondi Regni; e dopo ne' triboli, e rancori d'amare liti ricorsa: stravagante stagione, liti strani e diversi, intempestiva opportunità, nuovi e bizzarri umori.[7]

Readers who are drawn to the volume by the promise of an unusual interaction between the textual journey and Tassoni's physical travels throughout Europe, however, are bound to be largely disappointed. Only rarely, in fact, does the author establish a connection between his travels and his reading of the *Canzoniere*. In his discussion of the sonnet 'Ite, caldi sospiri, al freddo core' (*RVF*, 153),[8] for instance, he amusingly compares Petrarch's warm sighs with the extreme temperatures that force him to stop at Les Martigues:

> Ma viemmi da ridere, che mentre sto qui scrivendo [...] s'è gelata tutta questa marina, e tutto questo stagno di Martega di sorte, ch'egli ci vorrà altro, che sospiri a rompere il ghiaccio per uscirne.[9]

In another instance, he draws a comparison between 'L'aura gentil, che rasserena i poggi' (*RVF*, 194) and his own work:

> È sonetto che mostra appunto essere stato fatto per cammino, come le mie *Considerazioni*, benché a me cominci omai a parere di non essere più in cammino, essendo oggi ventitré giorni che io mi trovo gelato e confinato in questa maledetta Riviera.[10]

Finally, Tassoni's own entrance into Saragozza coincides with the very last poem of the *Canzoniere*,[11] thus perfecting the comparison between the textual journey and the author's physical itinerary.

These isolated instances are not enough to sustain Tassoni's presentation of

---

7   'Reader, this is a travel book, woven in the depths of winter, partly between the waves and the rocks of a stormy sea, partly between the cliffs and the shores of two sterile kingdoms; and later reexamined among the tribulations and the animosity of bitter disputes. The season was strange, the lands different and foreign, the occasion untimely, and the humors new and bizarre' (Tassoni, *Considerazioni*, fol. †3)

8   All references are from Francesco Petrarca, *Canzoniere*, ed. by Marco Santagata (Milan: Mondadori, 1996).

9   'And I almost laugh when I notice that, while I am busy writing, the sea and the pond of Les Martigues have frozen in such a way that it will take more than sighs to break the ice and get out' (Tassoni, *Considerazioni*, p. 228).

10   'This is a sonnet that seems to have been composed whilst travelling, like these *Considerazioni* of mine, although I am beginning to feel that I am no longer travelling, as for the past twenty-three days I have been frozen and confined by this accursed river' (Tassoni, *Considerazioni*, p. 265).

11   Tassoni, *Considerazioni*, p. 460.

the volume as an 'opera di viaggio'.[12] The few scholars who have discussed the *Considerazioni*, all believe it unlikely that Tassoni could have penned such an erudite work without consulting several sources. Even if the author began his work in 1602, during his trip to Spain, he must have completed and revised it during the years between the end of the journey and the granting of the *imprimatur* in 1608.[13] Indeed, Tassoni himself seems to allude to two phases in his writing when he says that *Considerazioni* was 'tessuta' in the depths of winter and later 'ricorsa' among various troubles. This is confirmed by Orazio Bacci's careful analysis of the manuscript, that he divides into two parts written at different times ('parte antica' and 'parte nuova').[14]

As he does not intend to write for the 'idiots',[15] and as he trusts that virtually everyone in his audience must own a copy of the *Canzoniere*, Tassoni does not provide the full text of Petrarch's poems. He proceeds with a methodical examination that numbers sonnets, ballads, sextains, songs, and madrigals according to their position in the sequence of poems with a similar metric structure. The standard division between poems written during Laura's life and after her death is strongly underlined, as the numbering starts again with the first poem of the new section. 'Oimè il bel viso, oimè il soave sguardo' (*RVF*, 267) therefore becomes Sonnet 1 of the Second Part. Although some of the poems only receive cursory attention, Tassoni's decision to consider all of them is striking in light of the censorship that had struck Petrarch's work in the sixteenth century. While the entire *Canzoniere* was scrutinized with suspicion during the Counter-Reformation, explicit condemnation was reserved for the sonnets in which Petrarch had criticized the corruption of the clergy. Published in 1580, the Parma *Index Librorum Prohibitorum* banned three poems ('Fiamma dal ciel su le tue treccie piova' [*RVF*, 136], 'L'avara Babilonia à colmo il sacco' [*RVF*, 137], and 'Fontana di dolore, albergo d'ira' [*RVF*, 138]), while in 1590 the condemnation was extended to a fourth sonnet, 'De l'empia Babilonia, ond'è fuggita' (*RVF*, 114). The Index compiled in 1593 under Pope Clement VIII reiterated the ban of these poems, which resulted in their omission from most of the subsequent editions of the *Canzoniere* until 1722.[16] In light of these events, it is certainly remarkable that Tassoni included all the incriminated poems in the *Considerazioni*, thus restoring the integrity of Petrarch's work. Sonnet 114 ('De l'empia Babilonia') is hastily

---

12   Andrea Lazzarini (see his chapter in this volume) points out that the published version of *Considerazioni* contains fewer allusions to the journey compared to the manuscript, which suggests Tassoni's decreasing confidence in this narrative strategy.

13   Orazio Bacci points out that Tassoni's request for the *imprimatur* dates back to the end of 1606, which seems to indicate that by that time the author already believed the volume ready to be printed. See Orazio Bacci, *Le Considerazioni sopra le Rime del Petrarca di Alessandro Tassoni* (Florence: Loescher and Seber, 1887), p. 5.

14   Bacci, pp. 6–7. On the philological issues related to *Considerazioni* see also Daniele, pp. 221–22, and Lazzarini's chapter in this volume.

15   Tassoni, *Considerazioni sul Petrarca* (1609), p. 6.

16   See Luisa Avellini, 'Proposte per il Petrarca all'"Indice" negli anni del papato Boncompagni', in *Italianistica*, 33.2 (2004), 133–41. On Pier Paolo Vergerio's role in these events see María Luisa Cerrón Puga, 'Nel labirinto di Babilonia. Vergerio artefice della censura di Petrarca,' in *Annali della Scuola Normale Superiore di Pisa. Classe di Lettere e Filosofia*, 5th ser., 1.2 (2009), 387–424.

dismissed: its condemnation, Tassoni claims, was not a great loss for poetry.[17] The cryptic Latin quote that follows, however, seems to allude to a different kind of damage. 'Manebant etiam tum vestigia morientis libertatis' [There remained even yet some traces of dying liberty], Tassoni writes, quoting Tacitus (*Annals*, I. 74).[18] As Gabriele Bucchi has demonstrated, Tassoni was an attentive reader of Tacitus. The Latin historian provided, among other things, 'testimonianza di esempi virtuosi ed eroici da opporre alla meschinità del presente' [testimony of virtuous and heroic examples in opposition to the pettiness of the present].[19] The enigmatic quote from Tacitus could therefore be interpreted as a reference to the traces ('vestigia') of the original *Canzoniere* that Tassoni inserts in the *Considerazioni* by listing the banned sonnet, and/or even to Tassoni's surreptitious expression of intellectual freedom that led to the inclusion of the incriminated poem. The other three censored sonnets are grouped together and only briefly described:

> In questi tre sonetti il Petrarca lavora di straforo, e dà il cardo alla Corte di Roma, perciò come scandalosi si tralasciano.[20]

Tassoni's only comment concerns a possible alternative interpretation of these three sonnets, that is dismissed as 'di poco giudizio' [foolish]. While preserving the integrity of Petrarch's work and stressing the 'scandalous' potential of the banned sonnets, Tassoni is careful to avoid the controversy that a thorough discussion of the poems could ignite. Following in the author's cautious footsteps Ludovico Antonio Muratori, in his 1711 edition of *Considerazioni*, reproduced these same passages without adding any comments on his part.[21]

The objective of *Considerazioni*, as stated in its first pages, is twofold: on the one hand, Tassoni intends to depart from the unconditional veneration that many pay to Petrarch by stressing features of his poems that no one should imitate; on the other, he plans to shed light on obscure or misunderstood passages, which, he maintains, will highlight the poet's originality. Tassoni declares from the outset that his real polemical target is not Petrarch but his followers, a statement that most critics have taken at face value but that is hard to justify in light of the fact that the author's disapproval is exclusively reserved for the *Canzoniere* and not for its many imitations. Furthermore, as Giosuè Carducci pointed out, an attack against Petrarch's followers seems oddly anachronistic at the beginning of the seventeenth century, when the phenomenon of *Petrarchismo* was on the wane.[22] It is as if Tassoni

17   Tassoni, *Considerazioni*, p. 174.
18   Tacitus, *Annals*, trans. by John Jackson (Cambridge, MA: Harvard University Press, 1937), p. 371.
19   Gabriele Bucchi, 'La tragedia (e la farsa) delle cose umane: Tassoni e Tacito', *Studi secenteschi*, 56 (2015), 3–29 (p. 8).
20   'In these three sonnets Petrarch acts secretively and criticizes the Roman court. Therefore, since they are scandalous, we will ignore them' (Tassoni, *Considerazioni*, p. 213).
21   Ludovico Antonio Muratori, in *Le Rime di Francesco Petrarca, riscontrate co i testi a penna della Libreria Estense, e co i fragmenti dell'originale d'esso poeta. S'aggiungono le Considerazioni rivedute e ampliate d'Alessandro Tassoni, le annotazioni di Girolamo Muzio, e le osservazioni di Lodovico Antonio Muratori* (Modena: Soliani, 1711), p. 243 and p. 308.
22   Giosuè Carducci, in *Rime di Francesco Petrarca sopra argomenti storici morali e diversi* (Livorno: Vigo,

needed a justification for his own painstaking attention to Petrarch's work in the new historical and cultural context. At the beginning of the seventeenth century, writing a commentary on the *Canzoniere* seems to have become an enterprise in need of a justification, however polemical.

Paradoxically, the *Considerazioni* would turn out to be the only complete commentary of the *Canzoniere* in the seventeenth century,[23] and would enjoy renewed fame when Ludovico Antonio Muratori republished it together with Girolamo Muzio's *Annotazioni* and his own notes. In the preface, Muratori shares words of praise for the *Considerazioni*, and takes issue only with its author's insistence on focusing on Petrarch's flaws, rather than his talent.[24] Muratori does not simply reproduce the 1609 *princeps*, but he complements it with the notes that Tassoni had written on his personal copy of the volume, presumably in view of a second edition. In this revised version, Tassoni's commentary would continue to circulate, as Muratori's work was republished in 1727, 1741, 1759, 1762, 1821–22, 1826–27, 1832, and 1837.[25]

The real importance of Tassoni's volume therefore lies in its contributions to Petrarch's exegesis. While the *pars destruens* of the *Considerazioni* — the irreverent and at times offensive attack on Petrarch — created much noise but eventually dissipated, its *pars costruens* — the erudite commentary of the *Canzoniere* — would constitute a valuable critical resource for future generations of readers and scholars.

Tassoni's careful analysis of Petrarch's poetry leads him to defend the poet against the accusation of having borrowed too freely from his precursors, be they Tuscan or Provençal. He is also generous in his praise of particular poems, such as 'In qual parte del ciel, in qual ydea' (*RVF*, 159) and 'Po, ben può tu portartene la scorza' (*RVF*, 180), both of which are qualified as 'bellissimo'.[26] 'Stiamo, Amor, a veder la Gloria nostra' (*RVF*, 192) clearly shows having been penned by a 'maestro dell'arte;'[27] 'Levòmmi il mio pensier in parte ov'era' is among the most excellent examples of lyrical poetry.[28] Commenting on the 'Canzoni Sorelle' — the three songs devoted to Laura's eyes [*RVF*, 70, 71, and 72] — Tassoni goes as far as to say that they alone would have earned Petrarch the poetic laurel, and promises to discuss them at length in a future work.[29] Highest admiration is indeed reserved for Petrarch's *canzoni*, whether they deal with love or other themes — though 'Verdi panni, sanguigni, oscuri o persi' (*RVF*, 29] is criticized as 'oscura e sconvolta'

1876), p. xxix.

23   See Bacci, p. 27. On seventeenth-century commentaries on specific poems in Petrarch's *Canzoniere*, see Simona Morando, 'Petrarca al vaglio degli affetti. Su alcuni commenti primo-secenteschi', *Lettere italiane*, 63.4 (2011), 505–33.

24   Muratori, p. viii.

25   See Pietro Puliatti, *Bibliografia di Alessandro Tassoni* (Florence: Sansoni, 1969), I, 66–76.

26   Tassoni, *Considerazioni*, pp. 233 and 251–52.

27   Tassoni, *Considerazioni*, p. 264.

28   Tassoni, *Considerazioni*, p. 383.

29   Tassoni, *Considerazioni*, pp. 128–29. A similar — and similarly unfulfilled — promise concludes the last installment in the controversy, *La tenda rossa*, where Girolamo Nomisenti announces Tassoni's plan of praising Petrarch's poetry in a separate volume (*La tenda rossa*, p. 269).

[obscure and distraught].[30] The opening lines of the seventh stanza of 'O aspectata in ciel beata e bella' (*RVF*, 28) elicit the highest praise:

> Meraviglie del Petrarca son queste, che non si leggono altrove; ristrignere in così pochi versi, e con tanta chiarezza, e grazia, e maestà, l'ambizioso, ed infelice passaggio di Serse sull'Ellesponto.[31]

Tassoni ends his work on a peculiar and almost contradictory note, defending Petrarch's last *canzone* against its detractors.

These occasional displays of admiration clash with instances of bitter criticism. At times, Tassoni finds Petrarch inconsistent in his depiction of Laura, as he oscillates between attributing an almost supernatural quality to his beloved ('O delle donne altero e raro mostro', he writes in *RVF*, 347) and treating her as a most ordinary woman ('femina è cosa mobil per natura'; *RVF*, 183).[32] Tassoni also takes issue with Petrarch's tendency to create contrast: 'Quando io movo i sospiri a chiamar voi' (*RVF*, 5), for instance, begins with praise only to end with silence, which strikes Tassoni as a useless contradiction ('contraddizioni spigolate senza profitto') and makes him wish Petrarch had omitted the sonnet from his collection altogether.[33] Nor does Petrarch's celebrated elegance escape the author's criticism: the quartets of 'Ai pie' de' colli ove la bella vesta' (*RVF*, 8), Tassoni writes, are more convoluted than the Devil's tail;[34] 'S'i' 'l dissi mai, ch'i' vegna in odio a quella' and 'Verdi panni, sanguigni, oscuri o persi' (respectively *RVF*, 206 and 29):

> sono come due cortiggiane alle quali il soperchio liscio abbia fatto cadere i capegli e marcirsi i denti; percioché la troppa squisitezza delle rime ha loro storpiati i concetti.[35]

Tassoni found the second of these two *canzoni* particularly disagreeable, as the final line of its fourth stanza seemed 'appicccicatali con lo sputo per far rima' [to be glued with spit just to form a rhyme].[36]

The greatest criticism, however, is reserved not for Petrarch's *canzoni* but for his sonnets,[37] which, Tassoni claims, must have been published by somebody other than Petrarch[38] and are like chickens at a market, with a good one always sitting

---

30   Tassoni, *Considerazioni*, p. 67.

31   'These are prodigies of Petrarch that cannot be read elsewhere; to condense in so few verses, and with such clarity, grace, and majesty, Xerxes's ambitious and ill-fated crossing over the Hellespont' (Tassoni, *Considerazioni*, p. 65).

32   Tassoni, *Considerazioni*, p. 254.

33   Tassoni, *Considerazioni*, p. 23. Another sonnet that Tassoni wishes Petrarch had omitted is *RVF*, 251: 'O misera et horribil visïone!' (*Considerazioni*, p. 332).

34   Tassoni, *Considerazioni*, p. 30.

35   '[...] are like two courtesans whose excessive care has caused their hair to shed and their teeth to rot; the extreme sophistication of their rhymes has distorted their meaning' (Tassoni, *Considerazioni*, p. 276).

36   Tassoni, *Considerazioni*, p. 278.

37   'Grande in ogni modo è la differenza che si conosce tra le canzoni ed i sonetti di questo poeta' [The difference between the poet's *canzoni* and his sonnets, however, is great] (Tassoni, *Considerazioni*, p. 98).

38   Tassoni, *Considerazioni*, p. 360.

next to a bad one.[39] Some seem to have been written hastily — like 'Poco era ad appressarsi agli occhi miei' (*RVF*, 51)[40] — or haphazardly — like 'Quando giugne per gli occhi al cor profondo' (*RVF*, 94).[41] 'Lasso, quante fïate Amor m'assale' (*RVF*, 109) feels like a 'spugna secca' [a dry sponge],[42] while 'Se 'l sasso, ond'è piú chiusa questa valle' (*RVF*, 117) is childish and could only be appreciated in Petrarch's times, when 'ogni ronzino passava per destriere'[43] [any nag was mistaken for a courser]. Tassoni is clearly more at ease with expressing scorn than praise, as he professes his admiration for Petrarch in rather generic terms, whereas he seizes with glee and colourfully exploits any opportunity to expose flaws and censor mishaps.

The first sonnet of the *Canzoniere*, 'Voi ch'ascoltate in rime sparse il suono', receives particular scrutiny. Tassoni chastises the lack of elegance of l. 11 ('Di me medesmo meco mi vergogno') and the prosaic cadence of l. 4 ('Quand'era in parte altr'uom da quel ch'i' sono'). As far as the content is concerned, Tassoni takes issue with the faulty logic that leads Petrarch to call 'giovanil' [youthful] an 'errore' [error] that had lasted twenty-one years, and to interpret shame and knowledge as the results of 'vaneggiar' [wandering].

In its irreverent attack on tradition, the *Considerazioni* anticipate some of the themes that Tassoni would develop in his *Pensieri*, published in 1612.[44] In this work, Tassoni publicly voiced his reservations concerning the first *Vocabolario degli Accademici della Crusca* [*Dictionary of the Crusca Academy*], published just a few months earlier. He was harshly critical of the solution to the *questione della lingua* (the attempt to provide a unified set of linguistic norms for the entire Italian peninsula) that the *Vocabolario* promoted.[45] In particular, Tassoni challenged the idea, at the core of the *Accademia*'s linguistic philosophy, that fourteenth-century Florentine (or Tuscan, as Tassoni used the two terms interchangeably) should be taken as a model. Tassoni's answer to the question 'Se trecento anni sono meglio si scrivesse in volgare italiano o nell'età presente' [whether written Italian was better three hundred years ago or in the present day] conveys the author's faith in the perfectibility of human inventions, and in the progress that time inevitably brings forth:

> Le lingue, come gli uomini stessi, nascono rozze, e tanto più rozza è da credere, che questa nostra nascesse, quanto ch'ella ebbe origine dalla corruzione della latina e d'altre varie straniere e barbare, che si meschiarono insieme nelle miserie d'Italia [...] È ben vero, che i nominati autori [nel *Vocabolario*] con

39 Tassoni, *Considerazioni*, p. 207.
40 Tassoni, *Considerazioni*, pp. 102 and 150.
41 Tassoni, *Considerazioni*, p. 150.
42 Tassoni, *Considerazioni*, p. 170.
43 Tassoni, *Considerazioni*, p. 176.
44 For a more complete treatment of this aspect of Tassoni's thought in the context of his life and other works see Laura Benedetti, 'Alessandro Tassoni', in *Dictionary of Literary Biography: Italian Writers of the Seventeenth Century*, ed. by Albert N. Mancini and Glenn Palen Pierce (Detroit, MI: Thomson Gale, 2008), pp. 255–63.
45 On the relationship between Tassoni and the Accademia della Crusca, see Pietro Puliatti, 'Il pensiero linguistico di Tassoni e la Crusca', in *Studi Secenteschi*, 26 (1985), 3–23; Bruno Arcudi, 'Alessandro Tassoni and the Accademia della Crusca', in *Forum Italicum*, 6 (1972), 378–92; and Paul B. Diffley, 'Tassoni's Linguistic Writings', in *Studi secenteschi*, 33 (1992), 67–92.

miglior giudicio degli altri cercaron di fare scelta delle frasi e voci, che loro parver più belle; ma sì non la seppero, né potero eglino far perfetta, che i moderni non abbiano trovato che riprendere, aggiugnere, moderare e lasciare, seguitando, oltre la ragione, anche l'uso, che è il vero giudice e padron delle lingue.[46]

The language used by the Medieval Florentine chronicler Giovanni Villani (c. 1280–1348) seemed to Tassoni less elegant and precise than that of Francesco Guicciardini (1483–1540), while Boccaccio's style, in his view, could only be imitated by creative writers, not by secretaries or authors of philosophical or political treatises. Throughout the discussion, Tassoni is firm in his refusal of an archaic and strictly literary solution to the *questione della lingua*. A similar attitude inspires the document *Incognito da Modana contro ad alcune voci del Vocabolario della Crusca* [*Unknown from Modana versus Some Words in the Crusca Dictionary*], which, however, was exclusively addressed to the *Accademia della Crusca*, and not destined for public circulation. Here Tassoni's tone is more sarcastic, both in the introduction (where the *Vocabolario* is defined as 'grandemente pernizioso alla gioventù e a' forestieri' [highly dangerous for youth and foreigners])[47] and in the annotations to individual entries, that range from witty to salacious. For instance, while the *Vocabolario della Crusca* prudishly defines 'culo' [ass] as 'parte del corpo con la quale si siede' [part of the body with which one sits], Tassoni is quick to comment: 'Nel mio paese si caca col culo e si siede con le natiche. Non so a Firenze' [where I come from, we use the ass to shit and the buttocks to sit. I don't know about Florence].[48] Himself a member of the *Accademia della Crusca* since 1598, Tassoni resented the extensive inclusion of obsolete terms in the *Vocabolario*: far from representing the true inclination of the *Accademia* at large, the archaisms constituted, in his view, the result of a 'mero capriccio d'alcuni particolari' [mere whim of some individuals].[49]

Tassoni's criticism of Petrarch's *Canzoniere* must therefore be interpreted as a prelude to a full-fledged attack on the linguistic, literary, and philosophical tradition that Petrarch seemed to embody, while the controversy that was about to ensue was another front of the battle in which he engaged, during the same years, against the principle of imitation. Like the *Pensieri* and the pamphlet against the Accademia della Crusca, the *Considerazioni* display reluctance to grant traditional authorities acritical and unconditioned power over modern creativity.

It was perhaps Tassoni's attitude and irreverence, more than the specific

---

46   'Languages, like men themselves, are born unrefined, which is all the more true for our language, that originated from the corruption of Latin and other barbarian and foreign languages, that were mixed together in the misery of Italy [...] It is true that the authors quoted [in the *Vocabolario*], more than the others, tried to choose phrases and terms that they considered more beautiful. But they did not know how, nor were they able to make a perfect choice. Modern authors thus found it necessary to criticize, add, moderate and drop, following not only reason, but also custom, which is the real judge and master of languages' (Alessandro Tassoni, *Varietà di pensieri* [Modena: Verdi, 1612], pp. 555–56).
47   Alessandro Tassoni, *Incognito da Modana contro alcune voci del Vocabolario della Crusca*, in Id., *Scritti inediti*, ed. by Pietro Puliatti (Modena: Aedas Muratoriana, 1975), pp. 125–49 (p. 127).
48   Tassoni, *Incognito da Modana*, p. 135.
49   Tassoni, *Incognito da Modana*, p. 126.

objections concerning particular passages, that prompted Giuseppe degli Aromatari to pick up his pen in defence of Petrarch. The result was the *Risposte*, published in Padua in 1611. The work is introduced by Giovan Battista Bottini's letter to Marco Antonio Salvucci.[50] Bottini claims to have obtained a sample of Aromatari's work and decided to publish it in order to please Salvucci, who had originally requested it. He also describes Aromatari as a twenty-year-old man who had taken a break from his medical studies to answer Tassoni's criticism. This may serve as a justification of the fact that, in spite of the title, the *Risposte* only deals with the first ten poems examined by Tassoni, and one fourth of the book is devoted to a rebuttal of Tassoni's criticism of Petrarch's first sonnet. The discussion, however, is not limited to Petrarch. In particular, Aromatari upholds the authority of Aristotle's *Poetics* that Tassoni had instead considered a mere draft:

> Che la *Poetica* d'Aristotele poi sia uno abbozzamento, questa è un'opinione seminata dal Castelvetri; e è stata da tanti, e tanti con tante, e sì efficaci ragioni ributtata; che se non si sciolgono quelle, io non posso crederla per abbozzo a un semplice detto del Signor Tassoni.[51]

It is a revealing passage. Aromatari clearly shows that the debate goes beyond a mere assessment of Petrarch's poetic ability and involves many ('tanti, e tanti') interpreters of Aristotle, whose authority he holds in greater esteem than that of his interlocutor. While usually respectful, Aromatari is also fearless, and becomes increasingly self-assured as the work progresses, to the point of accusing Tassoni of deliberately altering Petrarch's lines to prove his point, and of pretending to forget his own findings when such omissions help him strengthen a particular interpretation.[52]

Ever so inclined to challenge all authorities, Tassoni did not, however, tolerate criticism of his own work, which led to another chapter in the controversy, the *Avvertimenti*. Writing under the pseudonym of Crescenzio Pepe, Tassoni accused Aromatari of having lied about his age, of having misrepresented Tassoni's work, of having taken too long to answer the *Considerazioni* and of having done so with the help of the entire city of Padua. The latter accusation referred to Tassoni's suspicion that Aromatari was little more than a spokesperson for Padua's Aristotelian circle and in particular for his professor, philosopher Cesare Cremonini. In order to make the topic more lively, Tassoni resorts to a dialogical format. Speaking on Tassoni's

---

50   Information about these other two men involved in the controversy is scant. Marco Antonio Salvucci is described as a 'buon letterato perugino' by Giovan Battista Vermignoli (*Biografia degli scrittori e notizie delle opere loro*, [Perugia: Vincenzo Bartelli e Giovanni Costantini, 1828], t. I, part I, p. 235), but very little has survived of his work. Marco Antonio Bonciario's volume *Idyllia et selectarum epistolarum centuria nova: cum decuriis duabus* (Perugia: Marco Naccarino, 1607) contains both a letter from Bonciario to Salvucci and a short piece by Salvucci himself (respectively at pp. 108 and 311–13).
51   'The idea that Aristotle's *Poetics* is but a draft is an opinion spread by Castelvetro. It has been refuted by many with many and very persuasive arguments; until these arguments are proven wrong, I cannot consider it a draft just because Signor Tassoni says so' (Aromatari, *Risposte*, p. 47). Tassoni had referred to Aristotle's *Poetics* as an 'abbozzamento' in *Considerazioni*, p. 20. For Daniele, Tassoni's irreverence toward Petrarch was only a consequence of his rejection of Aristotle's authority (p. 225).
52   Aromatari, *Risposte*, pp. 72 and 93.

behalf, Crescenzio Pepe quotes and rebuts several passages from the *Risposte*, but he keeps his own voice too, which allows him to admit, somewhat begrudgingly, some mistakes on Tassoni's part.[53] It is clear, however, that Petrarch's exegesis is no longer the author's primary concern. He is more interested in mocking his adversary for his use of Greek, reiterating his view on the limits of Aristotle's *Poetics*, and impressing readers with his puns.[54]

The debate was obviously becoming acrimonious, as demonstrated by the fact that in his new response, *Dialoghi*, Giuseppe Aromatari, now writing under the pseudonym of Falcidio Melampodio, asks for the protection of Cardinal Alessandro d'Este. It was also becoming more and more difficult for readers — and perhaps for the authors themselves — to orient themselves, to follow and distinguish between the arguments of the two contenders and those of their fictional spokespersons. Even Aromatari shows some uncertainty in the organization of his material. First, he — or, rather, his spokesperson, Falcidio Melampodio — states that he will use codes to indicate the origin of the different arguments — using the letter A to for the *Avvertimenti*, C for the *Considerazioni*, R for the *Risposte* — but he then switches to a different narrative strategy. He pretends to fall asleep and to see Crescenzio Pepe in a dream. The work is therefore structured as a dialogue between Falcidio and Pepe with the added complication that later in the volume Falcidio wakes up, has dinner, and a man at his table volunteers to play the role of Crescenzio Pepe to continue the conversation.

It was easy for Tassoni to mock his rival's convoluted strategy in the last instalment of the debate, *La tenda rossa*. Here the tone becomes openly derogatory and bellicose, which may explain why the volume bears on its cover a false place of publishing — Frankfurt — rather than the real one — Modena. The fictional author is a servant of Tassoni — as if the author could not stoop to answering his opponent directly — and the title contains a not-so-veiled threat:

> [Il Re dei Tartari] nelle sue guerre metteva la prima giornata una tenda bianca in segno di general perdono. E se 'l nimico non si rendeva, mettea la seconda giornata una tenda rossa ch'era indizio di morte a tutti coloro c'avessero prese l'armi. Ma se questo poi non bastava, mettea la terza giornata una tenda nera, che dinotava l'ultimo sterminio di ogni età, d'ogni sesso.[55]

Continuing the war metaphor, Tassoni names his arguments as blows delivered with different weapons. He also moves farther and farther away from the issues at hand to address his opponent's alleged lack of respect in challenging the *Considerazioni*.

It is hard for modern readers to see what could have prompted such heated responses on Tassoni's part, except for his notoriously irascible temperament and oversized opinion of himself. There is even evidence that Tassoni, at least in one

---

53   Pepe, p. 179.

54   Pepe, pp. 59, 127–28, and 76.

55   '[The King of Tartars] during his wars, on the first day, pitched a white tent as a sign of general forgiveness. If the enemy did not surrender, on the second day he pitched a red tent to indicate the death of those who would fight against him. If that did not suffice, on the third day he pitched a black tent that signified the death of everybody, regardless of age or sex' (Tassoni, *La tenda rossa*, pp. 2–3).

case, had found Aromatari's objections very sound and planned to incorporate them into a subsequent edition of his work. In discussing the sonnet 'Que' ch'infinita providentia et arte' (*RVF*, 4) in the *Considerazioni*, Tassoni had criticized Petrarch's choice to compare Rome not to Bethlehem, but to the entire Judea. Aromatari, quoting Bottini, had instead maintained that Petrarch did not intend to establish a comparison but simply provide three examples of humility — the apostle John, Christ, and Laura.[56] In the Muratori edition of the *Considerazioni* — which, as previously mentioned, incorporates Tassoni's handwritten notes to his personal copy of the volume — Tassoni himself subscribes to this interpretation. Bypassing Aromatari, he appropriates Bottini's view of that particular passage:

> Il Signor Giovan Battista Bottini tiene che 'l Petrarca in quello Sonetto non faccia comparazione, ma rechi solamente tre esempi, o casi che vogliam dirli, ne' quali abbia Dio maravigliosamente esaltato l'umiltà [...], la quale esposizione non può se non lodarsi.[57]

Obviously Aromatari, Bottini, and Tassoni are not radically different in their premises and criteria, which could have kept the discussion within the boundaries of civility. But Tassoni's scorn at having to tolerate the fastidious and usually impeccable objections of an unknown student of medicine, together with his suspicion of having become the target of a Paduan conspiracy, led him to abandon all restraint and furiously lash out at his opponent. Furthermore, as noticed by Leto Alessandri,[58] Tassoni took the controversy to a much more dangerous level. In *La tenda rossa*, he seems to be targeting not so much Giuseppe Aromatari but rather his teacher, the renowned Aristotelian scholar Cesare Cremonini whom, as previously mentioned, he suspected of having instigated the *Risposte*. The relationship between Aromatari and Cremonini was indeed strong and well documented. Leonello Leonelli reported that young Aromatari, on his way from Perugia to Montpellier to study medicine, was so struck by Cremonini's lectures in Padua that he never resumed his journey to France.[59] Cremonini's prestige was indisputable and international. His lessons attracted intellectuals of the calibre of Justus Lipsius and Gabriel Naudé,[60] but also put him at the forefront of the debate on intellectual freedom. During forty years of teaching, Cremonini, among other things, defended his university from the influence of the Jesuits[61] and established

---

56   Aromatari, pp. 48–49.

57   'Signor Giovan Battista Bottini claims that Petrarch in that sonnet is not making a comparison but simply alleging three examples, or instances if you prefer to call them so, in which God has wonderfully extolled humility [...] Such an explanation can only be praised' (Muratori, p. 16).

58   Leto Alessandri, 'Giuseppe degli Aromatari, difensore del Petrarca contro Alessandro Tassoni', in *Atti dell'Accademia properziana del Subiasio in Assisi*, 2.8–9–10 (1904), 121–68 (pp. 142–44).

59   Leonello Leonelli, *Giuseppe Aromatari. Letterato, medico, naturalista* (Assisi: Froebel, 1887), p. 6.

60   Gabriel Naudé left a memorable portrait of Cesare Cremonini in *Naudeana et Patiniana* (Amsterdam: François Vander Plaatz, 1703), pp. 53–57.

61   Already in 1591 — the same year he started teaching in Padua — Cremonini travelled to Venice to voice the concerns of his university about the competition of the Jesuits. See Charles B. Schmitt, 'Cesare Cremonini', in *Dizionario biografico degli italiani* (Rome: Istituto dell'Enciclopedia Italiana, 1960–), xxx (1984), <http://www.treccani.it/enciclopedia/cesare-cremonini_(Dizionario-Biografico)/> [accessed 25 April 2019]; and Maria Assunta Del Torre, *Studi su Cesare Cremonini*.

himself as a formidable and uncompromising interpreter of Aristotle. This activity did not escape the attention of the Inquisition, that monitored his teachings from 1604 to 1626. The main charge against Cremonini was that, following Aristotle, he had gone as far as denying the immortality of the soul. Cremonini's standard line of defence was to separate philosophy from theology and to affirm his right to teach all of Aristotle's works, including those that contained opinions contrary to Christian doctrine. This is precisely the line of defence that Tassoni debunks in *La tenda rossa*:

> Aristotile, e Alessandro, noi ancor li vogliam per maestri; ma non già in tutte le cose come volete voi, perché non siamo Eretici [...]. Ma forse verrete con la solita goffa distinzione, ch'altro è parlar filosoficamente, altro come teologo. [...] *Verum non est contrarium vero.* O è falsa la dottrina d'Aristotele, e d'Alessandro; o è falsa la Teologia. Rispondete a questo dilemma.[62]

This attack arrived at a time when Cremonini was facing the harshest scrutiny. His volume *Disputatio de coelo: adiecta est apologia dictorum Aristotelis de via lactea, de facie in orbe lunae*, in fact, was published in 1613, the same year as *La tenda rossa*, and immediately prompted two notes from the Inquisition. The first of these documents listed forty passages that were deemed questionable, while the second recommended a new and revised edition that would modify the incriminated passages and include the author's firm condemnation of Aristotelian principles in disagreement with catholic doctrine.[63] In his response Cremonini reiterated his distinction between St. Thomas's authority as a theologian — which he claimed undisputable — and his role as an interpreter of Aristotle which could, on the contrary, be subject to debate.[64]

An analysis of the development of the controversy that would continue to set Cremonini at odds with the Inquisition until the philosopher's death in 1631 falls beyond the scope of this essay. It is important to point out, however, that Tassoni's sly remarks threatened the reputation of both Aromatari and Cremonini at a particularly perilous time. Tassoni's behaviour is all the more disconcerting in light of his cautious treatment of Petrarch's four banned sonnets, which reveals his awareness of the dangers of openly challenging religious authorities. His accusations are renewed and made even more precise towards the end of *La tenda rossa*, where Nomisenti refuses to introduce more examples to criticize his opponent because, he claims, he has already wasted enough time:

> Parendomi d'haver gittato pur troppo tempo e carta questi due mesi, massimamente scrivendo contra persona che parte per Inghilterra a concordar

---

Cosmologia e logica nel tardo aristotelismo padovano (Padua: Antenore, 1968), pp. 16–17.

62 'We also want to follow the teachings of Aristotle and Alexander, but not all of them, because we are not heretics [...] But perhaps you will come up with your usual awkward distinction that speaking like a philosopher is one thing, speaking like a theologian is another thing [...] Truth cannot be the contrary of the truth. Either Aristotle and Alexander's philosophy is false, or theology is. Solve this dilemma' (Tassoni, *La tenda rossa*, p. 8).

63 The notes from the Inquisition are included in Léopold Mabillaud, *Étude historique sur la philosophie de la Renaissance en Italie (Cesare Cremonini)* (Paris: Hachette, 1881), pp. 349–57. See also Del Torre, pp. 53–63.

64 Mabillaud, p. 361.

Calvino con Alessandro Afrodiseo.[65]

Tassoni's report of Aromatari's journey is not only tendentious but also incorrect, as it does not appear that the doctor accepted King James's invitation to England.[66] Unable to reply to his opponent with critical and rhetorical arguments, Tassoni resorts to intimidation, ending his volume with a clear threat:

> Guardinsi pur essi come censurano i Principi e i Religiosi, che importa più, che il censurare i Poeti. E di questo sia detto assai.[67]

Enough said, indeed. Tassoni had taken the controversy to a domain where arguing could have had dangerous repercussions. It was paradoxical, for a writer who was so ready to mock tradition and authorities, to invoke the power of the Inquisition against those who had dared oppose him. If Aromatari wrote a new reply, he wisely decided not to publish it.[68] He went on to become a celebrated physician, while his brave attempt to discuss Petrarch's poetry would earn him the plaque that to this day decorates a home in Assisi, in memory of the 'letterato che difese il Petrarca' [the man of letters who took Petrarch's defence].[69]

---

65   'It seems to me that I wasted even too much time and paper in these two months, especially writing against somebody who is leaving for England to reconcile Calvin with Alexander of Aphrodisia' (Tassoni, *La tenda rossa*, p. 268).

66   Aromatari seems to have turned down the invitation precisely for religious reasons (Leonelli, p. 7). Tassoni himself realized his mistake — though he did not seem to consider it very relevant — in a letter that he wrote to Annibale Sassi on 31 October 1613 (see Tassoni, *Lettere*, p. 117).

67   'They should mind how they criticize noble and religious people, which has more serious consequences than criticizing poets. Enough said' (Tassoni, *La tenda rossa*, p. 269).

68   In two letters dated 9 April 1614 and 4 June 1614, both addressed to Annibale Sassi, Tassoni mentions a possible answer that Aromatari was preparing with Cremonini's help (Tassoni, *Lettere*, I, pp. 135 and 145). Puliatti reports that Aromatari filed and then withdrew a lawsuit against Tassoni (*Bibliografia*, I, p. 86).

69   According to Francesco Santucci, however, the house that bears the inscription is not the one where Aromatari was born ('L'antica famiglia degli Aromatari', in *Giuseppe Aromatari nel quarto centenario della nascita*, ed. by Giuseppe Catanzaro, Otello Ciacci, and Francesco Santucci [Assisi: Accademia Properziana del Subasio, 1987], pp. 7–39 [pp. 29–33]).

CHAPTER 9

'Nobiltà dello stile' and 'grandezza e rarità del pensiero': Petrarch and the Petrarchists in Apostolo Zeno's *Giornale de' letterati italiani* (1710–18)[1]

Giacomo Vagni

1. Introduction

The 'Giornale de' letterati italiani' was founded by Apostolo Zeno, Scipione Maffei, and Antonio Vallisneri in 1710, and was published quarterly in Venice by the printer Hertz, who was able to distribute it all over Italy.[2] It was published regularly in Venice, in forty tomes, until 1727, and then sporadically, in 1733, 1739, and 1740. Between 1710 and 1718 the Journal was supervised by Zeno, who also handled directly, with his brother Pier Caterino, the literary and historical subjects, while Maffei coordinated the legal contributions, and Vallisneri the medical.[3]

The journal was the product of a Northern-Italy erudite élite, rooted in Veneto but closely linked with the scholars active in Emilia and Tuscany, and with the literary and ecclesiastical authorities in Rome.[4] Following the tradition of erudite

1   This research was developed at the University of Lausanne as part of the project 'Lirici del Cinquecento da Crescimbeni a Croce. Il petrarchismo come mito fondativo della modernità letteraria italiana', funded by the SNSF (project ID: PZ00P1_174066).
2   Brendan Dooley, 'The *Giornale de' Letterati d'Italia* (1710–40): Journalism and "Modern" Culture in the Early Eighteenth-Century Veneto', *Studi Veneti*, 6 (1982), 229–70 (pp. 248–49). See also Brendan Dooley, *Science, Politics, and Society in Eighteenth-Century Veneto. The 'Giornale de' letterati' and its World* (New York; London: Garland, 1991); *Il 'Giornale de' letterati d'Italia' trecento anni dopo. Scienza, storia, arte, identità (1710–2010). Atti del convegno (Padova, Venezia, Verona, 17–19 novembre 2010)*, ed. by Enza del Tedesco (Pisa-Rome: Fabrizio Serra, 2012); *Indici del 'Giornale de' Letterati d'Italia'*, ed. by Michela Fantato, foreword by Corrado Viola (Pisa-Rome: Fabrizio Serra, 2012).
3   Giuseppe Ricuperati, 'Giornali e società nell'Italia dell'Ancien Régime', in Valerio Castronovo, Giuseppe Ricuperati, and Carlo Capra, *La stampa italiana dal Cinquecento all'Ottocento* (Bari: Laterza, 1976), pp. 117–64 (p. 129, with a complete list of names and tasks of the editorial board and of the collaborators).
4   Andrea Battistini, 'La cultura del primo Settecento', in *Storia generale della letteratura italiana*, ed.

journalism, it propagated information about the most important recent books in all kind of disciplines. The journal provided synthesis that aimed toward objectivity: the critical point lay in the choice of the works to be digested more than on explicit claims about their value.[5] In this sense limiting its range of interests to Italian publications was itself a basic form of criticism, justified as a response to the widespread lack of knowledge about the activities of Italians scholars, and by the wish to sustain the ongoing reform of Italian culture.[6]

The term 'literature', as was common in the eighteenth century, covered the whole range of culture: the main part of the journal (especially after the departure of Apostolo Zeno for Vienna, in 1718) was dedicated to sciences.[7] But the debate on poetry and language was no less important: the task of renovating the whole Italian culture could not be accomplished without dealing also with the decadence of the 'belle lettere'.[8] Therefore, the thirty or so issues published in the eight years of Apostolo Zeno's supervision represent a privileged viewpoint on the reception of the lyric poetry tradition in early eighteenth-century culture.[9]

The nineteenth-century reception of Petrarchism as the 'chronic disease' of Italian culture would turn upside down the judgement of the Arcadian age:[10] nonetheless, some of the issues dealt with in the early eighteenth-century discussions anticipated certain patterns that were to structure the modern understanding of that phenomenon.[11] Therefore, this essay will consider what the Journal published about Medieval and Renaissance lyric poetry in the years of Zeno's supervision: the extended period represents an emblematic and influential experience in this context, and will permit us to deepen our awareness of how critical reflection on Petrarchism was conducted in a crucial moment for the constitution of the modern history of Italian literature.

---

by Nicola Borsellino and Walter Pedullà, VII: *Il secolo riformatore. Poesia e ragione nel Settecento* (Milan: Motta, 2004), pp. 28–115.

5   See Scipione Maffei, *Letterati d'Italia. Introduzione al 'Giornale' (1710)*, ed. by Francesca Brunetti, with an essay by Cesare De Michelis (Venice: Marsilio, 2009).

6   From a wider point of view, as argues Dooley ('The *Giornale*', p. 230): 'the *Giornale* represented a final attempt to counterbalance the intellectual hegemony of centralized transalpine nation-states by creating an independent unity within Italian letters'; see also Françoise Waquet, *'Per la gloria e onore dell'Italia'. Sur le contexte idéologique du 'Giornale'*, in *Il 'Giornale de' letterati d'Italia' trecento anni dopo*, pp. 13–20.

7   Ricuperati, p. 146.

8   Ricuperati, p. 137.

9   Michele Mari, *La critica letteraria nel Settecento* (Milan: Ledizioni, 2013), pp. 9–35. See also Giuseppe Nicoletti, 'Agli esordi del petrarchismo arcadico: appunti per un capitolo di storia letteraria fra Sei e Settecento', in *Il Petrarchismo nel Settecento e nell'Ottocento*, ed. by Sandro Gentili and Luigi Trenti (Rome: Bulzoni, 2006), pp. 31–66.

10   See Arturo Graf, *Attraverso il Cinquecento* (Turin; Florence: Loescher, 1888).

11   See Amedeo Quondam, 'Sul Petrarchismo. Dieci anni dopo', in *Petrarca, l'Italia, l'Europa. Sulla varia fortuna di Petrarca. Atti del Convegno di studi (Bari, 20–22 maggio 2015)*, ed. by Elisa Tinelli, foreword by Davide Canfora (Bari: Edizioni di Pagina), pp. 243–58; and Simone Albonico, 'Appunti su "forma" e "materia" nella poesia di Pietro Bembo e del suo tempo', in *Lirica in Italia 1494–1530. Esperienze ecdotiche e percorsi storiografici. Atti del Convegno (Friburgo, 8–9 giugno 2016)*, ed. by Uberto Motta and Giacomo Vagni (Bologna: I libri di Emil, 2017), pp. 73–100.

2. The Journal between Erudition, Literary History, and the 'Orsi-Bouhours Quarrel'

The introduction of the first issue praised the French journal *Mémoires de Trévoux* for its contribution to learning and religion, and added that the only point it was missing 'for its full perfection' was a proper engagement in studying 'Italian literature and its history', since its judgement on this subject was based 'on valueless perspectives, or on the trust of people who lacked any knowledge of our best authors':

> Una sola cosa per l'intiera sua perfezione pare da desiderarsi, ed è che alcuno di que' pregiatissimi Soggetti si compiacesse d'impiegar qualche tempo nell'istruirsi a fondo della Letteratura Italiana e dell'Istoria di essa: conciosiaché mal corrispondono alla purgatezza del rimanente i loro giudizi del gusto Italiano nell'Eloquenza e nella Poesia, formati e sopra cose di nessun prezzo, e su la fede d'alcuni che la minima notizia non ebbero degli ottimi nostri Autori.[12]

If they knew Italian culture, continued the author (Scipione Maffei), the Jesuits that edited the *Mémoires* would have seen that 'the balance' they 'so charitably wish' to Italians had been born in Italy along with its vernacular poetry, had gained perfection in the fourteenth century and never really left the country, not even in periods of decadence such as the fifteenth and seventeenth centuries:

> Vedrebbero allora che quel buon senso ch'essi con tanta carità ci vanno augurando nacque fra noi al nascere di nostra Lingua, e già nel Secolo del 1300 a perfezione era giunto; vedrebbero ch'egli non mancò in Italia giammai, benché nel XV Secolo alquanto meno si coltivasse, e benché nel XVII in alcuna Provincia patisse disastro; e vedrebbero finalmente ch'egli fiorisce ancora oggigiorno quanto in altro tempo mai fosse, come il Giornale ch'ora intraprendesi darà loro facilmente a vedere.[13]

The journal assumed the task of showing Europe how the 'buon senso' was still flourishing in Italy. As we see, the influence of French culture, and at the same time, competition with it, marked the journal's attitude and programme from its very beginning.[14]

Louis XIV's French classicists had developed a cultural politics aiming to present their culture as the fulfilment of Italian Renaissance, finally ratifying the superiority of the 'moderns' upon the 'ancients'.[15] On the contrary, Italian modern poetry appeared to them as dominated by artifice and bad taste: the very opposite of the values of rational clarity they searched in literature. Before the end of seventeenth century, Italian scholars identified Father Dominique Bohours's book *La Manière de bien penser dans les ouvrages d'esprit* (Paris: Veuve Mabre-Cramoisy, 1687) as the synthesis and the symbol of such an attack, and dedicated themselves

---

12   *Il Giornale de' letterati italiani*, I (1710), 13–67 (pp. 24–27).
13   Ibid.
14   Waquet, p. 18.
15   Cesare de Michelis, 'All'origine del *Giornale de' letterati d'Italia*', in *Il 'Giornale de' letterati d'Italia' trecento anni dopo*, pp. 21–28 (pp. 23–24). See also *La Querelle des Anciens et des Modernes*, ed. by Anne-Marie Lecoq, preceded by 'Les abeilles et le araignées', essay by Marc Fumaroli, with an afterword by Jean-Robert Armogathe (Paris: Gallimard, 2001).

to its deconstruction.[16] In the introduction cited above we can easily recognize the figure of the French Jesuit behind the sketch of people 'lacking any knowledge of our best authors'. Bouhours was indeed explicitly accused of inadequate proficiency in the study of the best Italian poets in the next issue of the *Giornale*, that included a review of the Italian 'official' reply to his text, the *Considerazioni sopra un famoso libro Franzese intitolato 'La Manière de bien penser'* by Giovan Gioseffo Orsi (Bologna, Pisarri: 1703; but 1704). Summarizing Orsi's arguments, the reviewer explained that he had defended Tasso and Bonarelli and left aside 'others though famous', because they had not been criticized by Bouhours, 'who maybe did not know many excellent imitators of Petrarch, and maybe not even the Master of Lyrical Poetry himself'.[17] The name of Petrarch, besides, had already been implicitly evoked by Maffei when he stated that Italian language and taste attained their perfection in the fourteenth century. Since its very foundation, as we see, the journal's claim against the charge of the decadence of Italian culture could not help recalling the father of Italian lyrical poetry.

After a long review of Orsi's *Considerazioni* against Bouhours, an even longer account was dedicated to the 'literary disputes' about it.[18] The journal — not surprisingly — fully sustained Orsi's position, stating that his whole work stood out for an 'excellent judgment' and a 'remarkable temperance'.[19] An apparently neutral résumé of the objections to Orsi was followed by punctual replies in favour of him. The nationalistic background of the operation ensured that, paradoxically enough, the journalist attacked not the French Jesuits of Trévoux — who according to him rightly attempted to defend their homeland — but instead Francesco Montani of Pesaro, who by publishing anonymously a pamphlet against Orsi's dialogues had betrayed the Italian cause.[20]

The reasons for a 'struggle between nations' frankly overtook literary ones,

---

16   See Maria Grazia Accorsi and Elisabetta Graziosi, 'Da Bologna all'Europa: la polemica Orsi-Bouhours', *La rassegna della letteratura italiana*, 93 (1989), 84–136; Corrado Viola, *Tradizioni letterarie a confronto. Italia e Francia nella polemica Orsi-Bouhours* (Verona: Fiorini, 2001); and Corrado Viola, *Osservazioni sul canone nell'età dell'Arcadia e Tradizioni letterarie a confronto nella polemica Orsi-Bohours* (Verona: QuiEdit, 2009), pp. 39–57.

17   'Non si ragiona di altri benché celebri, che in gran numero ha avuti la Nazione Italiana, perché altri non sono stati criticati dal P[adre] B[ouhours], il quale per avventura non aveva cognizione di tanti eccellenti imitatori del Petrarca, e né pur quasi dello stesso Maestro della Lirica Poesia', *Giornale de' letterati d'Italia*, 2 (1710), 151 (see also pp. 121–22).

18   *Giornale de' letterati d'Italia*, 2 (1710), 116–61, and 3 (1710), 77–194.

19   *Giornale de' letterati d'Italia*, 2 (1710), 161: 'In tutta l'Opera spicca un sommo giudizio, e una singolare moderazione: cosa assai difficile a praticarsi, particolarmente da chi scrive in materia di contese letterarie'.

20   *Giornale de' Letterati d'Italia*, 3 (1710), 79–80. The book against which the Journal argued was [Francesco Montani], *Lettera toccante le Considerazioni sopra la maniera di ben pensare scritta da un accademico *** al signor conte di *** l'anno 1705* (Venice: Basejo, 1709). An account was also given of the *Lettere di diversi autori in proposito delle Considerazioni del marchese Giovan Gioseffo Orsi sopra il famoso libro franzese [...]* (Bologna: Pisarri, 1707), where we find a lot of scholars involved with the Journal, such as Apostolo Zeno, Ludovico A. Muratori, Eustachio Manfredi, and Anton Maria Salvini (see Viola, *Tradizioni*, p. x).

putting aside apparent differences.[21] Orsi's strategy to defend Italian honour — tacitly endorsed, or at least not questioned by the Journal — stood basically on the long-established principle of 'autorizzamento': the exhibition of *loci paralleli* from Latin authors or from Petrarch to defend the verses Bouhours found baroque and artificial aimed to demonstrate both the ignorance of the Frenchman and the irrefutable 'pedigree' of the Italian poets. Such a criterion was anything but up to date: Muratori's reflection on 'buon gusto', carefully digested by the Journal in the first two tomes, had largely passed by this traditional form of criticism.[22] But in the context of the controversy, they could still go along almost peacefully. Together with the historical pattern fixed by Crescimbeni's *L'istoria della volgar poesia* (Rome: Chracas, 1698), they represented three different (but not incompatible) ways to achieve the same aim: the redeeming of Italian literature and tradition against French presumption.

Such an attempt at putting together conflicting positions and methods was not determined just for tactical reasons: rather, it was at the core of the Journal's attempt to renew and finally reunite the Italian *res publica litterarum*.[23] The quarrels between Muratori and Fontanini on one side, and the Arcadia schism on the other would have shortly put under threat such an illusion even inside the editorial board of the journal: but the very first issues still displayed an effort to present the Italian scholars' front as tight and compact.[24]

Despite the wide and ecumenical outlook of this project, the editorial board of the *Giornale* was first of all the expression of a Northern Italian cultural élite highly influenced by Benedictine seventeenth-century erudition.[25] This kind of sensibility plainly appeared in the opening statement of the 'Novelle letterarie' of tome five (1711).[26] Citing a passage of Father Louis Ellies du Pin's *Nouvelle bibliothèque des auteurs ecclésiastiques* (Paris: Pralard, 1686–91), the journalist blamed the present tendency to prefer modern vernacular 'trifles' to 'solid erudition', so provoking the loss of the 'infinite profit' that may be gained with the publication of 'unpublished works of the highest value' or of annotated editions of ancient authors:

> Saravvi tal città che abbonderà di rarissimi antichi Manoscritti, e che si pregerà di Soggetti eccellenti nella critica e nelle lingue, e con tutto ciò non vi si stamperanno che Operette volgari e Sonetti. La cecità nostra in questa parte è incredibile e portentosa, poiché tralasciando il danno che ne proviene agli studi,

21   For Voltaire's definition of the Orsi-Bohours quarrel as a 'querelle des anciens et des modernes', which had turned to a 'querelle entre nations', see Viola, *Tradizioni*, pp. xi–xii.

22   Viola, *Tradizioni*, pp. 394–95. Lamindo Pritanio's *Riflessioni sopra il Buon Gusto intorno le Scienzie e le Arti* (Venice: Pavino, 1708) were reviewed in *Giornale de' letterati d'Italia*, 1 (1710), 283–316; Lodovico A. Muratori, *Della perfetta poesia italiana [...]*, 2 vols (Modena: Soliani, 1706), II (1710), 162–90.

23   Ricuperati, pp. 125–26.

24   Silvia Tatti, 'Il *Giornale* e Roma: lo scisma d'Arcadia', in *Il 'Giornale de' letterati d'Italia' trecento anni dopo*, pp. 311–20.

25   Paolo Golinelli, '"Nemo solus satis sapit". Dal *Giornale de' letterati* del Bacchini al *Giornale de' letterati d'Italia*', in *Il 'Giornale de' letterati d'Italia' trecento anni dopo*, pp. 145–54 (p. 152).

26   The 'Novelle letterarie', in the final part of each issue, reported briefly the news of the books freshly published or in print.

confinati perciò nelle bagattelle, e tralasciando la gloria che volontariamente cediamo alle altre Provincie, egli è manifesto che ci venghiamo in questo modo a privare d'un utile infinito che potrebbe ritrarsene, così dal pubblicare cose inedite di sommo pregio, come dal fare edizioni d'Autori antichi, accresciute, e illustrate, e collazionate con tanti preziosi codici che nelle librerie inutilmente marciscono.[27]

Philologically accurate editions, whether of unpublished works or of annotated classical texts, were the most desirable outcome of the scholars' efforts, and a basic feature to regain Italian supremacy in European culture. The need to boost such endeavours was not the least of the Journal's concerns. The judgment on modern writers' editions, as we will see, was established on these same criteria, enhancing above all publication of the unpublished, biographical reconstructions based on new documents, and annotations to texts. The more general aim of such an attitude was the (re)construction of a tradition, a tradition established more on the material base of books and documents than on the spiritual connections between abstract ideas.

This same stance emerges in a subtle but explicit way in the long digest of the works 'concerning the history of vernacular poetry' of Giovan Mario Crescimbeni.[28] A substantial introductory note stated that his essential contribution to the knowledge of the 'qualities of our language and of our poetry' and to the 'promotion of the good use' of it was not only due to 'the famous Assembly of Arcadia' he founded and coordinated, but above all to his writings.[29] Crescimbeni's 'erudite' publications were lined up with the Journal's battles: a new understanding of the Italian poetic tradition appeared to be a fundamental step for the reform of culture.[30] Among Crescimbeni's works, what best met the journalist's taste and gained the most explicit praise was the fifth book of the 'Commentari'. It was 'the most intriguing and the most useful' work, because it included 'the report of the efforts made concerning the works of many vernacular poets' — that is, an outline of lessons, annotations, and commentaries 'that made us know the beauties of our poetry'.[31]

The recourse to late sixteenth-century commentaries and academic lessons was highly appreciated and strongly advised for modern editions of past authors.[32]

27   *Giornale de' letterati d'Italia*, 5 (1711), 382–83. We find similar terms in Muratori's early scripts: see Corrado Viola, *Canoni d'Arcadia. Muratori Maffei Lemene Ceva Quadrio* (Pisa: ETS, 2009), p. 35.

28   *Giornale de' letterati d'Italia*, 6 (1711), pp. 174–261; the review was completed, after the printing of the last books of the 'Commentari', in t. XI (1712), 269–89.

29   See *Giornale de' letterati d'Italia*, 6 (1711), p. 174: 'Il Sig. Canonico Crescimbeni ha molto contribuito sì a far conoscere i pregi della nostra Lingua, e della nostra Poesia, sì a promoverne nell'Italia il buon uso. A tal effetto non tanto egli è concorso con lo stabilimento della celebre Radunanza degli Arcadi, della quale egli è perpetuo Custode, quanto co' propri componimenti in diversi tempi da lui pubblicati'.

30   Tatti, pp. 318–20. Apostolo Zeno's letters show he himself had projected the writing of a history of Italian literature which he never accomplished: see Fabio Danelon, 'Scrivere per un nuovo pubblico (giornalismo e storiografia letteraria nel primo Settecento). Dopo il *Giornale de' letterati d'Italia*: gli *Scrittori d'Italia* di Giammaria Mazzucchelli', in *Il 'Giornale de' letterati d'Italia' trecento anni dopo*, 247–57 (p. 254).

31   *Giornale de' letterati d'Italia*, 6 (1711), 181–82.

32   On sixteenth-century exegesis of lyric poetry see Pietro Petteruti Pellegrino, *La negligenza dei*

An example is the digest of the *opera omnia* of one of the most important poets of the Arcadian canon, Giovanni Della Casa (Florence: Manni, 1707).[33] Reviewing the book, the journalist praised the reference to past commentary exploited by the modern editor, and argued that these were not 'the only outstanding efforts elaborated by distinguished men upon Casa's rhymes'.[34] He acquainted the reader with about ten more sources (mostly expositions and academic lectures) on the subject, stating that 'if a collection of the complete works of Monsignor Della Casa was ever thought of again — as it seems to be in the desire of some amateurs of fine literature — it could exploit, if not all of them, at least some of the following [documents], which would be of great help to demonstrate the eminence [of this opus]'.[35]

3. Petrarch and the Rights of Criticism

Between the Journal's references, the Modenese Ludovico Antonio Muratori's influence cannot be overestimated.[36] His production in the poetic field was carefully described: the first tome extensively summarized his 'Progetto della nuova Repubblica Letteraria d'Italia' (1703) and the writings that had discussed it;[37] the second and third respectively reviewed his *Della Perfetta Poesia Italiana* (Modena: Soliani, 1706)[38] and the essays that dealt with it;[39] the eighth digested his new edition of Petrarch's *Canzoniere*.[40]

Muratori's Petrarch edition is a key point for the critic on the *Canzoniere* in eighteenth century.[41] Thus, it is worth seeing how the work was received by the Journal, to see whether or not its pioneering proposals were understood and enhanced. A first brief notice on the edition to come was given in the 'Novelle letterarie' of the second tome.[42] It was presented as a philologically accurate work, with new textual variants from two manuscripts from the Biblioteca Estense

---

poeti. Indagini sull'esegesi lirica dei moderni nel Cinquecento (Rome: Bulzoni, 2013); and *Il poeta e il suo pubblico. Lettura e commento dei testi lirici nel Cinquecento. Convegno internazionale di studi (Ginevra, 15–17 maggio 2008)*, ed. by Massimo Danzi and Roberto Leporatti (Genève: Droz, 2012).

33   *Giornale de' letterati d'Italia*, 4 (1710), 164–211.

34   *Giornale de' letterati d'Italia*, 4 (1710), 172: 'Queste però non sono le sole considerabili fatiche lavorate da uomini insigni sopra le Rime del Casa'.

35   See ibid.: 'Se mai di tutte l'Opere di Monsig. della Casa nuovamente Raccolta si meditasse, come pare che in persona amatrice delle buone lettere ve n'abbia talento, si potrebbe fars'uso, se non di tutte, almeno di alcuna delle seguenti, che molto gioverebbono ad illustrarle'.

36   Ricuperati, p. 134.

37   *Giornale de' letterati d'Italia*, 1 (1710), 267–320.

38   *Giornale de' letterati d'Italia*, 2 (1710), 162–90.

39   *Giornale de' letterati d'Italia*, 3 (1710), 375–94.

40   *Giornale de' letterati d'Italia*, 8 (1711), 177–98.

41   See Mario Fubini, 'Le *Osservazioni* del Muratori al Petrarca e la critica letteraria nell'età dell'Arcadia', in *Dal Muratori al Baretti. Studi sulla critica e sulla cultura del Settecento* (Rome-Bari: Laterza, 1975), I, 49–173; Roberto Tissoni, *Il commento ai classici italiani nel Sette e nell'Ottocento (Dante e Petrarca). Edizione riveduta* (Padua: Antenore, 1993), pp. 11–30; Viola, *Tradizioni*, pp. 391–417; Rossella Bonfatti, *L'«erario» della modernità. Muratori tra etica ed estetica* (Bologna: Clueb, 2010).

42   *Giornale de' letterati d'Italia*, 2 (1710), 506–07.

compared with the author's originals from Ubaldini's edition (Rome: Grignani, 1642), and the annotations of Alessandro Tassoni (Modena: Cassiani, 1609) and Girolamo Muzio (Venice: Dusinelli, 1582), in addition to Muratori's. One remark of the journalist touched on what would be a major problem in presenting Muratori's work, his criticism of many of Petrarch's poems 'that was going to stir up a hornets' nest':

> Seguitano le *Considerazioni* del Sig. Muratori intorno alle virtù Poetiche del Petrarca, senza però tacersi quel tanto che talvolta sembra meno lodevole nelle medesime: colla qual impresa ben vedesi ch'egli più che mai farà per istuzzicare, come suol dirsi, il vespaio.[43]

The same theme was resumed in the extended review: this was clearly perceived as the most problematic point, that above all deserved and needed a defence. The journalist lingered again on Muratori's (and Tassoni's) detection of 'imperfections' in Petrarch's writings, claiming that the author's task was surely not the questioning of the poet's authority — even if he had indeed censored many of his poems:

> Egli bene spesso mostra che le opposizioni del Tassoni al Petrarca non sono di molto peso: tanto è lontano che egli abbia voluto scriver quest'Opera per dir male di questo poeta; anzi, non molto dopo protesta esser più desideroso di lodarlo 'da per tutto' che di biasimarlo, 'ancorché' dic'egli 'poche volte': il che non so se gli verrà fatto buono dagli amatori del Petrarca, essendo vero che i componimenti ove il Sig. Muratori si ferma con la censura sono in assai maggior numero di quelli ove secondo lui non apparisce difetto.[44]

The reviewer found it appropriate to reiterate the issue one more time in the conclusion of his paper, highlighting that Muratori's attitude in judging Petrarch was sincere and unbiased — and so, in turn, demanded an unbiased reading, so to understand how his notes were 'useful and praiseworthy' for the comprehension and imitation of the Master:

> chi leggerà attentamente queste *Osservazioni*, e senz'alcuna passione o prevenzione contraria, le giudicherà utili e lodevoli, e riporrà il loro Autore nel numero di quelli che meglio si sono affaticati per illustrare i componimenti di questo Poeta e per agevolarne agli studiosi la più lodevole imitazione.[45]

The Journal had already offered a similar reflection on the topic in the 'Novelle letterarie' of the sixth tome, when announcing the publishing of the book. These lines had been written — if not by Muratori himself — by someone that sharply and openly supported him, and constituted the first apology, right after the printing, of his work on the *Canzoniere*. 'However strange such a severe examination may seem to Petrarch's worshippers', it attacked caustically, 'they should consider whether it has been conducted with righteousness and fairness', only to detect 'the beauties and the glitches' of this 'excellent example' of poetry — a poetry composed, nonetheless, by 'a man', exposed as everyone else 'to imperfections':

---

43   *Giornale de' letterati d'Italia*, 2 (1710), 507.
44   *Giornale de' letterati d'Italia*, 8 (1711), 179.
45   *Giornale de' letterati d'Italia*, 8 (1711), 197–99.

per quanto possa parere strano a i veneratori del Petrarca il severo esame che se ne fa dal Sig. Muratori, eglino però hanno esattamente e senza passione a riflettere se quell'esame sia fatto su le norme del giusto, e debbono anzi ricevere a buon grado l'intenzione retta di lui, che non per altro si è dato a ricercar le bellezze e i difetti di questo Poeta, il quale ciò non ostante sarà sempre un ottimo ed eccellente esemplare, se non acciocché quegli che si pongono ad imitarlo e studiarlo si fermino con lo studio e con l'imitazione in quelle cose che lo rendono incomparabile, e meno si lambicchino il cervello sopra di quelle che pur ci fanno conoscere che il Petrarca era uomo, cioè soggetto ad imperfezioni, e che egli scriveva in un tempo e in una lingua in cui ancora e' non avea chi imitare.[46]

What is for us the most original and ground-breaking point in Muratori's method — the recourse to critical judgment, instead of tradition, to value the writing of the most eminent Italian poet — was perhaps too subtle to be directly picked up by most of the readers (even consenting ones, as it is proved by Orsi's unpublished apology of the book).[47] The problem of judgment with arguments not openly stated by the annotator did not go unnoticed by the Journal, but it was quickly solved by making reference to the theoretical part of *Della perfetta poesia italiana* (already digested in tome two), where the author had largely explained his method.[48]

What seemed more urgent, even to those who approved and enhanced what Muratori was trying to do, was not to discuss the theoretical foundation of literary criticism, but to justify his right to criticize Petrarch's poems as driven by the pedagogical wish to contribute to better imitation. Such an effort to explain that Muratori did not intend to challenge the pre-eminence of Petrarch is consistent with the Journal's programme: the generation of scholars such as Crescimbeni, Zeno, and Muratori himself had sketched for the first time a linear and coherent path in Italian history that directly linked modern poetry to its fourteenth- and sixteenth-century origins. This freshly shaped history of Italian literature allowed both the claim of Italian 'primogeniture' in the rebirth of *humanae litterae*, and the possibility of giving it continuity into modern times. As Petrarch was the recognized forefather of this rebirth, any attempt to question his authority would have had repercussions on the whole construction. It was, therefore, important to make clear — as Muratori himself tried to do in the foreword to his edition — that his objections to Petrarch's poems aimed to guarantee a stronger and better imitation: they were thus justified, consistently enough, as a way to reinforce Petrarch's authority.

On the other hand, as usual in the Journal's digests dealing with past authors, the main part of the review was dedicated to the poet's biography, sometimes integrating Muratori's with (minor) corrections and new information.[49] In addition

---

46   *Giornale de' letterati d'Italia*, 6 (1711), 513–14.

47   Viola, *Tradizioni*, pp. 397–99.

48   *Giornale de' letterati d'Italia*, 8 (1711), p. 181. Some of the philosophical premises of Muratori's reflection on 'buon gusto' were to find in the 'Introduction' to his *Riflessioni sopra il Buon Gusto intorno le Scienzie e le Arti* (Venice: Pavino, 1708), written by the Journal's collaborator Bernardo Trevisan and carefully summarized in *Giornale de' letterati d'Italia*, 1 (1710), 283–316.

49   One of the very few remarks on the edition concerned indeed the writing of Petrarch's life — the journalist, though judging it as 'one of the most exact' ever written, contested the lack

a few remarks concerned the layout of the annotated text and the completeness of the annotation. The journalist mentioned that the first reason why Muratori had reprinted the *Canzoniere* was that he had been given a copy of the rarest version of the *Considerazioni* of Alessandro Tassoni, 'reviewed and expanded from the author himself after the printing'.[50] The journalist regretted that Tassoni's additions were not clearly distinguished from the others, and that Muratori had just reproduced Tassoni's selection of Girolamo Muzio's notes instead of reporting all of them, since their source (the *Battaglie per diffesa dell'italica lingua*, published in 1582) was nowadays hard to find.[51]

Such an extreme scrupulousness, far from being mere pedantry, was completely coherent with the Journal's programme and values. This attention to biographical and philological features, rooted through Muratori in the Maurine tradition and not neglectful of some Renaissance examples, was the outcome of a specific perception of the connections between the past (to be discovered with a factual and carefully documented historical analysis) and the present.[52] The 'variorum' form of annotation, inspired by the humanists' tradition, gave the sense of the on-going chain of scholars — a selected community extending in both space and time — that had been working on the text. Such a tradition, carefully reconstructed and meticulously represented on the page, was the way both to canonize the text and to authorize modern critical activity on it.

Nonetheless, for Muratori — as well as for the reviewer who reported the statement with implicit agreement — the connection with such a tradition was active and not at all obliging. Tassoni had written an 'opera di buona critica', thus worth re-printing, while those who had preceded him had not, because they limited themselves to 'grammar and erudition', without indicating the 'beauties and flaws' of Petrarch's poems. The chain of tradition was a basic medium to guarantee the status of the opus, and was necessary at first for its comprehension, but the interpreter had the right and the duty to value and judge it.[53]

The rights of critique were discussed again some years later, in the review of another book involving judgment on Petrarch. Tomes twenty-six and twenty-seven contained a long digest of a work that is today almost completely forgotten: the second volume of the *Saggi de' letterati esercizi de' Filergiti di Forlì* (Forlì: Selva, 1714).[54] The review opened with effusive praise of the Academy of the Filergiti,

---

of footnotes for sources: 'Non può negarsi [...] che quella, la quale è stata qui compilata dal Sig. Muratori, non sia una delle più esatte, che abbiamo, come che a molti non piaccia il tralasciamento delle citazioni, e de' fonti, su' quali egli ha fondata di quando in quando la sua narrazione'; *Giornale de' letterati d'Italia*, 8 (1711), 186.

50   *Giornale de' letterati d'Italia*, 8 (1711), 178–79.

51   *Giornale de' letterati d'Italia*, 8 (1711), 183–84. The printed sources cited by the journalist are: *Considerazioni sopra le Rime del Petrarca d'Alessandro Tassoni [...] Aggiuntavi nel fine una scelta dell'Annotazioni del Muzio ristrette, e parte esaminate* (Modena: Cassiani, 1609) and *Battaglie di Hieronimo Mutio Giustinopolitano, per diffesa dell'italica lingua [...] Et alcune bellissime annotationi sopra il Petrarca* (Venice: Dusinelli, 1582).

52   Viola, *Canoni*, pp. 54–56, and 78–79.

53   *Giornale de' letterati d'Italia*, 8 (1711), 178–79.

54   *Giornale de' letterati d'Italia*, 26 (1716), 186–228, and 27 (1716), 324–54.

implicitly compared with institutions such as the Crusca and the Arcadia.[55] A very long summary was then dedicated to the first part of the book: a collection of twenty-four lessons on imitation proposed by the 'prince' of the Academy, Fabrizio Antonio Monsignani. The next issue gave space to the rest of the essay: ten papers that dealt with one Petrarch sonnet each, and the reprint of a hundred and seven sonnets 'transportati al morale' (that is, re-written as texts of moral philosophy) by the secretary of the Academy, Ottavio Petrignani.[56]

The discussion of Petrarch's poems is probably the most novel and interesting part of the book.[57] The outline was fixed: a *pars destruens* entrusted to a member of the Academy, who tried to demonstrate the errors committed by the poet, and the reply of Petrignani, where Petrarch's choices were explained and interpreted to show the poem's excellence. The poems to be discussed were the Sonnets 109–18 of the ancient editions, that corresponded respectively to *RVF*, 140, 141, 143–48, 151, and 150. The choice showed openly the purely rhetorical nature of the exercise: those who had the task of attacking Petrarch did not choose a poem they actually found poorly written, but rather had to criticize a text they were given, assigned from a pre-fixed series. This dialectic and otiose feature gained the journalist's praise — in a statement that may be the clearest description of literary criticism (of its scope and tools) that we can find in the Journal.[58] Censures and apologies, argued the journalist, were 'always unfair' because partial, while literary criticism had above all to be unbiased. Thus, the disinterested nature of the dialectic exercise performed by the Filergiti guaranteed the absence of passions that could misdirect the judgment, thus allowing access to the poetry's kernel, its inner and hidden truth:

> Non sappiamo se maggiore sia la disgrazia degli Scrittori più celebri per esser di continuo soggette l'Opere loro alla censura degli uomini, anche nelle cose dove sono più degni di lode, o pur la loro fortuna per esser queste difese anche nelle cose dove sono potuti ingannarsi. Certo è che in ciò che riguarda e la censura e la difesa la critica è sempre ingiusta, perché serve più a far conoscere la passione

---

55   See *Giornale de' letterati d'Italia*, 26 (1716), 186–87: 'Molte sono le Adunanze e le Accademie letterate d'Italia, ma la maggior parte di queste si perde o in esaminare certi problemi più plausibili per la novità che utili per l'argomento, o in recitare sonetti e altre poesie dove più si trovi di acume che di buon gusto. [...] Non è già per questo che alcune non ne abbia l'Italia le quali tendono a più alto segno, e trattano cose e più importanti e più gloriose al lor nome e alla loro nazione. In queste ora si cercano nuovi lumi per le scienze e per le buone arti, ora si studia di levare certi pregiudici che possono guastare la poesia e la eloquenza, ora si procura di mettere in chiaro le buone regole del nostro volgare idioma e di ritornarlo a quella perfezione e bellezza che tempo fa gli hanno dato i nostri migliori maestri e scrittori'.

56   The 'moralized' sonnets had already been published in *Saggio di letterati esercizi de gli accademici Filergiti di Forlì [...] raccolti da Ottaviano Petrignani* (Forlì: Selva, 1699), with the approval of Carlo Mario Maggi, whose literary line clearly inspired Petrignani; the journalist reported a letter of Maggi to Petrignani, where the Milanese stated that 'the dignity of the subject' was the only dignity that Petrarch's poems were lacking, and added: 'Questo è 'l giudicio che ne diede il Maggi, e a questo noi pure ci sottoscriviamo senz'alcun timore di allontanarci dal vero'; *Giornale de' letterati d'Italia*, 27 (1716), 351–53.

57   This same part escaped to Graziosi, pp. 161–62, who recall the book and Petrignani's link with Maggi.

58   The statement was probably in debt with a page of Muratori's dedicated to the first volume of the Filergiti's essays (Forlì: Selva, 1699): Muratori, *Della perfetta poesia*, IV, 186.

che il vero, e più tosto che instruire, confonde, e partorisce più del profitto l'errore. Quando però avviene che si esamini un componimento a puro oggetto di letterario esercizio, e affinché se ne scuopra interamente il midollo per utile o insegnamento di chi vuole imitarlo, non si può abbastanza commendarne l'esame, massimamente ove questo esca di mano a persone dotte e intendenti.[59]

4. Publishing and Judging the Petrarchists

These writings taken together form a kind of coherent map of the main interests of the *Giornale* concerning Italian poetry. First and foremost, as already outlined, was the theme most considered in the context of the debate between Italians and French about the excellence of the respective traditions. The rejection of the seventeenth-century Baroque, typical of the Arcadia programme, was adopted through Muratori and Orsi as a way to reaffirm the excellence of the noblest Italian tradition that was born with Petrarch and had reached its apex with Tasso.[60] The defence of Tasso against charges of rhetorical affectation had been the first move of an Italian scholar closely linked to the Journal, Giusto Fontanini, who composed *L'Aminta di Torquato Tasso difeso e illustrato* (Rome: Zenobi and Placo, 1700). The discussion on Tasso's verses had therefore continued to be one of the most debated topics in the whole development of the Orsi-Bouhours quarrel. The apology for the author of *Gerusalemme liberata* quickly shifted toward a wider consideration of the full lyric tradition, so providing the basis — following Crescimbeni's inputs — for what would become the history of Italian literature.[61]

This polemical and apologetic posture was far from neutral, and had major consequences for the larger reflection on literary tradition. Even the key concepts of 'âge d'or' and of 'grand siècle', though at their origin typical of Renaissance eulogies, were readopted under the influence of the model of the 'classic age' of Louis XIV,[62] creating a model of the development of Italian literature based on a sequence of centuries, a sequence that seemed to follow a sinusoidal trend, articulated on centuries of glory (the fourteenth, sixteenth, and eighteenth) and of decadence (the fifteenth and seventeenth).

Moreover, the renewed acknowledgement of the Italian Renaissance as the golden age of literature was closely linked not only with an apology for Italy's past culture but also with its present awakening after the Baroque parenthesis. This apologetic bias constituted an ambiguous but productive feature when judging Petrarch's sixteenth-century imitators. It integrated (and complicated) the Journal's erudite impartial approach with modern urgencies, and it fashioned a form of criticism that claimed a tight affinity with its object. A similar setting prompted a sympathetic outlook on authors, enhancing their (supposedly) common values, and in the meantime, introducing categories largely in debt, for dialectical reasons, to a concurrent tradition, that of the French rationalistic classicism.[63]

---

59   *Giornale de' letterati d'Italia*, 27 (1716), 325–26.
60   Viola, *Osservazioni*, pp. 11–13 and 34.
61   Tatti, pp. 319–20.
62   Viola, *Tradizioni*, p. VIII.
63   Viola, *Tradizioni*, p. XII.

This implied the definition of a canon of authors able both to redeem the Italian tradition and to offer a model for modern literature. The importance of modern editions of ancient lyric poets was explicitly linked, in the first issue of the Journal, to the quarrel against 'the French and other foreign nations', who believed 'that Italians are only keen on exaggerations, sophistications, wordplays, and platitudes alike':

> Quando i Francesi ed altre nazioni forastiere si fanno ad esaminare il gusto degl'Italiani in quella spezie di Poesia che Lirica comunemente appelliamo, credono che a questi altro non piaccia se non Gonfiezze, Raffinamenti, Scherzi di parole e simili inezie, le quali per verità non meno che altrove furono nell'Italia, ma solo per qualche tempo nel secolo oltrepassato, in riputazione ed in uso. Per questa cagione eglino considerano il Marini, l'Achillini e simil turba di gente come que' soli che tengano ancora nella nostra Poesia il principato ed il credito, e pensano col discoprire la debolezza di questi di renderci tutti del nostro cattivo gusto convinti.[64]

The present times, continued the journalist, had seen the publishing of many books that 'clearly showed that the lyrical poetry practiced here, as well as the other genres of poetry, is made of a truly stronger alloy, and may resist the harder tests'.[65] He was going to digest seven editions of good poetry, aiming to show how the 'good taste' was strongly rooted in Italian history and had not been abandoned in contemporary literature.[66]

Between 1710 and 1718 we find about twenty editions of ancient poets and four anthologies fully digested in the journal or mentioned in the 'Novelle letterarie'. Most of them were published in Bologna, by the same printer, Pisarri, who had published Orsi's response to Bouhours: Buonaccorso da Montemagno (Pisarri, 1709), Agostino Staccoli (Pisarri, 1709), Giovanni Guidiccioni (Barbiroli, 1709), Angelo di Costanzo (Barbiroli, 1709; and Pisarri, 1712), Giovan Girolamo de' Rossi (Pisarri, 1711), Luigi Tansillo (Pisarri, 1711), Anton Francesco Raineri (Pisarri, 1712), and Francesco Maria Molza (Pisarri, 1713). All of them appeared as imitators of Petrarch, and all of them except Buonaccorso and Staccoli were sixteenth-century poets. The Journal covered the whole series of ancient vernacular lyric poems edited by the milieu of the 'Colonia Renia' and the 'Accademia degli

---

64   *Giornale de' letterati d'Italia*, 1 (1710), 179–80.
65   'Negli ultimi anni sonsi veduti molti libri d'insegnamento e di pratica, i quali dimostrano chiaramente, che la Lirica che tra noi si professa, non meno che gli altri generi di Poesia sono di assai miglior lega, e stanno a prova del più difficile esperimento' (ibid.).
66   They were 'componimenti di alcuni Rimatori sì de' passati secoli, come del nostro, i quali col loro esempio servano insieme ad altri di eccitamento, ad altri di disinganno' (ibid.). The collection was entitled 'Alcuni Rimatori Italiani stampati ultimamente', and had a sequel, two years later, with the review of four more new books: *Giornale de' letterati d'Italia*, 1 (1710), 179–221, and 11 (1712), 93–163. After Apostolo Zeno's departure for Vienna in 1718, the series continued with an important shift in the title ('Rimatori italiani ultimamente stampati, le cui opere sono citate nella Crusca'), that explicitly linked the choice of the books to digest with their presence in the Crusca Vocabulary: see *Giornale de' letterati d'Italia*, 32 (1719), 227–369; 33.1 (1721), 230–377; and 33.2 (1722), 172–232 on Alamanni and Rucellai; 34 (1723), 38–81 on Giusto de' Conti; 35 (1724), 223–46 on Dante; 36 (1724), 206–29 on Buonaccorso da Montemagno sr. and jr.; 38.1 (1727), 132–60 on Chiabrera.

Abbandonati' under the direction of Eustachio Manfredi.[67] It was undoubtedly the most important venture in the field of sixteenth-century lyric poetry in these years. The soul of the Journal, Apostolo Zeno, had some part in it: the digest of Guidiccioni's edition explicitly cited as a source an important manuscript received from Zeno by the editor.[68]

The operation, by the way, reflected a certain affinity with the trend prompted by the Journal. They were small size editions with plain, un-annotated texts: not yet the glorious 'editio variorum' hoped for, but still a first attempt to circulate the good models of Renaissance poetry. The most important edition published by Pisarri, however, was the first part of the *Scelta di Sonetti, e Canzoni de' più eccellenti rimatori d'ogni secolo* (1709), praised by the Journal as 'the most copious, the best ordered, the most perfect' collection ever published, where 'the quantity of the poems did not undermine their quality'.[69] The accurately selected texts were disposed in a chronological order — a choice openly appreciated by the reviewer (almost certainly Apostolo Zeno). In this way, he stated, 'you may see what Italian poetry had been in any time not through a report or by a speculation, but by experience and practice'.[70] It is clear how such a book could be considered in line with the project of rethinking Italian tradition that the Journal openly promoted: Zeno defined the anthology as a sort of 'perceptible history' of Italian literature, able to 'show the dissimilarity' of literary tastes in the different periods.[71]

The Journal also gave a particular attention to a second important pole for lyric poetry printing: Florence. Here, under the imprint of academics such as Anton Maria Salvini and Giovan Battista Baldinotti, had been published the *opera omnia* of Giovanni Della Casa (Manni, 1707) mentioned above,[72] the poems of Giusto de' Conti (Guiducci and Franchi, 1715), and those of Buonaccorso da Montemagno Sr. and Jr. (Manni, 1718), for the first time distinguished as two different persons.[73]

---

67   Graziosi, pp. 96–105 and 207–25. On Manfredi see: Andrea Campana, *Eustachio Manfredi e le dinamiche della poesia d'occasione* (Bologna: Patron, 2018) and Andrea Donnini, 'Eustachio Manfredi rimatore', *Giornale storico della letteratura italiana*, 178 (2001), 205–57. The notice of the publication of the poems of Manfredi himself (Bologna: Pisarri, 1713) and of Domenico Maria Mazza (Bologna: Pisarri, 1713) was given in the 'Novelle letterarie' of tome 17 (1714), 407–09.
68   *Giornale de' letterati d'Italia*, 1 (1710), 194.
69   See *Giornale de' letterati d'Italia*, 1 (1710), 217: 'Confessandola tutti la più copiosa, la più ordinata, e la più perfetta di quante mai se ne fossero in alcun tempo vedute. In essa la quantità de' componimenti non pregiudica alla loro bontà'. On the *Scelta* see Amedeo Quondam, *Petrarchismo mediato. Per una critica della forma 'antologia'* (Rome: Bulzoni, 1974).
70   'Quello che v'ha di particolare in questa bella Scelta, si è l'ordine Cronologico ch'ella serba: cosicché non già per relazione o per congettura, ma per pratica ed uso si vede qual fosse l'Italiana Poesia di ogni tempo, e se n'ha, per così dire, un'Istoria sensibile' (ibid.).
71   Zeno cited as very significant a passage where the editor sentenced that 'altro è importante a leggersi negli antichi, altro ne' moderni'; *Giornale de' letterati d'Italia*, 1 (1710), 220.
72   *Giornale de' letterati d'Italia*, 4 (1711), 164–211. The work is also mentioned in the 'Novelle letterarie' of tomes 6 (1710), 394–95; and 22 (1715), 445–46.
73   The two editions were announced in the 'Novelle letterarie' of tome 22 (1715); for their reviews, see note 66. Furthermore, the Journal reviewed the editions of sixteenth-century minor poets Tommaso Baldinotti (Pisa: Bindi, 1702) and Petronio Barbati (Foligno: Campitelli, 1712), and the anthologies *Raccolta di Rime di Poeti Napoletani* (Naples: Parrino, 1701) and *Rime scelte de' poeti illustri de' nostri tempi* (Lucca: Frediani, 1709). In the 'Novelle letterarie' it was also given notice of

It was a more restricted number of poets: the Florentines offered a meaningful selection of Petrarch's imitators, published in annotated editions. Della Casa, himself a Florentine, was one of the most important (if not the most important) authors in the Arcadia canon. Buonaccorso da Montemagno the elder and Giusto de' Conti were believed — as was argued by the journalist — to be almost contemporaries of Petrarch, and therefore considered among the very first to follow the Master's path.

In the Journal we may also trace the first steps of the venture of the brothers Gaetano and Giannantonio Volpi with the printer Giuseppe Comino in Padua, who from the 1720s would become one of the most important promoters of the publication of sixteenth-century authors in Italy. Curiously enough we already find a brief notice of Giannantonio Volpi in the first issue's 'Novelle letterarie', mentioned as a doctor in laws from Bergamo who was about to publish an annotated edition of Catullus, Tibullus, and Propertius.[74] Some years later, in the 'Novelle letterarie' of tome twenty-eight, the establishment of a new printing-house in Padova was announced, coordinated by the Volpi brothers, who were about to publish the *opera omnia* of Andrea Navagero, a friend and collaborator of Pietro Bembo and Aldo Manuzio.[75] The edition, assured the journalist, was going to be the 'most beautiful, and as correct as possible'.[76] The next issue of the Journal digested the work.[77] The reviewer highlighted how the choice of such a scholar — a cultivated and elegant Latin writer, and a Venetian aristocrat that combined within himself civic engagement, Christian piety, and a noble cult for friendship — was indeed a telling one, which indicated the route the printers wanted to pursue.[78]

The Journal's report of Volpi's enterprise showed more than a simple affinity: it revealed a direct link with the editors that allowed the *Giornale* to anticipate a preview of their publications in the 'Novelle letterarie' of tome thirty, after having praised the publishing of Luigi Alamanni's *La coltivazione* and Giovanni Rucellai's *Le api* (Padua: Comino, 1718).[79] The Volpi brothers would collect the inheritance of the Pisarri editions of the years 1709–13, showing a similar wish to disseminate sixteenth-century literature: but their annotated release, edited with strict philological attention, showed the influence of the model supported and promoted

'il Coppetta' (Perugia: Ciani and Desideri, 1720), Ludovico Ariosto (London: Pickard, 1716), and Gabriello Chiabrera (Rome: Salvioni, 1718).

74   *Giornale de' letterati d'Italia*, 1 (1710), 449–50.

75   *Giornale de' letterati d'Italia*, 28 (1717), 437–38.

76   'Nella nuova stamperia [...] hanno principiato i direttori di essa a dar prova del loro ottimo gusto con la raccolta di tutte le Opere dell'insigne Andrea Navagero, Senatore Veneziano, sì latine, che italiane, le quali presentemente stanno sotto il torchio. Si può assicurare il pubblico, che la edizione sarà bellissima, e al maggior segno corretta' (ibid.).

77   *Giornale de' letterati d'Italia*, 29 (1717), 86–122.

78   *Giornale de' letterati d'Italia*, 29 (1717), 87–88 and 94–95. The reviewer highlighted Navagero's practice of vernacular poetry, and narrated 'a particularità degna di osservazione': when he was the ambassador of Venice at the court of the Emperor Charles V, he became a friend of Juan Boscán, teaching him how to compose 'Sonetti, e altri componimenti alla foggia degl'Italiani': Boscán would have convinced Garcilaso de la Vega to do the same, thus introducing Petrarchism in Spain; see *Giornale de' letterati d'Italia*, 29 (1717), 100–01.

79   *Giornale de' letterati d'Italia*, 29 (1718), 426–27; for the reviews of Alamanni and Rucellai, see note 66.

(among others, within the same milieu) by the Journal. The Volpi editions marked an important step toward the canonization of sixteenth-century Petrarchism that would fulfil the premises put by Crescimbeni and Muratori on historiographical and theoretical grounds.[80] Along with the annotated 'opera omnia' of Bembo and Della Casa promoted in a context strongly linked with that of the Journal and published in Venice in 1728–29, they would promote the eighteenth-century canonization of some of the more important authors of the Italian Renaissance.[81]

The ensemble of the Journal's digests traces a coherent overview, where the sixteenth century generally appears as the age of perfection for vernacular poetry, and the fifteenth (even more than the seventeenth) that of the worst decadence. Agostino Staccoli from Urbino, who lived in the second half of the Quattrocento, 'had flourished [...] at the peak of barbarity'.[82] For the little-known poems of Giovan Girolamo de' Rossi, instead, it was enough 'to think that they were composed in the heart of the sixteenth century to believe they were good'.[83] Nonetheless, the appreciation for 'the golden age of Leo X' and of Petrarchism was not unconditional. Reviewing the edition of the poems of Petronio Barbati from Foligno (born about 1500, died in 1554), the author was praised for having been guided more by a 'free and fertile fantasy' than by a 'scrupulous imitation' — the latter being an 'almost universal custom in that age, where few had been able to move a step out of the footprints of someone else':

> Scrive egli su lo stile del Petrarca e de' buoni autori, ma non in guisa che di quando in quando non corra una strada del tutto sua. Vi si scorge un ingegno che si lascia guidare, ma con giudicio, più da sé stesso che dagli altri, e più da una fantasia libera e feconda che da una scrupolosa imitazione, costume quasi universale ai poeti di quell'età, pochi de' quali hanno saputo muovere un passo che su le altrui vestigie non fosse.[84]

To merit full praise a poet had to be elegant, serious, and original: this was not the case for many of the sixteenth-century imitators of Petrarch. Within the Renaissance tradition a more restricted canon was identified that largely corresponded with the one proposed by Crescimbeni: a canon that leant towards the second half of the

---

80   See Lorenzo Baldacchini, 'Comino, Giuseppe', in *Dizionario biografico degli italiani* (Rome: Istituto dell'Enciclopedia italiana, 1960–), XXVII (1982), <http://www.treccani.it/enciclopedia/giuseppe-comino_(Dizionario-Biografico)/>[accessed 27 April 2019].

81   See Amelia Juri, 'Anton Federigo Seghezzi editore delle *Opere* di Pietro Bembo (Venice, Hertzhauser, 1729): prime osservazioni sul commento ai poeti rinascimentali nel Settecento'; and Giacomo Vagni, 'I poeti del Cinquecento nelle prose di Parini e Bettinelli', in *Forme della critica letteraria nel Settecento. Atti del Convegno (Losanna, 13–14 ottobre 2016)*, ed. by Gabriele Bucchi and Carlo Enrico Roggia (Ravenna: Longo, 2017), pp. 33–46 and 65–77. Along with Casa and Bembo, we should also remember the *opera omnia* of Trissino edited in the very same years by Scipione Maffei: *Tutte le opere di Giovan Giorgio Trissino gentiluomo vicentino non più raccolte* (Verona: Vallarsi, 1729).

82   *Giornale de' letterati d'Italia*, I (1710), 187; it was therefore stated that Staccoli had probably been the best fifteenth-century poet after Lorenzo il Magnifico, and that he had been working hard 'to be an imitator of Petrarch', without feeling ashamed 'to appear so' (ibid.).

83   See *Giornale de' letterati d'Italia*, II (1712), 109: 'Per quello che spetta al giudizio che possiamo dare di questi suoi componimenti poetici, basta generalmente considerarli nati nel fiore del XVI secolo per crederli buoni'.

84   *Giornale de' letterati d'Italia*, II (1712), 154–55.

Cinquecento more than towards its beginning. Poets like Tansillo and di Costanzo (beside, of course, Della Casa) were the ones praised with greater and more explicit enthusiasm.

Angelo di Costanzo (1507?–1591) was declared 'one of the most excellent genii of the sixteenth century'.[85] His poems were described and interpreted with words mindful of Crescimbeni's *Bellezze della volgar poesia* that summarized the ideal model of poetry the Journal wanted to promote. He 'combined the nobility of the style with the prominence and the refinement of the thought'[86] and he had not been one of those 'who stuck so religiously to Petrarch' that they were only able 'to think or say what he had already thought or said'.[87] The elegance and the technical ability upon which the analysis often enthused could not, in Zeno's intention, substitute or overshadow the importance of the matter of the poems, substantiated with moral philosophy. Poetry had to give — in classical Horatian terms — pleasure and convenience, 'utile' and 'dulce': and even the lyric love poems had to demonstrate a sound and in some way original form of thinking. Similar terms were used for Giovanni Guidiccioni (1500–41), explaining that he had sometimes been obscure because he most enjoyed 'thinking deeply' about what he was writing, and aimed at driving his readers toward further reflections.[88]

Luigi Tansillo (1510–68) earned one of the longest reviews in the series of the 'Rimatori italiani antichi'.[89] The book was presented as a 'little, but golden and precious' collection of poems of someone who reached the level 'of the most famous poets' with his sonnets, and outdid them all with his *canzoni*.[90] Even if the journalist contested Stigliani's *boutade* that Tansillo was better than Petrarch ('all these eulogies [...] will not make us admire the copy more than the original'), his judgment on his production was, by all means, favourable.[91] An important part of the argument was meant to demonstrate that the obscene poem 'Il Vendemmiatore' was not at all representative of his production, but was indeed an offspring of his youth ('parto giovanile') that the mature poet sincerely regretted. All his other poems, even the love ones, were instead the output of a very temperate writing ('una castigatissima penna'): the poet's declaration to pope Paolo IV, that his rhymes had been sometimes frivolous but his life had always been honourable, was for the journalist to be believed.[92] Literary excellence had to be associated with spotless

---

85   See *Giornale de' letterati d'Italia*, I (1710), 204: 'Uno de' più eccellenti ingegni del secolo XVI'.

86   See *Giornale de' letterati d'Italia*, I (1710), 205–06: 'Per aver congiunta alla nobiltà dello stile anche la grandezza e rarità del pensiero'.

87   'Lavora di suo, e per così dire, di pianta, e non è stato un di quegli, che stanno attaccati sì religiosamente al Petrarca, che non sappiano né pensare né dire se non quanto da questo sia stato detto o pensato' (ibid.).

88   See *Giornale de' letterati*, I (1710), 195: 'Basterà riflettere, che Mons. Guidiccione niente più apprezza, che pensar bene tutto quello che dice, e dirlo in maniera che più ne resti a pensar a chi legge'.

89   *Giornale de' letterati*, II (1712), 110–54.

90   See *Giornale de' letterati*, II (1712), 110.

91   See *Giornale de' letterati*, II (1712), 113: 'Tutte queste lodi, e molte altre, che troviamo date alle poesie del Tansillo, non faranno nulladimeno, che da noi si apprezzi la copia, vie più che l'originale'.

92   See *Giornale de' letterati*, II (1712), 131: 'Fu [...] la carta | vana talor, la vita sempre onesta'.

morality and an exemplary active life: he tried hard to show that Tansillo was 'not less valorous than learned'.[93]

For Zeno — as for Muratori — the link between morality and rhetoric (between life and writing) had a basic contribution in literary judgment. The promotion of aesthetic qualities tangled with ethical values was a key issue for the redemption of a literary tradition charged with triviality, and the idea of a moral superiority of the Italian Renaissance culture, regained by the moderns against the superficiality of a large part of the seventeenth-century literature, was often raised in the Journal.

When it was possible, moreover, it was used to counter the French accusations. An example was a newly published French translation of the seventeenth-century treatise by Emanuele Tesauro, *La filosofia morale* (Bruxelles: Foppens, 1713), that raised the irony of the journalist: 'In a time, when some of our books have already lost the reputation they used to have when we were children, we have to see them translated into foreign languages'.[94] For him, however, the question to be raised was not primarily about the opportunity to revive an out-dated baroque essay (that indeed continued to have a certain popularity even in Italy), but that of the moral poverty inextricably linked to its style 'metaforico e concettoso', inadequate to carry the comparison with the elegant and thoughtful sixteenth-century prose:

> Regalo assai migliore avrebbe fatto il Padre Croset ai Cavalieri di Malta, se avesse tradotto il *Cortegiano* del Castiglione, il *Galateo* del Casa, la *Vita politica* e il *Soliloquio* del nostro Paruta, o l'*Educazione cristiana* di Silvio Antoniano: opere sode, nelle quali con la necessaria gravità si tratta della vita morale e civile propria e degna di un qualsisia Cavaliere.[95]

For us it may be surprising to find the book on the Christian education of pupils written by the Filippo Neri's disciple Silvio Antoniano on the instance of Carlo Borromeo,[96] mentioned together with the works of the Venetian diplomat Paolo Paruta[97] and with such classic Renaissance works as the *Cortegiano* and the *Galateo*. Here is not the place to discuss in full the complex framework of this series of 'works of sound doctrine, where the moral and civil life is debated with the appropriate gravity'. It will be enough to notice how the series sketched a short canon of sixteenth-century prose, from its courtly beginning until its post-Tridentine ending. For Zeno (if he was the author) these works represented, however different they could appear, a successful combination of style and matter, where the excellence of the form plainly corresponded to the importance of the

---

93 See *Giornale de' letterati*, 11 (1712), 137: 'Era il Tansillo non meno valoroso, che letterato'.
94 See *Giornale de' letterati*, 11 (1712), 398. The treatise was often reprinted in the 1670s and 1680s, but its fortune was still conspicuous even in the first years of the new century: see Denise Aricò, *Il Tesauro in Europa: Studi sulle traduzioni della Filosofia morale* (Bologna: CLUEB, 1987).
95 *Giornale de' letterati d'Italia*, 17 (1714), 398–99.
96 Paolo Prodi, 'Antoniano, Silvio', in *Dizionario biografico degli italiani*, III (1961), <http://www.treccani.it/enciclopedia/silvio-antoniano_(Dizionario-Biografico)/> [accessed 27 April 2019]; and Elisabetta Patrizi, *Silvio Antoniano: un umanista ed educatore nell'età del rinnovamento cattolico (1540–1603)* (Macerata: EUM, 2010). The *editio princeps* had been printed in Verona by Delle Donne and Stringari in 1584.
97 Gino Benzoni, 'Paruta, Paolo', in *Dizionario biografico degli italiani*, LXXXI (2014), <http://www.treccani.it/enciclopedia/paolo-paruta_%28Dizionario-Biografico%29/> [accessed 27 April 2019].

subject. The same accord — achieved in an exemplary way by the Renaissance prose — was sought in sixteenth-century lyric poetry, to offer an adequate model for modern writers.

If compared with the modern reception of Renaissance literature, the latter seems to be the major point of difference. The scepticism for 'superstitious imitation' and the mistrust of Petrarchism as a form of 'mass literature' have some important early eighteenth-century classicist antecedents. What is really hard to find in the Arcadian age, on the contrary, is the conception of Renaissance culture as the expression of a corrupt and vacuous society, only devoted to the formal beauty of arts. The paradigm of the moral indignity of that world, firstly introduced by Rousseau and Herder and then fully developed after the Napoleonic age, would strongly influence studies on Petrarchism right into the twentieth century.[98] The recourse to eighteenth-century sources, as the examples of scholars like Carlo Dionisotti and Amedeo Quondam show, has been a major tool to overtake the Risorgimento's prejudices and gain a more comprehensive overview of the age of Classicism.[99] Following their lesson, eighteenth-century books and editions are still an essential tool for studying sixteenth-century poetry. Nevertheless, in recent times it has become more evident that some bias affected even the proclaimed neutrality of the erudite milieu of the *primo Settecento*. This growing awareness is showing that some of the still unresolved critical questions about the lyric poetry inspired by Petrarch have deep roots, far deeper than De Sanctis's censures. A full reconstruction of the genealogy of the modern judgement on Petrarchism (from eighteenth century to modern times) has not yet been written. This could be a survey of some interest, for a better understanding of how modern Italian literature has wanted to shape her identity through a peculiar rewriting of her Renaissance origins.

---

98   Eugenio Garin, *La cultura del Rinascimento. Dietro il mito dell'età nuova* (Milan: Il Saggiatore, 2000), pp. 5–8.
99   Franco Tomasi, Stefano Verdino, and Carlo Vecce, *Il 'tardo Rinascimento': tradizioni di genere e canone degli autori*, in *I cantieri dell'italianistica. Ricerca, didattica e organizzazione agli inizi del XXI secolo. Atti del XVII congresso dell'ADI (Rome Sapienza, 18–21 settembre 2013)*, ed. by Beatrice Alfonzetti, Guido Baldassarri, and Franco Tomasi (Rome: Adi editore, 2014), <http://www.italianisti.it/Atti-di-Congresso?pg=cms&ext=p&cms_codsec=14&cms_codcms=581> [accessed 25 April 2019].

INDEX

www.ingramcontent.com/pod-product-compliance
Lightning Source LLC
Chambersburg PA
CBHW080842250626

47161CB00010B/3161